LINUX
Network Administrator's Guide

WITHDRAWN ERAU-PRESCOTT LIBRARY

Other Linux resources from O'Reilly

Related titles

Apache Cookbook	Linux Server Security
DNS and BIND Cookbook	Network Troubleshooting Tools
Linux Server Cookbook	Running Linux
Linux Server Hacks	Using Samba

Linux Books Resource Center

linux.oreilly.com is a complete catalog of O'Reilly's books on Linux and Unix and related technologies, including sample chapters and code examples.

ONLamp.com is the premier site for the open source web platform: Linux, Apache, MySQL, and either Perl, Python, or PHP.

Conferences

O'Reilly brings diverse innovators together to nurture the ideas that spark revolutionary industries. We specialize in documenting the latest tools and systems, translating the innovator's knowledge into useful skills for those in the trenches. Visit *conferences.oreilly.com* for our upcoming events.

Safari Bookshelf (*safari.oreilly.com*) is the premier online reference library for programmers and IT professionals. Conduct searches across more than 1,000 books. Subscribers can zero in on answers to time-critical questions in a matter of seconds. Read the books on your Bookshelf from cover to cover or simply flip to the page you need. Try it today with a free trial.

LINUX
Network Administrator's Guide

THIRD EDITION

Tony Bautts, Terry Dawson,
and Gregor N. Purdy

O'REILLY®

Beijing · Cambridge · Farnham · Köln · Paris · Sebastopol · Taipei · Tokyo

Linux Network Administrator's Guide, Third Edition

by Tony Bautts, Terry Dawson, and Gregor N. Purdy

Copyright © 2005 O'Reilly Media, Inc. All rights reserved.
Copyright © 1995 Olaf Kirch. Copyright © 2000 Terry Dawson. Copyright on O'Reilly printed version © 2000 O'Reilly Media, Inc. Rights to copy the O'Reilly printed version are reserved.

Printed in the United States of America.

Published by O'Reilly Media, Inc., 1005 Gravenstein Highway North, Sebastopol, CA 95472.

O'Reilly books may be purchased for educational, business, or sales promotional use. Online editions are also available for most titles (*safari.oreilly.com*). For more information, contact our corporate/institutional sales department: (800) 998-9938 or *corporate@oreilly.com*.

Editor:	Andy Oram
Production Editor:	Adam Witwer
Cover Designer:	Edie Freedman
Interior Designer:	David Futato

Printing History:

January 1995:	First Edition.
June 2000:	Second Edition.
February 2005:	Third Edition.

Nutshell Handbook, the Nutshell Handbook logo, and the O'Reilly logo are registered trademarks of O'Reilly Media, Inc. The *Linux* series designations, *Linux Network Administrator's Guide*, Third Edition, images of the American West, and related trade dress are trademarks of O'Reilly Media, Inc.

Many of the designations used by manufacturers and sellers to distinguish their products are claimed as trademarks. Where those designations appear in this book, and O'Reilly Media, Inc. was aware of a trademark claim, the designations have been printed in caps or initial caps.

While every precaution has been taken in the preparation of this book, the publisher and authors assume no responsibility for errors or omissions, or for damages resulting from the use of the information contained herein.

This work is licensed under the Creative Commons Attribution-NonCommercial-ShareAlike 2.0 License. To view a copy of this license, visit *http://creativecommons.org/licenses/by-sa/2.0/* or send a letter to Creative Commons, 559 Nathan Abbott Way, Stanford, California 94305, USA.

 This book uses RepKover,™ a durable and flexible lay-flat binding.

ISBN: 0-596-00548-2

[M]

Table of Contents

Preface

The Internet is now a household term in many countries and has become a part of life for most of the business world. With millions of people connecting to the World Wide Web, computer networking has moved to the status of TV sets and microwave ovens. You can purchase and install a wireless hub with just about an equal amount of effort. The Internet has unusually high media coverage, with weblogs often "scooping" traditional media outlets for news stories, while virtual reality environments such as online games and the rest have developed into the "Internet culture."

Of course, networking has been around for a long time. Connecting computers to form local area networks has been common practice, even at small installations, and so have long-haul links using transmission lines provided by telecommunications companies. A rapidly growing conglomerate of worldwide networks has, however, made joining the global village a perfectly reasonable option for nearly everyone with access to a computer. Setting up a broadband Internet host with fast mail and web access is becoming more and more affordable.

Talking about computer networks often means talking about Unix. Of course, Unix is not the only operating system with network capabilities, nor will it remain a frontrunner forever, but it has been in the networking business for a long time and will surely continue to be for some time to come. What makes Unix particularly interesting to private users is that there has been much activity to bring free Unix-like operating systems to the PC, such as NetBSD, FreeBSD, and Linux.

Linux is a freely distributable Unix clone for personal computers that currently runs on a variety of machines that includes the Intel family of processors, but also PowerPC architectures such as the Apple Macintosh; it can also run on Sun SPARC and Ultra-SPARC machines; Compaq Alphas; MIPS; and even a number of video game consoles, such as the Sony PlayStation 2, the Nintendo Gamecube, and the Microsoft Xbox. Linux has also been ported to some relatively obscure platforms, such as the Fujitsu AP-1000 and the IBM System 3/90. Ports to other interesting architectures are currently in progress in developers' labs, and the quest to move Linux into the embedded controller space promises success.

Linux was developed by a large team of volunteers across the Internet. The project was started in 1990 by Linus Torvalds, a Finnish college student, as an operating systems course project. Since that time, Linux has snowballed into a full-featured Unix clone capable of running applications as diverse as simulation and modeling programs, word processors, speech-recognition systems, World Wide Web browsers, and a horde of other software, including a variety of excellent games. A great deal of hardware is supported, and Linux contains a complete implementation of TCP/IP networking, including PPP, firewalls, and many features and protocols not found in any other operating system. Linux is powerful, fast, and free, and its popularity in the world beyond the Internet is growing rapidly.

The Linux operating system itself is covered by the GNU General Public License, the same copyright license used by software developed by the Free Software Foundation. This license allows anyone to redistribute or modify the software (free of charge or for a profit) as long as all modifications and distributions are freely distributable as well. The term "free software" refers to freedom of application, not freedom of cost.

Purpose and Audience for This Book

This book was written to provide a single reference for network administration in a Linux environment. Beginners and experienced users alike should find the information they need to cover nearly all important administration activities required to manage a Linux network configuration. The possible range of topics to cover is nearly limitless, so of course it has been impossible to include everything there is to say on all subjects. We've tried to cover the most important and common ones. Beginners to Linux networking, even those with no prior exposure to Unix-like operating systems, have found earlier editions of this book good enough to help them successfully get their Linux network configurations up and running and get them ready to learn more.

There are many books and other sources of information from which you can learn any of the topics covered in this book in greater depth. We've provided a bibliography when you are ready to explore more.

Sources of Information

If you are new to the world of Linux, there are a number of resources to explore and become familiar with. Having access to the Internet is helpful, but not essential.

Linux Documentation Project Guides

The Linux Documentation Project is a group of volunteers who have worked to produce books (guides), HOWTO documents, and manpages on topics ranging from installation to kernel programming.

Books

Linux Installation and Getting Started

By Matt Welsh, et al. This book describes how to obtain, install, and use Linux. It includes an introductory Unix tutorial and information on systems administration, the X Window System, and networking.

Linux System Administrators Guide

By Lars Wirzenius and Joanna Oja. This book is a guide to general Linux system administration and covers topics such as creating and configuring users, performing system backups, configuring of major software packages, and installing and upgrading software.

Linux System Adminstration Made Easy

By Steve Frampton. This book describes day-to-day administration and maintenance issues of relevance to Linux users.

Linux Programmers Guide

By B. Scott Burkett, Sven Goldt, John D. Harper, Sven van der Meer, and Matt Welsh. This book covers topics of interest to people who wish to develop application software for Linux.

The Linux Kernel

By David A. Rusling. This book provides an introduction to the Linux kernel, how it is constructed, and how it works. Take a tour of your kernel.

The Linux Kernel Module Programming Guide

By Ori Pomerantz. This guide explains how to write Linux kernel modules. This book also originated in the LDP. The text of the current version is released under the Creative Commons Attribution-Share Alike License, so it can be freely altered and distributed.

More manuals are in development. For more information about the LDP, consult their server at *http://www.linuxdoc.org/* or one of its many mirrors.

HOWTO documents

The Linux HOWTOs are a comprehensive series of papers detailing various aspects of the system—such as how to install and configure the X Window System software, or write in assembly language programming under Linux. These are available online at one of the many Linux Documentation Project mirror sites (see next section). See the file *HOWTO-INDEX* for a list of what's available.

You might want to obtain the *Installation HOWTO*, which describes how to install Linux on your system; the *Hardware Compatibility HOWTO*, which contains a list of hardware known to work with Linux; and the *Distribution HOWTO*, which lists software vendors selling Linux on diskette and CD-ROM.

Linux Frequently Asked Questions

The *Linux Frequently Asked Questions with Answers* (FAQ) contains a wide assortment of questions and answers about the system. It is a must-read for all newcomers.

Documentation Available via WWW

There are many Linux-based WWW sites available. The home site for the Linux Documentation Project can be accessed at *http://www.tldp.org/*.

Any additional information can probably be found with a quick Google search. It seems that almost everything has been tried and likely written up by someone in the Linux community.

Documentation Available Commercially

A number of publishing companies and software vendors publish the works of the Linux Documentation Project. Two such vendors are Specialized Systems Consultants, Inc. (SSC) (*http://www.ssc.com*) and Linux Systems Labs (*http://www.lsl.com*). Both companies sell compendiums of Linux HOWTO documents and other Linux documentation in printed and bound form.

O'Reilly Media publishes a series of Linux books. This one is a work of the Linux Documentation Project, but most have been authored independently:

Running Linux
   An installation and user guide to the system describing how to get the most out of personal computing with Linux.

Linux Server Security
   An excellent guide to configuring airtight Linux servers. Administrators who are building web servers or other bastion hosts should consider this book a great source of information.

Linux in a Nutshell
   Another in the successful "in a Nutshell" series, this book focuses on providing a broad reference text for Linux.

Linux iptables Pocket Reference
   A brief but complete compendium of features in the Linux firewall system.

Linux Journal and Linux Magazine

Linux Journal and *Linux Magazine* are monthly magazines for the Linux community, written and published by a number of Linux activists. They contain articles ranging from novice questions and answers to kernel programming internals. Even if you have Usenet access, these magazines are a good way to stay in touch with the Linux community.

Linux Journal is the oldest magazine and is published by SSC, for which details were listed in the previous section. You can also find the magazine at *http://www.linuxjournal.com/*.

LinuxMagazine is a newer, independent publication. The home web site for the magazine is *http://www.linuxmagazine.com/*.

Linux Usenet Newsgroups

If you have access to Usenet news, the following Linux-related newsgroups are available:

comp.os.linux.announce
> A moderated newsgroup containing announcements of new software, distributions, bug reports, and goings-on in the Linux community. All Linux users should read this group.

comp.os.linux.help
> General questions and answers about installing or using Linux.

comp.os.linux.admin
> Discussions relating to systems administration under Linux.

comp.os.linux.networking
> Discussions relating to networking with Linux.

comp.os.linux.development
> Discussions about developing the Linux kernel and system itself.

comp.os.linux.misc
> A catch-all newsgroup for miscellaneous discussions that don't fall under the previous categories.

There are also several newsgroups devoted to Linux in languages other than English, such as *fr.comp.os.linux* in French and *de.comp.os.linux* in German.

Linux Mailing Lists

There are a large number of specialist Linux mailing lists on which you will find many people willing to help with your questions.

The best-known of these is the Linux Kernel Mailing List. It's a very busy and dense mailing list, with an enormous volume of information posted daily. For more information, visit *http://www.tux.org/lkml*.

Linux User Groups

Many Linux User Groups around the world offer direct support to users, engaging in activities such as installation days, talks and seminars, demonstration nights, and other social events. Linux User Groups are a great way to meet other Linux users in your area. There are a number of published lists of Linux User Groups. One of the most comprehensive is Linux Users Groups Worldwide (*http://lugww.counter.li.org/index.cms*).

Obtaining Linux

There is no single distribution of the Linux software; instead, there are many distributions, such as Debian, Fedora, Red Hat, SUSE, Gentoo, and Slackware. Each distribution contains everything you need to run a complete Linux system: the kernel, basic utilities, libraries, support files, and applications software.

Linux distributions may be obtained via a number of online sources, such as the Internet. Each of the major distributions has its own FTP and web site. Some of these sites are as follows:

Debian
  http://www.debian.org/

Gentoo
  http://www.gentoo.org/

Red Hat
  http://www.redhat.com/

Fedora
  http://fedora.redhat.com/

Slackware
  http://www.slackware.com/

SUSE
  http://www.suse.com/

Many of the popular general WWW archive sites also mirror various Linux distributions. The best-known of these sites is *http://www.linuxiso.org*.

Every major distribution can be downloaded directly from the Internet, but Linux may be purchased on CD-ROM from an increasing number of software vendors. If your local computer store doesn't have it, perhaps you should ask them to stock it! Most of the popular distributions can be obtained on CD-ROM. Some vendors produce products containing multiple CD-ROMs, each of which provides a different Linux distribution. This is an ideal way to try a number of different distributions before settling on your favorite.

Filesystem Standards

In the past, one of the problems that afflicted Linux distributions, as well as the packages of software running on Linux, was the lack of a single accepted filesystem layout. This resulted in incompatibilities between different packages, and confronted users and administrators with the task of locating various files and programs.

To improve this situation, in August 1993, several people formed the Linux File System Standard Group (FSSTND). After six months of discussion, the group created a draft that presents a coherent filesystem structure and defines the location of the most essential programs and configuration files.

This standard was supposed to have been implemented by most major Linux distributions and packages. It is a little unfortunate that, while most distributions have made some attempt to work toward the FSSTND, there is a very small number of distributions that has actually adopted it fully. Throughout this book, we will assume that any files discussed reside in the location specified by the standard; alternative locations will be mentioned only when there is a long tradition that conflicts with this specification.

The Linux FSSTND continued to develop, but was replaced by the Linux File Hierarchy Standard (FHS) in 1997. The FHS addresses the multi-architecture issues that the FSSTND did not. The FHS can be obtained from *http://www.freestandards.org*.

Standard Linux Base

The vast number of different Linux distributions, while providing lots of healthy choices for Linux users, has created a problem for software developers—particularly developers of non-free software.

Each distribution packages and supplies certain base libraries, configuration tools, system applications, and configuration files. Unfortunately, differences in their versions, names, and locations make it very difficult to know what will exist on any distribution. This makes it hard to develop binary applications that will work reliably on all Linux distribution bases.

To help overcome this problem, a new project sprang up called the Linux Standard Base. It aims to describe a standard base distribution that complying distributions will use. If a developer designs an application to work with the standard base platform, the application will work with, and be portable to, any complying Linux distribution.

You can find information on the status of the Linux Standard Base project at its home web site at *http://www.linuxbase.org/.*

If you're concerned about interoperability, particularly of software from commercial vendors, you should ensure that your Linux distribution is making an effort to participate in the standardization project.

About This Book

When Olaf Kirche joined the LDP in 1992, he wrote two small chapters on UUCP and smail, which he meant to contribute to the System Administrator's Guide. Development of TCP/IP networking was just beginning, and when those "small chapters" started to grow, he wondered aloud whether it would be nice to have a Networking Guide. "Great!" everyone said. "Go for it!" So he went for it and wrote the first version of the Networking Guide, which was released in September 1993.

Olaf continued work on the Networking Guide and eventually produced a much enhanced version of the guide. Vince Skahan contributed the original sendmail mail chapter, which was completely replaced in that edition because of a new interface to the sendmail configuration.

In March of 2000, Terry Dawson updated Olaf's original, adding several new chapters and bringing it into the new millennium.

The version of the guide that you are reading now is a fairly large revision and update prompted by O'Reilly Media and undertaken by Tony Bautts. Tony has been enthusiastic Linux user and information security consultant for longer than he would care to admit. He is coauthor of several other computer security-related books and likes to give talks on the subject as well. Tony is a big proponent of Linux in the commercial environment and routinely attempts to convert people to Gentoo Linux. For this edition he has added a few new chapters describing features of Linux networking that have been developed since the second edition, plus a bunch of changes to bring the rest of the book up to date.

The three iptables chapters (Chapters 7, 8, and 9) were updated by Gregor Purdy for this edition.

The book is organized roughly along the sequence of steps that you have to take to configure your system for networking. It starts by discussing basic concepts of networks, and TCP/IP-based networks in particular. It then slowly works its way up from configuring TCP/IP at the device level to firewall, accounting, and masquerade configuration, to the setup of common applications such as SSH, Apache, and Samba. The email part features an introduction to the more intimate parts of mail transport and routing and the myriad of addressing schemes that you may be confronted with. It describes the configuration and management of sendmail, the most common mail transport agent, and IMAP, used for delivery to individual mail users.

Chapters on LDAP and wireless networking round out the infrastructure for modern network administration.

Of course, a book can never exhaustively answer all questions you might have. So if you follow the instructions in this book and something still does not work, please be patient. Some of your problems may be due to mistakes on our part (see "How to Contact Us," later in this Preface), but they also may be caused by changes in the networking software. Therefore, you should check the listed information resources first. There's a good chance that you are not alone with your problems, so a fix or at least a proposed workaround is likely to be known—this is where search engines are particularly handy! If you have the opportunity, you should also try to get the latest kernel and network release from *http://www.kernel.org*. Many problems are caused by software from different stages of development, which fail to work together properly. After all, Linux is a "work in progress."

The Official Printed Version

In Autumn 1993, Andy Oram, who had been around the LDP mailing list from almost the very beginning, asked Olaf about publishing this book at O'Reilly & Associates. He was excited about this book, but never imagined that it would become as successful as it has. He and Andy finally agreed that O'Reilly would produce an enhanced Official Printed Version of the Networking Guide, while Olaf retained the original copyright so that the source of the book could be freely distributed. This means that you can choose freely: you can get the various free forms of the document from your nearest LDP mirror site and print it out, or you can purchase the official printed version from O'Reilly.

Why, then, would you want to pay money for something you can get for free? Is Tim O'Reilly out of his mind for publishing something everyone can print and even sell themselves?* Is there any difference between these versions?

The answers are "It depends," "No, definitely not," and "Yes and no." O'Reilly Media does take a risk in publishing the Network Administrator's Guide, but it seems to have paid off for them (since they've asked us to do it two more times). We believe this project serves as a fine example of how the free software world and companies can cooperate to produce something both can benefit from. In our view, the great service O'Reilly provides the Linux community (apart from the book becoming readily available in your local bookstore) is that it has helped Linux become recognized as something to be taken seriously: a viable and useful alternative to other commercial operating systems. It's a sad technical bookstore that doesn't have at least one shelf stacked with O'Reilly Linux books.

---

* Note that while you are allowed to print out the online version, you may not run the O'Reilly book through a photocopier, much less sell any of its (hypothetical) copies.

Why are they publishing it? They see it as their kind of book. It's what they would hope to produce if they contracted with an author to write about Linux. The pace, level of detail, and style fit in well with their other offerings.

The point of the LDP license is to make sure no one gets shut out. Other people can print out copies of this book, and no one will blame you if you get one of these copies. But if you haven't gotten a chance to see the O'Reilly version, try to get to a bookstore or look at a friend's copy. We think you'll like what you see and will want to buy it for yourself.

So what about the differences between the printed and online versions? Andy Oram has made great efforts at transforming our ramblings into something actually worth printing. (He has also reviewed a few other books produced by the LDP, contributing whatever professional skills he can to the Linux community.)

Since Andy started reviewing the Networking Guide and editing the copies sent to him, the book has improved vastly from its original form, and with every round of submission and feedback, it improves again. The opportunity to take advantage of a professional editor's skill is not to be wasted. In many ways, Andy's contribution has been as important as that of the authors. The same is also true of the production staff, who got the book into the shape that you see now. All these edits have been fed back into the online version, so there is no difference in content.

Still, the O'Reilly version *will* be different. It will be professionally bound, and while you may go to the trouble to print the free version, it is unlikely that you will get the same quality result. Secondly, our amateurish attempts at illustration will have been replaced with nicely redone figures by O'Reilly's professional artists. Indexers have generated an improved index, which makes locating information in the book a much simpler process. If this book is something you intend to read from start to finish, you should consider reading the official printed version.

Overview

Chapter 1, *Introduction to Networking*, discusses the history of Linux and covers basic networking information on UUCP, TCP/IP, various protocols, hardware, and security. The next few chapters deal with configuring Linux for TCP/IP networking and running some major applications.

Chapter 2, *Issues of TCP/IP Networking*, examines IP a little more closely before we get our hands dirty with file editing and the like. If you already know how IP routing works and how address resolution is performed, you can skip this chapter.

Chapter 3, *Configuring the Serial Hardware*, deals with the configuration of your serial ports.

Chapter 4, *Configuring TCP/IP Networking*, helps you set up your machine for TCP/ IP networking. It contains installation hints for standalone hosts and those connected to a network. It also introduces you to a few useful tools you can use to test and debug your setup.

Chapter 5, *Name Service and Configuration*, discusses how to configure hostname resolution and explains how to set up a name server.

Chapter 6, *The Point-to-Point Protocol*, covers PPP and *pppd*, the PPP daemon.

Chapter 7, *TCP/IP Firewall*, extends our discussion on network security and describes the Linux TCP/IP firewall iptables. IP firewalling provides a means of very precisely controlling who can access your network and hosts.

Chapter 8, *IP Accounting*, explains how to configure IP Accounting in Linux so that you can keep track of how much traffic is going where and who is generating it.

Chapter 9, *IP Masquerade and Network Address Translation*, covers a feature of the Linux networking software called IP masquerade, or NAT, which allows whole IP networks to connect to and use the Internet through a single IP address, hiding internal systems from outsiders in the process.

Chapter 10, *Important Network Features*, gives a short introduction to setting up some of the most important network infrastructure and applications, such as SSH. This chapter also covers how services are managed by the inetd superuser and how you may restrict certain security-relevant services to a set of trusted hosts.

Chapter 11, *Administration Issues with Electronic Mail*, introduces you to the central concepts of electronic mail, such as what a mail address looks like and how the mail handling system manages to get your message to the recipient.

Chapter 12, *sendmail*, covers the configuration of *sendmail*, a mail transport agent that you can use for Linux.

Chapter 13, *Configuring IPv6 Networks*, covers new ground by explaining how to configure IPv6 and connect to the IPv6 backbone.

Chapter 14, *Configuring the Apache Web Server*, describes the steps necessary to build an Apache web server and host basic web services.

Chapter 15, *IMAP*, explains the steps necessary to configure an IMAP mail server, and discusses its advantages over the traditional POP mail solution.

Chapter 16, *Samba*, helps you understand how to configure your Linux server to play nicely in the Windows networking world—so nicely, in fact, that your Windows users might not be able to tell the difference.*

Chapter 17, *OpenLDAP*, introduces OpenLDAP and discusses the configuration and potential uses of this service

Chapter 18, *Wireless Networking*, finally, details the steps required to configure wireless networking and build a Wireless Access Point on a Linux server.

---

* The obvious joke here is left to the reader.

Conventions Used in This Book

All examples presented in this book assume that you are using an sh-compatible shell. The bash shell is sh compatible and is the standard shell of all Linux distributions. If you happen to be a csh user, you will have to make appropriate adjustments.

The following is a list of the typographical conventions used in this book:

Italic
> Used for file and directory names, program and command names, email addresses and pathnames, URLs, and for emphasizing new terms.

Boldface
> Used for machine names, hostnames, site names, and for occasional emphasis.

Constant Width
> Used in examples to show the contents of code files or the output from commands and to indicate environment variables and keywords that appear in code.

Constant Width Italic
> Used to indicate variable options, keywords, or text that the user is to replace with an actual value.

Constant Width Bold
> Used in examples to show commands or other text that should be typed literally by the user.

 Indicates a tip, suggestion, or general note.

 Text appearing in this manner offers a warning. You can make a mistake here that hurts your system or is hard to recover from.

Safari Enabled

 When you see a Safari® Enabled icon on the cover of your favorite technology book, that means the book is available online through the O'Reilly Network Safari Bookshelf.

Safari offers a solution that's better than e-books. It's a virtual library that lets you easily search thousands of top tech books, cut and paste code samples, download chapters, and find quick answers when you need the most accurate, current information. Try it for free at *http://safari.oreilly.com*.

How to Contact Us

We have tested and verified the information in this book to the best of our ability, but you may find that features have changed (or even that we have made mistakes!). Please let us know about any errors you find, as well as your suggestions for future editions, by writing to:

O'Reilly Media, Inc.
1005 Gravenstein Highway North
Sebastopol, CA 95472
(800) 998-9938 (in the United States or Canada)
(707) 829-0515 (international or local)
(707) 829-0104 (fax)

You can send us messages electronically. To be put on the mailing list or request a catalog, send email to:

info@oreilly.com

To ask technical questions or comment on the book, send email to:

bookquestions@oreilly.com

We have a web site for the book, where we'll list examples, errata, and any plans for future editions. You can access this page at:

http://www.oreilly.com/catalog/linag3

For more information about this book and others, see the O'Reilly web site:

http://www.oreilly.com

Acknowledgments

This edition of the Networking Guide owes much to the outstanding work of Olaf, Vince, and Terry. It is difficult to appreciate the effort that goes into researching and writing a book of this nature until you've had a chance to work on one yourself. Updating the book was a challenging task, but with an excellent base to work from, it was an enjoyable one.

This book owes very much to the numerous people who took the time to proofread it and help iron out many mistakes. Phil Hughes, John Macdonald, and Kenneth Geisshirt all provided very helpful (and on the whole, quite consistent) feedback on the content of the third edition of this book. Andres Sepúlveda, Wolfgang Michaelis, and Michael K. Johnson offered invaluable help on the second edition. Finally, the book would not have been possible without the support of Holger Grothe, who provided Olaf with the Internet connectivity he needed to make the original version happen.

Terry thanks his wife, Maggie, who patiently supported him throughout his participation in the project despite the challenges presented by the birth of their first child, Jack. Additionally, he thanks the *many* people of the Linux community who either nurtured or suffered him to the point at which he could actually take part and actively contribute. "I'll help you if you promise to help someone else in return."

Tony would like to thank Linux gurus Dan Ginsberg and Nicolas Lidzborski for their support and technical expertise in proofreading the new chapters. Additionally, he thanks Katherine for her input with each chapter, when all she really wanted to do was check her email. Thanks to Mick Bauer for getting me involved with this project and supporting me along the way. Finally, many thanks to the countless Linux users who have very helpfully documented their perils in getting things to work, not to mention the countless others who respond on a daily basis to questions posted on the mailing lists. Without this kind of community support, Linux would be nowhere.

## CHAPTER 1

Introduction to Networking

History

The idea of networking is probably as old as telecommunications itself. Consider people living in the Stone Age, when drums may have been used to transmit messages between individuals. Suppose caveman A wants to invite caveman B over for a game of hurling rocks at each other, but they live too far apart for B to hear A banging his drum. What are A's options? He could 1) walk over to B's place, 2) get a bigger drum, or 3) ask C, who lives halfway between them, to forward the message. The last option is called *networking*.

Of course, we have come a long way from the primitive pursuits and devices of our forebears. Nowadays, we have computers talk to each other over vast assemblages of wires, fiber optics, microwaves, and the like, to make an appointment for Saturday's soccer match.* In the following description, we will deal with the means and ways by which this is accomplished, but leave out the wires, as well as the soccer part.

We define a network as a collection of *hosts* that are able to communicate with each other, often by relying on the services of a number of dedicated hosts that relay data between the participants. Hosts are often computers, but need not be; one can also think of X terminals or intelligent printers as hosts. A collection of hosts is also called a *site*.

Communication is impossible without some sort of language or code. In computer networks, these languages are collectively referred to as *protocols*. However, you shouldn't think of written protocols here, but rather of the highly formalized code of behavior observed when heads of state meet, for instance. In a very similar fashion, the protocols used in computer networks are nothing but very strict rules for the exchange of messages between two or more hosts.

---

* The original spirit of which (see above) still shows on some occasions in Europe.

TCP/IP Networks

Modern networking applications require a sophisticated approach to carry data from one machine to another. If you are managing a Linux machine that has many users, each of whom may wish to simultaneously connect to remote hosts on a network, you need a way of allowing them to share your network connection without interfering with each other. The approach that a large number of modern networking protocols use is called *packet switching*. A packet is a small chunk of data that is transferred from one machine to another across the network. The switching occurs as the datagram is carried across each link in the network. A packet-switched network shares a single network link among many users by alternately sending packets from one user to another across that link.

The solution that Unix systems, and subsequently many non-Unix systems, have adopted is known as TCP/IP. When learning about TCP/IP networks, you will hear the term *datagram*, which technically has a special meaning but is often used interchangeably with packet. In this section, we will have a look at underlying concepts of the TCP/IP protocols.

Introduction to TCP/IP Networks

TCP/IP traces its origins to a research project funded by the United States Defense Advanced Research Projects Agency (DARPA) in 1969. The ARPANET was an experimental network that was converted into an operational one in 1975 after it had proven to be a success.

In 1983, the new protocol suite TCP/IP was adopted as a standard, and all hosts on the network were required to use it. When ARPANET finally grew into the Internet (with ARPANET itself passing out of existence in 1990), the use of TCP/IP had spread to networks beyond the Internet itself. Many companies have now built corporate TCP/IP networks, and the Internet has become a mainstream consumer technology. It is difficult to read a newspaper or magazine now without seeing references to the Internet; almost everyone can use it now.

For something concrete to look at as we discuss TCP/IP throughout the following sections, we will consider Groucho Marx University (GMU), situated somewhere in Freedonia, as an example. Most departments run their own Local Area Networks, while some share one and others run several of them. They are all interconnected and hooked to the Internet through a single high-speed link.

Suppose your Linux box is connected to a LAN of Unix hosts at the mathematics department, and its name is **erdos**. To access a host at the physics department, say **quark**, you enter the following command:

```
$ ssh quark.school.edu
Enter password:
Last login: Wed Dec  3 18:21:25 2003 from 10.10.0.1
quark$
```

At the prompt, you enter your password. You are then given a shell[*] on **quark**, to which you can type as if you were sitting at the system's console. After you exit the shell, you are returned to your own machine's prompt. You have just used one of the instantaneous, interactive applications that uses TCP/IP: secure shell.

While being logged into **quark**, you might also want to run a graphical user interface application, like a word processing program, a graphics drawing program, or even a World Wide Web browser. The X Windows System is a fully network-aware graphical user environment, and it is available for many different computing systems. To tell this application that you want to have its windows displayed on your host's screen, you will need to make sure that you're SSH server and client are capable of tunneling X. To do this, you can check the *sshd_config* file on the system, which should contain a line like this:

```
X11Forwarding yes
```

If you now start your application, it will tunnel your X Window System applications so that they will be displayed on your X server instead of **quark**'s. Of course, this requires that you have X11 runnning on **erdos**. The point here is that TCP/IP allows **quark** and **erdos** to send X11 packets back and forth to give you the illusion that you're on a single system. The network is almost transparent here.

Of course, these are only examples of what you can do with TCP/IP networks. The possibilities are almost limitless, and we'll introduce you to more as you read on through the book.

We will now have a closer look at the way TCP/IP works. This information will help you understand how and why you have to configure your machine. We will start by examining the hardware and slowly work our way up.

Ethernets

The most common type of LAN hardware is known as *Ethernet.* In its simplest form, it consists of a single cable with hosts attached to it through connectors, taps, or transceivers. Simple Ethernets are relatively inexpensive to install, which together with a net transfer rate of 10, 100, 1,000, and now even 10,000 megabits per second (Mbps), accounts for much of its popularity.

Ethernets come in many flavors: *thick*, *thin*, and *twisted pair*. Older Ethernet types such as thin and thick Ethernet, rarely in use today, each use a coaxial cable, differing in diameter and the way you may attach a host to this cable. Thin Ethernet uses a T-shaped "BNC" connector, which you insert into the cable and twist onto a plug on the back of your computer. Thick Ethernet requires that you drill a small hole into

---

[*] The shell is a command-line interface to the Unix operating system. It's similar to the DOS prompt in a Microsoft Windows environment, albeit much more powerful.

the cable and attach a transceiver using a "vampire tap." One or more hosts can then be connected to the transceiver. Thin and thick Ethernet cable can run for a maximum of 200 and 500 meters, respectively, and are also called 10-base2 and 10-base5. The "base" refers to "baseband modulation" and simply means that the data is directly fed onto the cable without any modem. The number at the start refers to the speed in megabits per second, and the number at the end is the maximum length of the cable in hundreds of metres. Twisted pair uses a cable made of two pairs of copper wires and usually requires additional hardware known as *active hubs*. Twisted pair is also known as 10-baseT, the "T" meaning twisted pair. The 100 Mbps version is known as 100-baseT, and not surprisingly, 1000 Mbps is called 1000-baseT or gigabit.

To add a host to a thin Ethernet installation, you have to disrupt network service for at least a few minutes because you have to cut the cable to insert the connector. Although adding a host to a thick Ethernet system is a little complicated, it does not typically bring down the network. Twisted pair Ethernet is even simpler. It uses a device called a _hub_ or _switch_ that serves as an interconnection point. You can insert and remove hosts from a hub or switch without interrupting any other users at all.

Thick and thin Ethernet deployments are somewhat difficult to find anymore because they have been mostly replaced by twisted pair deployments. This has likely become a standard because of the cheap networking cards and cables—not to mention that it's almost impossible to find an old BNC connector in a modern laptop machine.

Wireless LANs are also very popular. These are based on the 802.11a/b/g specification and provide Ethernet over radio transmission. Offering similar functionality to its wired counterpart, wireless Ethernet has been subject to a number of security issues, namely surrounding encryption. However, advances in the protocol specification combined with different encryption keying methods are quickly helping to alleviate some of the more serious security concerns. Wireless networking for Linux is discussed in detail in Chapter 18.

Ethernet works like a bus system, where a host may send packets (or *frames*) of up to 1,500 bytes to another host on the same Ethernet. A host is addressed by a 6-byte address hardcoded into the firmware of its Ethernet network interface card (NIC). These addresses are usually written as a sequence of two-digit hex numbers separated by colons, as in **aa:bb:cc:dd:ee:ff**.

A frame sent by one station is seen by all attached stations, but only the destination host actually picks it up and processes it. If two stations try to send at the same time, a _collision_ occurs. Collisions on an Ethernet are detected very quickly by the electronics of the interface cards and are resolved by the two stations aborting the send, each waiting a random interval and re-attempting the transmission. You'll hear lots of stories about collisions on Ethernet being a problem and that utilization of Ethernets is only about 30 percent of the available bandwidth because of them. Collisions on

Ethernet are a *normal* phenomenon, and on a very busy Ethernet network you shouldn't be surprised to see collision rates of up to about 30 percent. Ethernet networks need to be more realistically limited to about 60 percent before you need to start worrying about it.*

Other Types of Hardware

In larger installations, or in legacy corporate environments, Ethernet is usually not the only type of equipment used. There are many other data communications protocols available and in use. All of the protocols listed are supported by Linux, but due to space constraints we'll describe them briefly. Many of the protocols have HOWTO documents that describe them in detail, so you should refer to those if you're interested in exploring those that we don't describe in this book.

One older and quickly disappearing technology is IBM's Token Ring network. Token Ring is used as an alternative to Ethernet in some LAN environments, and runs at lower speeds (4 Mbps or 16 Mbps). In Linux, Token Ring networking is configured in almost precisely the same way as Ethernet, so we don't cover it specifically.

Many national networks operated by telecommunications companies support packet-switching protocols. Previously, the most popular of these was a standard named X.25. It defines a set of networking protocols that describes how data terminal equipment, such as a host, communicates with data communications equipment (an X.25 switch). X.25 requires a synchronous data link and therefore special synchronous serial port hardware. It is possible to use X.25 with normal serial ports if you use a special device called a *Packet Assembler Disassembler* (PAD). The PAD is a standalone device that provides asynchronous serial ports and a synchronous serial port. It manages the X.25 protocol so that simple terminal devices can make and accept X.25 connections. X.25 is often used to carry other network protocols, such as TCP/IP. Since IP datagrams cannot simply be mapped onto X.25 (or vice versa), they are encapsulated in X.25 packets and sent over the network. There is an implementation of the X.25 protocol available for Linux, but it will not be discussed in depth here.

A protocol commonly used by telecommunications companies is called *Frame Relay*. The Frame Relay protocol shares a number of technical features with the X.25 protocol, but is much more like the IP protocol in behavior. Like X.25, Frame Relay requires special synchronous serial hardware. Because of their similarities, many cards support both of these protocols. An alternative is available that requires no

---

* The Ethernet FAQ at *http://www.faqs.org/faqs/LANs/ethernet-faq/* talks about this issue, and a wealth of detailed historical and technical information is available at Charles Spurgeon's Ethernet web site at *http://www.ethermanage.com/ethernet/ethernet.html/*.

special internal hardware, again relying on an external device called a Frame Relay Access Device (FRAD) to manage the encapsulation of Ethernet packets into Frame Relay packets for transmission across a network. Frame Relay is ideal for carrying TCP/IP between sites. Linux provides drivers that support some types of internal Frame Relay devices.

If you need higher-speed networking that can carry many different types of data, such as digitized voice and video, alongside your usual data, *Asynchronous Transfer Mode* (ATM) is probably what you'll be interested in. ATM is a new network technology that has been specifically designed to provide a manageable, high-speed, low-latency means of carrying data and control over the Quality of Service (QoS). Many telecommunications companies are deploying ATM network infrastructure because it allows the convergence of a number of different network services into one platform, in the hope of achieving savings in management and support costs. ATM is often used to carry TCP/IP. The *Networking HOWTO* offers information on the Linux support available for ATM.

Frequently, radio amateurs use their radio equipment to network their computers; this is commonly called *packet radio*. One of the protocols used by amateur radio operators is called AX.25 and is loosely derived from X.25. Amateur radio operators use the AX.25 protocol to carry TCP/IP and other protocols, too. AX.25, like X.25, requires serial hardware capable of synchronous operation, or an external device called a *Terminal Node Controller* to convert packets transmitted via an asynchronous serial link into packets transmitted synchronously. There are a variety of different sorts of interface cards available to support packet radio operation; these cards are generally referred to as being "Z8530 SCC based," named after the most popular type of communications controller used in the designs. Two of the other protocols that are commonly carried by AX.25 are the NetRom and Rose protocols, which are network layer protocols. Since these protocols run over AX.25, they have the same hardware requirements. Linux supports a fully featured implementation of the AX.25, NetRom, and Rose protocols. The *AX25 HOWTO* is a good source of information on the Linux implementation of these protocols.

Other types of Internet access involve dialing up a central system over slow but cheap serial lines (telephone, ISDN, and so on). These require yet another protocol for transmission of packets, such as SLIP or PPP, which will be described later.

The Internet Protocol

Of course, you wouldn't want your networking to be limited to one Ethernet or one point-to-point data link. Ideally, you would want to be able to communicate with a host computer regardless of what type of physical network it is connected to. For example, in larger installations such as Groucho Marx University, you usually have a number of separate networks that have to be connected in some way. At GMU, the math department runs two Ethernets: one with fast machines for professors and graduates, and another with slow machines for students.

This connection is handled by a dedicated host called a *gateway* that handles incoming and outgoing packets by copying them between the two Ethernets and the FDDI fiber optic cable. For example, if you are at the math department and want to access **quark** on the physics department's LAN from your Linux box, the networking software will not send packets to **quark** directly because it is not on the same Ethernet. Therefore, it has to rely on the gateway to act as a forwarder. The gateway (named **sophus**) then forwards these packets to its peer gateway **niels** at the physics department, using the backbone network, with **niels** delivering it to the destination machine. Data flow between **erdos** and **quark** is shown in Figure 1-1.

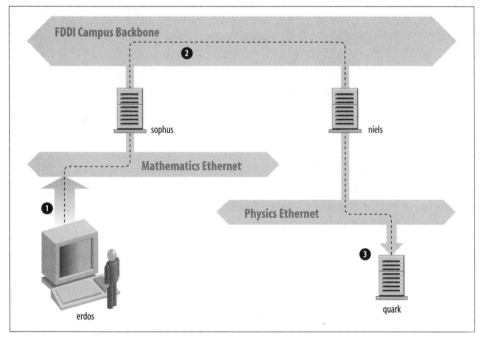

Figure 1-1. The three steps of sending a datagram from erdos to quark

This scheme of directing data to a remote host is called *routing*, and packets are often referred to as datagrams in this context. To facilitate things, datagram exchange is governed by a single protocol that is independent of the hardware used: IP, or *Internet Protocol*. In Chapter 2, we will cover IP and the issues of routing in greater detail.

The main benefit of IP is that it turns physically dissimilar networks into one apparently homogeneous network. This is called internetworking, and the resulting "meta-network" is called an *internet*. Note the subtle difference here between *an* internet and *the* Internet. The latter is the official name of one particular global internet.

Of course, IP also requires a hardware-independent addressing scheme. This is achieved by assigning each host a unique 32-bit number called the *IP address*. An IP address is usually written as four decimal numbers, one for each 8-bit portion, separated by dots. For example, **quark** might have an IP address of **0x954C0C04**, which would be written as **149.76.12.4**. This format is also called *dotted decimal notation* and sometimes *dotted quad notation*. It is increasingly going under the name IPv4 (for Internet Protocol, Version 4) because a new standard called IPv6 offers much more flexible addressing, as well as other modern features. It will be at least a year after the release of this edition before IPv6 is in use.

You will notice that we now have three different types of addresses: first there is the host's name, like **quark**, then there is an IP address, and finally, there is a hardware address, such as the 6-byte Ethernet address. All these addresses somehow have to match so that when you type *ssh quark*, the networking software can be given **quark**'s IP address; and when IP delivers any data to the physics department's Ethernet, it somehow has to find out what Ethernet address corresponds to the IP address.

We will deal with these situations in Chapter 2. For now, it's enough to remember that these steps of finding addresses are called *hostname resolution*, for mapping hostnames onto IP addresses, and *address resolution*, for mapping the latter to hardware addresses.

IP over Serial Lines

On serial lines, a "de facto" standard exists known as *Serial Line IP* (SLIP). A modification of SLIP known as *Compressed SLIP* (CSLIP), performs compression of IP headers to make better use of the relatively low bandwidth provided by most serial links. Another serial protocol is *Point-to-Point Protocol* (PPP). PPP is more modern than SLIP and includes a number of features that make it more attractive. Its main advantage over SLIP is that it isn't limited to transporting IP datagrams, but is designed to allow just about any protocol to be carried across it. This book discusses PPP in Chapter 6.

The Transmission Control Protocol

Sending datagrams from one host to another is not the whole story. If you log in to **quark**, you want to have a reliable connection between your *ssh* process on **erdos** and the shell process on **quark**. Thus, the information sent to and fro must be split into packets by the sender and reassembled into a character stream by the receiver. Trivial as it seems, this involves a number of complicated tasks.

A very important thing to know about IP is that, by intent, it is not reliable. Assume that 10 people on your Ethernet started downloading the latest release of the Mozilla web browser source code from GMU's FTP server. The amount of traffic generated might be too much for the gateway to handle because it's too slow and it's tight on

memory. Now if you happen to send a packet to **quark**, **sophus** r
buffer space for a moment and therefore unable to forward it. IP so'
by simply discarding it. The packet is irrevocably lost. It is therefc
ity of the communicating hosts to check the integrity and compi
and retransmit it in case of error.

This process is performed by yet another protocol, *Transmission Control F*
(TCP), which builds a reliable service on top of IP. The essential property of TCP is
that it uses IP to give you the illusion of a simple connection between the two processes on your host and the remote machine so that you don't have to care about
how and along which route your data actually travels. A TCP connection works
essentially like a two-way pipe that both processes may write to and read from.
Think of it as a telephone conversation.

TCP identifies the end points of such a connection by the IP addresses of the two
hosts involved and the number of a *port* on each host. Ports may be viewed as attachment points for network connections. If we are to strain the telephone example a little more, and you imagine that cities are like hosts, one might compare IP addresses
to area codes (where numbers map to cities), and port numbers to local codes (where
numbers map to individual people's telephones). An individual host may support
many different services, each distinguished by its own port number.

In the *ssh* example, the client application (*ssh*) opens a port on **erdos** and connects to
port 22 on **quark**, to which the sshd server is known to listen. This action establishes a TCP connection. Using this connection, *sshd* performs the authorization procedure and then spawns the shell. The shell's standard input and output are
redirected to the TCP connection so that anything you type to *ssh* on your machine
will be passed through the TCP stream and be given to the shell as standard input.

The User Datagram Protocol

Of course, TCP isn't the only user protocol in TCP/IP networking. Although suitable for applications like *ssh*, the overhead involved is prohibitive for applications
like NFS, which instead uses a sibling protocol of TCP called *User Datagram Protocol* (UDP). Just like TCP, UDP allows an application to contact a service on a certain
port of the remote machine, but it doesn't establish a connection for this. Instead,
you use it to send single packets to the destination service—hence its name.

Assume that you want to request a small amount of data from a database server. It
takes at least three datagrams to establish a TCP connection, another three to send
and confirm a small amount of data each way, and another three to close the connection. UDP provides us with a means of using only two datagrams to achieve almost
the same result. UDP is said to be connectionless, and it doesn't require us to establish and close a session. We simply put our data into a datagram and send it to the
server; the server formulates its reply, puts the data into a datagram addressed back

.o us, and transmits it back. While this is both faster and more efficient than TCP for simple transactions, UDP was not designed to deal with datagram loss. It is up to the application, a nameserver, for example, to take care of this.

More on Ports

Ports may be viewed as attachment points for network connections. If an application wants to offer a certain service, it attaches itself to a port and waits for clients (this is also called *listening* on the port). A client who wants to use this service allocates a port on its local host and connects to the server's port on the remote host. The same port may be open on many different machines, but on each machine only one process can open a port at any one time.

An important property of ports is that once a connection has been established between the client and the server, another copy of the server may attach to the server port and listen for more clients. This property permits, for instance, several concurrent remote logins to the same host, all using the same port 513. TCP is able to tell these connections from one another because they all come from different ports or hosts. For example, if you log in twice to **quark** from **erdos**, the first *ssh* client may use the local port 6464, and the second one could use port 4235. Both, however, will connect to the same port 513 on **quark**. The two connections will be distinguished by use of the port numbers used at **erdos**.

This example shows the use of ports as rendezvous points, where a client contacts a specific port to obtain a specific service. In order for a client to know the proper port number, an agreement has to be reached between the administrators of both systems on the assignment of these numbers. For services that are widely used, such as *ssh*, these numbers have to be administered centrally. This is done by the Internet Engineering Task Force (IETF), which regularly releases an RFC titled *Assigned Numbers* (RFC-1700). It describes, among other things, the port numbers assigned to well-known services. Linux uses a file called */etc/services* that maps service names to numbers.

It is worth noting that, although both TCP and UDP connections rely on ports, these numbers do not conflict. This means that TCP port 22, for example, is different from UDP port 22.

The Socket Library

In Unix operating systems, the software performing all the tasks and protocols described above is usually part of the kernel, and so it is in Linux. The programming interface most common in the Unix world is the Berkeley Socket Library. Its name derives from a popular analogy that views ports as sockets and connecting to a port as plugging in. It provides the bind call to specify a remote host, a transport protocol, and a service that a program can connect or listen to (using connect, listen, and accept). The socket library is somewhat more general in that it provides not only a class of TCP/IP-based sockets (the *AF_INET* sockets), but also a class that handles connections local to the machine (the *AF_UNIX* class). Some implementations can also handle other classes, like the Xerox Networking System (XNS) protocol or X.25.

In Linux, the socket library is part of the standard *libc* C library. It supports the *AF_INET* and *AF_INET6* sockets for TCP/IP and *AF_UNIX* for Unix domain sockets. It also supports *AF_IPX* for Novell's network protocols, *AF_ X25* for the X.25 network protocol, *AF_ATMPVC* and *AF_ATMSVC* for the ATM network protocol and *AF_AX25*, *AF_NETROM*, and *AF_ ROSE* sockets for Amateur Radio protocol support. Other protocol families are being developed and will be added in time.

Linux Networking

As it is the result of a concerted effort of programmers around the world, Linux wouldn't have been possible without the global network. So it's not surprising that in the early stages of development, several people started to work on providing it with network capabilities. A UUCP implementation was running on Linux almost from the very beginning, and work on TCP/IP-based networking started around autumn 1992, when Ross Biro and others created what has now become known as Net-1.

After Ross quit active development in May 1993, Fred van Kempen began to work on a new implementation, rewriting major parts of the code. This project was known as Net-2. The first public release, Net-2d, was made in the summer of 1993 (as part of the 0.99.10 kernel), and has since been maintained and expanded by several people, most notably Alan Cox. Alan's original work was known as Net-2Debugged. After heavy debugging and numerous improvements to the code, he changed its name to Net-3 after Linux 1.0 was released. The Net-3 code was further developed for Linux 1.2 and Linux 2.0. The 2.2 and later kernels use the Net-4 version network support, which remains the standard official offering today.

The Net-4 Linux Network code offers a wide variety of device drivers and advanced features. Standard Net-4 protocols include SLIP and PPP (for sending network traffic over serial lines), PLIP (for parallel lines), IPX (for Novell compatible networks), Appletalk (for Apple networks) and AX.25, NetRom, and Rose (for amateur radio networks). Other standard Net-4 features include IP firewalling (discussed in Chapter 7), IP accounting (Chapter 8), and IP Masquerade (Chapter 9). IP tunneling in a couple of different flavors and advanced policy routing are supported. A very large variety of Ethernet devices are supported, in addition to support for some FDDI, Token Ring, Frame Relay, and ISDN, and ATM cards.

Additionally, there are a number of other features that greatly enhance the flexibility of Linux. These features include interoperability with the Microsoft Windows network environment, in a project called Samba, discussed in Chapter 16, and an implementation of the Novell NCP (NetWare Core Protocol).[*]

Different Streaks of Development

There have been, at various times, varying network development efforts active for Linux.

Fred continued development after Net-2Debugged was made the official network implementation. This development led to the Net-2e, which featured a much revised design of the networking layer. Fred was working toward a standardized Device Driver Interface (DDI), but the Net-2e work has ended now.

Yet another implementation of TCP/IP networking came from Matthias Urlichs, who wrote an ISDN driver for Linux and FreeBSD. For this driver, he integrated some of the BSD networking code in the Linux kernel. That project, too, is no longer being worked on.

There has been a lot of rapid change in the Linux kernel networking implementation, and change is still the watchword as development continues. Sometimes this means that changes also have to occur in other software, such as the network configuration tools. While this is no longer as large a problem as it once was, you may still find that upgrading your kernel to a later version means that you must upgrade your network configuration tools, too. Fortunately, with the large number of Linux distributions available today, this is a quite simple task.

The Net-4 network implementation is now a standard and is in use at a very large number of sites around the world. Much work has been done on improving the performance of the Net-4 implementation, and it now competes with the best implementations available for the same hardware platforms. Linux is proliferating in the Internet Service Provider environment, and is often used to build cheap and reliable World Wide Web servers, mail servers, and news servers for these sorts of organizations. There is now sufficient development interest in Linux that it is managing to keep abreast of networking technology as it changes, and current releases of the Linux kernel offer the next generation of the IP protocol, IPv6, as a standard offering, which will be discussed at greater detail in Chapter 13.

Where to Get the Code

It seems odd now to remember that in the early days of the Linux network code development, the standard kernel required a huge patch kit to add the networking support to it. Today, network development occurs as part of the mainstream Linux kernel development process. The latest stable Linux kernels can be found on *ftp://ftp.*

---

[*] NCP is the protocol on which Novell file and print services are based.

kernel.org in */pub/linux/kernel/v2.x/*, where *x* is an even number. The latest experimental Linux kernels can be found on *ftp://ftp.kernel.org* in */pub/linux/kernel/v2.y/*, where y is an odd number. The kernel.org distributions can also be accessed via HTTP at *http://www.kernel.org*. There are Linux kernel source mirrors all over the world.

Maintaining Your System

Throughout this book, we will mainly deal with installation and configuration issues. Administration is, however, much more than that—after setting up a service, you have to keep it running, too. For most services, only a little attendance will be necessary, while some, such as mail, require that you perform routine tasks to keep your system up to date. We will discuss these tasks in later chapters.

The absolute minimum in maintenance is to check system and per-application logfiles regularly for error conditions and unusual events. Often, you will want to do this by writing a couple of administrative shell scripts and periodically running them from *cron*. The source distributions of some major applications contain such scripts. You only have to tailor them to suit your needs and preferences.

The output from any of your *cron* jobs should be mailed to an administrative account. By default, many applications will send error reports, usage statistics, or logfile summaries to the *root* account. This makes sense only if you log in as *root* frequently; a much better idea is to forward *root*'s mail to your personal account by setting up a mail alias as described in Chapters 11 and 12.

However carefully you have configured your site, Murphy's Law guarantees that some problem *will* surface eventually. Therefore, maintaining a system also means being available for complaints. Usually, people expect that the system administrator can at least be reached via email as *root*, but there are also other addresses that are commonly used to reach the person responsible for a specific aspect of maintenence. For instance, complaints about a malfunctioning mail configuration will usually be addressed to *postmaster*, and problems with the news system may be reported to *newsmaster* or *usenet*. Mail to *hostmaster* should be redirected to the person in charge of the host's basic network services, and the DNS name service if you run a nameserver.

System Security

Another very important aspect of system administration in a network environment is protecting your system and users from intruders. Carelessly managed systems offer malicious people many targets. Attacks range from password guessing to Ethernet snooping, and the damage caused may range from faked mail messages to data loss or violation of your users' privacy. We will mention some particular problems when discussing the context in which they may occur and some common defenses against them.

This section will discuss a few examples and basic techniques for dealing with system security. Of course, the topics covered cannot treat all security issues in detail; they merely serve to illustrate the problems that may arise. Therefore, reading a good book on security is an absolute must, especially in a networked system.

System security starts with good system administration. This includes checking the ownership and permissions of all vital files and directories and monitoring use of privileged accounts. The COPS program, for instance, will check your filesystem and common configuration files for unusual permissions or other anomalies. Another tool, Bastille Linux, developed by Jay Beale and found at *http://www.bastille-linux. org*, contains a number of scripts and programs that can be used to lock down a Linux system. It is also wise to use a password suite that enforces certain rules on the users' passwords that make them hard to guess. The shadow password suite, now a default, requires a password to have at least five letters and to contain both upper- and lowercase numbers, as well as nonalphabetic characters.

When making a service accessible to the network, make sure to give it "least privilege"; don't permit it to do things that aren't required for it to work as designed. For example, you should make programs setuid to **root** or some other privileged account only when necessary. Also, if you want to use a service for only a very limited application, don't hesitate to configure it as restrictively as your special application allows. For instance, if you want to allow diskless hosts to boot from your machine, you must provide *Trivial File Transfer Protocol* (TFTP) so that they can download basic configuration files from the */boot* directory. However, when used unrestrictively, TFTP allows users anywhere in the world to download any world-readable file from your system. If this is not what you want, restrict TFTP service to the */boot* directory (we'll come back to this in Chapter 10). You might also want to restrict certain services to users from certain hosts, say from your local network. In Chapter 10, we introduce *tcpd*, which does this for a variety of network applications. More sophisticated methods of restricting access to particular hosts or services will be explored in Chapter 7.

Another important point is to avoid "dangerous" software. Of course, any software you use can be dangerous because software may have bugs that clever people might exploit to gain access to your system. Things like this happen, and there's no complete protection against it. This problem affects free software and commercial products alike.* However, programs that require special privilege are inherently more dangerous than others because any loophole can have drastic consequences.† If you

---

* There have been commercial Unix systems (that you have to pay lots of money for) that came with a setuid root shell script, which allowed users to gain **root** privilege using a simple standard trick.

† In 1988, the RTM worm brought much of the Internet to a grinding halt, partly by exploiting a gaping hole in some programs, including the *sendmail* program. This hole has long since been fixed.

---

install a setuid program for network purposes, be doubly careful to check the documentation so that you don't create a security breach by accident.

Another source of concern should be programs that enable login or command execution with limited authentication. The *rlogin*, *rsh*, and *rexec* commands are all very useful, but offer very limited authentication of the calling party. Authentication is based on trust of the calling hostname obtained from a nameserver (we'll talk about these later), which can be faked. Today it should be standard practice to disable the *r* commands completely and replace them with the *ssh* suite of tools. The *ssh* tools use a much more reliable authentication method and provide other services, such as encryption and compression, as well.

You can never rule out the possibility that your precautions might fail, regardless of how careful you have been. You should therefore make sure that you detect intruders early. Checking the system logfiles is a good starting point, but the intruder is probably clever enough to anticipate this action and will delete any obvious traces he or she left. However, there are tools like *tripwire*, written by Gene Kim and Gene Spafford, that allow you to check vital system files to see if their contents or permissions have been changed. *tripwire* computes various strong checksums over these files and stores them in a database. During subsequent runs, the checksums are recomputed and compared to the stored ones to detect any modifications.

Finally, it's always important to be proactive about security. Monitoring the mailing lists for updates and fixes to the applications that you use is critical in keeping current with new releases. Failing to update something such as Apache or OpenSSL can lead directly to system compromise. One fairly recent example of this was found with the Linux Slapper worm, which propagated using an OpenSSL vulnerability. While keeping up to date can seem a daunting and time-consuming effort, administrators who were quick to react and upgrade their OpenSSL implementations ended up saving a great deal of time because they did not have to restore compromised systems!

## CHAPTER 2

Issues of TCP/IP Networking

In this chapter we turn to the configuration decisions that you'll need to make when connecting your Linux machine to a TCP/IP network, including dealing with IP addresses, hostnames, and routing issues. This chapter gives you the background you need in order to understand what your setup requires, while the next chapters cover the tools that you will use.

To learn more about TCP/IP and the reasons behind it, refer to the three-volume set *Internetworking with TCP/IP* (Prentice Hall) by Douglas R. Comer. For a more detailed guide to managing a TCP/IP network, see *TCP/IP Network Administration* (O'Reilly) by Craig Hunt.

Networking Interfaces

To hide the diversity of equipment that may be used in a networking environment, TCP/IP defines an abstract *interface* through which the hardware is accessed. This interface offers a set of operations that is the same for all types of hardware and basically deals with sending and receiving packets.

For each peripheral networking device, a corresponding interface has to be present in the kernel. For example, Ethernet interfaces in Linux are called by such names as *eth0* and *eth1*; PPP (discussed in Chapter 6) interfaces are named *ppp0* and *ppp1*; and FDDI interfaces are given names such as *fddi0* and *fddi1*. These interface names are used for configuration purposes when you want to specify a particular physical device in a configuration command, and they have no meaning beyond this use.

Before being used by TCP/IP networking, an interface must be assigned an IP address that serves as its identification when communicating with the rest of the world. This address is different from the interface name mentioned previously; if you compare an interface to a door, the address is like the nameplate pinned on it.

Other device parameters may be set, such as the maximum size of datagrams that can be processed by a particular piece of hardware, which is referred to as *Maximum*

Transfer Unit (MTU). Other attributes will be introduced later. Fortunately, most attributes have sensible defaults.

IP Addresses

As mentioned in Chapter 1, the IP networking protocol understands addresses as 32-bit numbers. Each machine must be assigned a number unique to the networking environment. If you are running a local network that does not have TCP/IP traffic with other networks, you may assign these numbers according to your personal preferences. There are some IP address ranges that have been reserved for such private networks. These ranges are listed in Table 2-1. However, for sites on the Internet, numbers are assigned by a central authority, the *Network Information Center* (NIC).

IP addresses are split up into four 8-bit numbers called *octets* for readability. For example, **quark.physics.groucho.edu** has an IP address of **0x954C0C04**, which is written as **149.76.12.4**. This format is often referred to as *dotted quad notation*.

Another reason for this notation is that IP addresses are split into a *network number*, which is contained in the leading octets, and a *host number*, which is the remainder. When applying to the NIC for IP addresses, you are not assigned an address for each single host you plan to use. Instead, you are given a network number and allowed to assign all valid IP addresses within this range to hosts on your network according to your preferences.

The size of the host partly depends on the size of the network. To accommodate different needs, several classes of networks have been defined, with different places to split IP addresses. The class networks are described here:

Class A
> Class A comprises networks **1.0.0.0** through **127.0.0.0**. The network number is contained in the first octet. This class provides for a 24-bit host part, allowing roughly 1.6 million hosts per network.

Class B
> Class B contains networks **128.0.0.0** through **191.255.0.0**; the network number is in the first two octets. This class allows for 16,320 nets with 65,024 hosts each.

Class C
> Class C networks range from **192.0.0.0** through **223.255.255.0**, with the network number contained in the first three octets. This class allows for nearly 2 million networks with up to 254 hosts.

Classes D, E, and F
> Addresses falling into the range of **224.0.0.0** through **254.0.0.0** are either experimental or are reserved for special purpose use and don't specify any network. IP

Multicast, which is a service that allows material to be transmitted to many points on an internet at one time, has been assigned addresses from within this range.

If we go back to the example in Chapter 1, we find that **149.76.12.4**, the address of **quark**, refers to host **12.4** on the class B network **149.76.0.0**.

You may have noticed that not all possible values in the previous list were allowed for each octet in the host part. This is because octets **0** and **255** are reserved for special purposes. An address where all host part bits are 0 refers to the network, and an address where all bits of the host part are 1 is called a *broadcast address*. This refers to all hosts on the specified network simultaneously. Thus, **149.76.255.255** is not a valid host address, but refers to all hosts on network **149.76.0.0**.

A number of network addresses are reserved for special purposes. **0.0.0.0** and **127.0.0.0** are two such addresses. The first is called the *default route*, and the second is the *loopback address*. The default route is a place holder for the router your local area network uses to reach the outside world.

Network **127.0.0.0** is reserved for IP traffic local to your host. Usually, address **127.0.0.1** will be assigned to a special interface on your host, the *loopback interface*, which acts like a closed circuit. Any IP packet handed to this interface from TCP or UDP will be returned as if it had just arrived from some network. This allows you to develop and test networking software without ever using a "real" network. The loopback network also allows you to use networking software on a standalone host. This may not be as uncommon as it sounds; for instance, services such as MySQL, which may only be used by other applications resident on the server, can be bound to the local host interface to provide an added layer of security.

Some address ranges from each of the network classes have been set aside and designated "reserved" or "private" address ranges. Sometimes referred to as RFC-1918 addresses, these are reserved for use by private networks and are not routed on the Internet. They are commonly used by organizations building their own intranet, but even small networks often find them useful. The reserved network addresses appear in Table 2-1.

Table 2-1. IP address ranges reserved for private use

Class	Networks
A	10.0.0.0 through 10.255.255.255
B	172.16.0.0 through 172.31.0.0
C	192.168.0.0 through 192.168.255.0

Classless Inter-Domain Routing

Classless Inter-Domain routing (CIDR), discussed more in Chapter 4, is a newer and more efficient method of allocating IP addresses. With CIDR, network administrators can assign networks containing as few as two IP addresses, rather than the previous method of assigning an entire 254 addresses with a class C block. CIDR was designed for a number of reasons, but the primary reasons are the rapid depletion of IP addresses and various capacity issues with the global routing tables.

CIDR addresses are written using a new notation, not surprisingly called the CIDR block notation. An example is **172.16.0.0/24**, which represents the range of addresses from **172.16.0.0** to **172.16.0.255**. The 24 in the notation means that there are 24 address bits set, which leaves usable 8 bits of the 32-bit IP address. To reduce the number of addresses in this range, we could add three to the number of address bits, giving us a network address of **172.16.0.0/27**. This means that we would now have only five usable host bits, giving us a total of 32 addresses. CIDR addresses can also be used to create ranges larger than a class C. For example, removing two bits from the above 24-bit network example yields **172.16.0.0/22**. This provides a network space a network of 1,024 addresses, four times the size of a traditional class C space. Some common CIDR configurations are shown in Table 2-2.

Table 2-2. Common CIDR block notations

CIDR block prefix	Host bits	Number of addresses
/29	3 bits	8
/28	4 bits	16
/27	5 bits	32
/25	6 bits	128
/24	8 bits	256
/22	10 bits	1024

Address Resolution

Now that you've seen how IP addresses are composed, you may be wondering how they are used on an Ethernet or Token Ring network to address different hosts. After all, these protocols have their own addresses to identify hosts that have absolutely nothing in common with an IP address, don't they? Right.

A mechanism is needed to map IP addresses onto the addresses of the underlying network. The mechanism used is the *Address Resolution Protocol* (ARP). In fact, ARP is not confined to Ethernet or Token Ring, but is used on other types of networks, such as the amateur radio AX.25 protocol. The idea underlying ARP is exactly what most people do when they have to find Mr. X in a throng of 150 people: the person who wants him calls out loudly enough that everyone in the room can hear her, expecting him to respond if he is there. When he responds, she knows which person he is.

When ARP wants to find the Ethernet address corresponding to a given IP address, it uses an Ethernet feature called *broadcasting*, in which a datagram is addressed to all stations on the network simultaneously. The broadcast datagram sent by ARP contains a query for the IP address. Each receiving host compares this query to its own IP address and if it matches, returns an ARP reply to the inquiring host. The inquiring host can now extract the sender's Ethernet address from the reply. A useful utility to assist you in determining ARP addresses on your network is the *arp* utility. When run without any options, the command will return output similar to the following:

```
vbrew root # arp
Address              HWtype  HWaddress          Flags Mask        Iface
172.16.0.155         ether   00:11:2F:53:4D:EF  C                 eth0
172.16.0.65          ether   00:90:4B:C1:4A:E5  C                 eth0
vlager.vbrew.com     ether   00:10:67:00:C3:7B  C                 eth1
172.16.0.207         ether   00:0B:DB:53:E7:D4  C                 eth0
```

It is also possible to request specific ARP addresses from hosts on your network, and should it be necessary, network administrators can also modify, add, or remove ARP entries from their local cache.

Let's talk a little more about ARP. Once a host has discovered an Ethernet address, it stores it in its ARP cache so that it doesn't have to query for it again the next time it wants to send a datagram to the host in question. However, it is unwise to keep this information forever; the remote host's Ethernet card may be replaced because of technical problems, so the ARP entry would become invalid. Therefore, entries in the ARP cache are discarded after some time to force another query for the IP address.

Sometimes it is also necessary to find the IP address associated with a given Ethernet address. This happens when a diskless machine wants to boot from a server on the network, which is a common situation on Local Area Networks. A diskless client, however, has virtually no information about itself—except for its Ethernet address! So it broadcasts a message containing a request asking a boot server to provide it with an IP address. There's another protocol for this situation named *Reverse Address Resolution Protocol* (RARP). Along with the BOOTP protocol, it serves to define a procedure for bootstrapping diskless clients over the network.

IP Routing

We now take up the question of finding the host that datagrams go to based on the IP address. Different parts of the address are handled in different ways; it is your job to set up the files that indicate how to treat each part.

IP networks

When you write a letter to someone, you usually put a complete address on the envelope specifying the country, state, and Zip Code. After you put it in the mailbox, the post office will deliver it to its destination: it will be sent to the country indicated, where the national service will dispatch it to the proper state and region. The advantage of this hierarchical scheme is obvious: wherever you post the letter, the local postmaster knows roughly which direction to forward the letter, but the postmaster doesn't care which way the letter will travel once it reaches its country of destination.

IP networks are structured similarly. The whole Internet consists of a number of proper networks, called *autonomous systems*. Each system performs routing between its member hosts internally so that the task of delivering a datagram is reduced to finding a path to the destination host's network. As soon as the datagram is handed to *any* host on that particular network, further processing is done exclusively by the network itself.

Subnetworks

This structure is reflected by splitting IP addresses into a host and network part, as explained earlier in this chapter. By default, the destination network is derived from the network part of the IP address. Thus, hosts with identical IP network numbers should be found within the same network.[*]

It makes sense to offer a similar scheme *inside* the network, too, since it may consist of a collection of hundreds of smaller networks, with the smallest units being physical networks like Ethernets. Therefore, IP allows you to subdivide an IP network into several *subnets*.

A subnet takes responsibility for delivering datagrams to a certain range of IP addresses. It is an extension of the concept of splitting bit fields, as in the A, B, and C classes. However, the network part is now extended to include some bits from the host part. The number of bits that are interpreted as the subnet number is given by the so-called *subnet mask*, or *netmask*. This is a 32-bit number too, which specifies the bit mask for the network part of the IP address.

The campus network of Groucho Marx University (GMU) is an example of such a network. It has a class B network number of **149.76.0.0**, and its netmask is therefore **255.255.0.0**.

Internally, GMU's campus network consists of several smaller networks, such as various departments' LANs. So the range of IP addresses is broken up into 254 subnets, **149.76.1.0** through **149.76.254.0**. For example, the department of Theoretical Physics has been assigned **149.76.12.0**. The campus backbone is a network in its

---

[*] Autonomous systems are slightly more general. They may comprise more than one IP network.

own right, and is given **149.76.1.0**. These subnets share the same IP network number, while the third octet is used to distinguish between them. They will thus use a subnet mask of **255.255.255.0**.

Figure 2-1 shows how **149.76.12.4**, the address of **quark**, is interpreted differently when the address is taken as an ordinary class B network and when used with subnetting.

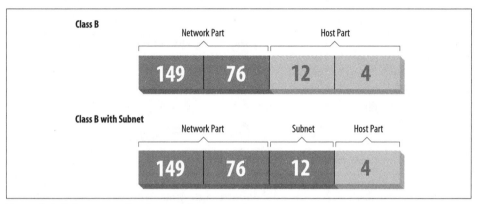

Figure 2-1. Subnetting a class B network

It is worth noting that *subnetting* (the technique of generating subnets) is only an *internal division* of the network. Subnets are generated by the network owner (or the administrators). Frequently, subnets are created to reflect existing boundaries, be they physical (between two Ethernets), administrative (between two departments), or geographical (between two locations), and authority over each subnet is delegated to some contact person. However, this structure affects only the network's internal behavior and is completely invisible to the outside world.

Gateways

Subnetting is not only a benefit to the organization; it is frequently a natural consequence of hardware boundaries. The viewpoint of a host on a given physical network, such as an Ethernet, is a very limited one: it can only talk to the host of the network it is on. All other hosts can be accessed only through special-purpose machines called *gateways*. A gateway is a host that is connected to two or more physical networks simultaneously and is configured to switch packets between them.

Figure 2-2 shows part of the network topology at GMU. Hosts that are on two subnets at the same time are shown with both addresses.

Different physical networks have to belong to different IP networks for IP to be able to recognize if a host is on a local network. For example, the network number **149. 76.4.0** is reserved for hosts on the mathematics LAN. When sending a datagram to **quark**, the network software on **erdos** immediately sees from the IP address **149.76.**

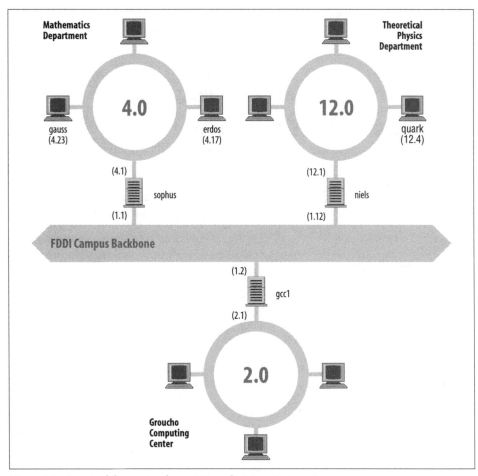

Figure 2-2. A part of the net topology at Groucho Marx University

12.4 that the destination host is on a different physical network, and therefore can be reached only through a gateway (**sophus** by default).

sophus itself is connected to two distinct subnets: the Mathematics department and the campus backbone. It accesses each through a different interface, *eth0* and *fddi0*, respectively. Now, what IP address do we assign it? Should we give it one on subnet **149.76.1.0** or on **149.76.4.0**?

The answer is: "both." **sophus** has been assigned the address **149.76.1.1** for use on the **149.76.1.0** network and address **149.76.4.1** for use on the **149.76.4.0** network. A gateway must be assigned one IP address for each network it belongs to. These addresses—along with the corresponding netmask—are tied to the interface through which the subnet is accessed. Thus, the interface and address mapping for **sophus** would be as shown in Table 2-3.

Table 2-3. Sample interfaces and addresses

Interface	Address	Netmask
eth0	149.76.4.1	255.255.255.0
fddi0	149.76.1.1	255.255.255.0
lo	127.0.0.1	255.0.0.0

The last entry describes the loopback interface *lo*, which we talked about earlier in this chapter.

Generally, you can ignore the subtle difference between attaching an address to a host or its interface. For hosts that are on one network only, such as **erdos**, you would generally refer to the host as having this-and-that IP address, although strictly speaking, it's the Ethernet interface that has this IP address. The distinction is really important only when you refer to a gateway.

The Routing Table

We now focus our attention on how IP chooses a gateway to use to deliver a datagram to a remote network.

We have seen that **erdos**, when given a datagram for **quark**, checks the destination address and finds that it is not on the local network. **erdos** therefore sends the datagram to the default gateway **sophus**, which is now faced with the same task. **sophus** recognizes that **quark** is not on any of the networks it is connected to directly, so it has to find yet another gateway to forward it through. The correct choice would be **niels**, the gateway to the physics department. **sophus** thus needs information to associate a destination network with a suitable gateway.

IP uses a table for this task that associates networks with the gateways by which they may be reached. A catch-all entry (the *default route*) must generally be supplied too; this is the gateway associated with network **0.0.0.0**. All destination addresses match this route, since none of the 32 bits are required to match, and therefore packets to an unknown network are sent through the default route. On **sophus**, the table might look as shown in Table 2-4.

Table 2-4. Sample routing table

Network	Netmask	Gateway	Interface
149.76.1.0	255.255.255.0	-	eth1
149.76.2.0	255.255.255.0	149.76.1.2	eth1
149.76.3.0	255.255.255.0	149.76.1.3	eth1
149.76.4.0	255.255.255.0	-	eth0
149.76.5.0	255.255.255.0	149.76.1.5	eth1
0.0.0.0	0.0.0.0	149.76.1.2	eth1

If you need to use a route to a network that **sophus** is directly connected to, you don't need a gateway; the gateway column here contains a hyphen.

It is possible to determine this information from the routing table by using the *route* command and the -n option, which will display IP addresses, rather than DNS names.

The process for identifying whether a particular destination address matches a route is a mathematical operation. The process is quite simple, but it requires an understanding of binary arithmetic and logic: a route matches a destination if the network address logically ANDed with the netmask precisely equals the destination address logically ANDed with the netmask.

Translation: a route matches if the number of bits of the network address specified by the netmask (starting from the left-most bit, the high order bit of byte one of the address) match that same number of bits in the destination address.

When the IP implementation is searching for the best route to a destination, it may find a number of routing entries that match the target address. For example, we know that the default route matches every destination, but datagrams destined for locally attached networks will match their local route, too. How does IP know which route to use? It is here that the netmask plays an important role. While both routes match the destination, one of the routes has a larger netmask than the other. We previously mentioned that the netmask was used to break up our address space into smaller networks. The larger a netmask is, the more specifically a target address is matched; when routing datagrams, we should always choose the route that has the largest netmask. The default route has a netmask of zero bits, and in the configuration presented above, the locally attached networks have a 24-bit netmask. If a datagram matches a locally attached network, it will be routed to the appropriate device in preference to following the default route because the local network route matches with a greater number of bits. The only datagrams that will be routed via the default route are those that don't match any other route.

You can build routing tables by a variety of means. For small LANs, it is usually most efficient to construct them by hand and feed them to IP using the route command at boot time (see Chapter 4). For larger networks, they are built and adjusted at runtime by routing daemons; these daemons run on central hosts of the network and exchange routing information to compute "optimal" routes between the member networks.

Depending on the size of the network, you'll need to use different routing protocols. For routing inside autonomous systems (such as the Groucho Marx campus), the *internal routing protocols* are used. The most prominent one of these is the *Routing Information Protocol* (RIP), which is implemented by the BSD routed daemon. For routing between autonomous systems, *external routing protocols* such as *External*

Gateway Protocol (EGP) or *Border Gateway Protocol* (BGP) have to be used; these protocols, including RIP, have been implemented in the University of Cornell's gated daemon.

Metric Values

We depend on dynamic routing to choose the best route to a destination host or network based on the number of *hops*. Hops are the gateways a datagram has to pass before reaching a host or network. The shorter a route is, the better RIP rates it. Very long routes with 16 or more hops are regarded as unusable and are discarded.

RIP manages routing information internal to your local network, but you have to run *gated* on all hosts. At boot time, gated checks for all active network interfaces. If there is more than one active interface (not counting the loopback interface), it assumes that the host is switching packets between several networks and will actively exchange and broadcast routing information. Otherwise, it will only passively receive RIP updates and update the local routing table.

When broadcasting information from the local routing table, *gated* computes the length of the route from the so-called *metric value* associated with the routing table entry. This metric value is set by the system administrator when configuring the route, and should reflect the actual route cost.* Therefore, the metric of a route to a subnet that the host is directly connected to should always be zero, while a route going through two gateways should have a metric of two. You don't have to bother with metrics if you don't use RIP or gated.

The Internet Control Message Protocol

IP has a companion protocol that we haven't talked about yet. This is the *Internet Control Message Protocol* (ICMP), used by the kernel networking code to communicate error messages to other hosts. For instance, assume that you are on **erdos** again and want to telnet to port 12345 on **quark**, but there's no process listening on that port. When the first TCP packet for this port arrives on **quark**, the networking layer will recognize this arrival and immediately return an ICMP message to **erdos** stating "Port Unreachable."

The ICMP protocol provides several different messages, many of which deal with error conditions. However, there is one very interesting message called the Redirect message. It is generated by the routing module when it detects that another host is using it as a gateway, even though a much shorter route exists. For example, after booting, the routing table of **sophus** may be incomplete. It might contain the routes

---

* The cost of a route can be thought of, in a simple case, as the number of hops required to reach the destination. Proper calculation of route costs can be a fine art in complex network designs.

to the math department's network, to the FDDI backbone, and the default route pointing at the Groucho Computing Center's gateway (**gcc1**). Thus, packets for **quark** would be sent to **gcc1** rather than to **niels**, the gateway to the physics department. When receiving such a datagram, **gcc1** will notice that this is a poor choice of route and will forward the packet to **niels**, meanwhile returning an ICMP Redirect message to **sophus** telling it of the superior route.

This seems to be a very clever way to avoid manually setting up any but the most basic routes. However, be warned that relying on dynamic routing schemes, be it RIP or ICMP Redirect messages, is not always a good idea. ICMP Redirect and RIP offer you little or no choice in verifying that some routing information is indeed authentic. This situation allows malicious good-for-nothings to disrupt your entire network traffic, or even worse. Consequently, the Linux networking code treats Network Redirect messages as if they were Host Redirects. This minimizes the damage of an attack by restricting it to just one host, rather than the whole network. On the flip side, it means that a little more traffic is generated in the event of a legitimate condition, as each host causes the generation of an ICMP Redirect message. It is generally considered bad practice to rely on ICMP redirects for anything these days.

Resolving Hostnames

As described earlier in this chapter, addressing in TCP/IP networking, at least for IP Version 4, revolves around 32-bit numbers. However, you will have a hard time remembering more than a few of these numbers. Therefore, hosts are generally known by "ordinary" names, such as **gauss** or **strange**. It becomes the application's duty to find the IP address corresponding to this name. This process is called *hostname resolution*. When an application needs to find the IP address of a given host, it relies on the library functions *gethostbyname(3)* and *gethostbyaddr(3)*. Traditionally, these and a number of related procedures were grouped in a separate library called the *resolverlibrary*; on Linux, these functions are part of the standard *libc*. Colloquially, this collection of functions is therefore referred to as "the resolver." Resolver name configuration is detailed in Chapter 5.

On a small network like an Ethernet or even a cluster of Ethernets, it is not very difficult to maintain tables mapping hostnames to addresses. This information is usually kept in a file named */etc/hosts*. When adding or removing hosts, or reassigning addresses, all you have to do is update the *hosts* file on all hosts. Obviously, this will become burdensome with networks that comprise more than a handful of machines.

On the Internet, address information was initially stored in a single *HOSTS.TXT* database, too. This file was maintained at the NIC, and had to be downloaded and installed by all participating sites. When the network grew, several problems with this scheme arose. Besides the administrative overhead involved in installing *HOSTS. TXT* regularly, the load on the servers that distributed it became too high. Even more severe, all names had to be registered with the NIC, which made sure that no name was issued twice.

This is why a new name resolution scheme was adopted in 1994: the *Domain Name System*. DNS was designed by Paul Mockapetris and addresses both problems simultaneously. We discuss the Domain Name System in detail in Chapter 5.

## CHAPTER 3

Configuring the Serial Hardware

The Internet is growing at an incredible rate. Much of this growth is attributed to Internet users who have cheap and easy access to DSL, cable, and other high-speed permanent network connections and who use protocols such as PPP to dial in to a network provider to retrieve their daily dose of email and news.

This chapter is intended to help all people who rely on modems to maintain their link to the outside world. We won't cover the mechanics of how to configure your modem, as you can find detailed documentation of this in many of the available modem HOWTO documents on the web. We will cover most of the Linux-specific aspects of managing devices that use serial ports. Topics include serial communications software, creating the serial device files, serial hardware, and configuring serial devices using the *setserial* and *stty* commands. Many other related topics are covered in the Serial HOWTO by David Lawyer.

Communications Software for Modem Links

There are a number of communications packages available for Linux. Many of these packages are *terminal programs*, which allow a user to dial in to another computer as if she were sitting in front of a simple terminal. The traditional terminal program for Unix-like environments is **kermit**. It is, however, ancient now, and would probably be considered difficult to use. There are more comfortable programs available that support features such as telephone-dialing dictionaries, script languages to automate dialing and logging in to remote computer systems, and a variety of file exchange protocols. One of these programs is **minicom**, which was modeled after some of the most popular DOS terminal programs. X11 users are accommodated, too. **seyon** is a fully featured X11-based communications program.

Terminal programs aren't the only type of serial communication programs available. Other programs let you connect to a host and download email in a single bundle, to read and reply to later at your leisure. This can save a lot of time and is especially useful if you are unfortunate enough to live in an area where your connectivity is time charged. All of the reading and replying time can be spent offline, and when you are ready, you can reconnect and upload your responses in a single bundle.

PPP is in-between, allowing both interactive and noninteractive use. Many people use PPP to dial in to their campus network or other Internet Service Provider to access the Internet. PPP (in the form of PPPoE) is also, however, commonly used over permanent or semipermanent connections like cable or DSL modems. We'll discuss PPPoE in Chapter 7.

Introduction to Serial Devices

The Unix kernel provides devices for accessing serial hardware, typically called *tty* devices (pronounced as it is spelled: T-T-Y).

This is an abbreviation for *Teletype device*, which used to be one of the major manufacturers of terminal devices in the early days of Unix. The term is used now for any character-based data terminal. Throughout this chapter, we use the term to refer exclusively to the Linux device files rather than the physical terminal.

Linux provides three classes of tty devices: serial devices, virtual terminals (all of which you can access by pressing Alt-F1 through Alt-F*nn* on the local console), and pseudo-terminals (similar to a two-way pipe, used by applications such as X11). The former were called tty devices because the original character-based terminals were connected to the Unix machine by a serial cable or telephone line and modem. The latter two were named after the tty device because they were created to behave in a similar fashion from the programmer's perspective.

PPP is most commonly implemented in the kernel. The kernel doesn't really treat the tty device as a network device that you can manipulate like an Ethernet device, using commands such as *ifconfig*. However, it does treat tty devices as places where network devices can be bound. To do this, the kernel changes what is called the "line discipline" of the tty device. PPP is a line discipline that may be enabled on tty devices. The general idea is that the serial driver handles data given to it differently, depending on the line discipline it is configured for. In its default line discipline, the driver simply transmits each character it is given in turn. When the PPP line discipline is selected, the driver instead reads a block of data, wraps a special header around it that allows the remote end to identify that block of data in a stream, and transmits the new data block. It isn't too important to understand this yet; we'll cover PPP in a later chapter, and it all happens automatically anyway.

Accessing Serial Devices

Like all devices in a Unix system, serial ports are accessed through device special files, located in the */dev* directory. There are two varieties of device files related to serial drivers, and there is one device file of each type for each port. The device will behave slightly differently, depending on which of its device files we open. We'll cover the differences because it will help you understand some of the configurations and advice that you might see relating to serial devices, but in practice you need to use only one of these. At some point in the future, one of them may even disappear completely.

The most important of the two classes of serial device has a major number of 4, and its device special files are named *ttyS0*, *ttyS1*, etc. The second variety has a major number of 5 and was designed for use when dialing out (calling out) through a port; its device special files are called *cua0*, *cua1*, etc. In the Unix world, counting generally starts at zero, while laypeople tend to start at one. This creates a small amount of confusion for people because COM1: is represented by */dev/ttyS0*, COM2: by */dev/ttyS1*, etc. Anyone familiar with IBM PC-style hardware knows that COM3: and greater were never really standardized anyway.

The *cua*, or "callout," devices were created to solve the problem of avoiding conflicts on serial devices for modems that have to support both incoming and outgoing connections. Unfortunately, they've created their own problems and are now likely to be discontinued. Let's briefly look at the problem.

Linux, like Unix, allows a device, or any other file, to be opened by more than one process simultaneously. Unfortunately, this is rarely useful with tty devices, as the two processes will almost certainly interfere with each other. Luckily, a mechanism was devised to allow a process to check if a tty device had already been opened by another device. The mechanism uses what are called *lock files*. The idea was that when a process wanted to open a tty device, it would check for the existence of a file in a special location, named similarly to the device it intends to open. If the file did not exist, the process created it and opened the tty device. If the file did exist, the process assumed that another process already had the tty device open and took appropriate action. One last clever trick to make the lock file management system work was writing the process ID (pid) of the process that had created the lock file into the lock file itself; we'll talk more about that in a moment.

The lock file mechanism works perfectly well in circumstances in which you have a defined location for the lock files and all programs know where to find them. Alas, this wasn't always the case for Linux. It wasn't until the Linux Filesystem Standard defined a standard location for lock files when tty lock files began to work correctly. At one time there were at least four, and possibly more, locations chosen by software developers to store lock files: */usr/spool/locks/*, */var/spool/locks/*, */var/lock/*, and */usr/lock/*. Confusion caused chaos. Programs were opening lock files in different locations that were meant to control a single tty device; it was as if lock files weren't being used at all.

The cua devices were created to provide a solution to this problem. Rather than relying on the use of lock files to prevent clashes between programs wanting to use the serial devices, it was decided that the kernel could provide a simple means of arbitrating who should be given access. If the ttyS device were already opened, an attempt to open the cua would result in an error that a program could interpret to mean the device was already being used. If the cua device were already open and an attempt was made to open the ttyS, the request would block; that is, it would be put on hold and wait until the cua device was closed by the other process. This worked quite well if you had a single modem that you had configured for dial-in access and you occasionally wanted to dial out on the same device. But it did not work very well in environments where you had multiple programs wanting to call out on the same device. The only way to solve the contention problem was to use lock files! Back to square one.

Suffice it to say that the Linux Filesystem Standard came to the rescue and now mandates that lock files be stored in the */var/lock* directory, and that by convention, the lock filename for the ttyS1 device, for instance, is *LCK..ttyS1*. The cua lock files should also go in this directory, but use of cua devices is now discouraged.

The cua devices will probably still be around for some time to provide a period of backward compatibility, but in time they will be retired. If you are wondering what to use, stick to the ttyS device and make sure that your system is Linux FSSTND compliant, or at the very least that all programs using the serial devices agree on where the lock files are located. Most software dealing with serial tty devices provides a compile-time option to specify the location of the lock files. More often than not, this will appear as a variable called something like LOCKDIR in the *Makefile* or in a configuration header file. If you're compiling the software yourself, it is best to change this to agree with the FSSTND-specified location. If you're using a precompiled binary and you're not sure where the program will write its lock files, you can use the following command to gain a hint:

```
strings binaryfile | grep lock
```

If the location found does not agree with the rest of your system, you can try creating a symbolic link from the lock directory that the foreign executable wants to use back to */var/lock/*. This is ugly, but it will work.

The Serial Device Special Files

Minor numbers are identical for both types of serial devices. If you have your modem on one of the ports COM1: through COM4:, its minor number will be the COM port number plus 63. If you are using special serial hardware, such as a high-performance multiple port serial controller, you will probably need to create special device files for it; it probably won't use the standard device driver. The *Serial HOWTO* should be able to assist you in finding the appropriate details.

Assume your modem is on COM2:. Its minor number will be 65, and its major number will be 4 for normal use. There should be a device called ttyS1 that has these numbers. List the serial ttys in the */dev/* directory. The fifth and sixth columns show the major and minor numbers, respectively:

```
$ ls -l /dev/ttyS*

0 crw-rw----    1 uucp      dialout    4,  64 Oct 13  1997 /dev/ttyS0
0 crw-rw----    1 uucp      dialout    4,  65 Jan 26 21:55 /dev/ttyS1
0 crw-rw----    1 uucp      dialout    4,  66 Oct 13  1997 /dev/ttyS2
0 crw-rw----    1 uucp      dialout    4,  67 Oct 13  1997 /dev/ttyS3
```

If there is no device with major number 4 and minor number 65, you will have to create one. Become the superuser and type:

```
# mknod -m 666 /dev/ttyS1 c 4 65
# chown uucp.dialout /dev/ttyS1
```

The various Linux distributions use slightly differing strategies for who should own the serial devices. Sometimes they will be owned by root, and other times they will be owned by another user. Most distributions have a group specifically for dial-out devices, and any users who are allowed to use them are added to this group.

Some people suggest making */dev/modem* a symbolic link to your modem device so that casual users don't have to remember the somewhat unintuitive *ttyS1*. However, you cannot use *modem* in one program and the real device filename in another. Their lock files would have different names and the locking mechanism wouldn't work.

Serial Hardware

RS-232 is currently the most common standard for serial communications in the PC world. It uses a number of circuits for transmitting single bits, as well as for synchronization. Additional lines may be used for signaling the presence of a carrier (used by modems) and for handshaking. Linux supports a wide variety of serial cards that use the RS-232 standard.

Hardware handshake is optional, but very useful. It allows either of the two stations to signal whether it is ready to receive more data, or if the other station should pause until the receiver is done processing the incoming data. The lines used for this are called *Clear to Send* (CTS) and *Request to Send* (RTS), respectively, which explains the colloquial name for hardware handshake: RTS/CTS.

The other type of handshake you might be familiar with is called XON/XOFF handshaking. XON/XOFF uses two nominated characters, conventionally Ctrl-S and Ctrl-Q, to signal to the remote end that it should stop and start transmitting data, respectively. While this method is simple to implement and okay for use by dumb terminals, it causes great confusion when you are dealing with binary data, as you may want to transmit those characters as part of your data stream, and not have them interpreted as flow control characters. It is also somewhat slower to take effect than hardware handshake. Hardware handshake is clean, fast, and recommended in preference to XON/XOFF when you have a choice.

In the original IBM PC, the RS-232 interface was driven by a UART chip called the 8250. PCs around the time of the 486 used a newer version of the UART called the 16450. It was slightly faster than the 8250. Nearly all Pentium-based machines have been supplied with an even newer version of the UART called the 16550. Some brands (most notably internal modems equipped with the Rockwell chip set) use completely different chips that emulate the behavior of the 16550 and can be treated similarly. Linux supports all of these in its standard serial port driver.[*]

The 16550 was a significant improvement over the 8250 and the 16450 because it offered a 16-byte FIFO buffer. The 16550 is actually a family of UART devices, comprising the 16550, the 16550A, and the 16550AFN (later renamed PC16550DN). The differences relate to whether the FIFO actually works; the 16550AFN is the one that is sure to work. There was also an NS16550, but its FIFO never really worked either.

The 8250 and 16450 UARTs had a simple 1-byte buffer. This means that a 16450 generates an interrupt for every character transmitted or received. Each interrupt takes a short period of time to service, and this small delay limits 16450s to a reliable maximum bit speed of about 9,600 bps in a typical ISA bus machine.

In the default configuration, the kernel checks the four standard serial ports, COM1: through COM4:. The kernel is also able to automatically detect what UART is used for each of the standard serial ports and will make use of the enhanced FIFO buffer of the 16550, if it is available.

Using the Configuration Utilities

Now let's spend some time looking at the two most useful serial device configuration utilities: *setserial* and *stty*.

The setserial Command

The kernel will make its best effort to correctly determine how your serial hardware is configured, but the variations on serial device configuration makes this determination difficult to achieve 100 percent reliably in practice. A good example of where this is a problem is the internal modems we talked about earlier. The UART they use has a 16-byte FIFO buffer, but it looks like a 16450 UART to the kernel device driver; unless we specifically tell the driver that this port is a 16550 device, the kernel will not make use of the extended buffer. Yet another example is that of the

---

[*] Note that we are not talking about WinModem™ here! WinModems have very simple hardware and rely completely on the main CPU of your computer instead of dedicated hardware to do all of the hard work. If you're purchasing a modem, it is our strongest recommendation to *not* purchase such a modem; get a real modem, though if you're stuck with a WinModem, there's hope! Check out *http://linmodems.org* for drivers, instructions, and the *LINMODEM HOWTO*.

dumb 4-port cards that allow sharing of a single IRQ among a number of serial devices. We may have to specifically tell the kernel which IRQ port it's supposed to use, and that IRQs may be shared.

setserial was created to configure the serial driver at runtime. The *setserial* command is most commonly executed at boot time from a script called *rc.serial* on some distributions, though yours may very. This script is charged with the responsibility of initializing the serial driver to accommodate any nonstandard or unusual serial hardware in the machine.

The general syntax for the *setserial* command is:

```
setserial device [parameters]
```

in which the device is one of the serial devices, such as ttyS0.

The *setserial* command has a large number of parameters. The most common of these are described in Table 3-1. For information on the remainder of the parameters, you should refer to the *setserial* manpage.

Table 3-1. setserial command-line parameters

Parameter	Description
port *port_number*	Specify the I/O port address of the serial device. Port numbers should be specified in hexadecimal notation, e.g., 0x2f8.
irq *num*	Specify the interrupt request line the serial device is using.
uart *uart_type*	Specify the UART type of the serial device. Common values are 16450, 16550, etc. Setting this value to none will disable this serial device.
fourport	Specifying this parameter instructs the kernel serial driver that this port is one port of an AST Fourport card.
spd_hi	Program the UART to use a speed of 57.6 kbps when a process requests 38.4 kbps.
spd_vhi	Program the UART to use a speed of 115 kbps when a process requests 38.4 kbps.
spd_normal	Program the UART to use the default speed of 38.4 kbps when requested. This parameter is used to reverse the effect of a spd_hi or spd_vhi performed on the specified serial device.
auto_irq	This parameter will cause the kernel to attempt to automatically determine the IRQ of the specified device. This attempt may not be completely reliable, so it is probably better to think of this as a request for the kernel to guess the IRQ. If you know the IRQ of the device, you should specify that it use the irq parameter instead.
autoconfig	This parameter must be specified in conjunction with the port parameter. When this parameter is supplied, setserial instructs the kernel to attempt to automatically determine the UART type located at the supplied port address. If the auto_irq parameter is also supplied, the kernel attempts to automatically determine the IRQ, too.
skip_test	This parameter instructs the kernel not to bother performing the UART type test during auto-configuration. This is necessary when the UART is incorrectly detected by the kernel.

A typical and simple *rc* file to configure your serial ports at boot time might look something like that shown in Example 3-1. Most Linux distributions will include something slightly more sophisticated than this one.

Example 3-1. rc.serial setserial commands

```
# /etc/rc.serial - serial line configuration script.
#
# Configure serial devices
/sbin/setserial /dev/ttyS0 auto_irq skip_test autoconfig
/sbin/setserial /dev/ttyS1 auto_irq skip_test autoconfig
/sbin/setserial /dev/ttyS2 auto_irq skip_test autoconfig
/sbin/setserial /dev/ttyS3 auto_irq skip_test autoconfig
#
# Display serial device configuration
/sbin/setserial -bg /dev/ttyS*
```

The -bg /dev/ttyS* argument in the last command will print a neatly formatted summary of the hardware configuration of all active serial devices. The output will look like that shown in Example 3-2.

Example 3-2. Output of setserial -bg /dev/ttyS command

```
/dev/ttyS0 at 0x03f8 (irq = 4) is a 16550A
/dev/ttyS1 at 0x02f8 (irq = 3) is a 16550A
```

The stty Command

The name *stty* probably means "set tty," but the *stty* command can also be used to display a terminal's configuration. Perhaps even more so than *setserial*, the *stty* command provides a bewildering number of characteristics that you can configure. We'll cover the most important of these in a moment. You can find the rest described in the *stty* manpage.

The *stty* command is most commonly used to configure terminal parameters, such as whether characters will be echoed or what key should generate a break signal. We explained earlier that serial devices are tty devices and the *stty* command is therefore equally applicable to them.

One of the more important uses of the *stty* for serial devices is to enable hardware handshaking on the device. We talked briefly about hardware handshaking earlier in this chapter. The default configuration for serial devices is for hardware handshaking to be disabled. This setting allows "three wire" serial cables to work; they don't support the necessary signals for hardware handshaking, and if it were enabled by default, they'd be unable to transmit any characters to change it.

Surprisingly, some serial communications programs don't enable hardware handshaking, so if your modem supports hardware handshaking, you should configure the modem to use it (check your modem manual for what command to use), and also configure your serial device to use it. The *stty* command has a crtscts flag that enables hardware handshaking on a device; you'll need to use this. The command is probably best issued from the *rc.serial* file (or equivalent) at boot time using commands such as those shown in Example 3-3.

Example 3-3. rc.serial stty commands

```
#
stty crtscts < /dev/ttyS0
stty crtscts < /dev/ttyS1
stty crtscts < /dev/ttyS2
stty crtscts < /dev/ttyS3
#
```

The *stty* command works on the current terminal by default, but by using the input redirection (<) feature of the shell, we can have *stty* manipulate any tty device. It's a common mistake to forget whether you are supposed to use < or >; modern versions of the *stty* command have a much cleaner syntax for doing this. To use the new syntax, we'd rewrite our sample configuration to look like that shown in Example 3-4.

Example 3-4. rc.serial stty commands using modern syntax

```
#
stty crtscts -F /dev/ttyS0
stty crtscts -F /dev/ttyS1
stty crtscts -F /dev/ttyS2
stty crtscts -F /dev/ttyS3
#
```

We mentioned that the *stty* command can be used to display the terminal configuration parameters of a tty device. To display all of the active settings on a tty device, use:

$ stty -a -F /dev/ttyS1

The output of this command, shown in Example 3-5, gives you the status of all flags for that device; a flag shown with a preceding minus, as in -crtscts, means that the flag has been turned off.

Example 3-5. Output of stty -a command

```
speed 19200 baud; rows 0; columns 0; line = 0;
intr = ^C; quit = ^\; erase = ^?; kill = ^U; eof = ^D; eol = <undef>;
        eol2 = <undef>; start = ^Q; stop = ^S; susp = ^Z; rprnt = ^R;
        werase = ^W; lnext = ^V; flush = ^O; min = 1; time = 0;
-parenb -parodd cs8 hupcl -cstopb cread clocal -crtscts
-ignbrk -brkint -ignpar -parmrk -inpck -istrip -inlcr -igncr -icrnl -ixon
        -ixoff -iuclc -ixany -imaxbel
-opost -olcuc -ocrnl onlcr -onocr -onlret -ofill -ofdel nl0 cr0 tab0
        bs0 vt0 ff0
-isig -icanon iexten echo echoe echok -echonl -noflsh -xcase -tostop
        -echoprt echoctl echoke
```

A description of the most important of these flags is given in Table 3-2. Each of these flags is enabled by supplying it to *stty* and disabled by supplying it to *stty* with the - character in front of it. Thus, to disable hardware handshaking on the ttyS0 device, you would use:

```
$ stty -crtscts -F /dev/ttyS0
```

Table 3-2. stty flags most relevant to configuring serial devices

Flags	Description
N	Set the line speed to N bits per second.
crtsdts	Enable/disable hardware handshaking.
ixon	Enable/disable XON/XOFF flow control.
clocal	Enable/disable modem control signals such as DTR/DTS and DCD. This is necessary if you are using a "three wire" serial cable because it does not supply these signals.
cs5 cs6 cs7 cs8	Set number of data bits to 5, 6, 7, or 8, respectively.
parodd	Enable odd parity. Disabling this flag enables even parity.
parenb	Enable parity checking. When this flag is negated, no parity is used.
cstopb	Enable use of two stop bits per character. When this flag is negated, one stop bit per character is used.
echo	Enable/disable echoing of received characters back to sender.

The next example combines some of these flags and sets the ttyS0 device to 19,200 bps, 8 data bits, no parity, and hardware handshaking with echo disabled:

```
$ stty 19200 cs8 -parenb crtscts -echo -F /dev/ttyS0
```

Serial Devices and the login: Prompt

It was once very common that a Unix installation involved one server machine and many "dumb" character mode terminals or dial-up modems. Today that sort of installation is less common, which is good news for many people interested in operating this way, because the "dumb" terminals are now very cheap to acquire. Dial-up modem configurations are no less common, but these days they would probably be used to support a PPP login (discussed in Chapter 6) rather than a simple login. Nevertheless, each of these configurations can make use of a simple program called a *getty* program.

The term *getty* is probably a contraction of "get tty." A *getty* program opens a serial device, configures it appropriately, optionally configures a modem, and waits for a connection to be made. An active connection on a serial device is usually indicated by the *Data Carrier Detect* (DCD) pin on the serial device being raised. When a connection is detected, the *getty* program issues a login: prompt, and then invokes the login program to handle the actual system login. Each of the virtual terminals (e.g., /dev/tty1) in Linux has a *getty* running against it.

There are a number of different *getty* implementations, each designed to suit some configurations better than others. The *getty* that we'll describe here is called *mgetty*, which is quite popular because it has all sorts of features that make it especially modem-friendly, including support for automatic fax programs and voice modems. We'll concentrate on configuring *mgetty* to answer conventional data calls and leave the rest for you to explore at your convenience.

Configuring the mgetty Daemon

The *mgetty* daemon is available in just about all Linux distributions in prepackaged form. The *mgetty* daemon differs from most other *getty* implementations in that it has been designed specifically for modems with the AT command set.

It still supports direct terminal connections but is best suited for dialup applications. Rather than using the DCD line to detect an incoming call, it listens for the RING message generated by modern modems when they detect an incoming call and are not configured for auto-answer.

The main executable program is called */usr/sbin/mgetty*, and its main configuration file is called */etc/mgetty/mgetty.config*. There are a number of other binary programs and configuration files that cover other *mgetty* features.

For most installations, configuration is a matter of editing the */etc/mgetty/ mgetty. config* file and adding appropriate entries to the */etc/inittab* file to execute *mgetty* automatically.

Example 3-6 shows a very simple *mgetty* configuration file. This example configures two serial devices. The first, */dev/ttyS0*, supports a Hayes-compatible modem at 38,400 bps. The second, */dev/ttyS0*, supports a directly connected VT100 terminal at 19,200 bps.

Example 3-6. Sample /etc/mgetty/mgetty.config file

```
#
# mgetty configuration file
#
# this is a sample configuration file, see mgetty.info for details
#
# comment lines start with a "#", empty lines are ignored
#
# ----- global section -----
#
# In this section, you put the global defaults, per-port stuff is below
#
# access the modem(s) with 38400 bps
speed 38400
#
# set the global debug level to "4" (default from policy.h)
debug 4
#
```

Example 3-6. Sample /etc/mgetty/mgetty.config file (continued)

```
# ----- port specific section -----
#
# Here you can put things that are valid only for one line, not the others
#
#
# Hayes modem connected to ttyS0: don't do fax, less logging
#
port ttyS0
  debug 3
  data-only y
#
# direct connection of a VT100 terminal which doesn't like DTR drops
#
port ttyS1
  direct y
  speed 19200
  toggle-dtr n
#
```

The configuration file supports global and port-specific options. In our example we used a global option to set the speed to 38,400 bps. This value is inherited by the ttyS0 port. Ports we apply *mgetty* to use this speed setting unless it is overwritten by a port-specific speed setting, as we have done in the ttyS1 configuration.

The debug keyword controls the verbosity of *mgetty* logging. The data-only keyword in the ttyS0 configuration causes *mgetty* to ignore any modem fax features, to operate just as a data modem. The direct keyword in the ttyS1 configuration instructs *mgetty* not to attempt any modem initialization on the port. Finally, the toggle-dtr keyword instructs *mgetty* not to attempt to hang up the line by dropping the *Data Terminal Ready* (DTR) pin on the serial interface; some terminals don't like this to happen.

You can also choose to leave the *mgetty.config* file empty and use command-line arguments to specify most of the same parameters. The documentation accompanying the application includes a complete description of the *mgetty* configuration file parameters and command-line arguments. See the following example.

We need to add two entries to the */etc/inittab* file to activate this configuration. The *inittab* file is the configuration file of the Unix System V *init* command. The *init* command is responsible for system initialization; it provides a means of automatically executing programs at boot time and re-executing them when they terminate. This is ideal for the goals of running a *getty* program.

```
T0:23:respawn:/sbin/mgetty ttyS0
T1:23:respawn:/sbin/mgetty ttyS1
```

Each line of the */etc/inittab* file contains four fields, separated by colons. The first field is an identifier that uniquely labels an entry in the file; traditionally it is two characters, but modern versions allow four. The second field is the list of run levels

---

at which this entry should be active. A run level is a means of providing alternate machine configurations and is generally implemented using trees of startup scripts stored in directories called */etc/rc1.d*, */etc/rc2.d*, etc. This feature is typically implemented very simply, and you should model your entries on others in the file or refer to your system documentation for more information. The third field describes when to take action. For the purposes of running a *getty* program, this field should be set to respawn, meaning that the command should be re-executed automatically when it dies. There are several other options, as well, but they are not useful for our purposes here. The fourth field is the actual command to execute; this is where we specify the *mgetty* command and any arguments we wish to pass it. In our simple example we're starting and restarting *mgetty* whenever the system is operating at either of run levels two or three, and are supplying as an argument just the name of the device we wish it to use. The *mgetty* command assumes the */dev/*, so we don't need to supply it.

This chapter was a quick introduction to *mgetty* and how to offer login prompts to serial devices. You can find more extensive information in the *Serial HOWTO*.

After you've edited the configuration files, you need to reload init to make the changes take effect. Simply send a hangup signal to the init process; it always has a process ID of one, so you can use the following command safely:

```
# kill -HUP 1
```

CHAPTER 4
Configuring TCP/IP Networking

In this chapter, we walk you through all the necessary steps to set up TCP/IP networking on your machine. Starting with the assignment of IP addresses, we slowly work our way through the configuration of TCP/IP network interfaces and introduce a few tools that come in handy when hunting down network installation problems.

Most of the tasks covered in this chapter will generally have to be done only once. Afterward, you have to touch most configuration files only when adding a new system to your network or reconfiguring your system entirely. Some of the commands used to configure TCP/IP, however, have to be executed each time the system is booted. This is usually done by invoking them from the system */etc/rc* scripts.

Commonly, the network-specific part of this procedure is contained in a script. The name of this script varies in different Linux distributions. In many older Linux distributions, it is known as *rc.net* or *rc.inet*. Sometimes you will also see two scripts named *rc.inet1* and *rc.inet2*; the former initializes the kernel part of networking and the latter starts basic networking services and applications. In modern distributions, the *rc* files are structured in a more sophisticated arrangement; here you may find scripts in the */etc/init.d/* (or */etc/rc.d/init.d/*) directory that create the network devices and other *rc* files that run the network application programs. This book's examples are based on the latter arrangement.

This chapter discusses parts of the script that configure your network interfaces. After finishing this chapter, you should have established a sequence of commands that properly configure TCP/IP networking on your computer. You should then replace any sample commands in the configuration scripts with your commands, make sure the script is executed from the basic *rc* script at startup time, and reboot your machine. The networking *rc* scripts that come along with your favorite Linux distribution should provide a solid example from which to work.

Understanding the /proc Filesystem

Linux 2.4 distributions rely on the *proc* filesystem for communicating with the kernel, 2.6 uses the new sysfs. Both interfaces permit access to kernel runtime information through a filesystem-like mechanism. For purposes of this chapter, we'll focus more on the */proc* filesystem, as it is currently more widely used. This filesystem, when mounted, can list files like any other filesystem, or display their contents. Typical items include the *loadavg* file, which contains the system load average, and *meminfo*, which shows current core memory and swap usage.

To this, the networking code adds the *net* directory. It contains a number of files that show things such as the kernel ARP tables, the state of TCP connections, and the routing tables. Most network administration tools get their information from these files.

The *proc* filesystem (or *procfs*, as it is also known) is usually mounted on */proc* at system boot time. The best method is to add the following line to */etc/fstab*:

```
# procfs mount point:
none  /proc  proc defaults
```

Then execute `mount /proc` from your */etc/rc* script.

The *procfs* is now configured into most kernels by default.

Installing the Tools

Prepackaged Linux distributions contain the major networking applications and utilities along with a coherent set of sample files. The only case in which you might have to obtain and install new utilities is when you install a new kernel release. Because they occasionally involve changes in the kernel networking layer, you will need to update the basic configuration tools. This update at least involves recompiling, but sometimes you may also be required to obtain the latest set of binaries. These binaries are available at their official home site at *ftp://ftp.inka.de/pub/comp/Linux/networking/NetTools/*, packaged in an archive called *net-tools-XXX.tar.gz*, where *XXX* is the version number.

If you want to compile and install the standard TCP/IP network applications yourself, you can obtain the sources from most Linux FTP servers. All modern Linux distributions include a fairly comprehensive range of TCP/IP network applications, such as World Wide Web browsers, Telnet and FTP programs, and other network applications such as talk. If you do find something that you need to compile yourself, the chances are good that it will compile under Linux from source quite easily if you follow the instructions included in the source package.

Setting the Hostname

Most, if not all, network applications rely on you to set the local host's name to some reasonable value. This setting is usually made during the boot procedure by executing the hostname command. To set the hostname to *name*, enter:

```
# hostname name
```

It is common practice to use the unqualified hostname without specifying the domain name. For instance, if we had a site called the Virtual Brewery (an imaginary but typical small network used in several chapters of this book) a host might be called **vale.vbrew.com** or **vlager.vbrew.com**. These are their official *fully qualified domain names* (FQDNs). Their local hostnames would be the first component of the name, such as **vale**. However, because the local hostname is frequently used to look up the host's IP address, you have to make sure that the resolver library is able to look up the host's IP address. This usually means that you have to enter the name in */etc/hosts*.

Some people suggest using the *domainname* command to set the kernel's idea of a domain name to the remaining part of the FQDN. This way you could combine the output from *hostname* and *domainname* to get the FQDN again. However, this is at best only half correct. *domainname* is generally used to set the host's NIS domain, which may be entirely different from the DNS domain to which your host belongs. Instead, to ensure that the short form of your hostname is resolvable with all recent versions of the *hostname* command, either add it as an entry in your local Domain Name Server or place the fully qualified domain name in the */etc/hosts* file. You may then use the --fqdn argument to the *hostname* command, and it will print the fully qualified domain name.

Assigning IP Addresses

If you configure the networking software on your host for standalone operation, you can safely skip this section, because the only IP address you will need is for the loopback interface, which is always **127.0.0.1**.

Things are a little more complicated with real networks such as Ethernets. If you want to connect your host to an existing network, you have to ask its administrators to give you an IP address on this network, though this is not always the case. Many networks now have a system of dynamically assigned IPs called *Dynamic Host Configuration Protocol* (DHCP), which we will discuss in the next section. When setting up a network all by yourself, you have to assign IP addresses by hand or by configuring a DHCP server. If you have a machine connected directly to the Internet, you will need to obtain an IP address from your ISP, DSL provider, or cable network.

Hosts within a local network usually share addresses from the same logical IP network, meaning that the first octets of their IP addresses are usually the same. If you have several physical networks, you have to either assign them different network numbers, or use subnetting to split your IP address range into several subnetworks. Subnetting will be revisited in the "Creating Subnets" section later in this chapter.

If your network is not connected to the Internet or will use network address translation to connect, you are free to choose any legal network address. Just make sure no packets from your internal network escape to the real Internet. To make sure no harm can be done even if packets *do* escape, you should use one of the network numbers reserved for private use. The *Internet Assigned Numbers Authority* (IANA) has set aside several network numbers from classes A, B, and C that you can use without registering. These addresses are valid only within your private network and are not routed between real Internet sites. The numbers are defined by RFC 1918 and are listed in Table 2-1 in Chapter 2. Note that the second and third blocks contain 16 and 256 networks, respectively.

Picking your addresses from one of these network numbers is not only useful for networks completely unconnected to the Internet; you can still implement restricted access to the Internet using a single host as a gateway. To your local network, the gateway is accessible by its internal IP address, while the outside world knows it by an officially registered address (assigned to you by your provider). We come back to this concept in connection with the IP masquerade facility in Chapter 9.

Throughout the remainder of the book, we will assume that the brewery's network manager uses a class B network number, say **172.16.0.0**. Of course, a class C network number would definitely suffice to accommodate both the brewery's and the winery's networks. We'll use a class B network here for the sake of simplicity; it will make the subnetting examples in the next section of this chapter a little more intuitive.

Using DHCP to Obtain an IP Address

Many networks now use the *Dynamic Host Configuration Protocol* (DHCP). This protocol runs on network layer two and listens for DHCP requests. The DHCP server has a predefined listing of IP address assigned by the network administrator, which can be assigned to users. When the DHCP receives a request for an IP address, it replies by issuing a DHCP lease. The lease means that the IP address is assigned to the requesting client for a predetermined amount of time. Busy networks often set the lease for a fixed number of hours to prevent the use of an address by an idle machine. Some networks set the threshold as low as two hours. Smaller networks may wish to set the DHCP lease times to a longer value, perhaps a day, or even a week. The value is entirely up to the network administrator and should be based on network usage.

To request a DHCP lease on a network, you will need to have the *dhcpcd* software. The latest version of the software can be obtained by visiting its home site *http:// www.phystech.com/download/dhcpcd.html*. There you will find the latest versions of the software as well as supporting documentation. Many modern Linux distributions will come with this software preinstalled and will even allow you to configure your interfaces with DHCP during the initial setup and configuration of the system.

Obtaining an IP address via DHCP is simple and is accomplished by issuing the following command:

```
vlager#  dhcpcd eth0
vlager#
```

The daemon will at this point, reconfigure your *eth0* interface, not only assigning an IP address, but also properly configuring the subnetting. Many DHCP servers will also provide default route and DNS information. In the case of the latter, your */etc/ resolv.conf* file will be rewritten with the updated DNS server information. If for some reason you do not want the daemon to rewrite your *resolv.conf* file, you can specify -R on the command line. There are a number of additional command-line options available for *dhcpcd*, which may be needed in some environments. For a list of these, please contact the *dhcpcd* manpage. The *resolv.conf* file will be discussed in greater detail in the chapter on DNS.

Running a DHCP server

With larger, more dynamic networks, DHCP is essential. However, in order for this service to be offered, the clients must receive their IP address from a DHCP server. While a number of routers, firewalls, and other network devices will offer this functionality, a network administrator may wish to consider using a Linux machine to provide it. Linux DHCP servers tend to provide a greater flexibility with their configuration options. There are a number of DHCP servers available, but one of the more popular and better recommended offerings comes from the ISC and can be found at *ftp://ftp.isc.org/isc/dhcp/*. The configuration and installation of this is very standard and uses the well-known *automake* configuration script. When the software has been compiled and installed, you are ready to begin configuration.

First, though, you need to make sure that your network interfaces are configured for multicast support. This is most easily checked by using the *ifconfig* command:

```
ticktock root # ifconfig
eth0      Link encap:Ethernet  HWaddr C0:FF:EE:C0:FF:EE
          inet addr:172.16.1.1  Bcast:172.16.1.255  Mask:255.255.255.0
          UP BROADCAST RUNNING MULTICAST  MTU:1500  Metric:1
          RX packets:80272 errors:0 dropped:0 overruns:0 frame:0
          TX packets:55339 errors:0 dropped:0 overruns:0 carrier:0
          collisions:0 txqueuelen:100
          RX bytes:8522502 (8.1 Mb)  TX bytes:9203192 (8.7 Mb)
          Interrupt:10 Base address:0x4000
```

If you don't see MULTICAST specified in the output, you need to reconfigure your kernel to support network multicast. The likelihood of this is slim because most kernel configurations contain this as a default option.

Now you're ready to write a *dhcpd.conf* file. A sample *dhcpd.conf* file looks like this:

```
# Sample DHCP Server Configuration
option domain-name "vbrew.com";
option domain-name-servers ns1.vbrew.com, ns2.vbrew.com;
default-lease-time 1600;
max-lease-time 7200;
log-facility local7;
# This is a very basic subnet declaration.
subnet 172.16.1.0 netmask 255.255.255.0 {
  range 172.16.1.10 172.16.1.50;
  option routers router1.vbrew.com;
}
```

This configuration will create which will assign addresses on the **172.16.1.0** network. It can assign a total of 40 IP addresses from **172.16.1.10** to **172.16.1.50**. The *option routers* and *domain-name-servers* commands allow you to set the default router and DNS servers for the clients.

Here's a brief listing of some of the more useful DHCP server configuration options:

option domain-name
Between quotes, you have the ability to specify the domain name for your network. This isn't necessary, but may be useful to speed up local name lookups.

option domain-name-servers
While considered optional, in most cases it is not. This is where the IP addresses or the FQDN domain name servers are listed.

default-lease-time
When a host asks for a lease and does not request a specific amount of time, this value, in seconds, is assigned.

max-lease-time
This option specifies the maximum amount of time that will be assigned as a lease.

fixed-address
The fixed address option lets you assign a fixed IP address to specific clients. This option is generally paired with the MAC address filtering options.

hardware Ethernet
With this option, network administrators can specify which MAC addresses will receive IP address allocations. This can be used to secure a DHCP range, or can be used to pair MAC addresses with specific IP addresses.

The DHCP server can use the client MAC address as a method to restrict or assign IP addresses. This type of configuration might be necessary in higher security environments where only known machines are to be assigned addresses. The following example shows how the DHCP server can assign a specific address to a host based on its MAC address, also important to note is that the range directive can be used here as well:

```
host vale {
    hardware ethernet 0:0f:d0:ee:ag:4e;
    fixed-address 172.16.1.55;
}
```

Make sure that your DHCP address pool ranges do not contain statically assigned addresses, otherwise IP address conflict problems are sure to follow.

Creating Subnets

To operate several Ethernets, you have to split your network into subnets. Note that subnetting is required only if you have more than one broadcast network—point-to-point links don't count. For instance, if you have one Ethernet, and one or more PPP links to the outside world, you don't need to subnet your network. This is explained in more detail in Chapter 6.

To accommodate the two Ethernets, the brewery's network manager decides to use 8 bits of the host part as additional subnet bits. This leaves another 8 bits for the host part, allowing for 254 hosts on each of the subnets. She then assigns subnet number 1 to the brewery and gives the winery number 2. Their respective network addresses are thus **172.16.1.0** and **172.16.2.0**. The subnet mask is **255.255.255.0**.

vlager, which is the gateway between the two networks, is assigned a host number of 1 on both of them, which gives it the IP addresses **172.16.1.1** and **172.16.2.1**, respectively.

Note that in this example we are using a class B network to keep things simple, but a class C network would be more realistic. With the new networking code, subnetting is not limited to byte boundaries, so even a class C network may be split into several subnets. For instance, you could use two bits of the host part for the netmask, giving you 4 possible subnets with 64 hosts on each.*

Writing Hosts and Networks Files

After you have subnetted your network, you should prepare for some simple sort of hostname resolution using the /etc/hosts file. If you are not going to use DNS or NIS for address resolution, you have to put all hosts in the hosts file.

---

* The first number on each subnet is the subnetwork address, and the last number on each subnet, is reserved as the broadcast address, so it's actually 62 hosts per subnet.

Even if you want to run DNS during normal operation, you should have some subset of all hostnames in *letc/hosts*. You should have some sort of name resolution, even when no network interfaces are running, for example, during boot time. This is not only a matter of convenience, but it allows you to use symbolic hostnames in your network *rc* scripts. Thus, when changing IP addresses, you only have to copy an updated *hosts* file to all machines and reboot, rather than edit a large number of *rc* files separately. Usually you put all local hostnames and addresses in *hosts*, adding those of any gateways and NIS servers used.

You should make sure that your resolver uses information from the *hosts* file only during initial testing. Sample files that come with your DNS software may produce strange results. To make all applications use *letc/hosts* exclusively when looking up the IP address of a host, you have to edit the *letc/host.conf* file. Comment out any lines that begin with the keyword order by preceding them with a hash sign, and insert the line:

```
order hosts
```

The configuration of the resolver library is covered in detail in Chapter 6.

The *hosts* file contains one entry per line, consisting of an IP address, a hostname, and an optional list of aliases for the hostname. The fields are separated by spaces or tabs, and the address field must begin in the first column. Anything following a hash sign (#) is regarded as a comment and is ignored.

Hostnames can be either fully qualified or relative to the local domain. For **vale**, you would usually enter the fully qualified name, **vale.vbrew.com**, and **vale** by itself in the *hosts* file, so that it is known by both its official name and the shorter local name.

This is an example how a *hosts* file at the Virtual Brewery might look. Two special names are included, **vlager-if1** and **vlager-if2**, which give the addresses for both interfaces used on **vlager**:

```
#
# Hosts file for Virtual Brewery/Virtual Winery
#
# IP            FQDN                 aliases
#
127.0.0.1       localhost
#
172.16.1.1      vlager.vbrew.com     vlager vlager-if1
172.16.1.2      vstout.vbrew.com     vstout
172.16.1.3      vale.vbrew.com       vale
#
172.16.2.1      vlager-if2
172.16.2.2      vbeaujolais.vbrew.com vbeaujolais
172.16.2.3      vbardolino.vbrew.com  vbardolino
172.16.2.4      vchianti.vbrew.com    vchianti
```

Just as with a host's IP address, you should sometimes use a symbolic name for network numbers, too. Therefore, the *hosts* file has a companion called */etc/networks* that maps network names to network numbers, and vice versa. At the Virtual Brewery, we might install a *networks* file as shown in the following.*

```
# /etc/networks for the Virtual Brewery
brew-net    172.16.1.0
wine-net    172.16.2.0
```

Interface Configuration for IP

After setting up your hardware as explained in Chapter 3, you have to make these devices known to the kernel networking software. A couple of commands are used to configure the network interfaces and initialize the routing table. These tasks are usually performed from the network initialization script each time you boot the system. The basic tools for this process are called *ifconfig* (where "if" stands for interface) and *route*.

ifconfig is used to make an interface accessible to the kernel networking layer. This involves the assignment of an IP address and other parameters, and activation of the interface, also known as "bringing up" the interface. Being active here means that the kernel will send and receive IP datagrams through the interface. The simplest way to invoke it is with:

```
ifconfig interface ip-address
```

This command assigns *ip-address* to *interface* and activates it. All other parameters are set to default values. For instance, the default network mask is derived from the network class of the IP address, such as **255.255.0.0** for a class B address. *ifconfig* is described in detail later in this chapter.

route allows you to add or remove routes from the kernel routing table. It can be invoked as:

```
route [add|del] [-net|-host] target [if]
```

The add and del arguments determine whether to add or delete the route to *target*. The -net and -host arguments tell the route command whether the target is a network or a host. The *if* argument is again optional, and allows you to specify to which network interface the route should be directed—the Linux kernel makes a sensible guess if you don't supply this information. This topic will be explained in more detail in succeeding sections.

---

* Note that names in *networks* must not collide with hostnames from the *hosts* file, or else some programs may produce strange results.

The Loopback Interface

Almost always, the very first interface to be activated is the loopback interface:

```
# ifconfig lo 127.0.0.1
```

Occasionally, you will see the dummy hostname **localhost** being used instead of the IP address. *ifconfig* will look up the name in the *hosts* file, where an entry should declare it as the hostname for **127.0.0.1**:

```
# Sample /etc/hosts entry for localhost
localhost      127.0.0.1
```

To view the configuration of an interface, you invoke **ifconfig**, giving it only the interface name as argument:

```
$ ifconfig lo
lo         Link encap:Local Loopback
           inet addr:127.0.0.1  Mask:255.0.0.0
           UP LOOPBACK RUNNING  MTU:3924  Metric:1
           RX packets:0 errors:0 dropped:0 overruns:0 frame:0
           TX packets:0 errors:0 dropped:0 overruns:0 carrier:0
           Collisions:0
```

As you can see, the loopback interface has been assigned a netmask of **255.0.0.0**, since **127.0.0.1** is a class A address.

Now you can almost start playing with your mini-network. What is still missing is an entry in the routing table that tells IP that it may use this interface as a route to destination **127.0.0.1**. This is accomplished by using:

```
# route add 127.0.0.1
```

Again, you can use localhost instead of the IP address, provided you've entered it into your */etc/hosts*.

Next, you should check that everything works fine, for example, by using *ping*. *ping* is the networking equivalent of a sonar device. The command is used to verify that a given address is actually reachable, and to measure the delay that occurs when sending a datagram to it and back again. The time required for this process is often referred to as the "round-trip time":

```
# ping localhost
PING localhost (127.0.0.1): 56 data bytes
64 bytes from 127.0.0.1: icmp_seq=0 ttl=255 time=0.4 ms
64 bytes from 127.0.0.1: icmp_seq=1 ttl=255 time=0.4 ms
64 bytes from 127.0.0.1: icmp_seq=2 ttl=255 time=0.4 ms
^C
--- localhost ping statistics ---
3 packets transmitted, 3 packets received, 0% packet loss
round-trip min/avg/max = 0.4/0.4/0.4 ms
#
```

When you invoke *ping* as shown here, it will continue emitting packets forever, unless interrupted by the user. The ^C marks the place where we pressed Ctrl-C.

The previous example shows that packets for **127.0.0.1** are properly delivered and a reply is returned to *ping* almost instantaneously. This shows that you have successfully set up your first network interface.

If the output you get from *ping* does not resemble that shown in the previous example, you are in trouble. Check any errors if they indicate that some file hasn't been installed properly. Check that the **ifconfig** and *route* binaries you use are compatible with the kernel release you run, and above all, that the kernel has been compiled with networking enabled (you see this from the presence of the */proc/net* directory). If you get an error message saying "Network unreachable," you probably got the **route** command wrong. Make sure you use the same address that you gave to **ifconfig**.

The steps previously described are enough to use networking applications on a standalone host. After adding the lines mentioned earlier to your network initialization script and making sure it will be executed at boot time, you may reboot your machine and try out various applications. For instance, *ssh localhost* should establish an *ssh* connection to your host, giving you an SSH login prompt.

However, the loopback interface is useful not only as an example in networking books, or as a test bed during development, but is actually used by some applications during normal operation.* Therefore, you always have to configure it, regardless of whether your machine is attached to a network or not.

Ethernet Interfaces

Configuring an Ethernet interface is pretty much the same as the loopback interface; it just requires a few more parameters when you are using subnetting.

At the Virtual Brewery, we have subnetted the IP network, which was originally a class B network, into class C subnetworks. To make the interface recognize this, the *ifconfig* incantation would look like this:

```
# ifconfig eth0 vstout netmask 255.255.255.0
```

This command assigns the *eth0* interface the IP address of **vstout** (172.16.1.2). If we omitted the netmask, **ifconfig** would deduce the netmask from the IP network class, which would result in an incorrect netmask of **255.255.0.0**. Now a quick check shows:

```
# ifconfig eth0
eth0        Link encap 10Mps Ethernet HWaddr  00:00:C0:90:B3:42
```

---

* For example, all applications based on RPC use the loopback interface to register themselves with the *portmapper* daemon at startup. These applications include NIS and NFS.

```
inet addr 172.16.1.2 Bcast 172.16.1.255 Mask 255.255.255.0
UP BROADCAST RUNNING  MTU 1500  Metric 1
RX packets 0 errors 0 dropped 0 overrun 0
TX packets 0 errors 0 dropped 0 overrun 0
```

You can see that **ifconfig** automatically sets the broadcast address (the Bcast field) to the usual value, which is the host's network number with all the host bits set. Also, the maximum transmission unit (the maximum size of IP datagrams the kernel will generate for this interface) has been set to the maximum size of Ethernet packets: 1,500 bytes. The defaults are usually what you will use, but all these values can be overridden if required, with special options that will be described under later in this chapter.

Just as for the loopback interface, you now have to install a routing entry that informs the kernel about the network that can be reached through *eth0*. For the Virtual Brewery, you might invoke route as:

```
# route add -net 172.16.1.0
```

At first this looks a little like magic, because it's not really clear how route detects which interface to route through. However, the trick is rather simple: the kernel checks all interfaces that have been configured so far and compares the destination address (**172.16.1.0** in this case) to the network part of the interface address (that is, the bitwise AND of the interface address and the netmask). The only interface that matches is *eth0*.

Now, what's that -net option for? This is used because **route** can handle both routes to networks and routes to single hosts (as you saw before with localhost). When given an address in dotted quad notation, **route** attempts to guess whether it is a network or a hostname by looking at the host part bits. If the address's host part is zero, **route** assumes it denotes a network; otherwise, **route** takes it as a host address. Therefore, **route** would think that **172.16.1.0** is a host address rather than a network number because it cannot know that we use subnetting. We have to tell **route** explicitly that it denotes a network, so we give it the -net flag.

Of course, the **route** command is a little tedious to type, and it's prone to spelling mistakes. A more convenient approach is to use the network names we defined in */etc/networks*. This approach makes the command much more readable; even the -net flag can be omitted because **route** knows that **172.16.1.0** denotes a network:

```
# route add brew-net
```

Now that you've finished the basic configuration steps, we want to make sure that your Ethernet interface is indeed running happily. Choose a host from your Ethernet, for instance **vlager**, and type:

```
# ping vlager
PING vlager: 64 byte packets
64 bytes from 172.16.1.1: icmp_seq=0. time=11. ms
64 bytes from 172.16.1.1: icmp_seq=1. time=7. ms
```

```
64 bytes from 172.16.1.1: icmp_seq=2. time=12. ms
64 bytes from 172.16.1.1: icmp_seq=3. time=3. ms
^C
----vstout.vbrew.com PING Statistics----
4 packets transmitted, 4 packets received, 0
round-trip (ms)  min/avg/max = 3/8/12
```

If you don't see similar output, something is broken. If you encounter unusual packet loss rates, this hints at a hardware problem, such as bad or missing terminators. If you don't receive any replies at all, you should check the interface configuration with *netstat*, described later in the chapter. The packet statistics displayed by *ifconfig* should tell you whether any packets have been sent out on the interface at all. If you have access to the remote host too, you should go over to that machine and check the interface statistics. This way you can determine exactly where the packets got dropped. In addition, you should display the routing information with route to see whether both hosts have the correct routing entry. *route* prints out the complete kernel routing table when invoked without any arguments (-n just makes it print addresses as dotted quad instead of using the hostname):

```
# route -n
Kernel routing table
Destination  Gateway  Genmask          Flags Metric Ref Use    Iface
127.0.0.1    *        255.255.255.255  UH    1      0   112    lo
172.16.1.0   *        255.255.255.0    U     1      0   10     eth0
```

The detailed meaning of these fields is explained later in the chapter. The Flags column contains a list of flags set for each interface. U is always set for active interfaces, and H says the destination address denotes a host. If the H flag is set for a route that you meant to be a network route, you have to reissue the route command with the -net option. To check whether a route you have entered is used at all, check to see if the Use field in the second to last column increases between two invocations of ping.

Routing Through a Gateway

In the previous section, we covered only the case of setting up a host on a single Ethernet. Quite frequently, however, one encounters networks connected to one another by gateways. These gateways may simply link two or more Ethernets but may also provide a link to the outside world, such as the Internet. In order to use a gateway, you have to provide additional routing information to the networking layer.

The Ethernets of the Virtual Brewery and the Virtual Winery are linked through such a gateway, namely the host **vlager**. Assuming that **vlager** has already been configured, we just have to add another entry to **vstout**'s routing table that tells the kernel it can reach all hosts on the winery's network through **vlager**. The appropriate incantation of **route** is shown below; the gw keyword tells it that the next argument denotes a gateway:

```
# route add wine-net gw vlager
```

Of course, any host on the winery network you wish to talk to must have a routing entry for the brewery's network. Otherwise you would only be able to send data to the winery network from the brewery network, but the hosts on the winery would be unable to reply.

This example describes only a gateway that switches packets between two isolated Ethernets. Now assume that **vlager** also has a connection to the Internet (say, through an additional SLIP link). Then we would want datagrams to *any* destination network other than the brewery to be handed to **vlager**. This action can be accomplished by making it the default gateway for **vstout**:

```
# route add default gw vlager
```

The network name **default** is shorthand for **0.0.0.0**, which denotes the default route. The default route matches every destination and will be used if there is no more specific route that matches. You do not have to add this name to *etc/networks* because it is built into **route**.

If you see high packet loss rates when pinging a host behind one or more gateways, this may hint at a very congested network. Packet loss is not so much due to technical deficiencies as to temporary excess loads on forwarding hosts, which makes them delay or even drop incoming datagrams.

Configuring a Gateway

Configuring a machine to switch packets between two Ethernets is pretty straightforward. Assume we're back at **vlager**, which is equipped with two Ethernet cards, each connected to one of the two networks. All you have to do is configure both interfaces separately, giving them their respective IP addresses and matching routes, and that's it.

It is quite useful to add information on the two interfaces to the *hosts* file as shown in the following example, so we have handy names for them, too:

```
172.16.1.1      vlager.vbrew.com    vlager vlager-if1
172.16.2.1      vlager-if2
```

The sequence of commands to set up the two interfaces is then:

```
# ifconfig eth0 vlager-if1
# route add brew-net
# ifconfig eth1 vlager-if2
# route add wine-net
```

If this sequence doesn't work, make sure your kernel has been compiled with support for IP forwarding enabled. One good way to do this is to ensure that the first number on the second line of */proc/net/snmp* is set to 1.

The Point-to-Point Interface

A PLIP link used to connect two machines is a little different from an Ethernet. PLIP links are an example of what are called *point-to-point* links, meaning that there is a single host at each end of the link. Networks like Ethernet are called *broadcast* networks. Configuration of point-to-point links is different because unlike broadcast networks, point-to-point links don't support a network of their own.

PLIP provides very cheap and portable links between computers. As an example, we'll consider the laptop computer of an employee at the Virtual Brewery that is connected to **vlager** via PLIP. The laptop itself is called **vlite** and has only one parallel port. At boot time, this port will be registered as *plip1*. To activate the link, you have to configure the *plip1* interface using the following commands:*

```
# ifconfig plip1 vlite pointopoint vlager
# route add default gw vlager
```

The first command configures the interface, telling the kernel that this is a point-to-point link, with the remote side having the address of **vlager**. The second installs the default route, using **vlager** as gateway. On **vlager**, a similar **ifconfig** command is necessary to activate the link (a **route** invocation is not needed):

```
# ifconfig plip1 vlager pointopoint vlite
```

Note that the *plip1* interface on **vlager** does not need a separate IP address, but may also be given the address **172.16.1.1**. Point-to-point networks don't support a network directly, so the interfaces don't require an address on any supported network. The kernel uses the interface information in the routing table to avoid any possible confusion.† Now we have configured routing from the laptop to the brewery's network; what's still missing is a way to route from any of the brewery's hosts to **vlite**. One particularly cumbersome way is to add a specific route to every host's routing table that names **vlager** as a gateway to **vlite**:

```
# route add vlite gw vlager
```

Dynamic routing offers a much better option for temporary routes. You could use *gated*, a routing daemon, which you would have to install on each host in the network in order to distribute routing information dynamically. The easiest option, however, is to use *proxy ARP* (Address Resolution Protocol). With proxy ARP, **vlager** will respond to any ARP query for **vlite** by sending its own Ethernet address. All packets for **vlite** will wind up at **vlager**, which then forwards them to the laptop. We will come back to proxy ARP in the section "Checking the ARP Tables," later in the chapter.

---

* Note that **pointopoint** is not a typo. It really is spelled like this.

† As a matter of caution, you should configure a PLIP link only after you have completely set up the routing table entries for your Ethernets. With some older kernels, your network route might otherwise end up pointing at the point-to-point link.

Current *net-tools* releases contain a tool called *plipconfig*, which allows you to set certain PLIP timing parameters. The IRQ to be used for the printer port can be set using the *ifconfig* command.

The PPP Interface

Although PPP links are only simple point-to-point links like PLIP connections, there is much more to be said about them. We discuss PPP in detail in Chapter 6.

IP Alias

The Linux kernel supports a feature that completely replaces the old dummy interface and serves other useful functions. IP Alias allows you to configure multiple IP addresses onto a physical device. In most cases, you could configure your host to look like many different hosts, each with its own IP address. This configuration is sometimes called *virtual hosting*, although technically it is also used for a variety of other techniques.*

To configure an alias for an interface, you must first ensure that your kernel has been compiled with support for IP Alias (check that you have a */proc/net/ip_alias* file; if not, you will have to recompile your kernel). Configuration of an IP alias is virtually identical to configuring a real network device; you use a special name to indicate it's an alias that you want. For example:

```
# ifconfig eth0:0 172.16.1.1
```

This command would produce an alias for the *eth0* interface with the address **172.16.1.1**. IP aliases are referred to by appending *:n* to the actual network device, in which "n" is an integer. In our example, the network device we are creating the alias on is *eth0*, and we are creating an alias numbered zero for it. This way, a single physical device may support a number of aliases.

Each alias may be treated as though it is a separate device, and as far as the kernel IP software is concerned, it will be; however, it will be sharing its hardware with another interface.

All About ifconfig

There are many more parameters to *ifconfig* than we have described so far. Its normal invocation is this:

```
ifconfig interface [address [parameters]]
```

---

* More correctly, using IP aliasing is known as network layer virtual hosting. It is more common in the WWW and STMP worlds to use application layer virtual hosting, in which the same IP address is used for each virtual host, but a different hostname is passed with each application layer request.

interface is the interface name, and *address* is the IP address to be assigned to the interface. This may be either an IP address in dotted quad notation or a name that *ifconfig* will look up in */etc/hosts*.

If `ifconfig` is invoked with only the interface name, it displays that interface's configuration. When invoked without any parameters, it displays all interfaces you have configured so far; a -a option forces it to show the inactive ones as well. A sample invocation for the Ethernet interface *eth0* may look like this:

```
# ifconfig eth0
eth0    Link encap 10Mbps Ethernet  HWaddr 00:00:C0:90:B3:42
        inet addr 172.16.1.2 Bcast 172.16.1.255 Mask 255.255.255.0
        UP BROADCAST RUNNING  MTU 1500  Metric 0
        RX packets 3136 errors 217 dropped 7 overrun 26
        TX packets 1752 errors 25 dropped 0 overrun 0
```

The MTU and Metric fields show the current maximum transmission unit size and metric value for that interface. The metric value is traditionally used by some operating systems to compute the cost of a route.

The RX and TX lines show how many packets have been received or transmitted error free, how many errors occurred, how many packets were dropped (probably because of low memory), and how many were lost because of an overrun. Receiver overruns usually occur when packets come in faster than the kernel can service the last interrupt. The flag values printed by *ifconfig* roughly correspond to the names of its command-line options; they will be explained later.

The following is a list of parameters recognized by *ifconfig*, with the corresponding flag names. Options that simply turn on a feature also allow it to be turned off again by preceding the option name by a dash (-).

up

> This option makes an interface accessible to the IP layer. This option is implied when an *address* is given on the command line. It may also be used to reenable an interface that has been taken down temporarily using the down option.
>
> This option corresponds to the flags UP and RUNNING.

down

> This option marks an interface inaccessible to the IP layer. This effectively disables any IP traffic through the interface. Note that this option also automatically deletes all routing entries that use this interface.

netmask *mask*

> This option assigns a subnet mask to be used by the interface. It may be given as either a 32-bit hexadecimal number preceded by 0x, or as a dotted quad of decimal numbers. While the dotted quad format is more common, the hexadecimal representation is often easier to work with. Netmasks are essentially binary, and it is easier to do binary-to-hexadecimal than binary-to-decimal conversion.

pointopoint *address*

This option is used for point-to-point IP links that involve only two hosts. This option is needed to configure SLIP or PLIP interfaces, for example. If a point-to-point address has been set, *ifconfig* displays the `POINTOPOINT` flag.

broadcast *address*

The broadcast address is usually made up from the network number by setting all bits of the host part. Some IP implementations (systems derived from BSD 4.2, for instance) use a different scheme in which all host part bits are cleared instead. The broadcast option adapts to these strange environments. If a broadcast address has been set, *ifconfig* displays the `BROADCAST` flag.

irq

This option allows you to set the IRQ line used by certain devices. This is especially useful for PLIP, but may also be useful for certain Ethernet cards.

metric *number*

This option may be used to assign a metric value to the routing table entry created for the interface. This metric is used by the RIP to build routing tables for the network.[*] The default metric used by *ifconfig* is zero. If you don't run a RIP daemon, you don't need this option at all; if you do, you will rarely need to change the metric value.

mtu *bytes*

This sets the Maximum Transmission Unit, which is the maximum number of octets the interface is able to handle in one transaction. For Ethernets, the MTU defaults to 1,500 (the largest allowable size of an Ethernet packet); for SLIP interfaces, it is 296. (There is no constraint on the MTU of SLIP links; this value is a good compromise.)

arp

This is an option specific to broadcast networks such as Ethernets or packet radio. It enables the use of the ARP to detect the physical addresses of hosts attached to the network. For broadcast networks, it is on by default. If ARP is disabled, *ifconfig* displays the `NOARP` flag.

-arp

This option disables the use of ARP on this interface.

promisc

This option puts the interface in promiscuous mode. On a broadcast network, this makes the interface receive all packets, regardless of whether they were destined for this host. This allows network traffic analysis using packet filters and

---

[*] RIP chooses the optimal route to a given host based on the "length" of the path. It is computed by summing up the individual metric values of each host-to-host link. By default, a hop has length 1, but this may be any positive integer less than 16. (A route length of 16 is equal to infinity. Such routes are considered unusable.) The **metric** parameter sets this hop cost, which is then broadcast by the routing daemon.

such, also called *Ethernet snooping*. Usually, this is a good technique for hunting down network problems that are otherwise hard to detect. Tools such as tcp-dump rely on this.

On the other hand, this option allows attackers to do nasty things, such as skim the traffic of your network for passwords. You can protect against this type of attack by prohibiting just anyone from plugging their computers into your Ethernet. You could also use secure authentication protocols, such as Kerberos or the secure shell login suite.* This option corresponds to the PROMISC flag.

-promisc
 This option turns promiscuous mode off.

allmulti
 Multicast addresses are like Ethernet broadcast addresses, except that instead of automatically including everybody, the only people who receive packets sent to a multicast address are those programmed to listen to it. This is useful for applications such as Ethernet-based video conferencing or network audio, to which only those interested can listen. Multicast addressing is supported by most, but not all, Ethernet drivers. When this option is enabled, the interface receives and passes multicast packets for processing. This option corresponds to the ALLMULTI flag.

-allmulti
 This option turns multicast addresses off.

The netstat Command

netstat is a useful tool for checking your network configuration and activity. It is in fact a collection of several tools lumped together. We discuss each of its functions in the following sections.

Displaying the routing table

When you invoke *netstat* with the -r flag, it displays the kernel routing table in the way we've been doing with route. On **vstout**, it produces:

```
# netstat -nr
Kernel IP routing table
Destination     Gateway       Genmask          Flags MSS Window  irtt Iface
127.0.0.1       *             255.255.255.255  UH      0 0          0 lo
172.16.1.0      *             255.255.255.0    U       0 0          0 eth0
172.16.2.0      172.16.1.1    255.255.255.0    UG      0 0          0 eth0
```

---

* OpenSSH can be obtained from *ftp://ftp.openbsd.org/OpenBSD/OpenSSH/portable*.

The -n option makes **netstat** print addresses as dotted quad IP numbers rather than the symbolic host and network names. This option is especially useful when you want to avoid address lookups over the network (e.g., to a DNS or NIS server).

The second column of **netstat**'s output shows the gateway to which the routing entry points. If no gateway is used, an asterisk is printed instead. The third column shows the "generality" of the route, i.e., the network mask for this route. When given an IP address to find a suitable route for, the kernel steps through each of the routing table entries, taking the bitwise AND of the address and the genmask before comparing it to the target of the route. The most specific match is used.

The fourth column displays the following flags that describe the route:

G   The route uses a gateway.

U   The interface to be used is up.

H   Only a single host can be reached through the route. For example, this is the case for the loopback entry **127.0.0.1**.

D   This route is dynamically created. It is set if the table entry has been generated by a routing daemon such as *gated* or by an ICMP redirect message (see Chapter 2).

M   This route is set if the table entry was modified by an ICMP redirect message.

!   The route is a reject route and datagrams will be dropped.

The next three columns show the MSS, Window, and irtt that will be applied to TCP connections established via this route. The MSS is the Maximum Segment Size and is the size of the largest datagram the kernel will construct for transmission via this route. The Window is the maximum amount of data the system will accept in a single burst from a remote host. The acronym *irtt* stands for "initial round trip time." The TCP protocol ensures that data is reliably delivered between hosts by retransmitting a datagram if it has been lost. The TCP protocol keeps a running count of how long it takes for a datagram to be delivered to the remote end and an acknowledgement to be received, so that it knows how long to wait before assuming a datagram needs to retransmitted; this process is called the round-trip time. The initial round-trip time is the value that the TCP protocol uses when a connection is first established. For most network types, the default value is okay, but for some slow networks, notably certain types of amateur packet radio networks, the time is too short and causes unnecessary retransmission. The irtt value can be set using the *route* command. Values of zero in these fields mean that the default is being used.

Finally, the last field displays the network interface that this route will use.

Displaying interface statistics

When invoked with the -i flag, *netstat* displays statistics for the network interfaces currently configured. If the -a option is also given, it prints *all* interfaces present in the kernel, not only those that have been configured currently. On **vstout**, the output from **netstat** will look like this:

```
# netstat -i
Kernel Interface table
Iface MTU Met  RX-OK RX-ERR RX-DRP RX-OVR  TX-OK TX-ERR TX-DRP TX-OVR Flags
lo      0   0   3185      0      0      0   3185      0      0      0 BLRU
eth0 1500   0 972633     17     20    120 628711    217      0      0 BRU
```

The MTU and Met fields show the current MTU and metric values for that interface. The RX and TX columns show how many packets have been received or transmitted error-free (RX-OK/TX-OK) or damaged (RX-ERR/TX-ERR); how many were dropped (RX-DRP/TX-DRP); and how many were lost because of an overrun (RX-OVR/TX-OVR).

The last column shows the flags that have been set for this interface. These characters are one-character versions of the long flag names that are printed when you display the interface configuration with *ifconfig*:

B   A broadcast address has been set.

L   This interface is a loopback device.

M   All packets are received (promiscuous mode).

O   ARP is turned off for this interface.

P   This is a point-to-point connection.

R   Interface is running.

U   Interface is up.

Displaying connections

netstat supports a set of options to display active or passive sockets. The options -t, -u, -w, and -x show active TCP, UDP, RAW, and Unix socket connections. If you provide the -a flag in addition, sockets that are waiting for a connection (i.e., listening) are displayed as well. This display will give you a list of all servers that are currently running on your system.

Invoking *netstat* -ta on **vlager** produces this output:

```
$ netstat -ta
Active Internet connections (servers and established)
Proto Recv-Q Send-Q Local Address        Foreign Address      State
tcp        0      0 localhost:mysql      *:*                  LISTEN
tcp        0      0 localhost:webcache   *:*                  LISTEN
tcp        0      0 *:www                *:*                  LISTEN
tcp        0      0 *:ssh                *:*                  LISTEN
tcp        0      0 *:https              *:*                  LISTEN
```

```
tcp      0      0 ::ffff:1.2.3.4:ssh   ::ffff:4.5.6.:49152 ESTABLISHED
tcp      0    652 ::ffff:1.2.3.4:ssh   ::ffff:4.5.6.:31996 ESTABLISHED
```

This output shows most servers simply waiting for an incoming connection. However, the fourth line shows an incoming SMTP connection from **vstout**, and the sixth line tells you there is an outgoing *telnet* connection to **vbardolino**.[*]

Using the -a flag by itself will display all sockets from all families.

Testing Connectivity with traceroute

A very simple way to test connectivity between hosts, and to verify routing paths is to use the *traceroute* tool. *traceroute* uses UDP datagrams (or ICMP if the -I option is specified) to determine the path which packets take over the network. The command can be invoked as follows:

```
# traceroute -n www.oreilly.com
traceroute to www.oreilly.com (208.201.239.37), 30 hops max, 40 byte packets
 1  22.44.55.23  187.714 ms  178.548 ms  177.132 ms
 2  206.171.134.130  186.730 ms  168.750 ms  150.769 ms
 3  216.102.176.193  168.499 ms  209.232.130.82  194.629 ms  209.232.130.28  185.999 ms
 4  151.164.243.121  212.852 ms  230.590 ms  132.040 ms
 5  151.164.240.134  80.049 ms  71.191 ms  53.450 ms
 6  151.164.40.150  45.320 ms  44.579 ms  176.651 ms
 7  151.164.191.82  168.499 ms  194.864 ms  149.789 ms
 8  151.164.248.90  80.065 ms  71.185 ms  88.922 ms
 9  69.22.143.178  228.883 ms  222.204 ms  179.093 ms
10  69.22.143.6  131.573 ms  89.394 ms  71.180 ms
 .
 .
```

Checking the ARP Tables

On some occasions, it is useful to view or alter the contents of the kernel's ARP tables, for example, when you suspect a duplicate Internet address is the cause for some intermittent network problem. The *arp* tool was made for situations like this. Its command-line options are:

```
arp [-v] [-t hwtype] -a [hostname]
arp [-v] [-t hwtype] -s hostname hwaddr
arp [-v] -d hostname [hostname]
```

All *hostname* arguments may be either symbolic hostnames or IP addresses in dotted quad notation.

---

[*] You can tell whether a connection is outgoing from the port numbers. The port number shown for the calling host will always be a simple integer. The host being called will use a well-known service port will be in use for which *netstat* uses the symbolic name such as smtp, found in */etc/services*. Of course, it is possible to specify your source port in a number of applications these days, so this isn't a guarantee!

The first invocation displays the ARP entry for the IP address or host specified, or all hosts known if no *hostname* is given. For example, invoking *arp* on **vlager** may yield something similar to:

```
# arp -e
Address             HWtype  HWaddress           Flags Mask    Iface
172.16.0.1                  (incomplete)                      eth0
172.16.0.155        ether   00:11:2F:38:4E:4F   C             eth0
172.16.0.69         ether   00:90:4B:F1:3A:B5   C             eth0
vale.vbrew.com      ether   00:10:67:30:C5:7B   C             eth1
172.16.0.207        ether   00:0B:DB:1A:C7:E2   C             eth0
```

which shows the Ethernet addresses of several hosts.

The -s option is used to permanently add *hostname*'s Ethernet address to the ARP tables. The *hwaddr* argument specifies the hardware address, which is by default expected to be an Ethernet address specified as six hexadecimal bytes separated by colons. You may also set the hardware address for other types of hardware, using the -t option.

For some reason, ARP queries for the remote host sometimes fail, for instance, when its ARP driver is buggy or there is another host in the network that erroneously identifies itself with that host's IP address; this problem requires you to manually add an IP address to the ARP table. Hard-wiring IP addresses in the ARP table is also a (very drastic) measure to protect yourself from hosts on your Ethernet that pose as someone else.

Invoking *arp* using the -d switch deletes all ARP entries relating to the given host. This switch may be used to force the interface to reattempt obtaining the Ethernet address for the IP address in question. This is useful when a misconfigured system has broadcasted wrong ARP information (of course, you have to reconfigure the broken host first).

The -s option may also be used to implement *proxy* ARP. This is a special technique through which a host, say **gate**, acts as a gateway to another host named **fnord** by pretending that both addresses refer to the same host, namely **gate**. It does so by publishing an ARP entry for **fnord** that points to its own Ethernet interface. Now when a host sends out an ARP query for **fnord**, **gate** will return a reply containing its own Ethernet address. The querying host will then send all datagrams to **gate**, which dutifully forwards them to **fnord**.

These contortions may be necessary when you want to access **fnord** from a DOS machine with a broken TCP implementation that doesn't understand routing too well. When you use proxy ARP, it will appear to the DOS machine as if **fnord** was on the local subnet, so it doesn't have to know about how to route through a gateway.

Another useful application of proxy ARP is when one of your hosts acts as a gateway to some other host only temporarily, for instance, through a dial-up link. In a previous example, we encountered the laptop **vlite**, which was connected to **vlager** through a PLIP link from time to time. Of course, this application will work only if the address of the host you want to provide proxy ARP for is on the same IP subnet as your gateway. **vstout** could proxy ARP for any host on the brewery subnet (**172. 16.1.0**), but never for a host on the winery subnet (**172.16.2.0**).

The proper invocation to provide proxy ARP for **fnord** is given below; of course, the given Ethernet address must be that of **gate**:

```
# arp -s fnord 00:00:c0:a1:42:e0 pub
```

The proxy ARP entry may be removed again by invoking:

```
# arp -d fnord
```

CHAPTER 5

Name Service and Configuration

As we discussed in Chapter 2, TCP/IP networking may rely on different schemes to convert names into addresses. The simplest way is to use a host table stored in */etc/ hosts*. This is useful only for a small LAN that is run by a single administrator and no IP traffic with the outside world. The format of the *hosts* file has already been described in Chapter 4.

While a *hosts* file approach may be appropriate on a small network, most administrators will need to investigate a DNS server. There are multiple services that you can use to resolve IP addresses. The most commonly used is the *Berkeley Internet Name Domain service* (BIND) Version 8.x. BIND v9.x has been available for some time now and seeks to add a variety of new features, as well as contend with security issues in BIND v8.x. The jump from BIND 8 to BIND 9 isn't quite as significant as was the leap from BIND 4 to 8; many of the configuration files and options are the same. Configuring BIND can be a real chore, but once you've done it, you can easily make changes in the network topology. On Linux, as on many other Unix-ish systems, BIND service is provided through a program called *named*. At startup, it loads a set of master files into its internal cache and waits for queries from remote or local user processes. There are different ways to set up BIND, and not all require you to run a nameserver on every host.

We will also discuss a simpler and more secure option, djbdns, written by David J. Bernstein. This resolver was written from scratch with security in mind and simplifies server setup in a number of ways, primarily by eliminating the need for multiple confusing zone files.

This chapter can do little more than give a rough sketch of how DNS works and how to operate a nameserver. It should be sufficient for readers with a small LAN and an Internet connection. For the most current information, you may want to check the documentation contained in the BIND or djbdns source packages, which supply manual pages, release notes, and in the BIND package, the *BIND Operator's Guide* (BOG). Don't let this name scare you off; it's actually a very useful document. For more comprehensive coverage of DNS and associated issues, you may find *DNS and BIND* by Paul Albitz and Cricket Liu (O'Reilly) a useful reference. DNS questions may be answered in a newsgroup called *comp.protocols.tcp-ip.domains*. For technical details, the Domain Name System is defined by RFC numbers 1033, 1034, and 1035.

The Resolver Library

The term *resolver* refers not to a special application, but to the resolver library. This is a collection of functions that can be found in the standard C library and are invoked by a wide range of networking applications. The central routines are *gethostbyname(2)* and *gethostbyaddr(2)*, which look up all IP addresses associated with a hostname, and vice versa. They may be configured to simply look up the information in *hosts*, or to query a number of DNS nameservers.

The resolver functions read configuration files when they are invoked. From these configuration files, they determine what databases to query, in which order, and other details relevant to how you've configured your environment. The older Linux standard library, libc, used */etc/host.conf* as its master configuration file, but since Version 2 of the GNU standard library, glibc, uses */etc/nsswitch.conf*.

The nsswitch.conf File

The *nsswitch.conf* file allows the system administrator to configure a wide variety of different databases. We'll limit our discussion to options that relate to host and network IP address resolution. You can easily find more information about the other features by reading the GNU standard library documentation.

Options in *nsswitch.conf* must appear on separate lines. Fields may be separated by whitespace (spaces or tabs). A hash sign (#) introduces a comment that extends to the next newline. Each line describes a particular service; hostname resolution is one of these. The first field in each line is the name of the database, ending with a colon. The database name associated with host address resolution is hosts. A related database is networks, which is used for resolution of network names into network addresses. The remainder of each line stores options that determine the way lookups for that database are performed.

The following options are available:

dns
> Use the DNS service to resolve the address. This makes sense only for host address resolution, not network address resolution. This mechanism uses the *fs* file that we'll describe later in the chapter.

files
> Search a local file for the host or network name and its corresponding address. This option uses the traditional */etc/hosts* and */etc/networks* files.

The order in which the services to be queried are listed determines the order in which they are queried when attempting to resolve a name. The query-order list is in the service description in the */etc/nsswitch.conf* file. The services are queried from left to right and by default searching stops when a resolution is successful.

A simple example of host and network database specification that would mimic our configuration using the older libc standard library is shown in Example 5-1.

Example 5-1. Sample nsswitch.conf file

```
# /etc/nsswitch.conf
#
# Example configuration of GNU Name Service Switch functionality.
# Information about this file is available in the `libc6-doc' package.

hosts:          dns files
networks:       files
```

This example causes the system to look up hosts first in the DNS and, if that can't find them, the */etc/hosts* file. Network name lookups would be attempted using only the */etc/networks* file.

You are able to control the lookup behavior more precisely using "action items" that describe what action to take given the result of the previous lookup attempt. Action items appear between service specifications and are enclosed within square brackets, [ ]. The general syntax of the action statement is:

    [[!] status = action ...]

There are two possible actions:

return

> Controls returns to the program that attempted the name resolution. If a lookup attempt was successful, the resolver will return with the details; otherwise, it will return a zero result.

continue

> The resolver will move on to the next service in the list and use it to attempt resolution.

The optional (!) character specifies that the status value should be inverted before testing; that is, it means "not."

The available status values on which we can act are as follows:

success

> The requested entry was found without error. The default action for this status is return.

notfound

> There was no error in the lookup, but the target host or network could not be found. The default action for this status is continue.

unavail

> The service queried was unavailable. This could mean that the *hosts* or *networks* file was unreadable for the `files` service or that a nameserver or NIS server did not respond for the `dns` or `nis` services. The default action for this status is `continue`.

tryagain

> This status means that the service is temporarily unavailable. For the *files* service, this would usually indicate that the relevant file was locked by some process. For other services, it may mean the server was temporarily unable to accept connections. The default action for this status is `continue`.

A simple example of how you might use this mechanism is shown in Example 5-2.

Example 5-2. Sample nsswitch.conf file using an action statement

```
# /etc/nsswitch.conf
#
# Example configuration of GNU Name Service Switch functionality.
# Information about this file is available in the `libc6-doc' package.

hosts:          dns [!UNAVAIL=return] files
networks:       files
```

This example attempts host resolution using DNS. If the return status is anything other than unavailable, the resolver returns whatever it has found. If, and only if, the DNS lookup attempt returns an unavailable status, the resolver attempts to use the local */etc/hosts*. This means that we should use the *hosts* file only if our nameserver is unavailable for some reason.

Configuring Nameserver Lookups Using resolv.conf

When configuring the resolver library to use the DNS name service for host lookups, you also have to tell it which nameservers to use. There is a separate file for this called *resolv.conf*. If this file does not exist or is empty, the resolver assumes the nameserver is on your local host.

To run a nameserver on your local host, you have to set it up separately, as will be explained in the following section, "How DNS Works." If you are on a local network and have the opportunity to use an existing nameserver, this should always be preferred. If you use a dialup IP connection to the Internet, you would normally specify the nameserver of your service provider in the *resolv.conf* file.

The most important option in *resolv.conf* is `nameserver`, which gives the IP address of a nameserver to use. If you specify several nameservers by giving the `nameserver` option several times, they are tried in the order given. You should therefore put the most reliable server first. The current implementation allows you to have up to three `nameserver` statements in *resolv.conf*. If no `nameserver` option is given, the resolver attempts to connect to the nameserver on the local host.

Two other options, `domain` and `search`, let you use shortcut names for hosts in your local domain. Usually, when just contacting another host in your local domain, you don't want to type in the fully qualified hostname, but use a name such as **gauss** on the command line and have the resolver tack on the **mathematics.groucho.edu** part.

This is just the `domain` statement's purpose. It lets you specify a default domain name to be appended when DNS fails to look up a hostname. For instance, when given the name **gauss**, the resolver first tries to find **gauss.** in DNS and fails, because there is no such top-level domain. When given **mathematics.groucho.edu** as a default domain, the resolver repeats the query for **gauss** with the default domain appended, this time succeeding.

That's just fine, you may think, but as soon you get out of the math department's domain, you're back to those fully qualified domain names. Of course, you would also want to have shorthands like **quark.physics** for hosts in the physics department's domain.

This is where the *search list* comes in. A search list can be specified using the `search` option, which is a generalization of the `domain` statement. Where the latter gives a single default domain, the former specifies a whole list of them, each to be tried in turn until a lookup succeeds. This list must be separated by blanks or tabs.

The `search` and `domain` statements are mutually exclusive and may not appear more than once. If neither option is given, the resolver will try to guess the default domain from the local hostname using the *getdomainname(2)* system call. If the local hostname doesn't have a domain part, the root domain is the default.

Assume you're at the Virtual Brewery and want to log in to **foot.groucho.edu**. By a slip of your fingers, you mistype **foot** as **foo**, which doesn't exist. GMU's nameserver will therefore tell you that it knows no such host. Using older search methods, the resolver used to keep trying the name with **vbrew.com** and **com** appended. The latter is problematic because **groucho.edu.com** might actually be a valid domain name. Their nameserver might then even find **foo** in their domain, pointing you to one of their hosts, which is not what you're looking for.

For some applications, these bogus host lookups can be a security problem. Therefore, you should usually limit the domains on your search list to your local organization or something comparable. At the mathematics department of Groucho Marx University, the search list would commonly be set to **maths.groucho.edu** and **groucho.edu**.

If default domains sound confusing to you, consider this sample *resolv.conf* file for the Virtual Brewery:

```
# /etc/resolv.conf
# Our domain
```

```
domain          vbrew.com
#
# We use vlager as central name server:
nameserver      172.16.1.1
```

When resolving the name **vale**, the resolver looks up **vale**. and, failing this, **vale. vbrew.com**.

Resolver Robustness

When running a LAN inside a larger network, you definitely should use central nameservers if they are available. The nameservers develop rich caches that speed up repeat queries, since all queries are forwarded to them. However, this scheme has a drawback: when a fire destroyed the backbone cable at one author's university, no more work was possible on his department's LAN because the resolver could no longer reach any of the nameservers. This situation caused difficulties with most network services, such as X terminal logins and printing.

Although it is not very common for campus backbones to go down in flames, one might want to take precautions against such cases.

One option is to set up a local nameserver that resolves hostnames from your local domain and forwards all queries for other hostnames to the main servers. Of course, this is applicable only if you are running your own domain.

Alternatively, you can maintain a backup host table for your domain or LAN in */etc/ hosts*. This is very simple to do. You simply ensure that the resolver library queries DNS first and the *hosts* file next. In the */etc/nsswitch.conf* file you'd use hosts: dns files to make the resolver fall back to the *hosts* file if the central nameserver is unreachable.

How DNS Works

DNS organizes hostnames in a domain hierarchy. A *domain* is a collection of sites that are related in some sense—because they form a proper network (e.g., all machines on a campus), because they all belong to a certain organization (e.g., the U.S. government), or because they're simply geographically close. For instance, universities are commonly grouped in the **edu** domain, with each university or college using a separate *subdomain*, below which their hosts are subsumed. Groucho Marx University the **groucho.edu** domain, while the LAN of the mathematics department is assigned **maths.groucho.edu**. Hosts on the departmental network would have this domain name tacked onto their hostname, so **erdos** would be known as **erdos.maths.groucho.edu**, which would be the FQDN (see "Setting the Hostname" in Chapter 4).

Figure 5-1 shows a section of the namespace. The entry at the root of this tree, which is denoted by a single dot, is quite appropriately called the *root domain* and encompasses all other domains. To indicate that a hostname is a FQDN, rather than a name relative to some (implicit) local domain, it is sometimes written with a trailing dot. This dot signifies that the name's last component is the root domain. Depending on its location in the name hierarchy, a domain may be called top-level, second-level, or third-level. More levels of subdivision occur, but they are rare. Table 5-1 lists several top-level domains that you may see frequently.

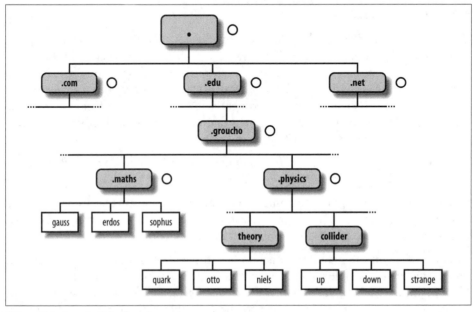

Figure 5-1. A part of the domain namespace

Table 5-1. Common top-level domains

Domain	Description
edu	(Mostly U.S.) educational institutions such as universities.
com	Commercial organizations and companies.
org	Noncommercial organizations.
net	Originally for gateways and other administrative entities, now commercial organizations and companies as well.
mil	U.S. military institutions.
gov	U.S. government institutions.
biz	For use by companies or commercial entities
name	Designated for individuals to use for personal web sites
info	Established for informational resource sites

Historically, the first four of these were assigned to the U.S., but changes in policy have meant that these domains, named global Top-Level Domains (gTLD), are now considered global in nature. Recent negotiations to broaden the range of gTLDs resulted in the last three additions. However, these new options have so far proven to be quite unpopular.

Outside the U.S., each country generally uses a top-level domain of its own named after the two-letter country code defined in ISO-3166. Finland, for instance, uses the **fi** domain; **fr** is used by France, **de** by Germany, and **aq** by Antarctica. Below this top-level domain, each country's NIC is free to organize hostnames in whatever way they want. Australia has second-level domains similar to the international top-level domains, named **com.au** and **edu.au**. Other countries, such as Germany, don't use this extra level, but have slightly long names that refer directly to the organizations running a particular domain. It's not uncommon to see hostnames such as *ftp://ftp. informatik.uni-erlangen.de*. Chalk that up to German efficiency.

Of course, these national domains do not necessarily mean that a host below that domain is actually located in that country; it means only that the host has been registered with that country's NIC. A Swedish manufacturer might have a branch in Australia and still have all its hosts registered with the **se** top-level domain.

This practice has become more popular in recent years, with countries such as Tuvalu (**tv**) and Togo (**to**) selling TLDs to enterprising agents who resell domain names such as **go.to** or **watch.tv**.

Organizing the namespace in a hierarchy of domain names nicely solves the problem of name uniqueness; with DNS, a hostname has to be unique only within its domain to give it a name different from all other hosts worldwide. Furthermore, fully qualified names are easy to remember. Taken by themselves, these are already very good reasons to split up a large domain into several subdomains.

DNS does even more for you than this. It also allows you to delegate authority over a subdomain to its administrators. For example, the maintainers at the Groucho Computing Center might create a subdomain for each department; we already encountered the math and physics subdomains above. When they find the network at the physics department too large and chaotic to manage from outside (after all, physicists are known to be an unruly bunch), they may simply pass control of the **physics. groucho.edu** domain to the administrators of this network. These administrators are free to use whatever hostnames they like and assign them IP addresses from their network in whatever fashion they desire, without outside interference.

To this end, the namespace is split up into zones, each rooted at a domain. Note the subtle difference between a zone and a domain: the domain **groucho.edu** encompasses all hosts at Groucho Marx University, while the zone **groucho.edu** includes only the hosts that are managed by the Computing Center directly—those at the mathematics department, for example. The hosts at the physics department belong to a different zone, namely **physics.groucho.edu**. In Figure 5-1, the start of a zone is marked by a small circle to the right of the domain name.

Name Lookups with DNS

At first glance, all this domain and zone fuss seems to make name resolution an awfully complicated business. After all, if no central authority controls what names are assigned to which hosts, how is a humble application supposed to know?

Now comes the really ingenious part about DNS. If you want to find the IP address of **erdos**, for example, DNS says, "Go ask the people who manage it, and they will tell you."

In fact, DNS is a giant distributed database. It is implemented by so-called nameservers that supply information on a given domain or set of domains. For each zone there are at least two, or at most a few, nameservers that hold all authoritative information on hosts in that zone. To obtain the IP address of **erdos**, all you have to do is contact the nameserver for the **groucho.edu** zone, which will then return the desired data.

Easier said than done, you might think. So how do I know how to reach the nameserver at Groucho Marx University? In case your computer isn't equipped with an address-resolving oracle, DNS provides for this, too. When your application wants to look up information on **erdos**, it contacts a local nameserver, which conducts a so-called iterative query for it. It starts off by sending a query to a nameserver for the root domain, asking for the address of **erdos.maths.groucho.edu**. The root nameserver recognizes that this name does not belong to its zone of authority, but rather to one below the **edu** domain. Thus, it tells you to contact an **edu** zone nameserver for more information and encloses a list of all edu nameservers along with their addresses. Your local nameserver will then go on and query one of those— for instance, **a.isi.edu**. In a manner similar to the root nameserver, **a.isi.edu** knows that the **groucho.edu** people run a zone of their own and points you to their servers. The local nameserver will then present its query for **erdos** to one of these, which will finally recognize the name as belonging to its zone and return the corresponding IP address.

This looks like a lot of traffic for looking up a measly IP address, but it's miniscule considering the speed of networking today. There's still room for improvement with this scheme, however.

To improve response time during future queries, the nameserver stores the information obtained in its local cache. So the next time anyone on your local network wants to look up the address of a host in the **groucho.edu** domain, your nameserver will go directly to the **groucho.edu** nameserver.*

---

* If information weren't cached, DNS would be as inefficient as any other method because each query would involve the root name servers.

Of course, the nameserver will not keep this information forever; it will discard it after some time. The expiration interval is called the *time to live* (ttl). Each datum in the DNS database is assigned such a ttl by administrators of the responsible zone.

Types of Nameservers

Nameservers that hold all information on hosts within a zone are called *authoritative* for this zone. Any query for a host within this zone will end up at one of these nameservers.

Authoritative servers must be fairly well synchronized. Thus, the zone's network administrator must make one the *primary* server, which loads its zone information from datafiles, and make the others *secondary* servers, which transfer the zone data from the primary server at regular intervals.

Having several nameservers distributes workload; it also provides backup. When one nameserver machine fails in a benign way, such as crashing or losing its network connection, all queries fall back to the other servers. Of course, this scheme doesn't protect you from server malfunctions that produce wrong replies to all DNS requests, such as from software bugs in the server program itself.

You can also run a nameserver that is not authoritative for any domain.* This is useful since the nameserver will still be able to conduct DNS queries for the applications running on the local network and cache the information. Hence, it is called a *caching-only* server.

The DNS Database

We have seen that DNS not only deals with IP addresses of hosts, but also exchanges information on nameservers. DNS databases may have, in fact, many different types of entries.

A single piece of information from the DNS database is called a *resource record* (RR). Each record has a type associated with it describing the sort of data it represents, and a class specifying the type of network it applies to. The latter accommodates the needs of different addressing schemes, including IP addresses (the IN class), Hesiod addresses (used by MIT's Kerberos system), and a few more. The prototypical resource record type is the A record, which associates a fully qualified domain name with an IP address.

A host may be known by more than one name. For example you might have a server that provides both FTP and World Wide Web servers, which you give two names: *ftp.machine.org* and *www.machine.org*. However, one of these names must be

---

* Well, almost. A nameserver has to provide at least name service for localhost and reverse lookups of **127.0. 0.1**.

identified as the official or *canonical* hostname, while the others are simply aliases referring to the official hostname. The difference is that the canonical hostname is the one with an associated A record, while the others only have a record of type CNAME that points to the canonical hostname.

We will not go through all record types here, but we will give you a brief example. Example 5-3 shows a part of the domain database that is loaded into the nameservers for the **physics.groucho.edu** zone.

Example 5-3. An excerpt from a BIND zone file for the physics department

```
; Authoritative Information on physics.groucho.edu.
$TTL 3D
@  IN  SOA niels.physics.groucho.edu. janet.niels.physics.groucho.edu. {
                    2004010200      ; serial no
                    8H              ; refresh
                    2H              ; retry
                    4W              ; expire
                    1D              ; default ttl
                }
;
; Name servers
            IN    NS     niels
            IN    NS     gauss.maths.groucho.edu.
gauss.maths.groucho.edu. IN A 149.76.4.23
;
; Theoretical Physics (subnet 12)
niels       IN    A      149.76.12.1
            IN    A      149.76.1.12
nameserver  IN    CNAME  niels
otto        IN    A      149.76.12.2
quark       IN    A      149.76.12.4
down        IN    A      149.76.12.5
iowa        IN    AAAA   2001:30fa::3
strange     IN    A      149.76.12.6
...
; Collider Lab. (subnet 14)
boson       IN    A      149.76.14.1
muon        IN    A      149.76.14.7
bogon       IN    A      149.76.14.12
...
```

Apart from the A and CNAME records, you can see a special record at the top of the file, stretching several lines. This is the SOA resource record signaling the *Start of Authority*, which holds general information on the zone that the server is authoritative for. The SOA record comprises, for instance, the default time to live for all records.

Note that all names in the sample file that do not end with a dot should be interpreted relative to the **physics.groucho.edu** domain. The special name (@) used in the SOA record refers to the domain name by itself.

We have seen earlier that the nameservers for the **groucho.edu** domain somehow have to know about the **physics** zone so that they can point queries to their nameservers. This is usually achieved by a pair of records: the NS record that gives the server's FQDN, and an A record that associates an address with that name. Since these records are what holds the namespace together, they are frequently called *glue records*. They are the only instances of records in which a parent zone actually holds information on hosts in the subordinate zone. The glue records pointing to the nameservers for **physics.groucho.edu** are shown in Example 5-4.

Example 5-4. An excerpt from a zone file for GMU

```
; Zone data for the groucho.edu zone.
....
;
; Glue records for the physics.groucho.edu zone
physics         IN    NS      niels.physics.groucho.edu.
                IN    NS      gauss.maths.groucho.edu.
niels.physics   IN    A       149.76.12.1
gauss.maths     IN    A       149.76.4.23
...
```

The BIND named.conf File

The primary configuration file of BIND is */etc/named.conf*. This style of configuration file has been in use by BIND since Version 8 replaced the old *named.boot* file.

The syntax is somewhat complex and supports a wide range of functions, but is fairly straightforward when configured to provide basic functionality. Example 5-5 shows a simple configuration file for the **vbrew** domain.

Example 5-5. The BIND named.conf file for vlager

```
// This is the primary configuration file for the BIND DNS server named.
//

options {
        directory "/var/cache/bind";
        allow-query { any; };
        recursion no;

zone "localhost" {
        type master;
        file "/etc/bind/db.local";
};

zone "127.in-addr.arpa" {
        type master;
        file "/etc/bind/db.127";
};
```

Example 5-5. The BIND named.conf file for vlager (continued)

```
zone "vbrew.com" {
        type master;
    allow-transfer { 10.10.0.5;
            172.16.90.4;
            1.2.3.4;
        };
        file "/etc/bind/db.vbrew.com";
};

zone "0.168.192.in-addr.arpa" {
        type master;
        file "/etc/bind/db.192.168.0";
};
```

If you take a close look, you will see that each of the statements is written similar to a C-like statement with attributes enclosed within { } characters in the *named.conf* file.

The comments, often indicated by a pound character (#) in Linux, are indicated by two forward slashes (//) instead.

One of the most important options in this configuration file is zone. This is how you tell BIND what it's supposed to know. Beneath zone is another very important option, allow-transfer. This option allows you to set the IP addresses permitted to perform a zone transfer. It is important to restrict this to authorized entities only because it contains a lot of information that could be useful to potential attackers. In the example configuration files, we've restricted zone transfers to the three IP addresses listed.

In the option statement, we've also disabled DNS recursion. This allows us to separate the DNS server functionality from the DNS cache functionality. For security reasons it's a good idea to do this. There have been many papers written on this subject, with one of the best explanations found at *http://cr.yp.to/djbdns/separation.html*. If you need recursive functionality, it is best to configure a caching-only server on an IP address separate from your DNS server. We'll discuss how to make a caching-only server with BIND a little bit later.

If you've decided that you can't live without recursion on the same server, there are ways within the *named.conf* to restrict recursion to specified domains. By using the allow-recursion option in place of the recursion no, you can specify a range of IP addresses allowed to perform recursive queries.

You've probably noticed that in this file we've included quite a few other entries than just the **vbrew.com** domain. These are present to be compliant with the specifications established in RFC 1912, "Common DNS Operational and Configuration Errors." This specification requests that sites be authoritative for the localhost forward and reverse zones, and for broadcast zones.

The BIND configuration supports many more options that we haven't covered here. If you'd like information all of the options, the best source of information is the documentation supplied with the BIND Version 8 or 9 source package.

The DNS Database Files

Master files included with *named*, zone files, always have a domain associated with them, which is called the *origin*. This is the domain name specified with the cache and primary options. Within a master file, you are allowed to specify domain and hostnames relative to this domain. A name given in a configuration file is considered *absolute* if it ends in a single dot; otherwise, it is considered relative to the origin. The origin by itself may be referred to using (@).

The data contained in a master file is split up in RRs, the smallest units of information available through DNS. Each RR has a type. A records, for instance, map a hostname to an IP address, and a CNAME record associates an alias for a host with its official hostname. Examples appear later in the chapter when a complete set of configuation and zone files are shown.

RR representations in master files share a common format:

    [domain] [ttl] [class] type rdata

Fields are separated by spaces or tabs. An entry may be continued across several lines if an opening brace occurs before the first newline and the last field is followed by a closing brace. Anything between a semicolon and a newline is ignored. A description of the format terms follows:

domain
> This term is the domain name to which the entry applies. If no domain name is given, the RR is assumed to apply to the domain of the previous RR.

ttl
> In order to force resolvers to discard information after a certain time, each RR is associated a time to live (*ttl*). The ttl field specifies the time in seconds that the information is valid after it has been retrieved from the server. It is a decimal number with at most eight digits.
>
> If no ttl value is given, the field value defaults to that of the *minimum* field of the preceding SOA record.

class
> This is an address class, such as IN for IP addresses or HS for objects in the Hesiod class. For TCP/IP networking, you have to specify IN.
>
> If no class field is given, the class of the preceding RR is assumed.

type

This describes the type of the RR. The most common types are A, SOA, PTR, and NS. The following sections describe the various types of RRs.

rdata

This holds the data associated with the RR. The format of this field depends on the type of RR. In the following discussion, it will be described for each RR separately.

The following is partial list of RRs to be used in DNS master files. There are a couple more of them that we will not explain; they are experimental and of little use, generally.

SOA

This RR describes a zone of authority. It signals that the records following the SOA RR contain authoritative information for the domain. Every master file included by a `primary` statement must contain an SOA record for this zone. The resource data contains the following fields:

origin

This field is the canonical hostname of the primary nameserver for this domain. It is usually given as an absolute name.

contact

This field is the email address of the person responsible for maintaining the domain, with the "@" sign replaced by a dot. For instance, if the responsible person at the Virtual Brewery were **janet**, this field would contain **janet. vbrew.com**.

serial

This field is the version number of the zone file, expressed as a single decimal number. Whenever data is changed in the zone file, this number should be incremented. A common convention is to use a number that reflects the date of the last update, with a version number appended to it to cover the case of multiple updates occurring on a single day, e.g., 2000012600 being update 00 that occurred on January 26, 2000.

The serial number is used by secondary nameservers to recognize zone information changes. To stay up to date, secondary servers request the primary server's SOA record at certain intervals and compare the serial number to that of the cached SOA record. If the number has changed, the secondary servers transfer the whole zone database from the primary server.

refresh

This field specifies the interval in seconds that the secondary servers should wait between checking the SOA record of the primary server. Again, this is a decimal number with at most eight digits.

Generally, the network topology doesn't change too often, so this number should specify an interval of roughly a day for larger networks, and even more for smaller ones.

retry

This number determines the intervals at which a secondary server should retry contacting the primary server if a request or a zone refresh fails. It must not be too low, or a temporary failure of the server or a network problem could cause the secondary server to waste network resources. One hour, or perhaps one-half hour, might be a good choice.

expire

This field specifies the time in seconds after which a secondary server should finally discard all zone data if it hasn't been able to contact the primary server. You should normally set this field to at least a week (604,800 seconds), but increasing it to a month or more is also reasonable.

minimum

This field is the default time to live value for resource records that do not explicitly contain one. The ttl value specifies the maximum amount of time other nameservers may keep the RR in their cache. This time applies only to normal lookups, and has nothing to do with the time after which a secondary server should try to update the zone information.

If the topology of your network does not change frequently, a week or even more is probably a good choice. If single RRs change more frequently, you could still assign them smaller ttls individually. If your network changes frequently, you may want to set *minimum* to one day (86,400 seconds).

A

This record associates an IP address with a hostname. The resource data field contains the address in dotted quad notation.

For each hostname, there must be only one A record. The hostname used in this A record is considered the *canonical* hostname. All other hostnames are aliases and must be mapped onto the canonical hostname using a CNAME record. If the canonical name of our host were **vlager**, we'd have an A record that associated that hostname with its IP address. Since we may also want another name associated with that address, say **news**, we'd create a CNAME record that associates this alternate name with the canonical name. We'll talk more about CNAME records shortly.

AAAA

This record is exactly the same as the A record, but is used exclusively for IPv6 addresses.

NS

NS records are used to specify a zone's primary server and all its secondary servers. An NS record points to a master nameserver of the given zone, with the resource data field containing the hostname of the nameserver.

You will meet NS records in two situations: the first is when you delegate authority to a subordinate zone; the second is within the master zone database of the subordinate zone itself. The sets of servers specified in both the parent and delegated zones should match.

The NS record specifies the name of the primary and secondary nameservers for a zone. These names must be resolved to an address so they can be used. Sometimes the servers belong to the domain, they are serving, which causes a "chicken-and-egg" problem; we can't resolve the address until the nameserver is reachable, but we can't reach the nameserver until we resolve its address. To solve this dilemma, we can configure special A records directly into the nameserver of the parent zone. The A records allow the nameservers of the parent domain to resolve the IP address of the delegated zone nameservers. These records are commonly called glue records because they provide the "glue" that binds a delegated zone to its parent. Refer to the "DNS Database" section earlier for an explanation of how this works.

CNAME

This record associates an alias with a host's canonical hostname. It provides an alternate name by which users can refer to the host whose canonical name is supplied as a parameter. The canonical hostname is the one the master file provides an A record for; aliases are simply linked to that name by a CNAME record, but don't have any other records of their own.

PTR

This type of record is used to associate names in the **in-addr.arpa** domain with hostnames. It is used for reverse mapping of IP addresses to hostnames. The hostname given must be the canonical hostname.

MX

This RR announces a *mail exchanger* for a domain. Mail exchangers are discussed in Chapter 11, "Mail Routing on the Internet." The syntax of an MX record is

    [*domain*] [*ttl*] [*class*] MX *preference host*

host names the MX for *domain*. Every MX has an integer *preference* associated with it. A mail transport agent that wants to deliver mail to *domain* tries all hosts that have an MX record for this domain until it succeeds. The one with the lowest preference value is tried first, and then the others, in order of increasing preference value.

HINFO

This record provides information on the system's hardware and software. Its syntax is:

```
[domain] [ttl] [class] HINFO hardware software
```

The *hardware* field identifies the hardware used by this host. Special conventions are used to specify this. If the field contains any blanks, it must be enclosed in double quotes. The *software* field names the operating system software used by the system. However, for security reasons, it's not a great idea to have this information publicly available, as it provides potentially valuable information to attackers. It's very uncommon to see it used lately, but some administrators like to use it to provide spurious or humorous information about their hosts.

Example HINFO records to describe machines look something like:

```
tao   36500 IN  HINFO  SEGA-DREAMCAST  LINUX2.6
cevad 36500 IN  HINFO  ATARI-104ST LINUX2.0
jedd  36500 IN  HINFO  TIMEX-SINCLAIR  LINUX2.6
```

Caching-Only named Configuration

There is a special type of *named* configuration that we'll talk about before we explain how to build a full nameserver configuration. It is called a *caching-only* configuration. It doesn't really serve a domain, but acts as a relay for all DNS queries produced on your host. The advantage of this scheme is that it builds up a cache so that only the first query for a particular host is actually sent to the nameservers on the Internet. Any repeated request will be answered directly from the cache in your local nameserver. It's also important to note here that a cache server should not be run from the same IP address as the DNS server.

A *named.conf* file for a caching-only server looks like this:

```
// Define networks to allow queries from.

acl allowednets { 192.168.99.0/24; 192.168.44.0/24; };
options {
    directory "/etc/bind";          // Working directory
    allow-query { allowednets; };
};

// Root server hints
zone "." { type hint;
      file "root.hint"; };

// Provide a reverse mapping for the loopback address 127.0.0.1
zone "0.0.127.in-addr.arpa" {
    type master;
    file "localhost.rev";
    notify no;
};
```

In addition to this *named.conf* file, you must set up the *root.hint* file with a valid list of root nameservers. You could copy and use Example 6.10 for this purpose, or, better yet, you could use a BIND tool called *dig* to get the most current version of this file. No other files are needed for a caching-only server configuration. We'll discuss *dig* in more detail later in this chapter, but for now, to obtain the information to create the *root.hint* file, you can use the following command:

```
vbrew# dig at e.root-servers.net . ns
```

Writing the Master Files

Examples 5-6, 5-7, 5-8, and 5-9 give sample configuration and zone files for a nameserver at the brewery, located on **vlager**. Due to the nature of the network discussed (a single LAN), the example is pretty straightforward.

The *root.hint* cache file shown in Example 5-6 shows sample hint records for a root nameserver. A typical cache file usually describes about a dozen nameservers. You can obtain the current list of nameservers for the root domain using the *dig* tool as described above.

Example 5-6. The root.hint file

```
; <<>> DiG 9.2.2 <<>> at e.root-servers.net . ns
;; global options:  printcmd
;; Got answer:
;; ->>HEADER<<- opcode: QUERY, status: NOERROR, id: 21972
;; flags: qr aa rd ra; QUERY: 1, ANSWER: 0, AUTHORITY: 1, ADDITIONAL: 0

;; QUESTION SECTION:
;at.                            IN      A

;; AUTHORITY SECTION:

;; Query time: 54 msec
;; SERVER: 206.13.28.12#53(206.13.28.12)
;; WHEN: Sat Jan 31 11:28:44 2004
;; MSG SIZE  rcvd: 83

;; Got answer:
;; ->>HEADER<<- opcode: QUERY, status: NOERROR, id: 8039
;; flags: qr rd ra; QUERY: 1, ANSWER: 1, AUTHORITY: 4, ADDITIONAL: 4

;; QUESTION SECTION:
;e.root-servers.net.            IN      A

;; ANSWER SECTION:
e.root-servers.net.     566162  IN      A       192.203.230.10

;; AUTHORITY SECTION:
ROOT-SERVERS.net.       134198  IN      NS      a.ROOT-SERVERS.net.
ROOT-SERVERS.net.       134198  IN      NS      f.ROOT-SERVERS.net.
```

Example 5-6. The root.hint file (continued)

```
ROOT-SERVERS.net.       134198  IN      NS      j.ROOT-SERVERS.net.
ROOT-SERVERS.net.       134198  IN      NS      k.ROOT-SERVERS.net.

;; ADDITIONAL SECTION:
a.ROOT-SERVERS.net.     566162  IN      A       198.41.0.4
f.ROOT-SERVERS.net.     566162  IN      A       192.5.5.241
j.ROOT-SERVERS.net.     566162  IN      A       192.58.128.30
k.ROOT-SERVERS.net.     566162  IN      A       193.0.14.129

;; Query time: 12 msec
;; SERVER: 206.13.28.12#53(206.13.28.12)
;; WHEN: Sat Jan 31 11:28:44 2004
;; MSG SIZE  rcvd: 196

;; Got answer:
;; ->>HEADER<<- opcode: QUERY, status: NOERROR, id: 61551
;; flags: qr rd ra; QUERY: 1, ANSWER: 13, AUTHORITY: 0, ADDITIONAL: 13

;; QUESTION SECTION:
;.                              IN      NS

;; ANSWER SECTION:
.                       479762  IN      NS      F.ROOT-SERVERS.NET.
.                       479762  IN      NS      B.ROOT-SERVERS.NET.
.                       479762  IN      NS      J.ROOT-SERVERS.NET.
.                       479762  IN      NS      K.ROOT-SERVERS.NET.
.                       479762  IN      NS      L.ROOT-SERVERS.NET.
.                       479762  IN      NS      M.ROOT-SERVERS.NET.
.                       479762  IN      NS      I.ROOT-SERVERS.NET.
.                       479762  IN      NS      E.ROOT-SERVERS.NET.
.                       479762  IN      NS      D.ROOT-SERVERS.NET.
.                       479762  IN      NS      A.ROOT-SERVERS.NET.
.                       479762  IN      NS      H.ROOT-SERVERS.NET.
.                       479762  IN      NS      C.ROOT-SERVERS.NET.
.                       479762  IN      NS      G.ROOT-SERVERS.NET.

;; ADDITIONAL SECTION:
F.ROOT-SERVERS.NET.     566162  IN      A       192.5.5.241
B.ROOT-SERVERS.NET.     566162  IN      A       192.228.79.201
J.ROOT-SERVERS.NET.     566162  IN      A       192.58.128.30
K.ROOT-SERVERS.NET.     566162  IN      A       193.0.14.129
L.ROOT-SERVERS.NET.     566162  IN      A       198.32.64.12
M.ROOT-SERVERS.NET.     566162  IN      A       202.12.27.33
I.ROOT-SERVERS.NET.     566162  IN      A       192.36.148.17
E.ROOT-SERVERS.NET.     566162  IN      A       192.203.230.10
D.ROOT-SERVERS.NET.     566162  IN      A       128.8.10.90
A.ROOT-SERVERS.NET.     566162  IN      A       198.41.0.4
H.ROOT-SERVERS.NET.     566162  IN      A       128.63.2.53
C.ROOT-SERVERS.NET.     566162  IN      A       192.33.4.12
G.ROOT-SERVERS.NET.     566162  IN      A       192.112.36.4

;; Query time: 17 msec
```

Example 5-6. The root.hint file (continued)

```
;; SERVER: 206.13.28.12#53(206.13.28.12)
;; WHEN: Sat Jan 31 11:28:44 2004
;; MSG SIZE  rcvd: 436
```

Example 5-7. The vbrew.com zone file

```
;
;                          Hosts at the brewery
;                    /etc/bind/zone/vbrew.com
;                          Origin is vbrew.com
;
$TTL 3D
@              IN  SOA   vlager.vbrew.com. janet.vbrew.com. (
                         200401206        ; serial, date + todays serial #
                         8H               ; refresh, seconds
                         2H               ; retry, seconds
                         4W               ; expire, seconds
                         1D )             ; minimum, seconds

           IN  NS    vlager.vbrew.com.
;
; local mail is distributed on vlager
                IN  MX    10 vlager
;
; loopback address
localhost.     IN  A     127.0.0.1
;
; Virtual Brewery Ethernet
vlager         IN  A     172.16.1.1
vlager-if1     IN  CNAME vlager
; vlager is also news server
news           IN  CNAME vlager
vstout         IN  A     172.16.1.2
vale           IN  A     172.16.1.3
;
; Virtual Winery Ethernet
vlager-if2     IN  A     172.16.2.1
vbardolino     IN  A     172.16.2.2
vchianti       IN  A     172.16.2.3
vbeaujolais    IN  A     172.16.2.4
;
; Virtual Spirits (subsidiary) Ethernet
vbourbon       IN  A     172.16.3.1
vbourbon-if1   IN  CNAME vbourbon
```

Example 5-8. The loopback zone file

```
;
; /etc/bind/zone/127.0.0      Reverse mapping of 127.0.0
;                             Origin is 0.0.127.in-addr.arpa.
;
;
```

Example 5-8. The loopback zone file (continued)

```
$TTL 3D
@              IN   SOA    vlager.vbrew.com. joe.vbrew.com. (
                          1          ; serial
                          360000     ; refresh: 100 hrs
                          3600       ; retry:   one hour
                          3600000    ; expire:  42 days
                          360000     ; minimum: 100 hrs
                          )
               IN   NS     vlager.vbrew.com.
1              IN   PTR    localhost.
```

Example 5-9. The vbrew reverse lookup file

```
;
;                       /etc/bind/zones/16.172.in-addr.arpa
;                            Origin is 16.172.in-addr.arpa.
;
$TTL 3D
@              IN   SOA    vlager.vbrew.com. joe.vbrew.com. (
                          16         ; serial
                          86400      ; refresh: once per day
                          3600       ; retry:   one hour
                          3600000    ; expire:  42 days
                          604800     ; minimum: 1 week
                          )
               IN   NS     vlager.vbrew.com.
; brewery
1.1            IN   PTR    vlager.vbrew.com.
2.1            IN   PTR    vstout.vbrew.com.
3.1            IN   PTR    vale.vbrew.com.
; winery
1.2            IN   PTR    vlager-if2.vbrew.com.
2.2            IN   PTR    vbardolino.vbrew.com.
3.2            IN   PTR    vchianti.vbrew.com.
4.2            IN   PTR    vbeaujolais.vbrew.com.
```

Verifying the Nameserver Setup

dig is the current nameserver query tool of choice, replacing the commonly known *nslookup*. It is flexible, fast, and can be used to query almost anything from a DNS server. The syntax for *dig* is very straightforward.

```
vbrew# dig nameserver name type
```

The command-line parameters are defined as follows:

nameserver

This is the name of the server that you are querying. It can be entered as a name or as an IP address. If you leave this blank, *dig* will use the DNS server listed in the *resolv.conf* file.

name

> This is the name of the DNS record that you want to look up.

type

> This is the type of query you want to execute. Common types are ANY, MX, and TXT. If left blank, *dig* will default to looking for an A record.

So, using this, if we wanted to see which servers handle mail for the Virtual Brewery, we would create the following *dig* query:

```
vbrew# dig vlager.vbrew.com MX

; <<>> DiG 9.2.2 <<>> vlager.vbrew.com MX
;; global options:  printcmd
;; Got answer:
;; ->>HEADER<<- opcode: QUERY, status: NOERROR, id: 40590
;; flags: qr rd ra; QUERY: 1, ANSWER: 0, AUTHORITY: 1, ADDITIONAL: 0

;; QUESTION SECTION:
;vlager.vbrew.com.        IN      MX

;; AUTHORITY SECTION:
vbrew.com.          10794   IN      SOA     vlager.vbrew.com. vlager.vbrew.com.
2003080803 10800 3600 604800 86400

;; Query time: 14 msec
;; SERVER: 192.168.28.12#53(192.168.28.12)
;; WHEN: Sun Feb  1 12:19:06 2004
;; MSG SIZE  rcvd: 104
```

Another example of an interesting query type which can be useful is the BIND version query. This is easily done with *dig* with the following syntax:

```
vlager# dig @vlager.vbrew.com version.bind. CHAOS TXT
.

.
; QUERY: 1, ANSWER: 1, AUTHORITY: 0, ADDITIONAL: 0

;; QUESTION SECTION:
;version.bind.                  CH      TXT

;; ANSWER SECTION:
VERSION.BIND.          0       CH      TXT     "BIND 8.2.2-P5"
.
.
```

Using nslookup

nslookup, while now deprecated, is still a good tool for checking the operation of your nameserver setup. It can be used both interactively with prompts and as a single command with immediate output. In the latter case, you simply invoke it as:

```
$ nslookup hostname
```

`nslookup` queries the nameserver specified in *resolv.conf* for *hostname*. (If this file names more than one server, `nslookup` chooses one at random.)

The interactive mode, however, is much more exciting. Besides looking up individual hosts, you may query for any type of DNS record and transfer the entire zone information for a domain.

When invoked without an argument, *nslookup* displays the nameserver it uses and enters interactive mode. At the prompt, you may type any domain name that you want to query. By default, it asks for class A records—those containing the IP address relating to the domain name.

You can look for record types by issuing:

```
> set type=type
```

in which *type* is one of the RRs names described earlier, or `ANY`.

For instance, you might have the following *nslookup* session:

```
$ nslookup
Default Server:  tao.linux.org.au
Address:  203.41.101.121

> metalab.unc.edu
Server:  tao.linux.org.au
Address:  203.41.101.121

Name:    metalab.unc.edu
Address:  152.2.254.81

>
```

The output first displays the DNS server being queried, and then the result of the query.

If you try to query for a name that has no IP address associated with it, but other records were found in the DNS database, `nslookup` returns with an error message saying "No type A records found." However, you can make it query for records other than type A by issuing the *set type* command. To get the SOA record of **unc.edu**, you would issue:

```
> unc.edu
Server:  tao.linux.org.au
Address:  203.41.101.121

*** No address (A) records available for unc.edu
> set type=SOA
> unc.edu
Server:  tao.linux.org.au
Address:  203.41.101.121

unc.edu
        origin = ns.unc.edu
```

```
            mail addr = host-reg.ns.unc.edu
            serial = 1998111011
            refresh = 14400 (4H)
            retry   = 3600 (1H)
            expire  = 1209600 (2W)
            minimum ttl = 86400 (1D)
unc.edu name server = ns2.unc.edu
unc.edu name server = ncnoc.ncren.net
unc.edu name server = ns.unc.edu
ns2.unc.edu      internet address = 152.2.253.100
ncnoc.ncren.net internet address = 192.101.21.1
ncnoc.ncren.net internet address = 128.109.193.1
ns.unc.edu       internet address = 152.2.21.1
```

In a similar fashion, you can query for MX records:

```
> set type=MX
> unc.edu
Server:  tao.linux.org.au
Address:  203.41.101.121

unc.edu preference = 0, mail exchanger = conga.oit.unc.edu
unc.edu preference = 10, mail exchanger = imsety.oit.unc.edu
unc.edu name server = ns.unc.edu
unc.edu name server = ns2.unc.edu
unc.edu name server = ncnoc.ncren.net
conga.oit.unc.edu       internet address = 152.2.22.21
imsety.oit.unc.edu      internet address = 152.2.21.99
ns.unc.edu       internet address = 152.2.21.1
ns2.unc.edu      internet address = 152.2.253.100
ncnoc.ncren.net internet address = 192.101.21.1
ncnoc.ncren.net internet address = 128.109.193.1
```

Using a type of ANY returns all resource records associated with a given name.

A practical application of **nslookup**, besides debugging, is to obtain the current list of root nameservers. You can obtain this list by querying for all NS records associated with the root domain:

```
> set type=NS
> .
Server:  tao.linux.org.au
Address:  203.41.101.121

Non-authoritative answer:
(root)  name server = A.ROOT-SERVERS.NET
(root)  name server = H.ROOT-SERVERS.NET
(root)  name server = B.ROOT-SERVERS.NET
(root)  name server = C.ROOT-SERVERS.NET
(root)  name server = D.ROOT-SERVERS.NET
(root)  name server = E.ROOT-SERVERS.NET
(root)  name server = I.ROOT-SERVERS.NET
(root)  name server = F.ROOT-SERVERS.NET
(root)  name server = G.ROOT-SERVERS.NET
```

```
(root)   name server = J.ROOT-SERVERS.NET
(root)   name server = K.ROOT-SERVERS.NET
(root)   name server = L.ROOT-SERVERS.NET
(root)   name server = M.ROOT-SERVERS.NET

Authoritative answers can be found from:
A.ROOT-SERVERS.NET      internet address = 198.41.0.4
H.ROOT-SERVERS.NET      internet address = 128.63.2.53
B.ROOT-SERVERS.NET      internet address = 128.9.0.107
C.ROOT-SERVERS.NET      internet address = 192.33.4.12
D.ROOT-SERVERS.NET      internet address = 128.8.10.90
E.ROOT-SERVERS.NET      internet address = 192.203.230.10
I.ROOT-SERVERS.NET      internet address = 192.36.148.17
F.ROOT-SERVERS.NET      internet address = 192.5.5.241
G.ROOT-SERVERS.NET      internet address = 192.112.36.4
J.ROOT-SERVERS.NET      internet address = 198.41.0.10
K.ROOT-SERVERS.NET      internet address = 193.0.14.129
L.ROOT-SERVERS.NET      internet address = 198.32.64.12
M.ROOT-SERVERS.NET      internet address = 202.12.27.33
```

To see the complete set of available commands, use the *help* command in **nslookup**.

Other Useful Tools

There are a few other tools that can help you with your tasks as a BIND administrator. We will briefly describe two of them here. Please refer to the documentation that comes with these tools for more information on how to use them.

hostcvt helps you with your initial BIND configuration by converting your */etc/hosts* file into master files for *named*. It generates both the forward (A) and reverse mapping (PTR) entries, and takes care of aliases. Of course, it won't do the whole job for you, as you may still want to tune the timeout values in the SOA record, for example, or add MX records. Still, it may save you a few aspirins. *hostcvt* is part of the BIND source, but can also be found as a standalone package.

After setting up your nameserver, you may want to test your configuration. Some good tools that make this job much simpler; the first is called *dnswalk*, which is a Perl-based package. The second is called *nslint*. They both examine your DNS database for common mistakes and verify that the information is consistent. Two other useful tools are *host*, which is a general purpose DNS database query tool. You can use this tool to manually inspect and diagnose DNS database entries.

This tool is likely to be available in prepackaged form. *dnswalk* and *nslint* are available in source from *http://www.visi.com/~barr/dnswalk/* and *ftp://ftp.ee.lbl.gov/nslint.tar.Z*. The *host*'s source code can be found at *ftp://ftp.nikhef.nl/pub/network/* and *ftp://ftp.is.co.za/networking/ip/dns/dig/*.

Alternatives to BIND

Those who have been concerned with the number of security vulnerabilities found in the BIND server through the years, or who prefer an easier DNS solution, may wish to investigate an alternative, djbdns. This software, written from scratch by D.J. Bernstein, provides a much more robust, simplified and secure framework for DNS. djbdns is easy to install and configure, and is much less complex than BIND, essentially the same functionality. In this next section, we'll cover the basics of installing and configuring a DNS server using djbdns. It is important to note that a djbdns DNS server is designed to be just that, a DNS server, meaning that by default it won't be resolving queries for machines outside of your authority. For that, you will need to build a separate caching server on a separate machine or IP address. As recommended earlier, caches and DNS servers should be separated for security reasons. To read more about this topic, please refer to the djbdns web site at *http://cr.yp.to/djbdns.html*.

Installing djbdns

To run djbdns, you first need to install another DJB program called daemontools, which is basically a collection of tools used to manage various Unix daemons. To view full documentation and source code for daemontools, visit its webpage at *http://cr.yp.to/daemontools.html*. When you've successfully downloaded the software, extract it to a directory on your machine and compile the software. daemontools comes with a script that will automatically compile and install the software. It can be launched as follows:

```
vlager# mkdir software
vlager# cd software
vlager# tar xzpf daemontools-0.76.tar.gz
vlager# cd admin/daemontools-0.76
vlager# package/install
```

When the script finishes, you can remove the installation directories, and begin installing the next dependency, ucspi-tcp, which is DJB's very own TCP client-server handling program. It is also very easy to install:

```
vlager# mkdir software
vlager# cd software
vlager# tar xzpf ucspi-tcp-0.88.tar.gz
vlager# cd ucspi-tcp-0.88
vlager# make
vlager# make setup check
```

This will install the software to the */usr/local* directory on your machine. You won't need to do anything else with the operation or configuration of this software for the moment.

Once it is installed, you are ready to install the djbdns software. The djbdns installation is accomplished using the same steps documented above for ucspi-tcp. This process will also install djbdns to the */usr/local* directory. You will need to make sure that the svscan process is running before configuring djbdns. svscan is part of the daemontools package and must be running for djbdns to function.

When you've verified that *svscan* is running, you can start the configuration of the DNS server. The first step is to create two user accounts, *tinydns* and *dnslog*. djbdns will use both of these to conduct its business, rather than run as root, as BIND installations often do.

Next, you will need to create a directory for your DNS server's configuration files and logs, and then configure it as follows:

```
vlager# mkdir /etc/tinydns
vlager# tinydns-conf tinydns dnslog /etc/tinydns 172.16.0.2
```

The IP address **172.16.0.2** in the example should be replaced with your DNS server's external IP address. Following this, *svscan* needs to be informed of the new service. This process accomplished with three commands:

```
vlager# ln -s /etc/tinydns /service
vlager# svstat /service/tinydns
```

This will complete the installation of your djbdns server; all that's left is to do is configure your hosts. Under BIND, this is where a majority of the complexity and confusion exists; dbjdns, however, makes adding new DNS records much easier.

Adding Hosts

You will need to configure your host information so that your DNS server is providing a service. The first step in this process is to establish yourself as an authority over your domain. For our example, the Virtual Brewery, we will want to configure our DNS server to answer all queries for the **vbrew.com** domain. Rather than hassle with long zone files, this can be done with a few short steps.

```
vlager# cd /service/tinydns/root
vlager# ./add-ns vlager.com 172.16.1.1
vlager# ./add-ns 1.16.172.in-addr.arpa 172.16.1.1
vlager# make
```

Now that the server will handle queries for our **vbrew** domain, we can use it to configure individual hosts on our network. Fortuantely, this is just as easy as the previous step. To associate an address to our favorite host, **vlager**, and to our web server, we need to use the following commands:

```
vlager# cd /service/tinydns/root
vlager# ./add-host vlager.vbrew.com 172.16.1.10
vlager# ./add-host www.vlager.com 172.16.1.11
vlager# ./add-alias mail.vbrew.com 172.16.1.10
vlager# make
```

Using the *add-host* command, we enter the FDQN followed by the IP addresss to create our DNS records. You might have noticed the other command used in the example, *add-alias*. This command adds an alias to an already assigned IP. In the example, we have our host **vlager** set to also answer to the name **mail**. This is useful if a server serves multiple purposes. Take special notice of the last command executed in the series, *make*. Things won't work if you forget to execute this command, since it is responsible for compiling the raw configuration file, into one readable by the server. If you're having problems with your installation, check this first.

The commands *add-host*, *add-ns*, and *add-alias* just edit the master djbdns configuration file called *data* located in */service/tinydns/root*. If you want to do this manually, you can just open the datafile in your browser and add the following lines:

```
=vlager.vbrew.com:172.16.1.10
=www.vlager.com:172.16.1.11
+mail.vbrew.com:172.16.1.10
```

You'll notice that the host entry lines begin with = and the alias lines begin with a + character. While the manual method does work, it adds more complexity, since you will now be required to also manually check your datafile for duplicate entries. Most administrators will just want to stick with the automated tools to avoid complications.

Installing an External DNS Cache

When you've successfully created your DNS server and have everything functioning properly, you may want to craete an external DNS cache, so hosts on your network can resolve the IP addresses of external machines. This is done by installing a DNS cache, which again with djbdns is simple. Assuming that you have *svscan* running, you must first create (or verify the existance of) two system accounts, one for the cache program and one for the logging mechanism. Though it isn't necessary to do so, it is a good idea to call them something meaningful, such as *dnscache* and *dnslog*, respectively.

Next, you'll need to determine the IP address on which to run your DNS cache. Remember this should be a different IP address than you're using for your DNS server. Now, as root, create a directory for the DNS service and configure it with the following commands:

```
vstout# mkdir /etc/dnscache
vstout# dnscache-conf dnscache dnslog /etc/dnscache <cache.ip.address>
```

Again, as root, you now need to inform svscan that you have a new service for it to run:

```
vstout# ln -s /etc/dnscache /service
```

Now, to be certain that the new service is running, wait a few moments and issue the following command:

```
vstout# svstat /service/dnscache
/service/dnscache: up (pid 1139) 149 seconds
```

When you've made certain that the service is running, you need to tell it which IP addresses are authorized to access the cache. In the case of the Virtual Brewery, we want to authorize the entire **172.16** network, so we'll enter the following command:

```
vstout# touch /etc/dnscache/root/ip/172.16
```

Of course, you'll want to make sure that your *letc/resolv.conf* knows about your new DNS cache. You can test to see whether or not your cache is working with nslookup, *dig*, or one of the included djbdns tools, *dnsip*:

```
vlager# dnsip www.google.com
216.239.57.104 216.239.57.99
vlager#
```

CHAPTER 6
The Point-to-Point Protocol

Point-to-point protocol (PPP) is a protocol used to send datagrams across a serial connection. In this chapter, we briefly cover its basic building blocks. We will also cover PPP over Ethernet (PPPoE), which is now commonly used by telecom providers to establish DSL sessions. There is also a comprehensive O'Reilly book on the topic, *Using & Managing PPP*, by Andrew Sun.

At the very bottom of PPP is the *High-Level Data Link Control* (HDLC) protocol, which defines the boundaries around the individual PPP frames and provides a 16-bit checksum.* A PPP frame is capable of holding packets from protocols other than IP, such as Novell's IPX or Appletalk. PPP achieves this by adding a protocol field to the basic HDLC frame that identifies the type of packet carried by the frame.

The *Link Control Protocol* (LCP) is used on top of HDLC to negotiate options pertaining to the data link. For instance, the *Maximum Receive Unit* (MRU) states the maximum datagram size that one side of the link agrees to receive.

An important step at the configuration stage of a PPP link is client authorization. Although it is not mandatory, it is really a must for dial-up lines in order to keep out intruders. Usually the called host (the server) asks the client to authorize itself by proving it knows some secret key. If the caller fails to produce the correct secret, the connection is terminated. With PPP, authorization works both ways; the caller may also ask the server to authenticate itself. These authentication procedures are totally independent of each other. There are two protocols for different types of authorization, which we will discuss further in this chapter: *Password Authentication Protocol* (PAP) and *Challenge Handshake Authentication Protocol* (CHAP).

Each network protocol that is routed across the data link (like IP and AppleTalk) is configured dynamically using a corresponding *Network Control Protocol* (NCP). To send IP datagrams across the link, both sides running PPP must first negotiate which

---

* In fact, HDLC is a much more general protocol devised by the International Standards Organization (ISO) and is also an essential component of the X.25 specification.

IP address each of them uses. The control protocol used for this negotiation is the *Internet Protocol Control Protocol* (IPCP).

Besides sending standard IP datagrams across the link, PPP also supports Van Jacobson header compression of IP datagrams. This technique shrinks the headers of TCP packets to as little as 3 bytes. It is more colloquially referred to as VJ header compression. The use of compression may be negotiated at startup time through IPCP, as well.

PPP on Linux

On Linux, PPP functionality is split into two parts: a kernel component that handles the low-level protocols (HDLC, IPCP, IPXCP, etc.) and the user space *pppd* daemon that handles the various higher-level protocols, such as PAP and CHAP. The current release of the PPP software for Linux contains the PPP daemon *pppd* and a program named *chat* that automates the dialing of the remote system.

The PPP kernel driver was written by Michael Callahan and reworked by Paul Mackerras. *pppd* was derived from a free PPP implementation for Sun and 386BSD machines that was written by Drew Perkins and others, and is maintained by Paul Mackerras. It was ported to Linux by Al Longyear. *chat* was written by Karl Fox.

PPP is implemented by a special line discipline. To use a serial line as a PPP link, you first establish the connection over your modem as usual and subsequently convert the line to PPP mode. In this mode, all incoming data is passed to the PPP driver, which checks the incoming HDLC frames for validity (each HDLC frame carries a 16-bit checksum), and unwraps and dispatches them. Currently, PPP is able to transport both the IP protocol, optionally using Van Jacobson header compression, and the IPX protocol.

pppd aids the kernel driver, performing the initialization and authentication phase that is necessary before actual network traffic can be sent across the link. *pppd*'s behavior may be fine-tuned using a number of options. As PPP is rather complex, it is impossible to explain all of them in a single chapter. This book therefore cannot cover all aspects of *pppd*, but only gives you an introduction. For more information, consult *Using & Managing PPP* or the *pppd* manpages, or *READMEs* in the *pppd* source distribution, which should help you sort out most questions this chapter fails to discuss. The *PPP HOWTO* might also be of use.

Probably the greatest help you will find in configuring PPP will come from other users of the same Linux distribution. PPP configuration questions are very common, so try your local usergroup mailing list or the IRC Linux channel. If your problems persist even after reading the documentation, you could try the *comp.protocols.ppp* newsgroup. This is the place where you can find most of the people involved in *pppd* development.

Running pppd

When you want to connect to the Internet through a PPP link, you have to set up basic networking capabilities, such as the loopback device and the resolver. Both have been covered in Chapters 4 and 5. You can simply configure the nameserver of your Internet Service Provider in the */etc/resolv.conf* file, but this will mean that every DNS request is sent across your serial link. This situation is not optimal; the closer (network-wise) you are to your nameserver, the faster the name lookups will be. An alternative solution is to configure a caching-only nameserver at a host on your network. This means that the first time you make a DNS query for a particular host, your request will be sent across your serial link, but every subsequent request will be answered directly by your local nameserver, and will be much faster. This configuration is described in Chapter 5.

As an introductory example of how to establish a PPP connection with *pppd*, assume you are at **vlager** again. First, dial in to the PPP server **c3po** and log in to the **ppp** account. **c3po** will execute its PPP driver. After exiting the communications program you used for dialing, execute the following command, substituting the name of the serial device you used for the ttyS3 shown here:

```
# pppd /dev/ttyS3 38400 crtscts defaultroute
```

This command flips the serial line *ttyS3* to the PPP line discipline and negotiates an IP link with **c3po**. The transfer speed used on the serial port will be 38,400 bps. The crtscts option turns on hardware handshake on the port, which is an absolute must at speeds above 9,600 bps.

The first thing *pppd* does after starting up is negotiate several link characteristics with the remote end using LCP. Usually, the default set of options *pppd* tries to negotiate will work, so we won't go into this here, except to say that part of this negotiation involves requesting or assigning the IP addresses at each end of the link.

For the time being, we also assume that **c3po** doesn't require any authentication from us, so the configuration phase is completed successfully.

pppd will then negotiate the IP parameters with its peer using IPCP, the IP control protocol. Since we didn't specify any particular IP address to *pppd* earlier, it will try to use the address obtained by having the resolver look up the local hostname. Both will then announce their addresses to each other.

Usually, there's nothing wrong with these defaults. Even if your machine is on an Ethernet, you can use the same IP address for both the Ethernet and the PPP interface. Nevertheless, *pppd* allows you to use a different address, or even to ask your peer to use some specific address. These options are discussed in "Choosing IP Addresses," later in this chapter.

After going through the IPCP setup phase, *pppd* will prepare your host's networking layer to use the PPP link. It first configures the PPP network interface as a point-to-point link, using *ppp0* for the first PPP link that is active, ppp1 for the second, and so on. Next, it sets up a routing table entry that points to the host at the other end of the link. In the previous example, *pppd* made the default network route point to **c3po**, because we gave it the defaultroute option.* The default route simplifies your routing by causing any IP datagram destined to a nonlocal host to be sent to **c3po**; this makes sense since it is the only way they can be reached. There are a number of different routing schemes *pppd* supports, which we will cover in detail later in this chapter.

Using Options Files

Before *pppd* parses its command-line arguments, it scans several files for default options. These files may contain any valid command-line arguments spread out across an arbitrary number of lines. Hash signs introduce comments.

The first options file is */etc/ppp/options*, which is always scanned when *pppd* starts up. Using it to set some global defaults is a good idea, because it allows you to keep your users from doing several things that may compromise security. For instance, to make *pppd* require some kind of authentication (either PAP or CHAP) from the peer, you add the auth option to this file. This option cannot be overridden by the user, so it becomes impossible to establish a PPP connection with any system that is not in your authentication databases. Note, however, that some options can be overridden; the connect string is a good example.

The other options file, which is read after */etc/ppp/options*, is *.ppprc* in the user's home directory. It allows each user to specify her own set of default options.

A sample */etc/ppp/options* file might look like this:

```
# Global options for pppd running on vlager.vbrew.com
lock                    # use UUCP-style device locking
auth                    # require authentication
usehostname             # use local hostname for CHAP
domain vbrew.com        # our domain name
```

The lock keyword makes *pppd* comply to the standard UUCP method of device locking. With this convention, each process that accesses a serial device, say */dev/ttyS3*, creates a lock file with a name such as *LCK..ttyS3* in a special lock-file directory to signal that the device is in use. This is necessary to prevent other programs, such as *minicom* or *uucico*, from opening the serial device while it is used by PPP.

---

* The default network route is installed only if none is already present.

The next three options relate to authentication and, therefore, to system security. The authentication options are best placed in the global configuration file because they are "privileged" and cannot be overridden by users' ~/.ppprc options files.

Using chat to Automate Dialing

One of the things that may have struck you as inconvenient in the previous example is that you had to establish the connection manually before you could fire up *pppd*. *pppd* relies on an external program or shell script to log in and connect to the remote system. The command to be executed can be given to *pppd* with the connect command-line option. *pppd* will redirect the command's standard input and output to the serial line.

The *pppd* software package is supplied with a very simple program called *chat*, which is capable of being used in this way to automate simple login sequences. We'll talk about this command in some detail.

If your login sequence is complex, you will need something more powerful than *chat*. One useful alternative you might consider is *expect*, written by Don Libes. It has a very powerful language based on Tcl and was designed exactly for this sort of application. Those of you whose login sequence requires, for example, challenge/response authentication involving calculator-like key generators will find *expect* powerful enough to handle the task. Since there are so many possible variations on this theme, we won't describe how to develop an appropriate *expect* script in this book. Suffice it to say, you'd call your *expect* script by specifying its name using the *pppd* connect option. It's also important to note that when the script is running, the standard input and output will be attached to the modem, not to the terminal that invoked *pppd*. If you require user interaction, you should manage it by opening a spare virtual terminal, or arrange some other means.

The *chat* command lets you specify a *chat* script. Basically, a *chat* script consists of an alternating sequence of strings that we expect to receive from the remote system, and the answers we are to send. We will call them *expect* and *send* strings, respectively. This is a typical excerpt from a *chat* script:

```
ogin: b1ff ssword: s3|<r1t
```

This script tells *chat* to wait for the remote system to send the login prompt and return the login name **b1ff**. We wait only for ogin: so that it doesn't matter if the login prompt starts with an uppercase or lowercase l, or if it arrives garbled. The following string is another expect string that makes *chat* wait for the password prompt and send our response password.

This is basically what *chat* scripts are all about. A complete script to dial up a PPP server would, of course, also have to include the appropriate modem commands. Assume that your modem understands the Hayes command set, and the server's telephone number is 318714. The complete *chat* invocation to establish a connection with **c3po** would then be:

```
$ chat -v '' ATZ OK ATDT318714 CONNECT '' ogin: ppp word: GaGariN
```

By definition, the first string must be an expect string, but as the modem won't say anything before we have kicked it, we make *chat* skip the first expect by specifying an empty string. We then send ATZ, the reset command for Hayes-compatible modems and wait for its response (OK). The next string sends the dial command along with the phone number to *chat* and expects the CONNECT message in response. This is followed by an empty string again because we don't want to send anything now, but rather wait for the login prompt. The remainder of the *chat* script works exactly as described previously. This description probably looks a bit confusing, but we'll see in a moment that there is a way to make *chat* scripts a lot easier to understand.

The -v option makes *chat* log all activities to the syslog daemon local2 facility.*

Specifying the *chat* script on the command line bears a certain risk because users can view a process's command line with the *ps* command. You can avoid this risk by putting the *chat* script in a file such as *dial-c3po*. You make *chat* read the script from the file instead of the command line by giving it the -f option, followed by the filename. This action has the added benefit of making our *chat* expect sequences easier to understand. To convert our example, our *dial-c3po* file would look like this:

```
   ''      ATZ
   OK      ATDT318714
   CONNECT ''
   ogin:   ppp
   word:   GaGariN
```

When we use a *chat* script file in this way, the string we expect to receive is on the left and the response we will send is on the right. They are much easier to read and understand when presented this way.

The complete *pppd* incantation would now look like this:

```
# pppd connect "chat -f dial-c3po" /dev/ttyS3 38400 -detach \
       crtscts modem defaultroute
```

Besides the connect option that specifies the dial-up script, we have added two more options to the command line: -detach, which tells *pppd* not to detach from the console and become a background process, and the modem keyword, which makes it perform modem-specific actions on the serial device, such as disconnecting the line before and after the call. If you don't use this keyword, *pppd* will not monitor the

---

* If you edit *syslog.conf* to redirect these log messages to a file, make sure this file isn't world readable, as *chat* also logs the entire *chat* script by default—including passwords.

port's DCD line and will therefore not detect whether the remote end hangs up unexpectedly.

The examples we have shown are rather simple; *chat* allows for much more complex scripts. For instance, it can specify strings on which to abort the *chat* with an error. Typical abort strings are messages such as BUSY or NO CARRIER that your modem usually generates when the called number is busy or doesn't answer. To make *chat* recognize these messages immediately rather than timing out, you can specify them at the beginning of the script using the ABORT keyword:

```
$ chat -v ABORT BUSY ABORT 'NO CARRIER' '' ATZ OK ...
```

Similarly, you can change the timeout value for parts of the *chat* scripts by inserting TIMEOUT options.

Sometimes you also need to have conditional execution for parts of the *chat* script: when you don't receive the remote end's login prompt, you might want to send a BREAK or a carriage return. You can achieve this by appending a subscript to an expect string. The subscript consists of a sequence of send and expect strings, just like the overall script itself, which are separated by hyphens. The subscript is executed whenever the expected string it is appended to is not received in time. In the example above, we would modify the *chat* script as follows:

```
ogin:-BREAK-ogin: ppp ssword: GaGariN
```

When *chat* doesn't see the remote system send the login prompt, the subscript is executed by first sending a BREAK and then waiting for the login prompt again. If the prompt now appears, the script continues as usual; otherwise, it will terminate with an error.

IP Configuration Options

IPCP is used to negotiate a number of IP parameters at link configuration time. Usually, each peer sends an IPCP configuration request packet, indicating which values it wants to change from the defaults and the new value. Upon receipt, the remote end inspects each option in turn and either acknowledges or rejects it.

pppd gives you a lot of control over which IPCP options it will try to negotiate. You can tune it through various command-line options that we will discuss in this section.

Choosing IP Addresses

All IP interfaces require that IP addresses be assigned to them; a PPP device always has an IP address. The PPP suite of protocols provides a mechanism that allows the automatic assignment of IP addresses to PPP interfaces. It is possible for the PPP program at one end of a point-to-point link to assign an IP address for the remote end to use, or each may use its own.

Some PPP servers that handle a lot of client sites assign addresses dynamically; addresses are assigned to systems only when calling in and are reclaimed after they have logged off again. This allows the number of IP addresses required to be limited to the number of dial-up lines. While limitation is convenient for managers of the PPP dial-up server, it is often less convenient for users who are dialing in. We discussed the way that hostnames are mapped to IP addresses by use of a database in Chapter 5. In order for people to connect to your host, they must know your IP address or the hostname associated with it. If you are a user of a PPP service that assigns you an IP address dynamically, this knowledge is difficult without providing some means of allowing the DNS database to be updated after you are assigned an IP address. Such systems do exist, but we won't cover them in detail here; instead, we will look at the preferable approach, which involves you being able to use the same IP address each time you establish a network connection.*

In the previous example, we had *pppd* dial up **c3po** and establish an IP link. No provisions were taken to choose a particular IP address on either end of the link. Instead, we let *pppd* take its default action. It attempts to resolve the local hostname, **vlager** in our example, to an IP address, which it uses for the local end, while letting the remote machine, **c3po**, provide its own. PPP supports several alternatives to this arrangement.

To ask for particular addresses, you generally provide *pppd* with the following option:

    local_addr:remote_addr

local_addr and *remote_addr* may be specified either in dotted quad notation or as hostnames.† This option makes *pppd* attempt to use the first address supplied as its own IP address, and the second as the peer's. If the peer rejects either of the addresses during IPCP negotiation, no IP link will be established.‡

If you are dialing in to a server and expect it to assign you an IP address, you should ensure that *pppd* does not attempt to negotiate one for itself. To do this, use the noipdefault option and leave the *local_addr* blank. The noipdefault option will stop *pppd* from trying to use the IP address associated with the hostname as the local address.

---

* More information on two dynamic host assignment mechanisms can be found at *http://www.dynip.com/*.

† Using hostnames in this option has consequences for CHAP authentication. Please refer to the section "The CHAP Secrets File" later in this chapter.

‡ The *ipcp-accept-local* and *ipcp-accept-remote* options instruct your *pppd* to accept the local and remote IP addresses being offered by the remote PPP, even if you've supplied some in your configuration. If these options are not configured, your *pppd* will reject any attempt to negotiate the IP addresses used.

If you want to set only the local address but accept any address the peer uses, simply leave out the *remote_addr* part. To make **vlager** use the IP address **130.83.4.27** instead of its own, give it **130.83.4.27:** on the command line. Similarly, to set the remote address only, leave the *local_addr* field blank. By default, *pppd* will then use the address associated with your hostname.

Routing Through a PPP Link

After setting up the network interface, *pppd* will usually set up a host route to its peer only. If the remote host is on a LAN, you certainly want to be able to connect to hosts "behind" your peer as well; in that case, a network route must be set up.

We have already seen that *pppd* can be asked to set the default route using the defaultroute option. This option is very useful if the PPP server you dialed up acts as your Internet gateway.

The reverse case, in which your system acts as a gateway for a single host, is also relatively easy to accomplish. For example, take some employee at the Virtual Brewery whose home machine is called **oneshot**. Let's also assume that we've configured **vlager** as a dial-in PPP server. If we've configured **vlager** to dynamically assign an IP address that belongs to the Brewery's subnet, we can use the proxyarp option with *pppd*, which will install a proxy ARP entry for **oneshot**. This automatically makes **oneshot** accessible from all hosts at the brewery and the winery.

However, things aren't always that simple. Linking two local area networks usually requires adding a specific network route because these networks may have their own default routes. Besides, having both peers use the PPP link as the default route would generate a loop, through which packets to unknown destinations would ping-pong between the peers until their time to live expired.

Suppose the Virtual Brewery opens a branch in another city. The subsidiary runs an Ethernet of its own using the IP network number **172.16.3.0**, which is subnet 3 of the brewery's class B network. The subsidiary wants to connect to the brewery's network via PPP to update customer databases. Again, **vlager** acts as the gateway for the brewery network and will support the PPP link; its peer at the new branch is called **vbourbon** and has an IP address of **172.16.3.1**.

When **vbourbon** connects to **vlager**, it makes the default route point to **vlager** as usual. On **vlager**, however, we will have only the point-to-point route to **vbourbon** and will have to specially configure a network route for subnet 3 that uses **vbourbon** as its gateway. We could do this manually using the *route* command by hand after the PPP link is established, but this is not a very practical solution. Fortunately, we can configure the route automatically by using a feature of *pppd* that we haven't discussed yet—the *ip-up* command. This command is a shell script or program located in */etc/ppp* that is executed by *pppd* after the PPP interface has been configured. When present, it is invoked with the following parameters:

```
ip-up iface device speed local_addr remote_addr
```

Table 6-1 summarizes the meaning of each of the arguments (in the first column, we show the number used by the shell script to refer to each argument).

Table 6-1. ip-up arguments

Name	Purpose
iface	The network interface used, e.g., ppp0
device	The pathname of the serial device file used (/dev/tty, if stdin/stdout are used)
speed	The speed of the serial device in bits per second
local_addr	The IP address of the link's remote end in dotted quad notation
remote_addr	The IP address of the remote end of the link in dotted quad notation

In our case, the *ip-up* script may contain the following code fragment:[*]

```
#!/bin/sh
case $5 in
172.16.3.1)            # this is vbourbon
        route add -net 172.16.3.0 gw 172.16.3.1;;
...
esac
exit 0
```

Similarly, */etc/ppp/ip-down* can be used to undo any actions of ip-up after the PPP link has been taken down again. So in our */etc/ppp/ip-down* script we would have a route command that removed the route we created in the */etc/ppp/ip-up* script.

However, the routing scheme is not yet complete. We have set up routing table entries on both PPP hosts, but so far none of the hosts on either network knows anything about the PPP link. This is not a big problem if all hosts at the subsidiary have their default route pointing at **vbourbon** and all brewery hosts route to **vlager** by default.

Link Control Options

We already encountered LCP, which is used to negotiate link characteristics and test the link.

The two most important options negotiated by LCP are the *Asynchronous Control Character Map* and the *Maximum Receive Unit*. There are a number of other LCP configuration options, but they are far too specialized to discuss here.

The Asynchronous Control Character Map, colloquially called the *async map*, is used on asynchronous links, such as telephone lines, to identify control characters that must be escaped (replaced by a specific two-character sequence) to avoid them

---

[*] If we wanted to have routes for other sites created when they dial in, we'd add appropriate case statements to cover those where the ... appears in the example.

being interpreted by equipment used to establish the link. For instance, you may want to avoid the XON and XOFF characters used for software handshake because a misconfigured modem might choke upon receipt of an XOFF. Other candidates include Ctrl-l (the *telnet* escape character). PPP allows you to escape any of the characters with ASCII codes 0 through 31 by specifying them in the async map.

The async map is a 32-bit-wide bitmap expressed in hexadecimal. The least significant bit corresponds to the ASCII NULL character, and the most significant bit corresponds to ASCII 31 decimal. These 32 ASCII characters are the control characters. If a bit is set in the bitmap, it signals that the corresponding character must be escaped before it is transmitted across the link.

To tell your peer that it doesn't have to escape all control characters, but only a few of them, you can specify an async map to *pppd* using the asyncmap option. For example, if only ^S and ^Q (ASCII 17 and 19, commonly used for XON and XOFF) must be escaped, use the following option:

```
asyncmap 0x000A0000
```

The conversion is simple as long as you can convert binary to hex. Lay out 32 bits in front of you. The right-most bit corresponds to ASCII 00 (NULL), and the left-most bit corresponds to ASCII 32 decimal. Set the bits corresponding to the characters you want escaped to one, and all others to zero. To convert that into the hexadecimal number *pppd* expects, simply take each set of 4 bits and convert them into hex. You should end up with eight hexadecimal figures. String them all together and preprend "0x" to signify it is a hexadecimal number, and you are done.

Initially, the async map is set to 0xffffffff—that is, all control characters will be escaped. This is a safe default, but is usually much more than you need. Each character that appears in the async map results in two characters being transmitted across the link, so escaping comes at the cost of increased link utilization and a corresponding performance reduction.

In most circumstances, an async map of 0x0 works fine. No escaping is performed.

The Maximum Receive Unit (MRU) signals to the peer the maximum size of HDLC frames that we want to receive. Although this may remind you of the Maximum Transfer Unit (MTU) value, these two have little in common. The MTU is a parameter of the kernel networking device and describes the maximum frame size that the interface is able to transmit. The MRU is more of an advice to the remote end not to generate frames larger than the MRU; the interface must nevertheless be able to receive frames of up to 1,500 bytes.

Choosing an MRU is therefore not so much a question of what the link is capable of transferring, but of what gives you the best throughput. If you intend to run interactive applications over the link, setting the MRU to values as low as 296 is a good idea, so that an occasional larger packet (say, from an FTP session) doesn't make your cursor "jump." To tell *pppd* to request an MRU of 296, you give it the option mru 296. Small MRUs, however, make sense only if you have VJ header compression (it is enabled by default), because otherwise you'd waste a large amount of your bandwidth just carrying the IP header for each datagram.

pppd also understands a couple of LCP options that configure the overall behavior of the negotiation process, such as the maximum number of configuration requests that may be exchanged before the link is terminated. Unless you know exactly what you are doing, you should leave these options alone.

Finally, there are two options that apply to LCP echo messages. PPP defines two messages, *Echo Request* and *Echo Response*. *pppd* uses this feature to check whether a link is still operating. You can enable this by using the lcp-echo-interval option together with a time in seconds. If no frames are received from the remote host within this interval, *pppd* generates an Echo Request and expects the peer to return an Echo Response. If the peer does not produce a response, the link is terminated after a certain number of requests are sent. This number can be set using the lcp-echo-failure option. By default, this feature is disabled altogether.

General Security Considerations

A misconfigured PPP daemon can be a devastating security breach. It can be as bad as letting anyone plug their machine into your Ethernet (and that can be very bad). In this section, we discuss a few measures that should make your PPP configuration safe.

> Root privilege is required to configure the network device and routing table. You will usually solve this by running pppd setuid **root**. However, pppd allows users to set various security-relevant options.

To protect against any attacks a user may launch by manipulating **pppd** options, you should set a couple of default values in the global */etc/ppp/options* file, like those shown in the sample file in "Using Options Files," earlier in this chapter. Some of them, such as the authentication options, cannot be overridden by the user, and thus provide reasonable protection against manipulations. An important option to protect is the connect option. If you intend to allow non-root users to invoke *pppd* to connect to the Internet, you should always add the connect and noauth options to the global options file */etc/ppp/options*. If you fail to do this, users will be able to execute arbitrary commands with root privileges by specifying the command as their connect command on the *pppd* line or in their personal options file.

Another good idea is to restrict which users may execute *pppd* by creating a group in */etc/group* and adding only those users who you wish to have the ability to execute the PPP daemon. You should then change group ownership of the *pppd* daemon to that group and remove the world execute privileges. To do this, assuming you've called your group **dialout**, you could use something like:

```
# chown root /usr/sbin/pppd
# chgrp dialout /usr/sbin/pppd
# chmod 4750 /usr/sbin/pppd
```

Of course, you have to protect yourself from the systems you speak PPP with, too. To fend off hosts posing as someone else, you should always require some sort of authentication from your peer. Additionally, you should not allow foreign hosts to use any IP address they choose, but restrict them to at most a few. The following section will deal with these topics in detail.

Authentication with PPP

With PPP, each system may require its peer to authenticate itself using one of two authentication protocols: the *Password Authentication Protocol* (PAP) or the *Challenge Handshake Authentication Protocol* (CHAP). When a connection is established, each end can request the other to authenticate itself, regardless of whether it is the caller or the callee. In the description that follows, we will loosely talk of "client" and "server" when we want to distinguish between the system sending authentication requests and the system responding to them. A PPP daemon can ask its peer for authentication by sending yet another LCP configuration request identifying the desired authentication protocol.

PAP Versus CHAP

PAP, which is offered by many Internet Service Providers, works basically the same way as the normal login procedure. The client authenticates itself by sending a username and a (optionally encrypted) password to the server, which the server compares to its secrets database. This technique is vulnerable to eavesdroppers, who may try to obtain the password by listening in on the serial line, and to repeated trial and error attacks.

CHAP does not have these deficiencies. With CHAP, the server sends a randomly generated "challenge" string to the client along with its hostname. The client uses the hostname to look up the appropriate secret, combines it with the challenge, and encrypts the string using a one-way hashing function. The result is returned to the server along with the client's hostname. The server now performs the same computation and acknowledges the client if it arrives at the same result.

CHAP also doesn't require the client to authenticate itself only at startup time, but sends challenges at regular intervals to make sure that the client hasn't been replaced by an intruder, for instance, by switching phone lines or because of a modem configuration error that causes the PPP daemon not to notice that the original phone call has dropped out and someone else has dialed in.

pppd keeps the secret keys for PAP and CHAP in two separate files called */etc/ppp/pap-secrets* and */etc/ppp/chap-secrets*. By entering a remote host in one or the other file, you have fine control over whether PAP or CHAP is used to authenticate yourself with your peer, and vice versa.

By default, *pppd* doesn't require authentication from the remote host, but it will agree to authenticate itself when requested by the remote host. Since CHAP is so much stronger than PAP, *pppd* tries to use the former whenever possible. If the peer does not support it, or if *pppd* can't find a CHAP secret for the remote system in its *chap-secrets* file, it reverts to PAP. If it doesn't have a PAP secret for its peer either, it refuses to authenticate altogether. As a consequence, the connection is shut down.

You can modify this behavior in several ways. When given the auth keyword, *pppd* requires the peer to authenticate itself. *pppd* agrees to use either CHAP or PAP as long as it has a secret for the peer in its CHAP or PAP database. There are other options to turn a particular authentication protocol on or off, but I won't describe them here.

If all systems you talk to with PPP agree to authenticate themselves with you, you should put the auth option in the global */etc/ppp/options* file and define passwords for each system in the *chap-secrets* file. If a system doesn't support CHAP, add an entry for it to the *pap-secrets* file. That way, you can make sure no unauthenticated system connects to your host.

The next two sections discuss the two PPP secrets files, *pap-secrets* and *chap-secrets*. They are located in */etc/ppp* and contain triplets of clients, servers, and passwords, optionally followed by a list of IP addresses. The interpretation of the client and server fields is different for CHAP and PAP, and also depends on whether we authenticate ourselves with the peer or whether we require the server to authenticate itself with us.

The CHAP Secrets File

When it has to authenticate itself with a server using CHAP, *pppd* searches the *chap-secrets* file for an entry with the client field equal to the local hostname, and the server field equal to the remote hostname sent in the CHAP challenge. When requiring the peer to authenticate itself, the roles are simply reversed: *pppd* then looks for an entry with the client field equal to the remote hostname (sent in the client's CHAP response), and the server field equal to the local hostname.

The following is a sample *chap-secrets* file for **vlager**:*

```
# CHAP secrets for vlager.vbrew.com
#
```

---

* The double quotes are not part of the secret; they merely serve to protect the whitespace within it.

```
# client          server           secret               addrs
#---------------------------------------------------------------------
vlager.vbrew.com  c3po.lucas.com   "Use The Source Luke" vlager.vbrew.com
c3po.lucas.com    vlager.vbrew.com "arttoo! arttoo!"      c3po.lucas.com
*                 vlager.vbrew.com "TuXdrinksVicBitter"   pub.vbrew.com
```

When **vlager** establishes a PPP connection with **c3po**, **c3po** asks **vlager** to authenticate itself by sending a CHAP challenge. *pppd* on **vlager** then scans *chap-secrets* for an entry with the client field equal to **vlager.vbrew.com** and the server field equal to **c3po.lucas.com**, and finds the first line shown in the example.* It then produces the CHAP response from the challenge string and the secret (Use The Source Luke), and sends it off to **c3po**.

pppd also composes a CHAP challenge for **c3po** containing a unique challenge string and its fully qualified hostname, **vlager.vbrew.com**. **c3po** constructs a CHAP response in the way we discussed, and returns it to **vlager**. *pppd* then extracts the client hostname (**c3po.vbrew.com**) from the response and searches the *chap-secrets* file for a line matching **c3po** as a client and **vlager** as the server. The second line does this, so *pppd* combines the CHAP challenge and the secret arttoo! arttoo!, encrypts them, and compares the result to **c3po**'s CHAP response.

The optional fourth field lists the IP addresses that are acceptable for the client named in the first field. The addresses can be given in dotted quad notation or as hostnames that are looked up with the resolver. For instance, if **c3po** asks to use an IP address during IPCP negotiation that is not in this list, the request is rejected and IPCP is shut down. In the sample file shown above, **c3po** is therefore limited to using its own IP address. If the address field is empty, any addresses are allowed; a value of "-" prevents the use of IP with that client altogether.

The third line of the sample *chap-secrets* file allows any host to establish a PPP link with **vlager** because a client or server field of * is a wildcard matching any hostname. The only requirements are that the connecting host must know the secret and that it must use the IP address associated with **pub.vbrew.com**. Entries with wildcard hostnames may appear anywhere in the secrets file, since *pppd* will always use the best match it can find for the server/client pair.

pppd may need some help forming hostnames. As explained before, the remote hostname is always provided by the peer in the CHAP challenge or response packet. The local hostname is obtained by calling the *gethostname(2)* function by default. If you have set the system name to your unqualified hostname, you also have to provide *pppd* with the domain name using the domain option:

```
# pppd domain vbrew.com
```

---

* This hostname is taken from the CHAP challenge.

This provision appends the Brewery's domain name to **vlager** for all authentication related activities. Other options that modify *pppd*'s idea of the local hostname are usehostname and name. When you give the local IP address on the command line using *local:remote* and *local* as a name instead of a dotted quad, *pppd* uses this as the local hostname.

The PAP Secrets File

The PAP secrets file is very similar to CHAP's. The first two fields always contain a username and a server name; the third holds the PAP secret. When the remote host sends its authentication information, *pppd* uses the entry that has a server field equal to the local hostname, and a user field equal to the username sent in the request. When it is necessary for us to send our credentials to the peer, *pppd* uses the secret that has a user field equal to the local username and the server field equal to the remote hostname.

A sample PAP secrets file might look like this:

```
# /etc/ppp/pap-secrets
#
# user          server        secret        addrs
vlager-pap      c3po          cresspahl     vlager.vbrew.com
c3po            vlager        DonaldGNUth   c3po.lucas.com
```

The first line is used to authenticate ourselves when talking to **c3po**. The second line describes how a user named **c3po** has to authenticate itself with us.

The name vlager-pap in the first column is the username that we send to **c3po**. By default, *pppd* picks the local hostname as the username, but you can also specify a different name by giving the user option followed by that name.

When picking an entry from the *pap-secrets* file to identify yourself to a remote host, *pppd* must know the remote host's name. As it has no way of finding that out, you must specify it on the command line using the remotename keyword followed by the peer's hostname. To use the above entry for authentication with **c3po**, for example, we must add the following option to *pppd*'s command line:

```
# pppd ... remotename c3po user vlager-pap
```

In the fourth field of the PAP secrets file (and all following fields), you can specify what IP addresses are allowed for that particular host, just as in the CHAP secrets file. The peer will be allowed to request only addresses from that list. In the sample file, the entry that **c3po** will use when it dials in—the line where **c3po** is the client—allows it to use its real IP address and no other.

Note that PAP is a rather weak authentication method, you should use CHAP instead whenever possible. We will therefore not cover PAP in greater detail here; if you are interested in using it, you will find more PAP features in the *pppd(8)* manpage.

Debugging Your PPP Setup

By default, *pppd* logs any warnings and error messages to *syslog*'s daemon facility. You have to add an entry to *syslog.conf* that redirects these messages to a file or even the console; otherwise, syslog simply discards them. The following entry sends all messages to */var/log/ppp-log*:

```
daemon.*                    /var/log/ppp-log
```

If your PPP setup doesn't work right away, you should look in this logfile. If the log messages don't help, you can also turn on extra debugging output using the debug option. This output makes *pppd* log the contents of all control packets sent or received to syslog. All messages then go to the daemon facility.

Finally, the most drastic way to check a problem is to enable kernel-level debugging by invoking *pppd* with the kdebug option. It is followed by a numeric argument that is the sum of the following values: 1 for general debug messages, 2 for printing the contents of all incoming HDLC frames, and 4 to make the driver print all outgoing HDLC frames. To capture kernel debugging messages, you must either run a *syslogd* daemon that reads the */proc/kmsg* file, or the *klogd* daemon. Either of them directs kernel debugging to the syslog kernel facility.

More Advanced PPP Configurations

While configuring PPP to dial in to a network like the Internet is the most common application, some users have more advanced requirements. In this section we'll talk about a few of the more advanced configurations possible with PPP under Linux.

PPP Server

Running *pppd* as a server is just a matter of configuring a serial tty device to invoke *pppd* with appropriate options when an incoming data call has been received. One way to do this is to create a special account, say **ppp**, and give it a script or program as a login shell that invokes *pppd* with these options. Alternatively, if you intend to support PAP or CHAP authentication, you can use the *mgetty* program to support your modem and exploit its "/AutoPPP/" feature.

To build a server using the login method, you add a line similar to the following to your */etc/passwd* file:[*]

```
ppp:x:500:200:Public PPP Account:/tmp:/etc/ppp/ppplogin
```

If your system supports shadow passwords, you also need to add an entry to the */etc/shadow* file:

---

[*] The *useradd* or *adduser* utility, if you have it, will simplify this task.

```
ppp:!:10913:0:99999:7:::
```

Of course, the UID and GID you use depends on which user you wish to own the connection, and how you've created it. You also have to set the password for the mentioned account using the *passwd* command.

The *ppplogin* script might look like this:

```
#!/bin/sh
# ppplogin - script to fire up pppd on login
mesg n
stty -echo
exec pppd -detach silent modem crtscts
```

The *mesg* command disables other users from writing to the tty by using, for instance, the *write* command. The *stty* command turns off character echoing. This command is necessary; otherwise, everything the peer sends would be echoed back to it. The most important *pppd* option given is -detach because it prevents *pppd* from detaching from the controlling tty. If we didn't specify this option, it would go to the background, making the shell script exit. This in turn would cause the serial line to hang up and the connection to be dropped. The silent option causes *pppd* to wait until it receives a packet from the calling system before it starts sending. This option prevents transmit timeouts from occurring when the calling system is slow in firing up its PPP client. The modem option makes *pppd* drive the modem control lines of the serial port. You should always turn this option on when using *pppd* with a modem. The crtscts option turns on hardware handshake.

Besides these options, you might want to force some sort of authentication—for example, by specifying auth on *pppd*'s command line or in the global options file. The manual page also discusses more specific options for turning individual authentication protocols on and off.

If you wish to use *mgetty*, all you need to do is configure *mgetty* to support the serial device your modem is connected to (see Chapter 3 for details), configure *pppd* for either PAP or CHAP authentication with appropriate options in its *options* file, and finally, add a section similar to the following to your */etc/mgetty/login.config* file:

```
# Configure mgetty to automatically detect incoming PPP calls and invoke
# the pppd daemon to handle the connection.
#
/AutoPPP/ -     ppp   /usr/sbin/pppd auth -chap +pap login
```

The first field is a special piece of magic used to detect that an incoming call is a PPP one. You must not change the case of this string; it is case sensitive. The third column is the username that appears in *who* listings when someone has logged in. The rest of the line is the command to invoke. In our example, we've ensured that PAP authentication is required, disabled CHAP, and specified that the system *passwd* file should be used for authenticating users. This is probably similar to what you'll want. Remember, you can specify the options in the *options* file or on the command line if you prefer.

Here is a small checklist of tasks to perform and the sequence you should perform them to get PPP dial in working on your machine. Make sure each step works before moving on to the next:

1. Configure the modem for auto-answer mode. On Hayes-compatible modems, this is performed using a command such as ATS0=3. If you're going to be using the *mgetty* daemon, this isn't necessary.

2. Configure the serial device with a *getty*-type of command to answer incoming calls. A commonly used *getty* variant is *mgetty*.

3. Consider authentication. Will your callers authenticate using PAP, CHAP, or system login?

4. Configure *pppd* as server as described in this section.

5. Consider routing. Will you need to provide a network route to callers? Routing can be performed using the *ip-up* script.

Demand Dialing

When there is IP traffic to be carried across the link, *demand dialing* causes your telephone modem to dial and to establish a connection to a remote host. Demand dialing is most useful when you can't leave your telephone line permanently switched to your Internet provider. For example, you might have to pay timed local calls, so it might be cheaper to have the telephone line switched on only when you need it and disconnected when you aren't using the Internet.

In the past, Linux solutions used the *diald* command, which worked well but was fairly tricky to configure. Versions 2.3.0 and later of the PPP daemon have built-in support for demand dialing and make it very simple to configure.

To configure *pppd* for demand dialing, all you need to do is add options to your *options* file or the *pppd* command line. Table 6-2 summarizes the options related to demand dialing.

Table 6-2. Demand dialing options

Option	Description
demand	This option specifies that the PPP link should be placed in demand dial mode. The PPP network device will be created, but the *connect* command will not be used until a datagram is transmitted by the local host. This option is mandatory for demand dialing to work.
active-filter *expression*	This option allows you to specify which data packets are to be considered active traffic. Any traffic matching the specified rule will restart the demand dial idle timer, ensuring that *pppd* waits again before closing the link. The filter syntax has been borrowed from the *tcpdump* command. The default filter matches all datagrams.
holdoff *n*	This option allows you to specify the minimum amount of time, in seconds, to wait before reconnecting this link if it terminates. If the connection fails while *pppd* believes it is in active use, it will be reestablished after this timer has expired. This timer does not apply to reconnections after an idle timeout.

Table 6-2. Demand dialing options (continued)

Option	Description
idle *n*	If this option is configured, *pppd* will disconnect the link whenever this timer expires. Idle times are specified in seconds. Each new active data packet will reset the timer.

A simple demand dialing configuration would therefore look something like this:

```
demand
holdoff 60
idle 180
```

This configuration would enable demand dialing, wait 60 seconds before reestablishing a failed connection, and drop the link if 180 seconds pass without any active data on the link.

Persistent Dialing

Persistent dialing is what people who have permanent dial-up connections to a network will want to use. There is a subtle difference between demand dialing and persistent dialing. With persistent dialing, the connection is automatically established as soon as the PPP daemon is started, and the persistent aspect comes into play whenever the telephone call supporting the link fails. Persistent dialing ensures that the link is always available by automatically rebuilding the connection if it fails.

You might be fortunate to not have to pay for your telephone calls; perhaps they are local and free, or perhaps they're paid by your company. The persistent dialing option is extremely useful in this situation. If you do have to pay for your telephone calls, then you have to be a little careful. If you pay for your telephone calls on a time-charged basis, persistent dialing is almost certainly not what you want; unless you're very sure you'll be using the connection fairly steadily 24 hours a day. If you do pay for calls, but they are not time charged, you need to be careful to protect yourself against situations that might cause the modem to endlessly redial. The *pppd* daemon provides an option that can help reduce the effects of this problem.

To enable persistent dialing, you must include the persist option in one of your *pppd* options files. Including this option alone is all you need to have *pppd* automatically invoke the command specified by the connect option to rebuild the connection when the link fails. If you are concerned about the modem redialing too rapidly (in the case of modem or server fault at the other end of the connection), you can use the holdoff option to set the minimum amount of time that *pppd* will wait before attempting to reconnect. This option won't solve the problem of a fault costing you money in wasted phone calls, but it will at least serve to reduce the impact of one.

A typical configuration might have persistent dialing options that look like this:

```
persist
holdoff 600
```

The holdoff time is specified in seconds. In our example, *pppd* waits a full five minutes before redialing after the call drops out.

It is possible to combine persistent dialing with demand dialing, using idle to drop the link if it has been idle for a specified period of time. We doubt many users would want to do so, but this scenario is described briefly in the *pppd* manpage, if you'd like to pursue it.

PPPoE Options in Linux

PPPoE has become much more important recently, as it is the connection method of choice by a number of DSL providers. Fortunately for Linux users, a number of functional options are available, most of which are easily configurable. PPPoE is nothing new; it is simply the same PPP as used over dial-up, except it is used over Ethernet.

For the purposes of this section, we'll assume that your DSL modem and equipment are properly configured and ready for use. More information on how this is accomplished can be found in the excellent Linux *DSL HOWTO*, written by David Fannin and Hal Burgiss (*http://www.tldp.org/HOWTO/DSL-HOWTO*). Additionally, we'll assume that the Ethernet card in your PC is installed and operational.

In most DSL environments the DSL modem is configured to be a bridge, meaning that it won't have an IP address. As a result of this, your server will be configured with a WAN IP address. Before enabling the WAN interface, you should make certain that you've patched all of the listening services on your machine. Additionally, you should consider using an IPtables or other firewall. Security when connecting directly to the Internet should be of the utmost importance. It has been reported that unpatched versions of some Linux distributions survive only a few hours on the Internet before they're compromised. Make sure you've done as much as possible to ensure that this doesn't happen to you!

PPPoE Clients

To get started with configuring PPPoE, you will need to obtain a PPPoE client. There are a number of clients available, including one from Roaring Penguin that has become very popular with many users and providers. It can be downloaded from *http://www.roaringpenguin.com* in both source format and as pre-compiled RPMs. When you've downloaded and compiled or installed the software, you are ready for configuration. The client software comes with a very easy to use configuration script called *adsl-setup*. It will ask you a number of questions about your system, network, and PPPoE user information. In some cases it will have already provided the answers, requiring you to only confirm!

However helpful, the script isn't foolproof, so we'll walk through a manual configuration. It's also a good idea, especially from the network administrator's viewpoint, to have a good idea of how software is configured, just in case something goes wrong in the future.

PPPoE manual client configuration

Configuring the client is pretty easy, especially if you've previously set up a standard PPP configuration. First, you'll need to edit the */etc/ppp/pap-secrets* file. You will need to replace the default values with your PPPoE username and password. The file will look something like this:

```
#User                    #Server        #Password       #IP
groucho@dslcompany.to    *              my_password     *
```

Next, open the */etc/ppp/pppoe.conf* file in your text editor. You will need to tell it both your WAN interface name, and your PPPoE username. The relevant lines in the file appear as follows:

```
# Ethernet card connected to ADSL modem
ETH=eth0

# ADSL user name.  You may have to supply "@provider.com"
USER=groucho@dslcompany.to
```

The file contains a number of additional configuration options. Unless you're really certain that you need to change these, you probably shouldn't. If you are determined to make some changes, refer to the PPP manpages for more information.

Lastly, if you haven't already configured your DNS servers in the */etc/resolv.conf* file, this should be done now. Detailed information about DNS configuration can be found in Chapter 5.

When you've finished with the configuration, you can now test the connection to see if it works. The *adsl-start* script is used specifically for this purpose. You can call it from the command line, or, ideally, include it in your system startup scripts. This is accomplished differently for almost every distribution. Consult documentation specific to your distribution for specifics on how to install startup scripts.

If the startup script completes without errors, you should be connected to the Internet. A quick and easy way to test this is to ping something that will answer. Success will look like this:

```
vlager# ping www.google.com
PING www.google.akadns.net (66.102.7.99) 56(84) bytes of data.
64 bytes from 66.102.7.99: icmp_seq=1 ttl=245 time=5.94 ms
64 bytes from 66.102.7.99: icmp_seq=2 ttl=245 time=5.02 ms
64 bytes from 66.102.7.99: icmp_seq=3 ttl=245 time=5.02 ms
ctrl-c
--- www.google.akadns.net ping statistics ---
3 packets transmitted, 3 received, 0% packet loss, time 2009ms
rtt min/avg/max/mdev = 5.028/5.333/5.945/0.440 ms
vlager#
```

Additionally, you can check the configuration by using *ifconfig*:

```
vlager# ifconfig -a
eth0      Link encap:Ethernet  HWaddr 00:08:02:F0:BB:0E
          UP BROADCAST RUNNING MULTICAST  MTU:1500  Metric:1
          RX packets:8701578 errors:6090 dropped:0 overruns:0 frame:5916
          TX packets:3888596 errors:0 dropped:0 overruns:0 carrier:0
          collisions:6289 txqueuelen:100
          RX bytes:1941625928 (1851.6 Mb)  TX bytes:1481305134 (1412.6 Mb)
          Interrupt:30

eth1      Link encap:Ethernet  HWaddr 00:90:27:FE:02:A0
          inet addr:10.10.0.254  Bcast:10.10.0.255  Mask:255.255.255.0
          UP BROADCAST RUNNING MULTICAST  MTU:1500  Metric:1
          RX packets:48920435 errors:0 dropped:0 overruns:0 frame:0
          TX packets:55211769 errors:0 dropped:0 overruns:2 carrier:9
          collisions:367030 txqueuelen:100
          RX bytes:2018181326 (1924.6 Mb)  TX bytes:1564406617 (1491.9 Mb)
          Interrupt:10 Base address:0x4000

ppp0      Link encap:Point-to-Point Protocol
          inet addr: 64.168.44.33 P-t-P:64.168.44.1  Mask:255.255.255.255
          UP POINTOPOINT RUNNING NOARP MULTICAST  MTU:1492  Metric:1
          RX packets: 8701576 errors:0 dropped:0 overruns:0 frame:0
          TX packets: 3888594 errors:0 dropped:0 overruns:0 carrier:0
          collisions:0 txqueuelen:10
```

If something isn't working properly at this point, check all of your connections, and ensure the DSL gear is properly configured. Additionally, recheck your username and password in the configuration files—a mistyped password is one of the most common configuration problems!

## CHAPTER 7

TCP/IP Firewall

Security is increasingly important for companies and individuals alike. The Internet provides them with a powerful tool to distribute information about themselves and obtain information from others, but it also exposes them to dangers from which they were previously exempt. Computer crime, information theft, and malicious damage are all potential dangers.

This chapter covers the Linux features for setting up a firewall, known both by its command interface (*iptables*) and its kernel subsystem name (*netfilter*). This firewall implementation was new in the 2.4 kernel and works substantially the same way in 2.6.

A malicious person who gains access to a computer system may guess system passwords or exploit the bugs and idiosyncratic behavior of certain programs to obtain a working account on that host. Once they are able to log in to the host, they may have access to sensitive information. In a commercial setting, stealing, deleting, or modifying information such as marketing plans, new project details, or customer information databases can cause significant damage to the company.

The safest way to avoid such widespread damage is to prevent unauthorized people from gaining network access to the host. This is where firewalls come in.

 Constructing secure firewalls is an art. It involves a good understanding of technology, but equally important, it requires an understanding of the philosophy behind firewall designs. We won't cover everything you need to know in this book; we strongly recommend you do some additional research before trusting any particular firewall design, including any we present here.

We will focus on the Linux-specific technical issues in this chapter. Later we will present a sample firewall configuration that should serve as a useful starting point in your own configuration, but as with all security-related matters, you'll want to make sure that you understand the information well enough to customize it to suit your needs and verify that the result is sufficient. Double-check the design, make sure that you understand it, and then modify it to suit your requirements. To be safe, be sure.

Methods of Attack

As a network administrator, it is important that you understand the nature of potential attacks on computer security. We'll briefly describe the most important types of attacks so that you can better understand precisely what the Linux IP firewall will protect you against. You should do some additional reading to ensure that you are able to protect your network against other types of attacks. Here are some of the more important methods of attack and ways of protecting yourself against them:

Unauthorized access

> This simply means that people who shouldn't be allowed to use your computer services are able to connect to and use them. For example, people outside your company might try to connect to your company accounting host or to your NFS server.

> There are various ways to avoid this attack by carefully specifying who can gain access through these services. You can prevent network access to all except the intended users.

Exploitation of known weaknesses in programs

> Some programs and network services were not originally designed with strong security in mind and are inherently vulnerable to attack. The BSD remote services (*rlogin*, *rexec*, etc.) are an example.

> The best way to protect yourself against this type of attack is to disable any vulnerable services or find alternatives. A good place to start is to only install, run and expose services that you absolutely have to. Start with no network services and work your way up from there. Use the *netstat* command to determine the ports that your host is listening on, make sure the list is as small as possible, and know exactly what each of them is for. Don't run any network services on the firewall host, with the possible exception of Secure Shell (SSH)

> Track bug databases and patch lists and keep your systems up to date. Two of the most popular bug databases are the Bugtraq database, available online at *http://www.securityfocus.com/bid* (see also *http://www.securityfocus.com/rss* for information on accessing Bugtraq via an RSS feed) and the Common Vulnerabilities and Exposures (CVE) database, available online at *http://cve.mitre.org/* (see also the RSS at *http://www.opensec.org/feeds/cve/latest.xml*). Most Linux distributors provide tools to download and install updates. Red Hat has a utility called *yum*, SuSE has a utility called YaST Online Update (YOU), and Debian uses *apt-get*.

SSH and iptables

With SSH and *iptables*, you have two easy ways to access hosts and services inside your network from the outside world without exposing them directly. First, you can run SSH on the firewall and use SSH's port forwarding feature to access internal hosts and services from the outside, without exposing them directly to the outside. Section 12.1 of Bob Toxen's book *Real World Linux Security,* Second Edition (Prentice Hall), has additional information on using SSH in this way. Second, you can use *iptables* Destination Network Address Translation to expose SSH for multiple servers as distinct ports on the firewall's public IP address, with the connections forwarded to the individual hosts inside the network. See Chapter 9 for more information on Network Address Translation.

Denial of service

Denial of service attacks cause the service or program to cease functioning or prevent others from making use of the service or program. These may be performed at the network layer by sending carefully crafted and malicious packets that cause network connections to fail. They may also be performed at the application layer, where carefully crafted application commands are given to a program that cause it to become extremely busy or stop functioning.

Preventing suspicious network traffic from reaching your hosts and preventing suspicious program commands and requests (this requires software that understands the underlying protocols, such as proxy servers) are the best ways of minimizing the risk of a denial of service attack. It's useful to know the details of the attack method, so you should educate yourself about each new attack as it gets publicized.

Spoofing

This type of attack involves one host or application pretending to be another. Typically the attacker's host pretends to be an innocent host by forging IP addresses in network packets. For example, a well-documented exploit of the BSD rlogin service can use this method to mimic a TCP connection from another host by guessing TCP sequence numbers.

To protect against this type of attack, verify the authenticity of packets and commands (a combination of filtering and proxy servers can help here). Prevent packet routing with invalid source addresses. Use operating systems (such as Linux) with unpredictable connection control mechanisms, such as TCP sequence numbers and the allocation of dynamic port addresses.

Putting hosts with operating systems that have insecure sequence number algorithms behind a Linux firewall performing Network Address Translation allows you to continue to use them with increased safety, since the firewall host will use its own sequence numbering algorithms for communication with the outside world.

Eavesdropping

This is the simplest type of attack. A host is configured to "listen" to and capture data not belonging to it (by putting its network interface into "promiscuous" mode and monitoring all packets traversing the network segment). Carefully written eavesdropping programs can take usernames and passwords from user login network connections. Broadcast networks such as unswitched Ethernet are especially vulnerable to this type of attack, although it does require physical access to the Ethernet network. Wireless networks have similar problems and can be more dangerous since physical access is not required; proximity is sufficient.

To protect against this type of threat, avoid use of broadcast network technologies and enforce the use of data encryption.

It is more complicated, but not impossible, to do packet sniffing in a switched environment. Some Ethernet switches have administrative settings or even failure modes that cause them to copy all packets to one or more of their ports.

IP firewalling is very useful in preventing or reducing unauthorized access, network layer denial of service, and IP spoofing attacks. It not very useful in avoiding exploitation of weaknesses in network services or programs and eavesdropping.

What Is a Firewall?

A firewall is a hardened and trusted host that acts as a *choke point* among a group of networks (usually a single private network and a single public network).* All network traffic among the affected networks is routed through the firewall. The firewall host is configured with a set of rules that determine which network traffic will be allowed to pass and which will be blocked (dropped without response) or refused (rejected with a response). In some large organizations, you may even find a firewall located inside their corporate network to segregate sensitive areas of the organization from employees in other areas. Many cases of computer crime originate within an organization, rather than from outside.

Firewalls can be constructed in a variety of ways. The most sophisticated arrangement involves a number of separate hosts and is known as a *perimeter network* or *demilitarized zone* (DMZ) network. Two hosts act as "filters" (sometimes called *chokes*) to allow only certain types of network traffic to pass, and between these chokes reside network servers such as an email (SMTP) server or a World Wide Web

---

* The term firewall comes from a device used to protect people from fire. The firewall is a shield of material resistant to fire that is placed between a potential fire and the people it is protecting.

(HTTP) proxy server. This configuration can be very safe and allows a great range of control over who can connect both from the inside to the outside and from the outside to the inside. This sort of configuration might be used by large organizations.

In many cases, though, people build firewalls that also provide other services (such as SMTP or HTTP). These are less secure because if someone exploits a weakness in one of the extra services running on the firewall, the entire network's security has been breached. The attacker could modify the firewall rules to allow more access and turn off accounting that might have otherwise alerted the network administrator that there was unusual network activity. Nevertheless, these types of firewalls are cheaper and easier to manage than the more sophisticated arrangement just described. Figure 7-1 illustrates the two most common firewall configurations.

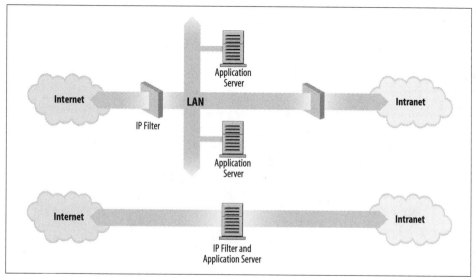

Figure 7-1. The two major classes of firewall design

The Linux kernel provides a range of built-in features that allow it to function as an IP firewall. The network implementation includes code (the *netfilter* subsystem) to do IP packet processing in a number of different ways, and provides a user-space mechanism (the iptables command) to configure what sort of rules you'd like to put in place. A Linux firewall is flexible enough to make it very useful in either of the configurations illustrated in Figure 7-1. Linux firewall software provides two other useful features that we'll discuss in separate chapters: IP Accounting (Chapter 8) and IP Masquerade and Network Address Translation (Chapter 9).

The three main classes of packet processing are filtering, mangling, and Network Address Translation (NAT). Filtering is simply deciding, at various points in the packet flow, whether or not to allow the packets through to the next stage. Packet mangling is a generic term for modifying packets as they move through the packet flow. NAT is a special application of mangling whereby source or destination IP addresses and/or ports are modified to transparently redirect traffic.

What Is IP Filtering?

IP filtering is simply a mechanism that decides which types of IP packets will be processed normally and which will be dropped or rejected. By *dropped* we mean that the packet is deleted and completely ignored, as if it had never been received. By *rejected* we mean that the firewall sends an ICMP response to the sender indicating a reason why the packet was rejected. You can apply many different sorts of criteria to determine which packets you wish to filter. Some examples of these are:

- Protocol type: TCP, UDP, ICMP, etc.
- Port number (for TCP/UPD)
- Packet type: SYN/ACK, data, ICMP Echo Request, etc.
- Packet source address: where it came from
- Packet destination address: where it is going to

It is important to understand at this point that IP filtering is a network layer facility. This means that it doesn't understand anything about the application using the network connections, only about the connections themselves. For example, you may deny users access to your internal network on the default Telnet port, but if you rely on IP filtering alone, you can't stop them from using the Telnet program with a port that you do allow to pass through your firewall. You can prevent this sort of problem by using proxy servers for each service that you allow across your firewall. The proxy servers understand the application that they were designed to proxy and can therefore prevent abuses, such as using the Telnet program to get past a firewall by using the World Wide Web port. If your firewall supports a World Wide Web proxy, outbound Telnet connections on the HTTP port will always be answered by the proxy and will allow only HTTP requests to pass. A large number of proxy-server programs exist. Some are free software and many others are commercial products. The *Firewall and Proxy Server HOWTO* (available online at *http://www.tldp.org/ HOWTO/Firewall-HOWTO.html*) discusses one popular set of these, but they are beyond the scope of this book.

The IP filtering rule set is made up of many combinations of the criteria listed previously. For example, let's imagine that you wanted to allow World Wide Web users within the Virtual Brewery network to have no access to the Internet except to use other sites' web servers. You would configure your firewall to allow forwarding of the following:

- Packets with a source address on Virtual Brewery network, a destination address of anywhere, and with a destination port of 80 (WWW)

- Packets with a destination address of Virtual Brewery network and a source port of 80 (WWW) from a source address of anywhere

Note that we've used two rules here. We have to allow our data to go out, but also the corresponding reply data to come back in. In practice, as we'll see in the chapter on IP masquerade and Network Address Translation (Chapter 9), *iptables* simplifies this and allows us to specify this in one command.

Netfilter and iptables

While developing the previous version of Linux IP firewalling (called `ipchains`), Paul "Rusty" Russell decided that IP firewalling should be less difficult. He set about the task of simplifying aspects of packet processing in the kernel firewalling code and produced a filtering framework that was both much cleaner and much more flexible. He called this new framework *netfilter*.

While *ipchains* was a vast improvement over its predecessor (*ipfwadm*) for the management of firewall rules, the way it processed packets was still complex, especially in conjunction with important features such as IP masquerade (discussed in Chapter 9) and other forms of address translation. Part of this complexity existed because IP masquerade and NAT were developed independently of the IP firewalling code and integrated later, rather than having been designed as a true part of the firewall code from the start. If a developer wanted to add yet more features in the packet-processing sequence, he would have had difficulty finding a place to insert the code and would have been forced to make changes in the kernel in order to do so.

netfilter addresses both the complexity and the rigidity of older solutions by implementing a generic framework in the kernel that streamlines the way packets are processed and provides a capability to extend filtering policy without having to modify the kernel. The *Linux 2.4 Packet Filtering HOWTO* (available online at *http://www.netfilter.org/documentation/HOWTO/packet-filtering-HOWTO.html*) offers a detailed list of the changes that have been made, so let's focus on the more practical aspects here.

To build a Linux IP firewall, it is necessary to have a kernel built with IP firewall (*netfilter*) support and the *iptables* user-space configuration utility. The *netfilter* code is the result of a large redesign of the packet handling flow in Linux. *netfilter* provides direct backward-compatible support for both of the two older Linux firewalling solutions (*ipfwadm* and *ipchains*), as well as a new command called *iptables*. In this book, we'll only cover *iptables*, but you can refer to previous editions of this book if you need to understand *ipfwadm* or *ipchains* rules.

Example iptables Commands

The *iptables* architecture groups network packet processing rules into *tables* by function (packet filtering, network address translation, and other packet mangling), each of which have *chains* (sequences) of processing *rules*. Rules consist of *matches* (used to determine which packets the rule will apply to) and *targets* (which determine what will be done with the matching packets).

iptables operates at OSI Layer 3 (Network). For OSI Layer 2 (Link), there are other technologies such as *ebtables* (Ethernet Bridge Tables). See *http://ebtables. sourceforge.net/* for more information.

This section will give a couple examples of *iptables* usage with high-level explanations. See the "iptables Concepts" section, later in the chapter, for additional information.

A packet-filtering example

This command could be used on a firewall to filter out all non-HTTP traffic, implementing the rules described in the earlier section, "What Is IP Filtering?", assuming eth0 is the Ethernet interface on the inside and eth1 is the Ethernet interface to the Internet.

```
iptables -t filter -P FORWARD DROP
iptables -t filter -A FORWARD -i eth0 -p tcp --dport 80 -j ACCEPT
iptables -t filter -A FORWARD -i eth1 -p tcp --sport 80 -j ACCEPT
```

The first command sets the default policy for the FORWARD chain of the filter table to DROP all packets. Table 7-1 shows how the second command means "allow all outbound HTTP requests." The third command is similar except that it means "allow all inbound HTTP responses."

Table 7-1. Decomposed example iptables command arguments

Component	Description
-t filter	Operate on the filter table (actually, the default)...
-A FORWARD	...by appending the following rule to its FORWARD chain.
-i eth0	Match packets coming in on the eth0 (inside) network interface...
-p tcp	...and using the tcp (TCP/IP) protocol
--dport 80	...and intended for port 80 on the (outside) destination host.
-j ACCEPT	Accept the packet for forwarding.

A Masquerading example

The previous section's packet filtering example doesn't make the best use of *iptables'* functionality. If you have a dynamic IP address on your Internet interface, you'd be better off using Masquerading (see Chapter 9 for more on Masquerading):

```
iptables -t nat -P POSTROUTING DROP
iptables -t nat -A POSTROUTING -o eth1 -p tcp --dport 80 -j MASQUERADE
```

A network translation example

This command could be used on a firewall to forward incoming HTTP traffic to a
web server on the internal network (see Chapter 9 for more on Network Address
Translation):

```
iptables -t nat -A PREROUTING -i eth1 -p tcp -dport 80 \
    -j DNAT --to-destination 192.168.1.3:8080
```

Table 7-2 shows what this sample *iptables* command means.

Table 7-2. Decomposed example iptables command arguments

Component	Description
-t nat	Operate on the nat (Network Address Translation) table…
-A PREROUTING	…by appending the following rule to its PREROUTING chain.
-i eth1	Match packets coming in on the eth1 network interface…
-p tcp	…and using the tcp (TCP/IP) protocol
--dport 80	…and intended for local port 80.
-j DNAT	Jump to the DNAT (Destination Network Address Translation) target…
--to-destination 192.168.1.3: 8080	…and change the destination address to **192.168.1.3** and destination port to 8080.

iptables Concepts

iptables defines five "hook points" in the kernel's packet processing pathways:
PREROUTING, INPUT, FORWARD, POSTROUTING, and OUTPUT. Built-in *chains* are attached to
these hook points; you can add a sequence of rules for each of them. Each of these
represents an opportunity to affect or monitor packet flow.

> It is common to refer to "the PREROUTING chain of the *nat* table," which
> makes it seem like chains belong to tables. But chains and tables are
> only partially correlated, and neither really "belongs" to the other.
> *Chains* represent hook points in the packet flow, and *tables* represent
> the types of processing that can occur. Figure 7-2 shows all the legal
> combinations, and the order in which they are encountered by pack-
> ets flowing through the system.

Packet Flow

Figure 7-2 shows how packets traverse the system. The boxes represent the *iptables*
chains, and inside each box is a list of the tables that have such a chain (in the order

in which they are invoked). All of these Table and Chain combinations are involved in packet mangling.

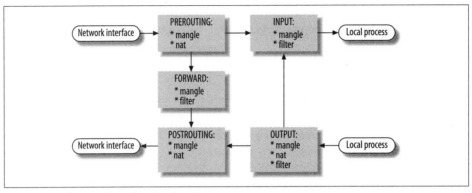

Figure 7-2. All network packet flow hook points

In Figure 7-3, the gray boxes represent chains and tables not involved in NAT.

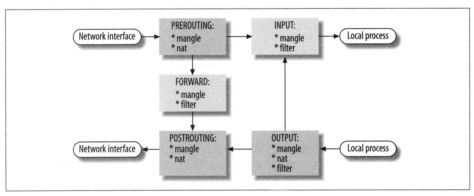

Figure 7-3. Network packet flow and hook points for NAT

Figure 7-4 shows how packets traverse the system for packet filtering.

Table 7-3 shows the five "hook points" and describes the points in the packet flow where they allow you to specify processing.

 For the curious, the hook points are defined in the kernel header file */usr/include/linux/netfilter_ipv4.h* with names such as NF_IP_FORWARD, NF_IP_LOCAL_{IN,OUT}, and NF_IP_{PRE,POST}_ROUTING.

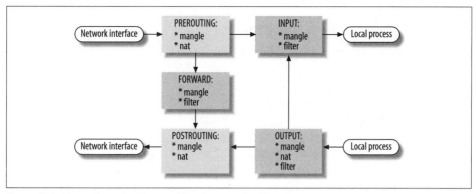

Figure 7-4. Network packet flow and hook points for filtering

Table 7-3. Hook points

	Allows you to process packets...
	flowing through a gateway computer, coming in one interface and going right back out another.
	just before they are delivered to a local process.
	just after they are generated by a local process.
ING	just before they go out a network interface.
NG	just as they arrive from a network interface (after dropping any packets resulting from the interface being in "promiscuous" mode, and after checksum validation).

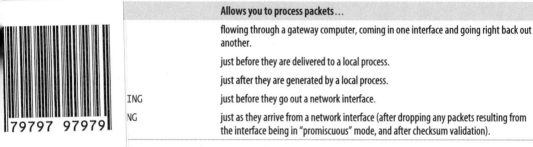

Your choice of chain will be based on where in the packet lifecycle you need to apply your rules. For example, if you want to filter outgoing packets, you generally do so in the OUTPUT chain, since the POSTROUTING chain is not associated with the filter table.

Three Ways We Can Do Filtering

Consider how a Unix host, or in fact any host capable of IP routing, processes IP packets. The basic steps, shown in Figure 7-5 are:

1. The IP packet is received.

   The incoming IP packet is examined to determine if it is destined for a process on this host.

2. If the packet is for this host, it is processed locally.

3. If it is not destined for this host (and IP forwarding is turned on), a search is made of the routing table for an appropriate route and the packet is forwarded to the appropriate interface or rejected if no route can be found.

4. Packets from local processes are sent to the routing software for forwarding to the appropriate interface.

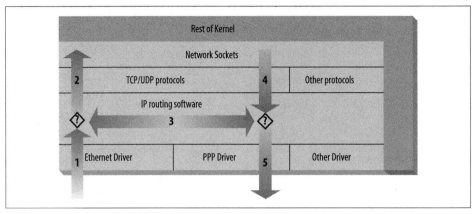

Figure 7-5. The stages of IP packet processing

The outgoing IP packet is examined to determine if there is a valid route for it to take; if not, it is dropped (ignored completely) or rejected (ignored after sending an ICMP message indicating there is no route to the destination host).

5. The IP packet is transmitted.

In our diagram, the flow 1 → 3 → 5 represents our host routing data between a host on our Ethernet network to a host reachable via our PPP link. The flows 1 → 2 and 4 → 5 represent the data input and output flows of a network program running on our local host. The flow 4 → 3 → 2 would represent data flow via a loopback connection. Naturally, data flows both into and out of network devices. The question marks on the diagram represent the points where the IP layer makes routing decisions.

The Linux kernel IP firewall is capable of applying filtering at various stages in this process. That is, you can filter the IP packets that come into your host, filter those packets being forwarded across your host, and filter those packets that are ready to be transmitted.

This may seem unnecessarily complicated at first, but it provides flexibility that allows some very sophisticated and powerful configurations to be built.

Tables

iptables comes with three built-in tables: `filter`, `mangle`, and `nat`. Each of these is preconfigured with chains corresponding to one or more of the hook points described in Table 7-4 and shown in Figure 7-2.

Table 7-4. Built-in tables

Table	Description
filter	Used to set policies for the type of traffic allowed into, through, and out of the computer. Unless you refer to a different table explicitly, *iptables* will operate on chains within this table by default.
	Its built-in chains are FORWARD, INPUT, and OUTPUT.
mangle	Used for specialized packet alteration, such as stripping off IP options (as with the IPV4OPTSSTRIP target extension).
	Its built-in chains are FORWARD, INPUT, OUTPUT, POSTROUTING, and PREROUTING.
nat	Used in conjunction with connection tracking to redirect connections for NAT, typically based on source or destination addresses.
	Its built-in chains are OUTPUT, POSTROUTING, and PREROUTING.

iptables arranges for the appropriate chains in these tables to be traversed by network packets based on the source and destination, and in the order depicted in Figure 7-2.

The default table is the filter table; If you do not specify an explicit table in an *iptables* command, filter is assumed.

Chains

Packets traverse chains, being presented to the chain's rules one at a time in order. If the packet does not match the rule's criteria, it moves on to the next rule in the chain. If a packet reaches the last rule in a chain and still does not match, the chain's policy is applied to it.

By default, each table has chains (initially empty) for some or all of the hook points. See Table 7-3 for a list of hook points, and Table 7-4 for a list of built-in chains for each table.

In addition, you can create your own custom chains to organize your rules.

A chain's *policy* is used to determine the fate of packets that reach the end of the chain without otherwise being sent to a specific target. Only the built-in targets ACCEPT and DROP (described in "Targets," later in this chaper) may be used as the policy for a built-in chain, and the default is ACCEPT. All user-defined chains have an implicit policy of RETURN, which cannot be changed.

If you want to have a more complicated policy target for a built-in chain, or a policy other than RETURN for a user-defined chain, you can add a rule to the end of the chain that matches all packets, with any target you like. You can set the chain's policy to DROP just in case you make a mistake in your catch-all rule, or to filter out traffic while you make modifications to your catch-all rule (by deleting it and re-adding it with changes).

Rules

An *iptables* rule consists of one or more *match* criteria to determine which network packets it will affect and a *target* specification that determines how the network packets will be affected. All match options must be satisfied for the rule to match a packet.

The system maintains packet and byte counters for every rule. Every time a packet reaches a rule and matches the rule's criteria, the packet counter is incremented and the byte counter is increased by the size of the matching packet.

Both the match and the target portion of the rule are optional. If there are no match criteria, all packets are considered to match. If there is no target specification, nothing is done to the packets (processing will proceed as if the rule did not exist except that the packet and byte counters will be updated). You can add such a "null" rule to the FORWARD chain of the filter table with the command iptables -t filter -A FORWARD.

Matches

There are a wide variety of matches available for use with *iptables*, although some are available only for kernels with certain features enabled. Generic Internet Protocol (IP) matches (such as protocol or source or destination address) are applicable to any IP packet.

In addition to the generic matches, *iptables* includes many specialized matches available through dynamically loaded extensions (you use the *iptables* -m or --match option to tell *iptables* that you want to use one of these extensions).

There is one match extension for dealing with a networking layer below the IP layer. The mac match extension matches based on Ethernet Media Access Controller (MAC) addresses.

Targets

Targets are used to specify the action to take when a rule matches a packet, and also to specify chain policies. There are four targets built into *iptables*, and extension modules that provide others. Table 7-5 describes these built-in targets.

Table 7-5. Built-in targets

Target	Description
ACCEPT	Let the packet through to the next stage of processing. Stop traversing the current chain, and start at the next stage shown in Figure 7-2.
DROP	Discontinue processing the packet completely. Do not check it against any other rules, chains, or tables. If you want to provide some feedback to the sender, then you can use the REJECT target extension.

Table 7-5. Built-in targets (continued)

Target	Description
QUEUE	Send the packet to userspace (i.e., code not in the kernel).
	See the `libipq` manpage for more information.
RETURN	From a rule in a user-defined chain, discontinue processing this chain, and resume traversing the calling chain at the rule following the one that had this chain as its target.
	From a rule in a built-in chain, discontinue processing the packet and apply the chain's policy to it.
	See the "Chains" section earlier in this chapter for more information about chain policies.

Setting Up Linux for Firewalling

The Linux kernel must be configured to support IP firewalling. There isn't much more to it than selecting the appropriate options when performing:

```
# make menuconfig
```

of your kernel.* In 2.4 kernels you should select the following options:

```
Networking options  --->
    [*] Network packet filtering (replaces ipchains)
        IP: Netfilter Configuration  --->
            .
            <M> Userspace queueing via NETLINK (EXPERIMENTAL)
            <M> IP tables support (required for filtering/masq/NAT)
            <M>    limit match support
            <M>    MAC address match support
            <M>    netfilter MARK match support
            <M>    Multiple port match support

            <M>    TOS match support
            <M>    Connection state match support
            <M>    Unclean match support (EXPERIMENTAL)
            <M>    Owner match support (EXPERIMENTAL)
            <M>    Packet filtering
            <M>      REJECT target support
            <M>      MIRROR target support (EXPERIMENTAL)
            .
            <M>    Packet mangling
            <M>      TOS target support
            <M>      MARK target support
            <M>    LOG target support
            <M> ipchains (2.2-style) support
            <M> ipfwadm (2.0-style) support
```

---

* Firewall packet logging is a special feature that writes a line of information about each datagram that matches a particular firewall rule out to a special device so you can see them.

Loading the Kernel Module

Before you can use the *iptables* command, you must load the *netfilter* kernel module that provides support for it. The easiest way to do this is to use the *modprobe* command as follows:

```
# modprobe ip_tables
```

Backward Compatibility with ipfwadm and ipchains

The remarkable flexibility of Linux *netfilter* is illustrated by its ability to emulate the *ipfwadm* and *ipchains* interfaces. Emulation makes the initial transition to the new generation of firewall software much easier (although you'd want to rewrite your rules as *iptables* eventually).

The two *netfilter* kernel modules called *ipfwadm.o* and *ipchains.o* provide backward compatibility for ipfwadm and ipchains. You may load only one of these modules at a time, and use one only if the *ip_tables.o* module is not loaded. When the appropriate module is loaded, *netfilter* works exactly like the former firewall implementation.

netfilter mimics the *ipchains* interface with the following commands:

```
# rmmod ip_tables
# modprobe ipchains
# ipchains options
```

Using iptables

The *iptables* command is extensible through dynamically loaded libraries. It is included in the *netfilter* source package available at *http://www.netfilter.org/*. It will also be included in any Linux distribution based on the 2.4 series kernels.

The *iptables* command is used to configure IP filtering and NAT (along with other packet-processing applications, including accounting, logging, and mangling). To facilitate this, there are two tables of rules called *filter* and *nat*. The filter table is assumed if you do not specify the -t option to override it. Five built-in chains are also provided. The INPUT and FORWARD chains are available for the *filter* table, the PREROUTING and POSTROUTING chains are available for the *nat* table, and the OUTPUT chain is available for both tables. In this chapter we'll discuss only the *filter* table. We'll look at the *nat* table in Chapter 9.

The general syntax of most *iptables* commands is:

```
# iptables command rule-specification extensions
```

Now we'll take a look at some options in detail, after which we'll review some examples.

Most of the options for the *iptables* command can be grouped into subcommands and rule match criteria. Table 7-6 describes the other options.

Table 7-6. iptables miscellaneous options

Option	Description
-c *packets bytes*	When combined with the -A, -I, or -R subcommand, sets the packet counter to *packets* and the byte counter to *bytes* for the new or modified rule.
--exact	Synonym for -x.
-h	Displays information on *iptables* usage. If it appears after -m *match* or -j *target*, then any additional help related to the extension *match* or *target* (respectively) is also displayed.
--help	Synonym for -h.
-j *target [options]*	Determines what to do with packets matching this rule. The *target* can be the name of a user-defined chain, one of the built-in targets, or an *iptables* extension (in which case there may be additional *options*).
--jump	Synonym for -j.
--line-numbers	When combined with the -L subcommand, displays numbers for the rules in each chain, so you can refer to the rules by index when inserting rules into (via -I) or deleting rules from (via -D) a chain. Be aware that the line numbering changes as you add and remove rules in the chain.
-m *match [options]*	Invoke extended *match*, possibly with additional *options*.
--match	Synonym for -m.
-M *cmd*	Used to load an *iptables* module (with new targets or match extensions) when appending, inserting, or replacing rules.
--modprobe=*cmd*	Synonym for -M.
-n	Displays numeric addresses and ports, instead of looking up domain names for the IP addresses and service names for the port numbers.
	This can be especially useful if your DNS service is slow or down.
--numeric	Synonym for -n.
--set-counters	Synonym for -c.
-t table	Performs the specified subcommand on *table*. If this option is not used, the subcommand operates on the filter table by default.
--table	Synonym for -t.
-v	Produces verbose output.
--verbose	Synonym for -v.
-x	Displays exact numbers for packet and byte counters, rather than the default abbreviated format with metric suffixes (K, M, or G).

Getting Help

iptables provides some source of online help. You can get basic information via the following commands:

```
iptables -h | --help
iptables -m match -h
iptables -j TARGET -h
man iptables
```

Sometimes there are contradictions among these sources of information.

The iptables Subcommands

Each *iptables* command can contain one subcommand, which performs an operation on a particular table (and, in some cases, chain). Table 7-7 lists the options that are used to specify the subcommand.

 The manpage for the *iptables* command in the 1.2.7a release shows a -C option in the synopsis section, but there is no -C option to the *iptables* command.

Table 7-7. iptables subcommand options

Option	Description
-A *chain rule*	Appends *rule* to *chain*.
--append	Synonym for -A.
-D *chain* [*index* | *rule*]	Deletes the rule at position *index* or matching *rule* from *chain*.
--delete	Synonym for -D.
--delete-chain	Synonym for -X.
-E *chain newchain*	Renames *chain* to *newchain*.
-F [*chain*]	Flushes (deletes) all rules from *chain* (or from all chains if no chain is given).
--flush	Synonym for -F.
-I *chain* [*index*] *rule*	Inserts *rule* into *chain*, at the front of the chain, or in front of the rule at position *index*.
--insert	Synonym for -I.
-L [*chain*]	Lists the rules for *chain* (or for all chains if no chain is given).
--list	Synonym for -L.
-N *chain*	Creates a new user-defined *chain*.
--new-chain	Synonym for -N. Commonly abbreviated --new.
-P *chain target*	Sets the default policy of the built-in *chain* to *target*. (applies to built-in chains and targets only).
--policy	Synonym for -P.
-R *chain index rule*	Replaces the rule at position *index* of *chain* with the new *rule*.
--rename-chain	Synonym for -E.
--replace	Synonym for -R.
-V	Displays the version of *iptables*.

Table 7-7. iptables subcommand options (continued)

Option	Description
--version	Synonym for -V.
-X [chain]	Deletes the user-defined chain, or all user-defined chains if none is given.
-Z chain	Zeros the packet and byte counters for chain (or for all chains if no chain is given).
--zero	Synonym for -Z.

Basic iptables Matches

iptables has a small number of built-in matches and targets and a set of extensions that are loaded if they are referenced. The matches for IP are considered built-in, and the others are considered match extensions (even though the icmp, tcp and udp match extensions are automatically loaded when the corresponding protocols are referenced with the -p built-in IP match option).

> Some options can have their senses inverted by using an optional exclamation point surrounded by spaces, immediately before the option. The options that allow this are annotated with [!]. Only the non-inverted sense is described in the sections that follow, since the inverted sense can be inferred from it.

Internet Protocol (IPv4) Matches

These built-in matches are available without a preceding -m argument to iptables. Table 7-8 shows the layout of the fields in an Internet Protocol (IPv4) packet. These fields are the subjects of various match and target extensions (including the set of built-in matches described in this section). Table 7-8 describes the options to this match.

Table 7-8. Internet Protocol match options

Option	Description
-d [!] addr[/mask]	Destination address addr (or range, if mask is given).
--destination	Synonym for -d.
--dst	Synonym for -d.
[!] -f	Second or further fragment of a packet that has undergone fragmentation.
	Connection tracking does automatic defragmentation, so this option is not often useful. If aren't using connection tracking, though, you can use it.
--fragments	Synonym for -f. Commonly abbreviated (including in the iptables manpage) --fragment.

Table 7-8. Internet Protocol match options (continued)

Option	Description
-i [!] *in*	Input interface *in* (if *in* ends with +, any interface having a name that starts with *in* will match).
--in-interface	Synonym for -i.
-o [!] *out*	Input interface *out* (if *out* ends with +, any interface having a name that starts with *out* will match).
--out-interface	Synonym for -o.
-p [!] *proto*	Protocol name or number *proto*.
	See Table 7-9 for a list of common protocol names and numbers. Your system's */etc/protocols* file will be consulted to map official names (in a case-insensitive manner) to numbers. The aliases in */etc/protocols* are not available.
	See also the official protocol list at *http://www.iana.org/assignments/protocol-numbers*.
	-p *protocol* includes an implicit -m *protocol* when *protocol* is one of icmp, tcp, or udp.
--protocol	Synonym for -p. Commonly abbreviated --proto.
-s [!] *addr*[/*mask*]	Source address *addr* (or range, if *mask* is given).
--source	Synonym for -s.
--src	Synonym for -s.

You can use the old-style dotted-quad notation for masks such as **192.168.1.0/255. 255.255.0**, or the newer Common Inter-Domain Routing (CIDR) notation such as **192.168.1.0/24** (see RFC 1591, available online at *http://www.rfc-editor.org/rfc/ rfc1519.txt*) for the address specifications of -s and -d.

Table 7-9. Common IP protocols

Name	Number(s)	Description
ALL	1, 6, 17	Equivalent to not specifying protocol at all
icmp	1	Internet Control Message Protocol
tcp	6	Transmission Control Protocol
udp	17	User Datagram Protocol

Ethernet Media Access Controller (MAC) Match

This match is based on the Media Access Controller (MAC) address of the source Ethernet interface. Table 7-10 describes the single option to this match.

This is actually not an IP match. Ethernet is at a lower level in the network architecture, but since many IP networks run over Ethernet, and the MAC information is available, this match extension is included anyway.

This match is available only if your kernel has been configured with CONFIG_IP_NF_MATCH_MAC enabled.

Table 7-10. MAC match options

Option	Description
--mac-source [!] *mac*	Match when the Ethernet frame source MAC field matches *mac*.
	The format is: *XX*:*XX*:*XX*:*XX*:*XX*:*XX*, where each *XX* is replaced by two hexadecimal digits.

Use this only with rules on the PREROUTING, FORWARD, or INPUT chains, and only for packets coming from Ethernet devices.

For example, to allow only a single Ethernet device to communicate over an interface (such as an interface connected to a wireless device):

```
iptables -A PREROUTING -i eth1 -m mac --mac-source ! 0d:bc:97:02:18:21 -j DROP
```

Internet Control Message Protocol Match

The Internet Control Message Protocol (ICMP) match extension is automatically loaded if -p icmp is used. Table 7-11 describes the options to this match.

Table 7-11. ICMP match options

Option	Description
--icmp-type [!] *typename*	Matches ICMP type *typename*
--icmp-type [!] *type*[/*code*]	Matches ICMP *type* and *code* given

You can find the official ICMP types and codes at the official database at *http://www. iana.org/assignments/icmp-parameters* (per RFC 3232, "Assigned Numbers: RFC 1700 is Replaced by an On-line Database," available online at *http://www.rfc-editor. org/rfc/rfc3232.txt*).

User Datagram Protocol Match

The User Datagram Protocol (UDP) match extension is automatically loaded if -p udp is used. Table 7-12 describes the options to this match.

Table 7-12. UDP match options

Option	Description
`--destination-port [!] port[:port]`	Match when the UDP destination port number is equal to *port* (if only one port is given) or in the inclusive range (if both *port*s are given).
	Ports can be specified by name (from your system's */etc/services* file) or number.
`--dport`	Synonym for `--destination-port`.
`--source-port [!] port[:port]`	Match when the UDP source port is equal to *port* (if only one *port* is given) or in the inclusive range (if both *port*s are given).
	Ports can be specified by name (from your system's */etc/services* file) or number.
`--sport`	Synonym for `--source-port`.

Transmission Control Protocol Match

The Transmission Control Protocol (TCP) match extension is automatically loaded if -p tcp is used. Table 7-13 describes the options to this match.

Table 7-13. TCP match options

Option	Description
`--destination-port`	Synonym for `--dport`.
`--dport [!] port[:port]`	Match when the TCP destination port number is equal to *port* (if only one port is given) or in the inclusive range (if both *port*s are given).
	Ports can be specified by name (from your system's */etc/services* file) or number.
`--mss value[:value]`	Match SYN and ACK packets when the value of the TCP protocol Maximum Segment Size (MSS) field is equal to *value* (if only one *value* is given) or in the inclusive range (if both *value*s are given).
	See also the tcpmss match extension.
`--source-port`	Synonym for `--sport`.
`--sport [!] port[:port]`	Match when the TCP source port is equal to *port* (if only one *port* is given) or in the inclusive range (if both *port*s are given).
	Ports can be specified by name (from your system's */etc/services* file) or number.
`[!] --syn`	Synonym for `--tcp-flags SYN,RST,ACK SYN`. Packets matching this are called "SYN" packets.
	This option can be used to construct rules to block incoming connections while permitting outgoing connections.
`--tcp-flags`	Check the *mask* flags, and match if only the *comp* flags are set.
`[!] mask comp`	The *mask* and *comp* arguments are comma-separated lists of flag names, or one of the two special values ALL and NONE.
`--tcp-option[!] num`	Match if TCP option *num* is set.

A Naive Example

Let's suppose that we have a network in our organization and that we are using a Linux-based firewall host to allow our users to be able to access WWW (HTTP on port 80 only, not HTTPS on port 443) servers on the Internet, but to allow no other traffic to be passed. The commands that follow could be used to set up a simple set of forwarding rules to implement this policy. Note, however, that while this example is simple, the NAT and Masquerading solutions discussed in Chapter 9 are more often used for this type of application.

If our network has a 24-bit network mask (class C) and has an address of **172.16.1. 0**, then we'd use the following *iptables* rules:

```
1  # modprobe ip_tables
2  # iptables -F FORWARD
3  # iptables -P FORWARD DROP
4  # iptables -A FORWARD -p tcp -s 0/0 --sport 80 \
        -d 172.16.1.0/24 --syn -j DROP
5  # iptables -A FORWARD -p tcp -s 172.16.1.0/24 \
        --dport 80 -d 0/0 -j ACCEPT
6  # iptables -A FORWARD -p tcp -d 172.16.1.0/24 \
        --sport 80 -s 0/0 -j ACCEPT
```

Lines 1–3 install *iptables* into the running kernel, flush the FORWARD chain of the filter table (the default table if no explicit table is mentioned in the *iptables* command's arguments), and sets the default policy for the FORWARD chain of the filter table to DROP.

Line 4 prevents Internet hosts establishing connection from to the internal network by dropping SYN packets (but only if the source port is 80 since those are the only ones that would be let through by later rules)

Line 5 allows all packets heading from the internal network to port 80 on any host to get out.

Line 6 allows all packets heading from port 80 on any host to hosts on the internal network through.

A Sample Firewall Configuration

We've discussed the fundamentals of firewall configuration. Let's now look at an easily customizable firewall configuration. In this example, the network **172.16.1.0/ 24** is treated as if it were a publicly routable network, but it is actually a private, non-routable network. We are using such a non-routable network in this example because we have to use *some* network, and we don't want to put a real publicly routable network number here. The commands shown would work for a real class C publicly routable network.

```bash
#!/bin/bash
###########################################################################
# This sample configuration is for a single host firewall configuration
# with no services supported by the firewall host itself.
###########################################################################
#
# USER CONFIGURABLE SECTION (Lists are comma-separated)
#
#   OURNET      Internal network address space
#   OURBCAST    Internal network broadcast address
#   OURDEV      Internal network interface name
#
#   ANYADDR     External network address space
#   EXTDEV      External network interface name
#
#   TCPIN       List of TCP ports to allow in (empty = all)
#   TCPOUT      List of TCP ports to allow out (empty = all)
#
#   UDPIN       List of TCP ports to allow in (empty = all)
#   UDPOUT      List of TCP ports to allow out (empty = all)
#
#   LOGGING     Set to 1 to turn logging on, else leave empty
#
###########################################################################

OURNET="172.29.16.0/24"
OURBCAST="172.29.16.255"
OURDEV="eth0"

ANYADDR="0/0"
EXTDEV="eth1"

TCPIN="smtp,www"
TCPOUT="smtp,www,ftp,ftp-data,irc"

UDPIN="domain"
UDPOUT="domain"

LOGGING=

###########################################################################
#
# IMPLEMENTATION
#
###########################################################################


#
# Install the modules
#

modprobe ip_tables
modprobe ip_conntrack # Means we won't have to deal with fragments

#
```

```
# Drop all packets destined for this host received from outside.
#

iptables -A INPUT -i $EXTDEV -j DROP


#
# Remove all rules on the FORWARD chain of the filter table, and set th
# policy for that chain to DROP.
#

iptables -F FORWARD                                  # Delete rules
iptables -P FORWARD DROP                             # Policy = DROP
iptables -A FORWARD -s $OURNET -i $EXTDEV -j DROP        # Anti-spoof
iptables -A FORWARD -p icmp -i $EXTDEV -d $OURBCAST -j DROP # Anti-Smurf


#
# TCP - ESTABLISHED CONNECTIONS
#
# We will accept all TCP packets belonging to an existing connection
# (i.e. having the ACK bit set) for the TCP ports we're allowing through.
# This should catch more than 95 % of all valid TCP packets.
#

iptables -A FORWARD -d $OURNET -p tcp --tcp-flags SYN,ACK ACK \
  -m multiport --dports $TCPIN -j ACCEPT

iptables -A FORWARD -s $OURNET -p tcp --tcp-flags SYN,ACK ACK \
  -m multiport --sports $TCPIN -j ACCEPT


#
# TCP - NEW INCOMING CONNECTIONS
#
# We will accept connection requests from the outside only on the
# allowed TCP ports.
#

iptables -A FORWARD -i $EXTDEV -d $OURNET -p tcp --syn \
  -m multiport --sports $TCPIN -j ACCEPT


#
# TCP - NEW OUTGOING CONNECTIONS
#
# We will accept all outgoing tcp connection requests on the allowed /
# TCP ports.
#

iptables -A FORWARD -i $OURDEV -d $ANYADDR -p tcp --syn \
  -m multiport --dports $TCPOUT -j ACCEPT


#
# UDP - INCOMING
#
# We will allow UDP packets in on the allowed ports and back.
#
```

```
iptables -A FORWARD -i $EXTDEV -d $OURNET -p udp \
  -m multiport --dports $UDPIN -j ACCEPT

iptables -A FORWARD  -i $EXTDEV -s $OURNET -p udp \
  -m multiport --sports $UDPIN -j ACCEPT

#
# UDP - OUTGOING
#
# We will allow UDP packets out to the allowed ports and back.
#

iptables -A FORWARD -i $OURDEV -d $ANYADDR -p udp \
  -m multiport --dports $UDPOUT -j ACCEPT

iptables -A FORWARD -i $OURDEV -s $ANYADDR -p udp \
  -m multiport --sports $UDPOUT -j ACCEPT

#
# DEFAULT and LOGGING
#
# All remaining packets fall through to the default
# rule and are dropped. They will be logged if you've
# configured the LOGGING variable above.
#

if [ "$LOGGING" ]
then
  iptables -A FORWARD -p tcp  -j LOG  # Log barred TCP
  iptables -A FORWARD -p udp  -j LOG  # Log barred UDP
  iptables -A FORWARD -p icmp -j LOG  # Log barred ICMP
fi
```

In many simple situations, to use the sample, all you have to do is edit the top section of the file labeled "USER CONFIGURABLE section" to specify which protocols and packets type you wish to allow in and out. For more complex configurations, you will need to edit the section at the bottom as well. Remember, this is a simple example, so scrutinize it very carefully to ensure it does what you want while implementing it.

References

There is enough material on firewall configuration and design to fill a whole book, and indeed here are some good references that you might like to read to expand your knowledge on the subject:

Real World Linux Security, Second Edition
> by Bob Toxen (Prentice Hall). A great book with broad coverage of many security topics, including firewalls.

Building Internet Firewalls, Second Edition

by E. Zwicky, S. Cooper, and D. Chapman (O'Reilly). A guide explaining how to design and install firewalls for Unix, Linux, and Windows NT, and how to configure Internet services to work with the firewalls.

Firewalls and Internet Security, Second Edition

by W. Cheswick, S. Bellovin, and A. Rubin (Addison Wesley). This book covers the philosophy of firewall design and implementation.

Practical Unix & Internet Security, Third Edition

by S. Garfinkel, G. Spafford, and A. Schwartz (O'Reilly). This book covers a wide variety of security topics for popular Unix variants (including Linux), such as forensics, intrusion detection, firewalls, and more.

Linux Security Cookbook

by D. Barrett, R. Silverman, and R. Byrnes (O'Reilly). This book provides over 150 ready-to-use scripts and configuration files for important security tasks such as time-of-day network access restrictions, web server firewalling, preventing IP spoofing, and much more.

Linux iptables Pocket Reference

by G. Purdy (O'Reilly). This book covers firewall concepts, Linux packet processing flows, and contains a complete reference to the *iptables* command, including an encyclopedic reference to match and target extensions, that you can use for advanced applications.

## CHAPTER 8

IP Accounting

In today's world of commercial Internet service, it is becoming increasingly important to know how much data you are transmitting and receiving on your network connections. If you are an Internet Service Provider and you charge your customers by volume, this will be essential to your business. If you are a customer of an Internet Service Provider that charges by data volume, you will find it useful to collect your own data to ensure the accuracy of your Internet charges.

There are other uses for network accounting that have nothing to do with dollars and bills. If you manage a server that offers a number of different types of network services, it might be useful to you to know exactly how much data is being generated by each one. This sort of information could assist you in making decisions, such as what hardware to buy or how many servers to run.

The Linux kernel provides a facility that allows you to collect all sorts of useful information about the network traffic it sees. This facility is called *IP accounting*.

Configuring the Kernel for IP Accounting

The Linux IP accounting feature is very closely related to the Linux firewall software. The places you want to collect accounting data are the same places that you would be interested in performing firewall filtering: into and out of a network host and in the software that does the routing of packets. If you haven't read the section on firewalls, now is probably a good time to do so, as we will be using some of the concepts described in Chapter 7.

Configuring IP Accounting

Because IP accounting is closely related to IP firewall, the same tool was designated to configure it, so the **iptables** command is used to configure IP accounting. The command syntax is very similar to that of the firewall rules, so we won't focus on it, but we will discuss what you can discover about the nature of your network traffic using this feature.

The general command syntax is:

```
# iptables -A chain rule-specification
```

The **iptables** command allows you to specify direction in a manner consistent with the firewall rules.

The commands are much the same as firewall rules, except that the policy rules do not apply here. We can add, insert, delete, and list accounting rules. In the case of *ipchains* and **iptables**, all valid rules are accounting rules, and any command that doesn't specify the -j option performs accounting only.

The rule specification parameters for IP accounting are the same as those used for IP firewalls. These are what we use to define precisely what network traffic we wish to count and total.

Accounting by Address

Let's work with an example to illustrate how we'd use IP accounting.

Imagine we have a Linux-based router that serves two departments at the Virtual Brewery. The router has two Ethernet devices, eth0 and eth1, each of which services a department; and a PPP device, ppp0, that connects us via a high-speed serial link to the main campus of the Groucho Marx University.

Let's also imagine that for billing purposes that we want to know the total traffic generated by each of the departments across the serial link, and for management purposes we want to know the total traffic generated between the two departments.

Table 8-1 shows the interface addresses we will use in our example:

Table 8-1. Interfaces and their addresses

Interface	Address	Netmask
eth0	172.16.3.0	255.255.255.0
eth1	172.16.4.0	255.255.255.0

To answer the question, "How much data does each department generate on the PPP link?", we could use a rule that looks like this:

```
# iptables -A FORWARD -i ppp0 -d 172.16.3.0/24
# iptables -A FORWARD -o ppp0 -s 172.16.3.0/24
# iptables -A FORWARD -i ppp0 -d 172.16.4.0/24
# iptables -A FORWARD -o ppp0 -s 172.16.4.0/24
```

The first two rules say, "Count all data traveling in either direction across the interface named ppp0 with a source or destination address of **172.16.3.0/24**." The second set of two rules do the same thing, but for the second Ethernet network at our site.

To answer the second question, "How much data travels between the two departments?", we need a rule that looks like this:

```
# iptables -A FORWARD -s 172.16.3.0/24 -d 172.16.4.0/24
# iptables -A FORWARD -s 172.16.4.0/24 -d 172.16.3.0/24
```

These rules will count all packets with a source address belonging to one of the department networks and a destination address belonging to the other.

Accounting by Service Port

Okay, let's suppose we also want a better idea of exactly what sort of traffic is being carried across our PPP link. We might, for example, want to know how much of the link the FTP, SMTP, and World Wide Web (HTTP) services are consuming.

A script of rules to enable us to collect this information might look like this:

```
#!/bin/sh
# Collect ftp, smtp and www volume statistics for data carried on our
# PPP link using iptables.
#
iptables -A FORWARD -i ppp0 -p tcp --sport 20:21
iptables -A FORWARD -o ppp0 -p tcp --dport 20:21
iptables -A FORWARD -i ppp0 -p tcp --sport smtp
iptables -A FORWARD -o ppp0 -p tcp --dport smtp
iptables -A FORWARD -i ppp0 -p tcp --sport www
iptables -A FORWARD -o ppp0 -p tcp --dport www
```

There are a couple of interesting features to this configuration. First, we've specified the protocol. When we specify ports in our rules, we must also specify a protocol because TCP and UDP provide separate sets of ports. Since all of these services are TCP based, we've specified it as the protocol. Second, we've specified the two services ftp and ftp-data in one command. The **iptables** command allows either single ports or ranges of ports, which is what we've used here. The syntax "20:21" means "ports 20 (ftp-data) through 21 (ftp)," and is how we encode ranges of ports in **iptables** (the tcp match extension allow you to use port names in range specifications, but the multiport match extension does not—and you are better off using numbers for ranges anyway so you don't accidentally include more ports than you intend). When you have a list of ports in an accounting rule, it means that any data received for any of the ports in the list will cause the data to be added to that entry's totals. Remembering that the FTP service uses two ports, the command port and the data transfer port; we've added them together to total the FTP traffic.

We can expand on the second point a little to give us a different view of the data on our link. Let's now imagine that we class FTP, SMTP, and World Wide Web (HTTP) traffic as essential traffic, and all other traffic as nonessential. If we were interested in seeing the ratio of essential traffic to nonessential traffic, we could do something like this:

```
# iptables -A FORWARD -i ppp0 -p tcp -m multiport \
    --sports ftp-data,ftp,smtp,www -j ACCEPT
# iptables -A FORWARD -j ACCEPT
```

The first rule would count our essential traffic while the second one would count everything else.

Alternatively, we can use user-defined chains (this would be useful if the rules for determining essential traffic were more complex):

```
# iptables -N a-essent
# iptables -N a-noness
# iptables -A a-essent -j ACCEPT
# iptables -A a-noness -j ACCEPT
# iptables -A FORWARD -i ppp0 -p tcp -m multiport \
    --sports ftp-data,ftp,smtp,www -j a-essent
# iptables -A FORWARD -j a-noness
```

Here we create two user-defined chains—one called a-essent, where we capture accounting data for essential services, and another called a-noness, where we capture accounting data for nonessential services. We then add rules to our forward chain that match our essential services and jump to the a-essent chain, where we have just one rule that accepts all packets and counts them. The last rule in our forward chain is a rule that jumps to our a-noness chain, where again we have just one rule that accepts all packets and counts them. The rule that jumps to the a-noness chain will not be reached by any of our essential services, as they will have been accepted in their own chain. Our tallies for essential and nonessential services will therefore be available in the rules within those chains. This is just one approach you could take; there are others.

This looks simple enough. Unfortunately, there is a small but unavoidable problem when trying to do accounting by service type. You will remember that we discussed the role the MTU plays in TCP/IP networking in an earlier chapter. The MTU defines the largest packet that will be transmitted on a network device. When a packet is received by a router that is larger than the MTU of the interface that needs to retransmit it, the router performs a trick called *fragmentation*. The router breaks the large packet into small pieces no longer than the MTU of the interface and then transmits these pieces. The router builds new headers to put in front of each of these pieces, and these are what the remote host uses to reconstruct the original data. Unfortunately, during the fragmentation process, the port is lost for all but the first fragment. This means that the IP accounting can't properly count fragmented packets. It can reliably count only the first fragment or unfragmented packets. To ensure that we capture the second and later fragments, we could use a rule like this:

```
# iptables -A FORWARD -i ppp0 -m tcp -p tcp -f
```

These won't tell us what the original port for this data was, but at least we are able to see how much of our data is fragments and account for the volume of traffic they consume.

 Connection tracking does automatic defragmenting, so this technique won't often be useful. But if you aren't doing connection tracking, you can use it.

Accounting of ICMP Packets

The ICMP protocol does not use service port numbers and is therefore a little bit more difficult to collect details on. ICMP uses a number of different types of packets. Many of these are harmless and normal, while others should only be seen under special circumstances. Sometimes people with too much time on their hands attempt to maliciously disrupt the network access of a user by generating large numbers of ICMP messages. This is commonly called *ping flooding* (the generic term for this type of denial of service attack is *packet flooding*, but ping flooding is a common one). While IP accounting cannot do anything to prevent this problem (IP firewalling can help, though!), we can at least put accounting rules in place that will show us if anybody has been trying.

ICMP doesn't use ports as TCP and UDP do. Instead ICMP has ICMP message types. We can build rules to account for each ICMP message type. We place the ICMP message and type number in place of the port field in the accounting commands.

An IP accounting rule to collect information about the volume of ping data that is being sent to you or that you are generating might look like this:

```
# iptables -A FORWARD -m icmp -p icmp --sports echo-request
# iptables -A FORWARD -m icmp -p icmp --sports echo-reply
# iptables -A FORWARD -m icmp -p icmp -f
```

The first rule collects information about the "ICMP Echo Request" packets (ping requests), and the second rule collects information about the "ICMP Echo Reply" packets (ping replies). The third rule collects information about ICMP packet fragments. This is a trick similar to that described for fragmented TCP and UDP packets.

If you specify source and/or destination addresses in your rules, you can keep track of where the pings are coming from, such as whether they originate inside or outside your network. Once you've determined where the rogue packets are coming from, you can decide whether you want to put firewall rules in place to prevent them or take some other action, such as contacting the owner of the offending network to advise them of the problem, or perhaps even taking legal action if the problem is a malicious act.

Accounting by Protocol

Let's now imagine that we are interested in knowing how much of the traffic on our link is TCP, UDP, and ICMP. We would use rules like the following:

```
# iptables -A FORWARD -i ppp0 -m tcp -p tcp
# iptables -A FORWARD -o ppp0 -m tcp -p tcp
# iptables -A FORWARD -i ppp0 -m udp -p udp
# iptables -A FORWARD -o ppp0 -m udp -p udp
# iptables -A FORWARD -i ppp0 -m icmp -p icmp
# iptables -A FORWARD -o ppp0 -m icmp -p icmp
```

With these rules in place, all of the traffic flowing across the ppp0 interface will be analyzed to determine whether it is TCP, UDP, or ICMP traffic, and the appropriate counters will be updated for each.

Using IP Accounting Results

It is all very well to be collecting this information, but how do we actually get to see it? To view the collected accounting data and the configured accounting rules, we use our firewall configuration commands, asking them to list our rules. The packet and byte counters for each of our rules are listed in the output.

Listing Accounting Data

The **iptables** command behaves very similarly to the *ipchains* command. Again, we must use the -v when listing tour rules to see the accounting counters. To list our accounting data, we would use:

```
# iptables -L -v
```

Just as for the *ipchains* command, you can use the -x argument to show the output in expanded format with unit figures.

Resetting the Counters

The IP accounting counters will overflow if you leave them long enough. If they overflow, you will have difficulty determining the value they actually represent. To avoid this problem, you should read the accounting data periodically, record it, and then reset the counters back to zero to begin collecting accounting information for the next accounting interval.

The **iptables** command provides you with a simple means of doing this:

```
# iptables -Z
```

You can even combine the list and zeroing actions together to ensure that no accounting data is lost in between:

```
# iptables -L -Z -v
```

This command will first list the accounting data and then immediately zero the counters and begin counting again. If you are interested in collecting and using this information regularly, you would probably want to put this command into a script that recorded the output and stored it somewhere, and execute the script periodically using the cron command.

Flushing the Rule Set

One last command that might be useful allows you to flush all the IP accounting rules that you have configured. This is most useful when you want to radically alter your rule set without rebooting the host.

The **iptables** command supports the -F argument, which flushes all the rules of the type you specify:

```
# iptables -F
```

This flushes all of your configured rules (not just your accounting rules), removing them all and saving you having to remove each of them individually.

Passive Collection of Accounting Data

One last trick you might like to consider: if your Linux host is connected to an Ethernet, you can apply accounting rules to all of the data from the segment, not only that which it is transmitted by or destined for it. Your host will passively listen to all of the data on the segment and count it.

You should first turn IP forwarding off on your Linux host so that it doesn't try to route the packets it receives.* You can do so by running this command:

```
# echo 0 >/proc/sys/net/ipv4/ip_forward
```

You should then enable *promiscuous mode* on your Ethernet interface using the *ifconfig* command. Enabling promiscuous mode for an Ethernet device causes it to deliver all packets to the operating system rather than only those with its Ethernet address as the destination. This is only relevant if the device is connected to a broadcast medium (such as unswitched Ethernet). For example, to enable promiscuous mode on interface eth1:

```
# ifconfig eth1 promisc
```

---

* This isn't a good thing to do if your Linux machine serves as a router. If you disable IP forwarding, it will cease to route! Do this only on a machine with a single physical network interface.

Now you can establish accounting rules that allow you to collect information about the packets flowing across your Ethernet without involving your Linux accounting host in the route at all.

## CHAPTER 9

IP Masquerade and Network Address Translation

You don't have to have a good memory to remember a time when only large organizations could afford to have a number of computers networked together by a LAN. Today network technology has dropped so much in price that two things have happened. First, LANs are now commonplace, even in many household environments. Certainly many Linux users will have two or more computers connected by some Ethernet. Second, network resources, particularly IP addresses, are now a scarce resource, and while they used to be free, they are now being bought and sold.

Most people with a LAN will probably also want an Internet connection that every computer on the LAN can use. The IP routing rules are strict in how they deal with this situation. Traditional solutions to this problem would have involved requesting an IP network address, perhaps a class C address for small sites, assigning each host on the LAN an address from this network and using a router to connect the LAN to the Internet.

In a commercialized Internet environment, this is an expensive proposition. First, you'd be required to pay for the network addresses that are assigned to you. Second, you'd probably have to pay your Internet Service Provider for the privilege of having a suitable route to your network put in place so that the rest of the Internet knows how to reach you. This might still be practical for companies, but domestic installations don't usually justify the cost.

Fortunately, Linux provides an answer to this dilemma. This answer involves a component of a group of advanced networking features called *Network Address Translation* (NAT). NAT describes the process of modifying the network addresses (and sometimes port numbers) contained with packet headers while they are in transit. This might sound odd at first, but we'll show that it is ideal for solving the problem we've just described. IP *masquerading* is the name given to one type of network address translation that allows all of the hosts on a private network to use the Internet at the price of a single dynamic IP address. When the single address is statically assigned, the same functionality goes by the name SNAT (*Source NAT*). We'll refer to both of these as "masquerading" in what follows.

IP masquerading allows you to use private (non-routable) IP network addresses for your hosts on your LAN and have your Linux-based router perform some clever, real-time translation of IP addresses and ports. When it receives a packet from a computer on the LAN, it takes note of the type of packet it is, (such as TCP, UDP or ICMP) and modifies the packet so that it looks like it was generated by the router host itself (and remembers that it has done so). It then transmits the packet onto the Internet with its single connection IP address. When the destination host receives this packet, it believes the packet has come from the routing host and sends any reply packets back to that address. When the Linux masquerade router receives a packet from its Internet connection, it looks in its table of established masqueraded connections to see if this packet actually belongs to a computer on the LAN, and if it does, it reverses the modification it did on the forward path and transmits the packet to the LAN computer. A simple example is illustrated in Figure 9-1.

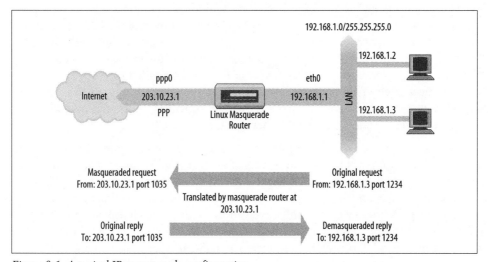

Figure 9-1. A typical IP masquerade configuration

We have a small Ethernet network using one of the reserved network addresses. The network has a Linux-based masquerade router providing access to the Internet. One of the workstations on the network (**192.168.1.3**) wishes to establish a connection to the remote host **209.1.106.178**. The workstation routes its packet to the masquerade router, which identifies this connection request as requiring masquerade services. It accepts the packet and allocates a port number to use (1035), substitutes its own IP address and port number for those of the originating host, and transmits the packet to the destination host. The destination host believes it has received a connection request from the Linux masquerade host and generates a reply packet. The masquerade host, on receiving this packet, finds the association in its masquerade table and reverses the substitution it performed on the outgoing packet. It then transmits the reply packet to the originating host.

The local host believes it is speaking directly to the remote host. The remote host knows nothing about the local host at all and believes it has received a connection from the Linux masquerade host. The Linux masquerade host knows these two hosts are speaking to each other, and on what ports, and performs the address and port translations necessary to allow communication.

This might all seem a little confusing, and it can be, but it works and is actually simple to configure. So don't worry if you don't understand all the details yet.

Side Effects and Fringe Benefits

The IP masquerade facility comes with its own set of side effects, some of which are useful and some of which might become bothersome.

None of the hosts on the supported network behind the masquerade router are ever directly seen; consequently, you need only one valid and routable IP address to allow all hosts to make network connections out onto the Internet. This has a downside: none of those hosts are visible from the Internet and you can't directly connect to them from the Internet; the only host visible on a masqueraded network is the masquerade host itself. This is important when you consider services such as mail or FTP. It helps determine what services should be provided by the masquerade host and what services it should proxy or otherwise treat specially.

However, you can use DNAT (*Destination NAT*) on the router to route inbound connections to certain ports to internal servers. This works great for web and mail servers. You can run those services on hosts on the private network, and use DNAT to forward inbound connections to port 80 and port 25 to the appropriate internal servers. This way, the router host is only involved in routing, not in providing any externally visible services. You can use the same technique to route incoming connections to a high-numbered port (say, 4022) to the Secure Shell (SSH) port (usually 22) on an internal host so you can SSH directly into one of your internal hosts through the router.

Because none of the masqueraded hosts are visible, they are relatively protected from attacks from outside. You can have one host serve as your firewall and masquerading router. Your whole network will be only as safe as your masquerade host, so you should use firewall rules to protect it and you should not run any other externally visible services on it.

IP masquerade will have some impact on the performance of your networking. In typical configurations this will probably be barely measurable. If you have large numbers of active masquerade sessions, though, you may find that the processing required at the masquerade host begins to impact your network throughput. IP masquerade must do a good deal of work for each packet compared to the process of conventional routing. That low-end host you have been planning on using as a masquerade host supporting a personal link to the Internet might be fine, but don't expect too much if you decide you want to use it as a router in your corporate network at Ethernet speeds.

Finally, some network services just won't work through masquerade, or at least not without a lot of help. Typically, these are services that rely on incoming sessions to work, such as some types of Direct Communications Channels (DCC), features in IRC, or certain types of video and audio multicasting services. Some of these services have specially developed "helper" kernel modules to provide solutions for these, and we'll talk about those in a moment. For others, it is possible that you will find no support, so be aware—it won't be suitable in all situations.

Configuring the Kernel for IP Masquerade

To use the IP masquerade facility, your kernel must be compiled with network packet filtering support. You must select the following options when configuring the kernel:

```
Networking options --->
 [M] Network packet filtering (replaces ipchains)
```

The *netfilter* package includes modules that help perform masquerading functions. For example, to provide connection tracking of FTP sessions, you'd load and use the *ip_conntrack_ftp* and *ip_nat_ftp.o* modules. This connection tracking support is required for masquerading to work correctly with protocols that involve multiple connections for one logical session, since masquerading relies on connection tracking.

Configuring IP Masquerade

If you've already read the firewall and accounting chapters, it probably comes as no surprise that the *iptables* command is used to configure the IP masquerade rules as well.

Masquerading is a special type of *packet mangling* (the technical term for modifying packets). You can masquerade only packets that are received on one interface that will be routed to another interface. To configure a masquerade rule, construct a rule very similar to a firewall forwarding rule, but with special options that tell the kernel to masquerade the packet. The *iptables* command uses -j MASQUERADE to indicate that packets matching the rule specification should be masqueraded (this is for a dynamic IP address; if you have a static IP address, use -j SNAT instead).

Let's look at an example. A computing science student at Groucho Marx University has a number of computers at home on a small Ethernet-based LAN. She has chosen to use one of the reserved private Internet network addresses for her network. She shares her accommodation with other students, all of whom have an interest in using the Internet. Because the students' finances are very tight, they cannot afford to use a permanent Internet connection, so instead they use a single Internet connection. They would all like to be able to share the connection to chat on IRC, surf the Web, and retrieve files by FTP directly to each of their computers—IP masquerade is the answer.

The student first configures a Linux host to support the Internet link and to act as a router for the LAN. The IP address she is assigned when she dials up isn't important. She configures the Linux router with IP masquerade and uses one of the private network addresses for her LAN: **192.168.1.0**. She ensures that each of the hosts on the LAN has a default route pointing at the Linux router.

The following *iptables* commands are all that are required to make masquerading work in her configuration:

```
# iptables -t nat -P POSTROUTING DROP
# iptables -t nat -A POSTROUTING -o ppp0 -j MASQUERADE
```

Now whenever any of the LAN hosts try to connect to a service on a remote host, their packets will be automatically masqueraded by the Linux masquerade router. The first rule in each example prevents the Linux host from routing any other packets and also adds some security.

To list the masquerade rules you have created, use the -L argument to the *iptables* command, as we described earlier while discussing firewalls:

```
# iptables -t nat -L
Chain PREROUTING (policy ACCEPT)
target     prot opt source              destination

Chain POSTROUTING (policy DROP)
target     prot opt source              destination
MASQUERADE  all  --  anywhere            anywhere          MASQUERADE

Chain OUTPUT (policy ACCEPT)
target     prot opt source              destination
```

Masquerade rules appear with a target of MASQUERADE.

Handling Nameserver Lookups

Handling domain nameserver lookups from the hosts on the LAN with IP masquerading has always presented a problem. There are two ways of accommodating DNS in a masquerade environment. You can tell each of the hosts to use the same DNS that the Linux router host does, and let IP masquerade do its magic on their DNS requests. Alternatively, you can run a caching nameserver on the Linux host and have each of the hosts on the LAN use the Linux host as their DNS. Although a more aggressive action, this is probably the better option because it reduces the volume of DNS traffic traveling on the Internet link and will be marginally faster for most requests, since they'll be served from the cache. The downside to this configuration is that it is more complex. The section "Caching-Only named Configuration" in Chapter 5 describes how to configure a caching nameserver.

More About Network Address Translation

The *netfilter* software is capable of many different types of NAT. IP masquerade is one simple application of it.

It is possible, for example, to build NAT rules that translate only certain addresses or ranges of addresses and leave all others untouched, or to translate addresses into pools of addresses rather than just a single address, as masquerade does. You can in fact use the *iptables* command to generate NAT rules that map just about anything, with combinations of matches using any of the standard attributes, such as source address, destination address, protocol type, port number, etc.

Translating the source address of a packet is referred to as Source NAT, or SNAT, in *iptables*. Translating the destination address of a packet is known as Destination NAT, or DNAT. SNAT and DNAT are targets that you may use with the *iptables* command to build more sophisticated rules.

CHAPTER 10
Important Network Features

After successfully setting up IP and the resolver (DNS), you then must look at the services you want to provide over the network. This chapter covers the configuration of a few simple network applications, including the *inetd* and *xinetd* servers and the programs from the *rlogin* family. We'll also deal briefly with the Remote Procedure Call interface, upon which services like the Network File System (NFS) are based. The configuration of NFS, however, is more complex and is not described in this book.

Of course, we can't cover all network applications in this book. If you want to install one that's not discussed here, please refer to the manual pages of the server for details.

The inetd Super Server

Programs that provide application services via the network are called network *daemons*. A daemon is a program that opens a port, most commonly a well-known service port, and waits for incoming connections on it. If one occurs, the daemon creates a child process that accepts the connection, while the parent continues to listen for further requests. This mechanism works well but has a few disadvantages; at least one instance of every possible service that you wish to provide must be active in memory at all times. In addition, the software routines that do the listening and port handling must be replicated in every network daemon.

To overcome these inefficiencies, most Unix installations run a special network daemon, what you might consider a "super server." This daemon creates sockets on behalf of a number of services and listens on all of them simultaneously. When an incoming connection is received on any of these sockets, the super server accepts the connection and spawns the server specified for this port, passing the socket across to the child to manage. The server then returns to listening.

The most common super server is called *inetd*, the Internet Daemon. It is started at system boot time and takes the list of services it is to manage from a startup file named */etc/inetd.conf*. In addition to those servers, there are a number of trivial services performed by *inetd* itself called *internal services*. They include *chargen*, which simply generates a string of characters, and *daytime*, which returns the system's idea of the time of day.

An entry in this file consists of a single line made up of the following fields:

```
service type protocol wait user server cmdline
```

Each of the fields is described in the following list:

service

Gives the service name. The service name has to be translated to a port number by looking it up in the */etc/services* file. This file will be described later in this chapter in the "The Services and Protocols Files" section later in this chapter.

type

Specifies a socket type, either stream (for connection-oriented protocols) or dgram (for datagram protocols). TCP-based services should therefore always use stream, while UDP-based services should always use dgram.

protocol

Names the transport protocol used by the service. This must be a valid protocol name found in the *protocols* file, explained later.

wait

This option applies only to dgram sockets. It can be either wait or nowait. If wait is specified, *inetd* executes only one server for the specified port at any time. Otherwise, it immediately continues to listen on the port after executing the server.

This is useful for "single-threaded" servers that read all incoming datagrams until no more arrive, and then exit. Most RPC servers are of this type and should therefore specify wait. The opposite type, "multithreaded" servers, allows an unlimited number of instances to run concurrently. These servers should specify nowait.

stream sockets should always use nowait.

user

This is the login ID of the user who will own the process when it is executing. This will frequently be the *root* user, but some services may use different accounts. It is a very good idea to apply the principle of least privilege here, which states that you shouldn't run a command under a privileged account if the program doesn't require this for proper functioning. For example, the NNTP news server runs as *news*, while services that may pose a security risk (such as tftp or finger) are often run as *nobody*.

server

  Gives the full pathname of the server program to be executed. Internal services are marked by the keyword *internal*.

cmdline

  This is the command line to be passed to the server. It starts with the name of the server to be executed and can include any arguments that need to be passed to it. If you are using the TCP wrapper, you specify the full pathname to the server here. If not, then you just specify the server name as you'd like it to appear in a process list. We'll talk about the TCP wrapper shortly.

  This field is empty for internal services.

A sample *inetd.conf* file is shown in Example 10-1. The finger service is commented out so that it is not available. This is often done for security reasons because it can be used by attackers to obtain names and other details of users on your system.

Example 10-1. A sample /etc/inetd.conf file

```
#
# inetd services
ftp       stream tcp nowait root /usr/sbin/ftpd      in.ftpd -l
telnet    stream tcp nowait root /usr/sbin/telnetd in.telnetd -b/etc/issue
#finger   stream tcp nowait bin   /usr/sbin/fingerd in.fingerd
#tftp     dgram  udp wait   nobody /usr/sbin/tftpd   in.tftpd
#tftp     dgram  udp wait   nobody /usr/sbin/tftpd   in.tftpd /boot/diskless
#login    stream tcp nowait root /usr/sbin/rlogind in.rlogind
#shell    stream tcp nowait root /usr/sbin/rshd     in.rshd
#exec     stream tcp nowait root /usr/sbin/rexecd  in.rexecd
#
#        inetd internal services
#
daytime  stream tcp nowait root internal
daytime  dgram  udp nowait root internal
time     stream tcp nowait root internal
time     dgram  udp nowait root internal
echo     stream tcp nowait root internal
echo     dgram  udp nowait root internal
discard  stream tcp nowait root internal
discard  dgram  udp nowait root internal
chargen  stream tcp nowait root internal
chargen  dgram  udp nowait root internal
```

The *tftp* daemon is shown commented out as well. *tftp* implements the *Trivial File Transfer Protocol* (TFTP), which allows someone to transfer any world-readable files from your system without password checking. This is especially harmful with the */etc/passwd* file, and even more so when you don't use shadow passwords.

tftp is commonly used by diskless clients and X terminals to download their code from a boot server. If you need to run the *tftpd* daemon for this reason, make sure to limit its scope to those directories from which clients will retrieve files; you will need to add those directory names to *tftpd*'s command line. This is shown in the second *tftp* line in the example.

The tcpd Access Control Facility

Since opening a computer to network access involves many security risks, applications are designed to guard against several types of attacks. Some security features, however, may be flawed (most drastically demonstrated by the RTM Internet worm, which exploited a hole in a number of programs, including old versions of the *sendmail* mail daemon), or do not distinguish between secure hosts from which requests for a particular service will be accepted and insecure hosts whose requests should be rejected. We've already briefly discussed the *finger* and *tftp* services. A network administrator would want to limit access to these services to "trusted hosts" only, which is impossible with the usual setup, for which *inetd* provides this service either to all clients or not at all.

A useful tool for managing host-specific access is *tcpd*, often called the daemon "wrapper." For TCP services you want to monitor or protect, it is invoked instead of the server program. *tcpd* checks whether the remote host is allowed to use that service, and only if this succeeds will it execute the real server program. *tcpd* also logs the request to the syslog daemon. Note that this does not work with UDP-based services.

For example, to wrap the *finger* daemon, you have to change the corresponding line in *inetd.conf* from this:

```
# unwrapped finger daemon
finger    stream tcp nowait bin   /usr/sbin/fingerd in.fingerd
```

to this:

```
# wrap finger daemon
finger stream tcp    nowait   root    /usr/sbin/tcpd   in.fingerd
```

Without adding any access control, this will appear to the client as the usual finger setup, except that any requests are logged to syslog's *auth* facility.

Two files called */etc/hosts.allow* and */etc/hosts.deny* implement access control. They contain entries that allow and deny access to certain services and hosts. When *tcpd* handles a request for a service such as *finger* from a client host named *biff.foobar.com*, it scans *hosts.allow* and *hosts.deny* (in this order) for an entry matching both the service and client host. If a matching entry is found in *hosts.allow*, access is granted and tcpd doesn't consult the *hosts.deny* file. If no match is found in the *hosts.allow* file, but a match is found in *hosts.deny*, the request is rejected by closing down the connection. The request is accepted if no match is found at all.

Entries in the access files look like this:

```
servicelist: hostlist [:shellcmd]
```

servicelist is a list of service names from */etc/services*, or the keyword ALL. To match all services except *finger* and *tftp*, use ALL EXCEPT finger, tftp.

hostlist is a list of hostnames, IP addresses, or the keywords ALL, LOCAL, UNKNOWN, or PARANOID. ALL matches any host, while LOCAL matches hostnames that don't contain a dot.* UNKNOWN matches any hosts whose name or address lookup failed. PARANOID matches any host whose hostname does not resolve back to its IP address.† A name starting with a dot matches all hosts whose domain is equal to this name. For example, .foobar.com matches **biff.foobar.com**, but not **nurks.fredsville.com**. A pattern that ends with a dot matches any host whose IP address begins with the supplied pattern, so **172.16.** matches **172.16.32.0**, but not **172.15.9.1**. A pattern of the form *n.n.n.n/m.m.m.m* is treated as an IP address and network mask, so we could specify our previous example as **172.16.0.0/255.255.0.0** instead. Lastly, any pattern beginning with a "/" character allows you to specify a file that is presumed to contain a list of hostname or IP address patterns, any of which are allowed to match. So a pattern that looked like */var/access/trustedhosts* would cause the *tcpd* daemon to read that file, testing if any of the lines in it matched the connecting host.

To deny access to the *finger* and *tftp* services to all but the local hosts, put the following in */etc/hosts.deny* and leave */etc/hosts.allow* empty:

```
in.tftpd, in.fingerd: ALL EXCEPT LOCAL, .your.domain
```

The optional *shellcmd* field may contain a shell command to be invoked when the entry is matched. This is useful to set up traps that may expose potential attackers. The following example creates a logfile listing the user and host connecting, and if the host is not **vlager.vbrew.com**, it will append the output of a finger to that host:

```
in.ftpd: ALL EXCEPT LOCAL, .vbrew.com : \
    echo "request from %d@%h: >> /var/log/finger.log; \
    if [ %h != "vlager.vbrew.com:" ]; then \
        finger -l @%h >> /var/log/finger.log \
    fi
```

The %h and %d arguments are expanded by *tcpd* to the client hostname and service name, respectively. Please refer to the *hosts_access(5)* manpage for details.

The xinetd Alternative

An alternative to the standard *inetd* has emerged and is now widely accepted. It is considered a more secure and robust program, and provides protection against some

---

* Usually only local hostnames obtained from lookups in */etc/hosts* contain no dots.

† While its name suggests it is an extreme measure, the PARANOID keyword is a good default, as it protects you against mailicious hosts pretending to be someone they are not. Not all tcpd are supplied with PARANOID compiled in; if yours is not, you need to recompile tcpd to use it.

DoS attacks used against *inetd*. The number of features offered by *xinetd* also makes it a more appealing alternative. Here is a brief list of features:

- Provides full-featured access control and logging
- Limits to the number of servers run at a single time
- Offers granular service-binding -services, which can be bound to specific IP addresses

xinetd is now a standard part of most Linux distributions, but if you need to find the latest source code or information, check the main distribution web site *http://www. xinetd.org*. If you are compiling, and use IPv6, you should make certain that you use the --with-inet6 option.

The configuration of *xinetd* is somewhat different, but not more complex than *inetd*. Rather than forcing one master configuration file for all services, *xinetd* can be configured to use a master configuration file, */etc/xinetd.conf*, and separate configuration files for each additional service configured. This, aside from simplifying configuration, allows for more granular configuration of each service, leading to *xinetd*'s greater flexibility.

The first file you'll need to configure is */etc/xinetd.conf*. A sample file looks like this:

```
# Sample configuration file for xinetd

defaults
{
        only_from      = localhost
        instances      = 60
        log_type       = SYSLOG authpriv info
        log_on_success = HOST PID
        log_on_failure = HOST
        cps            = 25 30
}

includedir /etc/xinetd.d
```

There are a number of options that can be configured, the options used above are:

only_from
> This specifies the IP addresses or hostnames from which you allow connections. In this example, we've restricted connections to the loopback interface only.

instances
> This sets the total number of servers that *xinetd* will run. Having this set to a reasonable number can help prevent malicious users from carrying out a DoS attack against your machine.

log_type SYSLOG|FILE
> This option allows you to set the type of logging you're planning to use. There are two options, syslog or file. The first, syslog, will send all log information to

the system log. The `file` directive will send logs to a file you specify. For a list of the additional options under each of these, see the *xinetd.conf* manpage.

`log_on_success`

With this option, you can set the type of information logged when a user connection is successful. Here's a list of some available suboptions:

`HOST`

This will log the remote host's IP address.

`PID`

This logs the new server's process ID.

`DURATION`

Enable this to have the total session time logged.

`TRAFFIC`

This option may be helpful for administrators concerned with network usage. Enabling this will log the total number of bytes in/out.

log_on_failure

`HOST`

This will log the remote host's IP address.

`ATTEMPT`

This logs all failed attempts to access services.

cps

Another security feature, this option will limit the incoming rate of connections to a service. It requires two options: the first is the number of connections per second which are allowed, and the second is the amount of time in seconds the service will be disabled.

Any of these options can be overridden in the individual service configuration files, which we're including in the */etc/xinetd.d* directory. These options set in the master configuration file will serve as default values. Configuration of individual services is also this simple. Here's an example of the FTP service, as configured for *xinetd*:

```
service ftp
{
        socket_type     = stream
        wait            = no
        user            = root
        server          = /usr/sbin/vsftpd
        server_args     = /etc/vsftpd/vsftpd.conf
        log_on_success  += DURATION USERID
        log_on_failure  += USERID
        nice            = 10
        disable         = no
}
```

The first thing you will want to note is that in the *xinetd.d* directory, the individual services tend to be helpfully named, which makes individual configuration files easier to identify and manage. In this case, the file is simply called *vsftp*, referring to the name of the FTP server we're using.

Taking a look at this example, the first active configuration line defines the name of the service that's being configured. Surprisingly, the service type is not defined by the *service* directive. The rest of the configuration is contained in brackets, much like functions in C. Some of the options used within the service configurations overlap those found in the defaults section. If an item is defined in the defaults and then defined again in the individual service configuration, the latter takes priority. There are a large number of configuration options available and are discussed in detail in the *xinetd.conf* manpage, but to get a basic service running, we need only a few:

socket_type

> This defines the type of socket used by the service. Administrators familiar with *inetd* will recognize the following available options, such as *stream*, *dgram*, *raw*, and *seqpacket*.

wait

> This option specifies whether the service is single or dual-threaded. yes means that the service is single threaded and that *xinetd* will start the service and then will stop handling requests for new connections until the current session ends. no means that new session requests can be processed.

user

> Here, you set the name of the user that will run the service.

server

> This option is used to specify location of the service that's being run.

server_args

> You can use this option to specify any additional options that need to be passed to the server.

nice

> This option determines the server priority. Again, this is an option that can be used to limit resources used by servers.

disable

> Really a very straightforward option, this determines whether or not the service is enabled.

The Services and Protocols Files

The port numbers on which certain "standard" services are offered are defined in the Assigned Numbers RFC. To enable server and client programs to convert service names to these numbers, at least part of the list is kept on each host; it is stored in a file called */etc/services*. An entry is made up like this:

```
service port/protocol   [aliases]
```

Here, *service* specifies the service name, *port* defines the port the service is offered on, and *protocol* defines which transport protocol is used. Commonly, the latter field is either *udp* or *tcp*. It is possible for a service to be offered for more than one protocol, as well as offering different services on the same port as long as the protocols are different. The *aliases* field allows you to specify alternative names for the same service.

Usually, you don't have to change the services file that comes along with the network software on your Linux system. Nevertheless, we give a small excerpt from that file in Example 10-2.

Example 10-2. A sample /etc/services file

```
# /etc/services

tcpmux          1/tcp                           # TCP port service multiplexer
echo            7/tcp
echo            7/udp
discard         9/tcp           sink null
discard         9/udp           sink null
systat          11/tcp          users
daytime         13/tcp
daytime         13/udp
netstat         15/tcp
qotd            17/tcp          quote
msp             18/tcp                          # message send protocol
msp             18/udp                          # message send protocol
chargen         19/tcp          ttytst source
chargen         19/udp          ttytst source
ftp-data        20/tcp
ftp             21/tcp
fsp             21/udp          fspd
ssh             22/tcp                          # SSH Remote Login Protocol
ssh             22/udp                          # SSH Remote Login Protocol
telnet          23/tcp
# 24 - private
smtp            25/tcp          mail
# 26 - unassigned
```

Like the services file, the networking library needs a way to translate protocol names—for example, those used in the services file—to protocol numbers understood by the IP layer on other hosts. This is done by looking up the name in the */etc/protocols* file. It contains one entry per line, each containing a protocol name, and the associated number. Having to touch this file is even more unlikely than having to meddle with */etc/services*. A sample file is given in Example 10-3.

Example 10-3. A sample /etc/protocols file

```
#
# Internet (IP) protocols
#
```

Example 10-3. A sample /etc/protocols file (continued)

```
ip        0      IP          # internet protocol, pseudo protocol number
icmp      1      ICMP        # internet control message protocol
igmp      2      IGMP        # internet group multicast protocol
tcp       6      TCP         # transmission control protocol
udp       17     UDP         # user datagram protocol
raw       255    RAW         # RAW IP interface

esp       50     ESP         # Encap Security Payload for IPv6
ah        51     AH          # Authentication Header for IPv6
skip      57     SKIP        # SKIP
ipv6-icmp 58     IPv6-ICMP   # ICMP for IPv6
ipv6-nonxt 59    IPv6-NoNxt  # No Next Header for IPv6
ipv6-opts 60     IPv6-Opts   # Destination Options for IPv6
rspf      73     RSPF        # Radio Shortest Path First.
```

Remote Procedure Call

The general mechanism for client-server applications is provided by the *Remote Procedure Call* (RPC) package. RPC was developed by Sun Microsystems and is a collection of tools and library functions. An important application built on top of RPC is NFS.

An RPC server consists of a collection of procedures that a client can call by sending an RPC request to the server along with the procedure parameters. The server will invoke the indicated procedure on behalf of the client, handing back the return value, if there is any. In order to be machine-independent, all data exchanged between client and server is converted to the *External Data Representation* format (XDR) by the sender, and converted back to the machine-local representation by the receiver. RPC relies on standard UDP and TCP sockets to transport the XDR formatted data to the remote host. Sun has graciously placed RPC in the public domain; it is described in a series of RFCs.

Sometimes improvements to an RPC application introduce incompatible changes in the procedure call interface. Of course, simply changing the server would crash all applications that still expect the original behavior. Therefore, RPC programs have version numbers assigned to them, usually starting with 1, and with each new version of the RPC interface, this counter will be bumped up. Often, a server may offer several versions simultaneously; clients then indicate by the version number in their requests which implementation of the service they want to use.

The communication between RPC servers and clients is somewhat peculiar. An RPC server offers one or more collections of procedures; each set is called a *program* and is uniquely identified by a *program number*. A list that maps service names to program numbers is usually kept in */etc/rpc*, an excerpt of which is shown in Example 10-4.

Example 10-4. A sample /etc/rpc file

```
#
# /etc/rpc - miscellaneous RPC-based services
#
portmapper      100000  portmap sunrpc
rstatd          100001  rstat rstat_svc rup perfmeter
rusersd         100002  rusers
nfs             100003  nfsprog
ypserv          100004  ypprog
mountd          100005  mount showmount
ypbind          100007
walld           100008  rwall shutdown
yppasswdd       100009  yppasswd
bootparam       100026
ypupdated       100028  ypupdate
```

In TCP/IP networks, the authors of RPC faced the problem of mapping program numbers to generic network services. They designed each server to provide both a TCP and a UDP port for each program and each version. Generally, RPC applications use UDP when sending data and fall back to TCP only when the data to be transferred doesn't fit into a single UDP datagram.

Of course, client programs need to find out to which port a program number maps. Using a configuration file for this would be too inflexible; since RPC applications don't use reserved ports, there's no guarantee that a port originally meant to be used by our database application hasn't been taken by some other process. Therefore, RPC applications pick any available port and register it with a special program called the *portmapper daemon*. The portmapper acts as a service broker for all RPC servers running on its machine. A client that wishes to contact a service with a given program number first queries the portmapper on the server's host, which returns the TCP and UDP port numbers the service can be reached at.

This method introduces a single point of failure, much like the *inetd* daemon does for the standard Berkeley services. However, this case is even a little worse because when the portmapper dies, all RPC port information is lost; this usually means that you have to restart all RPC servers manually or reboot the entire machine.

On Linux, the portmapper is called */sbin/portmap*, or sometimes */usr/sbin/rpc.portmap*. Other than making sure it is started from your network boot scripts, the portmapper doesn't require any configuration.

Configuring Remote Login and Execution

It's often very useful to execute a command on a remote host and have input or output from that command be read from, or written to, a network connection.

The traditional commands used for executing commands on remote hosts are *rlogin*, *rsh*, and *rcp*. We briefly discussed the security issues associated with it in Chapter 1 and suggested *ssh* as a replacement. The *ssh* package provides replacements called *ssh* and *scp*.

Each of these commands spawns a shell on the remote host and allows the user to execute commands. Of course, the client needs to have an account on the remote host where the command is to be executed. Thus, all these commands use an authentication process. The *r* commands use a simple username and password exchange between the hosts with no encryption, so anyone listening could easily intercept the passwords. The *ssh* command suite provides a higher level of security: it uses a technique called Public Key Cryptography, which provides authentication and encryption between the hosts to ensure that neither passwords nor session data are easily intercepted by other hosts.

It is possible to relax authentication checks for certain users even further. For instance, if you frequently have to log in to other machines on your LAN, you might want to be admitted without having to type your password every time. This was always possible with the *r* commands, but the *ssh* suite allows you to do this a little more easily. It's still not a great idea because it means that if an account on one machine is breached, access can be gained to all other accounts that user has configured for password-less login, but it is very convenient and people will use it.

Let's talk about removing the *r* commands and getting *ssh* to work instead.

Disabling the r Commands

Start by removing the *r* commands if they're installed. The easiest way to disable the old *r* commands is to comment out (or remove) their entries in the */etc/inetd.conf* file. The relevant entries will look something like this:

```
# Shell, login, exec and talk are BSD protocols.
shell    stream  tcp    nowait  root  /usr/sbin/tcpd /usr/sbin/in.rshd
login    stream  tcp    nowait  root  /usr/sbin/tcpd /usr/sbin/in.rlogind
exec     stream  tcp    nowait  root  /usr/sbin/tcpd /usr/sbin/in.rexecd
```

You can comment them by placing a # character at the start of each line, or delete the lines completely. Remember, you need to restart the *inetd* daemon for this change to take effect. Ideally, you should remove the daemon programs themselves, too.

Installing and Configuring ssh

OpenSSH is a free version of the *ssh* suite of programs; the Linux port can be found at *ftp://ftp.openbsd.org/pub/OpenBSD/OpenSSH/portable/* and in most modern Linux distributions.* We won't describe compilation here; good instructions are included in

---

* OpenSSH was developed by the OpenBSD project and is a fine example of the benefit of free software.

the source. If you can install it from a precompiled package, then it's probably wise to do so.

There are two parts to an *ssh* session. There is an *ssh* client that you need to configure and run on the local host and an ssh daemon that must be running on the remote host.

The ssh daemon

The *sshd* daemon is the program that listens for network connections from *ssh* clients, manages authentication, and executes the requested command. It has one main configuration file called */etc/ssh/sshd_config* and a special file containing a key used by the authentication and encryption processes to represent the host end. Each host and each client has its own key.

A utility called *ssh-keygen* is supplied to generate a random key. This is usually used once at installation time to generate the host key, which the system administrator usually stores in a file called */etc/ssh/ssh_host_key*. Keys can be of any length of 512 bits or greater. By default, *ssh-keygen* generates keys of 1,024 bits in length, and most people use the default. Using OpenSSH with SSH Version 2, you will need to generate RSA and DSA keys. To generate the keys, you would invoke the *ssh-keygen* command like this:

```
# ssh-keygen -t rsa1 -f /etc/openssh/ssh_host_key -N ""
# ssh-keygen -t dsa -f /etc/openssh/ssh_host_dsa_key -N ""
# ssh-keygen -t rsa -f /etc/openssh/ssh_host_rsa_key -N ""
```

You will be prompted to enter a passphrase if you omit the -N option. However, host keys must not use a passphrase, so just press the return key to leave it blank. The program output will look something like this:

```
Generating public/private dsa key pair.
Your identification has been saved in sshkey.
Your public key has been saved in sshkey.pub.
The key fingerprint is:
fb:bf:d1:53:08:7a:29:6f:fb:45:96:63:7a:6e:04:22 tb@eskimo 1024
```

You've probably noticed that three different keys were created. The first one, type rsa1, is used for SSH protocol Version 1, the next two types, rsa and dsa, are used for SSH protocol Version 2. It is recommended that SSH protocol Version 2 be used in place of SSH protocol Version 1 because of potential man-in-the-middle and other attacks against SSH protocol Version 1.

You will find at the end that two files have been created for each key. The first is called the private key, which must be kept secret and will be in */etc/openssh/ssh_host_key*. The second is called the public key and is one that you can share; it will be in */etc/openssh/ssh_host_key.pub*.

Armed with the keys for *ssh* communication, you need to create a configuration file. The *ssh* suite is very powerful and the configuration file may contain many options.

We'll present a simple example to get you started; you should refer to the *ssh* documentation to enable other features. The following code shows a safe and minimal *sshd* configuration file. The rest of the configuration options are detailed in the *sshd(8)* manpage:

```
#         $OpenBSD: sshd_config,v 1.59 2002/09/25 11:17:16 markus Exp $

#Port 22
Protocol 2
#ListenAddress 0.0.0.0
#ListenAddress ::

# HostKeys for protocol version 2
HostKey /etc/openssh/ssh_host_rsa_key
HostKey /etc/openssh/ssh_host_dsa_key

# Lifetime and size of ephemeral version 1 server key
#KeyRegenerationInterval 3600
#ServerKeyBits 768

# Authentication:

#LoginGraceTime 120
#PermitRootLogin yes
#StrictModes yes

#RSAAuthentication yes
#PubkeyAuthentication yes
# Change to yes if you don't trust ~/.ssh/known_hosts for
# RhostsRSAAuthentication and HostbasedAuthentication
#IgnoreUserKnownHosts no

# To disable tunneled clear text passwords, change to no here!
#PasswordAuthentication yes
#PermitEmptyPasswords no

# Change to no to disable s/key passwords
#ChallengeResponseAuthentication yes

#X11Forwarding no
#X11DisplayOffset 10
#X11UseLocalhost yes
#PrintMotd yes
#PrintLastLog yes
#KeepAlive yes
#UseLogin no
#UsePrivilegeSeparation yes
#PermitUserEnvironment no
MaxStartups 10
# no default banner path
#Banner /some/path
#VerifyReverseMapping no
```

```
# override default of no subsystems
Subsystem       sftp    /usr/lib/misc/sftp-server
```

It's important to make sure the permissions of the configuration files are correct to ensure that system security is maintained. Use the following commands:

```
# chown -R root:root /etc/ssh
# chmod 755 /etc/ssh
# chmod 600 /etc/ssh/ssh_host_rsa_key
# chmod 600 /etc/ssh/ssh_host_dsa_key
# chmod 644 /etc/ssh/sshd_config
```

The final stage of *sshd* administration daemon is to run it. Normally you'd create an *rc* file for it or add it to an existing one, so that it is automatically executed at boot time. The daemon runs standalone and doesn't require any entry in the */etc/inetd. conf* file. The daemon must be run as the *root* user. The syntax is very simple:

```
/usr/sbin/sshd
```

The *sshd* daemon will automatically place itself into the background when being run. You are now ready to accept *ssh* connections.

The ssh client

There are a number of *ssh* client programs: *slogin*, *scp*, and *ssh*. They each read the same configuration file, usually called */etc/openssh/ssh_config*. They each also read configuration files from the *.ssh* directory in the home directory of the user executing them. The most important of these files is the *.ssh/config* file, which may contain options that override those specified in the */etc/openssh/ssh_config* file, the *.ssh/identity* file, which contains the user's own private key, and the corresponding *.ssh/identity.pub* file, containing the user's public key. Other important files are *.ssh/known_hosts* and *.ssh/authorized_keys*; we'll talk about those in the next section, "Using ssh." First, let's create the global configuration file and the user key file.

/etc/ssh/ssh_config is very similar to the server configuration file. Again, there are lots of features that you can configure, but a minimal configuration looks like that presented in Example 10-5. The rest of the configuration options are detailed in the *sshd(8)* manpage. You can add sections that match specific hosts or groups of hosts. The parameter to the "Host" statement may be either the full name of a host or a wildcard specification, as we've used in our example, to match all hosts. We could create an entry that used, for example, Host *.vbrew.com to match any host in the **vbrew.com** domain.

Example 10-5. Example ssh client configuration file

```
#       $OpenBSD: ssh_config,v 1.19 2003/08/13 08:46:31 markus Exp $


# Site-wide defaults for various options

# Host *
```

Example 10-5. Example ssh client configuration file (continued)

```
#    ForwardAgent no
#    ForwardX11 no
#    RhostsRSAAuthentication no
#    RSAAuthentication yes
#    PasswordAuthentication yes
#    HostbasedAuthentication no
#    BatchMode no
#    CheckHostIP yes
#    AddressFamily any
#    ConnectTimeout 0
#    StrictHostKeyChecking ask
#    IdentityFile ~/.ssh/identity
#    IdentityFile ~/.ssh/id_rsa
#    IdentityFile ~/.ssh/id_dsa
#    Port 22
#    Protocol 2,1
#    Cipher 3des
#    Ciphers aes128-cbc,3des-cbc,blowfish-cbc,cast128-cbc,arcfour,aes192-cbc,aes2
56-cbc
#    EscapeChar ~
```

We mentioned in the server configuration section that every host and user has a key. The user's key is stored in his or her *~/.ssh/indentity* file. To generate the key, use the same *ssh-keygen* command we used to generate the host key, except this time you do not need to specify the name of the file in which you save the key. The *ssh-keygen* defaults to the correct location, but it prompts you to enter a filename in case you'd like to save it elsewhere. It is sometimes useful to have multiple identity files, so *ssh* allows this. Just as before, *ssh-keygen* will prompt you to entry a passphrase. Passphrases add yet another level of security and are a good idea. Your passphrase won't be echoed on the screen when you type it.

 There is no way to recover a passphrase if you forget it. Make sure it is something you will remember, but as with all passwords, make it something that isn't obvious, like a proper noun or your name. For a passphrase to be truly effective, it should be between 10 and 30 characters long and not be plain English prose. Try to throw in some unusual characters. If you forget your passphrase, you will be forced to generate a new key.

You should ask each of your users to run the *ssh-keygen* command just once to ensure their key file is created correctly. The ssh-keygen will create their *~/.ssh/* directories for them with appropriate permissions and create their private and public keys in *.ssh/identity* and *.ssh/identity.pub*, respectively. A sample session should look like this:

```
$ ssh-keygen
Key generation complete.
Enter file in which to save the key (/home/maggie/.ssh/identity):
```

```
Enter passphrase (empty for no passphrase):
Enter same passphrase again:
Your identification has been saved in /home/maggie/.ssh/identity.
Your public key has been saved in /home/maggie/.ssh/identity.pub.
The key fingerprint is:
1024 85:49:53:f4:8a:d6:d9:05:d0:1f:23:c4:d7:2a:11:67 maggie@moria
$
```

Now *ssh* is ready to run.

Using ssh

We should now have the *ssh* command and its associated programs installed and ready to run. Let's now take a quick look at how to run them.

First, we'll try a remote login to a host. The first time you attempt a connection to a host, the *ssh* client will retrieve the public key of the host and ask you to confirm its identity by prompting you with a shortened version of the public key called a finger-print.

The administrator at the remote host should have supplied you in advance with its public key fingerprint, which you should add to your *.ssh/known_hosts* file. If the remote administrator has not supplied you the appropriate key, you can connect to the remote host, but *ssh* will warn you that it does have a key and prompt you whether you wish to accept the one offered by the remote host. Assuming that you're sure no one is engaging in DNS spoofing and you are in fact talking to the correct host, answer yes to the prompt. The relevant key is then stored automatically in your *.ssh/known_hosts* and you will not be prompted for it again. If, on a future connection attempt, the public key retrieved from that host does not match the one that is stored, you will be warned, because this represents a potential security breach.

A first-time login to a remote host will look something like this:

```
$ ssh vlager.vbrew.com
The authenticity of host `vlager.vbrew.com' can't be established.
Key fingerprint is 1024 7b:d4:a8:28:c5:19:52:53:3a:fe:8d:95:dd:14:93:f5.
Are you sure you want to continue connecting (yes/no)? yes
Warning: Permanently added 'vchianti.vbrew.com,172.16.2.3' to the list of/
    known hosts.
maggie@vlager.vbrew.com's password:
Last login: Tue Feb  1 23:28:58 2004 from vstout.vbrew.com
$
```

You will be prompted for a password, which you should answer with the password belonging to the remote account, not the local one. This password is not echoed when you type it.

Without any special arguments, *ssh* will attempt to log in with the same user ID used on the local machine. You can override this using the -1 argument, supplying an alternate login name on the remote host. This is what we did in our example earlier in the book. Alternately, you can use the *userid@hostname.ext* format to specify a different username.

We can copy files to and from the remote host using the *scp* program. Its syntax is similar to the conventional cp with the exception that you may specify a hostname before a filename, meaning that the file path is on the specified host (It is also possible to use the *userid@hostname* format previously mentioned). The following example illustrates *scp* syntax by copying a local file called */tmp/fred* to the */home/maggie/* of the remote host **vlager.vbrew.com**:

```
$ scp /tmp/fred vlager.vbrew.com:/home/maggie/
maggie@vlager.vbrew.com's password:
fred                       100% |***************************| 50165   00:01 ETA
```

Again, you'll be prompted for a password. The *scp* command displays useful progress messages by default. You can copy a file from a remote host with the same ease; simply specify its hostname and file path as the source and the local path as the destination. It's even possible to copy a file from a remote host to some other remote host, but it is something you wouldn't normally want to do, because all of the data travels via your host.

You can execute commands on remote hosts using the *ssh* command. Again, its syntax is very simple. Let's have our user *maggie* retrieve the root directory of the remote host **vchianti.vbrew.com**. She'd do this with the following:

```
$ ssh vchianti.vbrew.com ls -CF /
maggie@vchianti.vbrew.com's password:
bin/    ftp/         mnt/    sbin/                            tmp/
boot/   home/        opt/    service/                         usr/
dev/    lib/         proc/   stage3-pentium3-1.4-20030726.tar.bz2  var/
etc/    lost+found/  root/
```

You can place *ssh* in a command pipeline and pipe program input/output to or from it just like any other command, except that the input or output is directed to or from the remote host via the *ssh* connection. Here is an example of how you might use this capability in combination with the *tar* command to copy a whole directory with subdirectories and files from a remote host to the local host:

```
$ ssh vchianti.vbrew.com "tar cf - /etc/" | tar xvf -
maggie@vchianti.vbrew.com's password:
etc/GNUstep
etc/Muttrc
etc/Net
etc/X11
etc/adduser.conf
..
..
```

Here we surrounded the command we will execute with quotation marks to make it clear what is passed as an argument to *ssh* and what is used by the local shell. This command executes the *tar* command on the remote host to archive the */etc/* directory and write the output to standard output. We've piped to an instance of the *tar* command running on our local host in extract mode reading from standard input.

Again, we were prompted for the password. Let's now configure our local *ssh* client so that it won't prompt for a password when connecting to the **vchianti.vbrew.com** host. We mentioned the *.ssh/authorized_keys* file earlier; this is where it is used. The *.ssh/authorized_keys* file contains the *public* keys on any remote user accounts that we wish to automatically log in to. You can set up automatic logins by copying the contents of the *.ssh/identity.pub* from the *remote* account into our local *.ssh/authorized_keys* file. It is vital that the file permissions of *.ssh/authorized_keys* allow only that you read and write it; anyone may steal and use the keys to log in to that remote account. To ensure the permissions are correct, change *.ssh/authorized_keys*, as shown:

```
$ chmod 600 ~/.ssh/authorized_keys
```

The public keys are a long *single* line of plain text. If you use copy and paste to duplicate the key into your local file, be sure to remove any end of line characters that might have been introduced along the way. The *.ssh/authorized_keys* file may contain many such keys, each on a line of its own.

The *ssh* suite of tools is very powerful, and there are many other useful features and options that you will be interested in exploring. Please refer to the manpages and other documentation that is supplied with the package for more information.

## CHAPTER 11

Administration Issues with Electronic Mail

Electronic mail transport has been one of the most prominent uses of networking since networks were devised. Email started as a simple service that copied a file from one machine to another and appended it to the recipient's *mailbox* file. The concept remains the same, although an ever-growing net, with its complex routing requirements and its ever increasing load of messages, has made a more elaborate scheme necessary.

Various standards of mail exchange have been devised. Sites on the Internet adhere to one laid out in RFC 822, augmented by some RFCs that describe a machine-independent way of transferring just about *anything*, including graphics, sound files, and special characters sets, by email.* CCITT has defined another standard, X.400. It is still used in some large corporate and government environments, but is progressively being retired.

Quite a number of mail transport programs have been implemented for Unix systems. One of the best known is *sendmail*, which was developed by Eric Allman at the University of California at Berkeley. Eric Allman now offers *sendmail* through a commercial venture, but the program remains free software. *sendmail* is supplied as the standard mail transfer agent (or MTA) in some Linux distributions. We describe *sendmail* configuration in Chapter 12.

sendmail supports a set of configuration files that have to be customized for your system. Apart from the information that is required to make the mail subsystem run (such as the local hostname), there are many parameters that may be tuned. *sendmail*'s main configuration file is very hard to understand at first. It looks as if your cat has taken a nap on your keyboard with the Shift key pressed. Luckily, modern configuration techniques take away a lot of the head scratching.

---

* Read RFC 1437 if you don't believe this statement!

When users retrieve mail on their personal systems, they need another protocol to use to contact the mail server. In Chapter 15 we discuss a powerful and increasingly popular type of server called IMAP.

In this chapter, we deal with what email is and what issues administrators have to deal with. Chapter 12 provides instructions on setting up *sendmail* for the first time. The information included should help smaller sites become operational, but there are several more options and you can spend many happy hours in front of your computer configuring the fanciest features.

For more information about issues specific to electronic mail on Linux, please refer to the *Electronic Mail HOWTO* by Guylhem Aznar. The source distribution of *sendmail* also contains extensive documentation that should answer most questions on setting it up.

What Is a Mail Message?

A mail message generally consists of a message body, which is the text of the message, and special administrative data specifying recipients, transport medium, etc., similar to what you see when you look at a physical letter's envelope.

This administrative data falls into two categories. In the first category is any data that is specific to the transport medium, such as the address of sender and recipient. It is therefore called the *envelope*. It may be transformed by the transport software as the message is passed along.

The second variety is any data necessary for handling the mail message, which is not particular to any transport mechanism, such as the message's subject line, a list of all recipients, and the date the message was sent. In many networks, it has become standard to prepend this data to the mail message, forming the so-called *mail header*. It is offset from the *mail body* by an empty line.* Most mail transport software in the Unix world use a header format outlined in RFC 822. Its original purpose was to specify a standard for use on the ARPANET, but since it was designed to be independent from any environment, it has been easily adapted to other networks, including many UUCP-based networks.

RFC 822 is only the lowest common denominator, however. More recent standards have been conceived to cope with growing needs such as data encryption, international character set support, and Multipurpose Internet Mail Extensions (MIME), described in RFC 1341 and other RFCs.

---

* It is customary to append a *signature* or *.sig* to a mail message, usually containing information on the author. It is offset from the mail message by a line containing "-- ", followed by a space. Netiquette dictates, "Keep it short."

In all these standards, the header consists of several lines separated by an end-of-line sequence. A line is made up of a field name, beginning in column one, and the field itself, offset by a colon and whitespace. The format and semantics of each field vary depending on the field name. A header field can be continued across a newline if the next line begins with a whitespace character such as tab. Fields can appear in any order.

A typical mail header may look like this:

```
Return-Path: <root@oreilly.com>
X-Original-To: spam@xtivix.com
Delivered-To: spam@ xtivix.com
Received: from smtp2.oreilly.com (smtp2.oreilly.com [209.58.173.10])
    by www.berkeleywireless.net (Postfix) with ESMTP id B05C520DF0A
    for <spam@ xtivix.com>; Wed, 16 Jul 2003 06:08:44 -0700 (PDT)
Received: (from root@localhost)
    by smtp2.oreilly.com (8.11.2/8.11.2) id h6GD5f920140;
    Wed, 16 Jul 2003 09:05:41 -0400 (EDT)
Date: Wed, 16 Jul 2003 09:05:41 -0400 (EDT)
Message-Id: <200307161305.h6GD5f920140@smtp2.oreilly.com>
From: Andy Oram <root@oreilly.com>
To: spam@ xtivix.com
Subject: Article on IPv6
```

Usually, all necessary header fields are generated by the mail reader you use, such as *elm*, *Outlook*, *Evolution*, or *pine*. However, some are optional and may be added by the user. *elm*, for example, allows you to edit part of the message header. Others are added by the mail transport software. If you look into a local *mailbox* file, you may see each mail message preceded by a "From" line (note: no colon). This is not an RFC 822 header; it has been inserted by your mail software as a convenience to programs reading the mailbox. To avoid potential trouble with lines in the message body that also begin with "From," it has become standard procedure to escape any such occurrence in the body of a mail message by preceding it with a > character.

This list is a collection of common header fields and their meanings:

From:
> This contains the sender's email address and possibly the "real name." Many different formats are used here, as almost every mailer wants to do this a different way.

To:
> This is a list of recipient email addresses. Multiple recipient addresses are separated by a comma.

Cc:
> This is a list of email addresses that will receive "carbon copies" of the message. Multiple recipient addresses are separated by a comma.

Bcc:

This is a list of hidden email addresses that will receive "carbon copies" of the message. The key difference between a "Cc:" and a "Bcc:" is that the addresses listed in a "Bcc:" will not appear in the header of the mail messages delivered to any recipient. It's a way of alerting recipients that you've sent copies of the message to other people without telling the others. Multiple recipient addresses are separated by a comma.

Subject:

Describes the content of the mail in a few words.

Date:

Supplies the date and time the mail was sent.

Reply-To:

Specifies the address that the sender wants the recipient's reply directed to. This may be useful if you have several accounts, but want to receive the bulk of mail only on the one you use most frequently. This field is optional.

Organization:

The organization that owns the machine from which the mail originates. If your machine is owned by you privately, either leave this out, or insert "private" or some complete nonsense. This field is not described by any RFC and is completely optional. Some mail programs support it directly, many don't.

Message-ID:

A string generated by the mail transport on the originating system. It uniquely identifies this message.

Received:

Every site that processes your mail (including the machines of sender and recipient) inserts such a field into the header, giving its site name, a message ID, time and date it received the message, which site it is from, and which transport software was used. These lines allow you to trace which route the message took, and you can complain to the person responsible if something went wrong.

X-anything:

No mail-related programs should complain about any header that starts with X-. It is used to implement additional features that have not yet made it into an RFC, or never will. For example, there was once a very large Linux mailing list server that allowed you to specify which channel you wanted the mail to go to by adding the string X-Mn-Key: followed by the channel name.

How Is Mail Delivered?

Generally, you will compose mail using a program such as *mail* or *mailx*, or more sophisticated ones such as *mutt*, *tkrat*, or *pine*. These programs are called *mail user agents* (MUAs). If you send a mail message, the interface program will in most cases hand it to another program for delivery. This is called the mail transport agent (MTA). On most systems the same MTA is used for both local and remote delivery and is usually invoked as */usr/sbin/sendmail*, or on non-FSSTND compliant systems as */usr/lib/sendmail*.

Local delivery of mail is, of course, more than just appending the incoming message to the recipient's mailbox. Usually, the local MTA understands aliasing (setting up local recipient addresses pointing to other addresses) and forwarding (redirecting a user's mail to some other destination). Also, messages that cannot be delivered must usually be *bounced*—that is, returned to the sender along with some error message.

For remote delivery, the transport software used depends on the nature of the link. Mail delivered over a network using TCP/IP commonly uses *Simple Mail Transfer Protocol* (SMTP), which is described in RFC 821. SMTP was designed to deliver mail directly to a recipient's machine, negotiating the message transfer with the remote side's SMTP daemon. Today it is common practice for organizations to establish special hosts that accept all mail for recipients in the organization and for that host to manage appropriate delivery to the intended recipient.

Email Addresses

Email addresses are made up of at least two parts. One part is the name of a *mail domain* that will ultimately translate to either the recipient's host or some host that accepts mail on behalf of the recipient. The other part is some form of unique user identification that may be the login name of that user, the real name of that user in "Firstname.Lastname" format, or an arbitrary alias that will be translated into a user or list of users. Other mail addressing schemes, such as X.400, use a more general set of "attributes" that are used to look up the recipient's host in an X.500 directory server.

How email addresses are interpreted depends greatly on what type of network you use. We'll concentrate on how TCP/IP networks interpret email addresses.

RFC 822

Internet sites adhere to the RFC 822 standard, which requires the familiar notation of *user@host.domain*, for which *host.domain* is the host's fully qualified domain name. The character separating the two is properly called a "commercial at" sign, but it helps if you read it as "at." This notation does not specify a route to the destination host. Routing of the mail message is left to the mechanisms we'll describe shortly.

Obsolete Mail Formats

Before moving on, let's have a look at the way things used to be. In the original UUCP environment, the prevalent form was *path!host!user*, for which *path* described a sequence of hosts the message had to travel through before reaching the destination *host*. This construct is called the *bang path* notation because an exclamation mark is colloquially called a "bang."

Other networks had still different means of addressing. DECnet-based networks, for example, used two colons as an address separator, yielding an address of *host::user*. The X.400 standard uses an entirely different scheme, describing a recipient by a set of attribute-value pairs, such as country and organization.

Lastly, on FidoNet, each user was identified by a code such as *2:320/204.9*, consisting of four numbers denoting zone (2 for Europe), net (320 referred to Paris and Banlieue), node (the local hub), and point (the individual user's PC). Fidonet addresses were mapped to RFC 822; the above, for example, was written as *Thomas. Quinot@p9.f204.n320.z2.fidonet.org*. Now aren't you glad we do things with simple domain names today?

How Does Mail Routing Work?

The process of directing a message to the recipient's host is called *routing*. Apart from finding a path from the sending site to the destination, it involves error checking and may involve speed and cost optimization.

On the Internet, the main job of directing data to the recipient host (once it is known by its IP address) is done by the IP networking layer.

Mail Routing on the Internet

On the Internet, the destination host's configuration determines whether any specific mail routing is performed. The default is to deliver the message to the destination by first determining what host the message should be sent to and then delivering it directly to that host. Most Internet sites want to direct all inbound mail to a highly available mail server that is capable of handling all this traffic and have it distribute the mail locally. To announce this service, the site publishes a so-called MX record for its local domain in its DNS database. MX stands for *Mail Exchanger* and basically states that the server host is willing to act as a mail forwarder for all mail addresses in the domain. MX records can also be used to handle traffic for hosts that are not connected to the Internet themselves. These hosts must have their mail passed through a gateway. This concept is discussed in greater detail in Chapter 6.

MX records are always assigned a *preference*. This is a positive integer. If several mail exchangers exist for one host, the mail transport agent will try to transfer the message to the exchanger with the lowest preference value, and only if this fails will it try a host with a higher value. If the local host is itself a mail exchanger for the destination address, it is allowed to forward messages only to MX hosts with a lower preference than its own; this is a safe way of avoiding mail loops. If there is no MX record for a domain, or no MX records left that are suitable, the mail transport agent is permitted to see if the domain has an IP address associated with it and attempt delivery directly to that host.

Suppose that an organization, say Foobar, Inc., wants all its mail handled by its machine **mailhub**. It will then have MX records like this in the DNS database:

```
green.foobar.com.        IN   MX     5     mailhub.foobar.com.
```

This announces **mailhub.foobar.com** as a mail exchanger for **green.foobar.com** with a preference of 5. A host that wishes to deliver a message to *joe@green.foobar.com* checks DNS and finds the MX record pointing at **mailhub**. If there's no MX with a preference smaller than 5, the message is delivered to **mailhub**, which then dispatches it to **green**.

This is a very simple description of how MX records work. For more information on mail routing on the Internet, refer to RFC 821, RFC 974, and RFC 1123.

CHAPTER 12
sendmail

It's been said that you aren't a *real* Unix system administrator until you've edited a *sendmail.cf* file. It's also been said that you're crazy if you've attempted to do so twice.

Fortunately, you no longer need to directly edit the cryptic *sendmail.cf* file. The new versions of *sendmail* provide a configuration utility that creates the *sendmail.cf* file for you based on much simpler macro files. You do not need to understand the complex syntax of the *sendmail.cf* file. Instead, you use the macro language to identify the features you wish to include in your configuration and specify some of the parameters that determine how that feature operates. A traditional Unix utility, called *m4*, then takes your macro configuration data and mixes it with the data it reads from template files containing the actual *sendmail.cf* syntax to produce your *sendmail.cf* file.

sendmail is an incredibly powerful mail program that is difficult to master. Any program whose definitive reference (*sendmail*, by Bryan Costales with Eric Allman, published by O'Reilly) is 1,200 pages long scares most people off. And any program as complex as *sendmail* cannot be completely covered in a single chapter. This chapter introduces *sendmail* and describes how to install, configure, and test it, using a basic configuration for the Virtual Brewery as an example. If the information presented here helps make the task of configuring *sendmail* less daunting for you, we hope you'll gain the confidence to tackle more complex configurations on your own.

Installing the sendmail Distribution

sendmail is included in prepackaged form in most Linux distributions. Despite this fact, there are some good reasons to install *sendmail* from source, especially if you are security conscious. *sendmail* changes frequently to fix security problems and to add new features. Closing security holes and using new features are good reasons to update the *sendmail* release on your system. Additionally, compiling *sendmail* from source gives you more control over the *sendmail* environment. Subscribe to the *sendmail-announce* mailing list to receive notices of new *sendmail* releases, and monitor the *http://www.sendmail.org/* site to stay informed about potential security threats and the latest *sendmail* developments.

Downloading sendmail Source Code

Download the *sendmail* source code distribution and the source code distribution signature file from *http://www.sendmail.org/current-release.html*, from any of the mirror sites, or from *ftp://ftp.sendmail.org/pub/sendmail/*. Here is an example using *ftp*:

```
# ftp ftp.sendmail.org
Connected to ftp.sendmail.org (209.246.26.22).
220 services.sendmail.org FTP server (Version 6.00LS) ready.
Name (ftp.sendmail.org:craig): anonymous
331 Guest login ok, send your email address as password.
Password: win@vstout.com
230 Guest login ok, access restrictions apply.
Remote system type is UNIX.
Using binary mode to transfer files.
ftp> cd /pub/sendmail
250 CWD command successful.
ftp> get sendmail.8.12.11.tar.gz
local: sendmail.8.12.11.tar.gz remote: sendmail.8.12.11.tar.gz
227 Entering Passive Mode (209,246,26,22,244,234)
150 Opening BINARY mode data connection for 'sendmail.8.12.11.tar.gz' (1899112
bytes).
226 Transfer complete.
1899112 bytes received in 5.7 secs (3.3e+02 Kbytes/sec)
ftp> get sendmail.8.12.11.tar.gz.sig
local: sendmail.8.12.11.tar.gz.sig remote: sendmail.8.12.11.tar.gz.sig
227 Entering Passive Mode (209,246,26,22,244,237)
150 Opening BINARY mode data connection for 'sendmail.8.12.11.tar.gz.sig' (152
bytes).
226 Transfer complete.
152 bytes received in 0.000949 secs (1.6e+02 Kbytes/sec)
```

If you do not have the current *sendmail* PGP keys on your key ring, download the PGP keys needed to verify the signature. Adding the following step to the ftp session downloads the keys for the current year:

```
ftp> get PGPKEYS
local: PGPKEYS remote: PGPKEYS
227 Entering Passive Mode (209,246,26,22,244,238)
150 Opening BINARY mode data connection for 'PGPKEYS' (61916 bytes).
226 Transfer complete.
61916 bytes received in 0.338 secs (1.8e+02 Kbytes/sec)
ftp> quit
221 Goodbye.
```

If you downloaded new keys, add the PGP keys to your key ring. In the following example, gpg (Gnu Privacy Guard) is used:

```
# gpg --import PGPKEYS
gpg: key 16F4CCE9: not changed
```

```
gpg: key 95F61771: public key imported
gpg: key 396F0789: not changed
gpg: key 678C0A03: not changed
gpg: key CC374F2D: not changed
gpg: key E35C5635: not changed
gpg: key A39BA655: not changed
gpg: key D432E19D: not changed
gpg: key 12D3461D: not changed
gpg: key BF7BA421: not changed
gpg: key A00E1563: non exportable signature (class 10) - skipped
gpg: key A00E1563: not changed
gpg: key 22327A01: not changed
gpg: Total number processed: 12
gpg:                 imported: 1  (RSA: 1)
gpg:                unchanged: 11
```

Of the twelve exportable keys in the *PGPKEYS* file, only one is exported to our key ring. The *not changed* comment for the other eleven keys shows that they were already installed on the key ring. The first time you import *PGPKEYS*, all twelve keys will be added to the key ring.

Before using the new key, verify its fingerprint, as in this gpg example:

```
# gpg --fingerprint 95F61771
pub  1024R/95F61771 2003-12-10 Sendmail Signing Key/2004 <sendmail@Sendmail.ORG>
     Key fingerprint = 46 FE 81 99 48 75 30 B1  3E A9 79 43 BB 78 C1 D4
```

Compare the displayed fingerprint against Table 12-1, which contains fingerprints for *sendmail* signing keys.

Table 12-1. Sendmail signing key fingerprints

Year	Fingerprint
1997	CA AE F2 94 3B 1D 41 3C 94 7B 72 5F AE 0B 6A 11
1998	F9 32 40 A1 3B 3A B6 DE B2 98 6A 70 AF 54 9D 26
1999	25 73 4C 8E 94 B1 E8 EA EA 9B A4 D6 00 51 C3 71
2000	81 8C 58 EA 7A 9D 7C 1B 09 78 AC 5E EB 99 08 5D
2001	59 AF DC 3E A2 7D 29 56 89 FA 25 70 90 0D 7E C1
2002	7B 02 F4 AA FC C0 22 DA 47 3E 2A 9A 9B 35 22 45
2003	C4 73 DF 4A 97 9C 27 A9 EE 4F B2 BD 55 B5 E0 0F
2004	46 FE 81 99 48 75 30 B1 3E A9 79 43 BB 78 C1 D4

If the fingerprint is correct, you can sign, and thus validate, the key. In this gpg example, we sign the newly imported *sendmail* key:

```
# gpg --edit-key 95F61771
gpg (GnuPG) 1.0.7; Copyright (C) 2002 Free Software Foundation, Inc.
This program comes with ABSOLUTELY NO WARRANTY.
This is free software, and you are welcome to redistribute it
under certain conditions. See the file COPYING for details.
```

```
gpg: checking the trustdb
gpg: checking at depth 0 signed=1 ot(-/q/n/m/f/u)=0/0/0/0/0/1
gpg: checking at depth 1 signed=1 ot(-/q/n/m/f/u)=1/0/0/0/0/0
pub  1024R/95F61771  created: 2003-12-10 expires: never      trust: -/q
(1). Sendmail Signing Key/2004 <sendmail@Sendmail.ORG>

Command> sign

pub  1024R/95F61771  created: 2003-12-10 expires: never      trust: -/q
            Fingerprint: 46 FE 81 99 48 75 30 B1  3E A9 79 43 BB 78 C1 D4

    Sendmail Signing Key/2004 <sendmail@Sendmail.ORG>

How carefully have you verified the key you are about to sign actually belongs to the
person named above?  If you don't know what to answer, enter "0".

    (0) I will not answer. (default)
    (1) I have not checked at all.
    (2) I have done casual checking.
    (3) I have done very careful checking.

Your selection? 3
Are you really sure that you want to sign this key
with your key: "Winslow Henson <win.henson@vstout.vbrew.com>"

I have checked this key very carefully.

Really sign? y

You need a passphrase to unlock the secret key for
user: "Winslow Henson <win.henson@vstout.vbrew.com>"
1024-bit DSA key, ID 34C9B515, created 2003-07-23

Command> quit
Save changes? y
```

After the *sendmail* keys have been added to the key ring and signed,[*] verify the *sendmail* distribution tarball. Here we use the *sendmail.8.12.11.tar.gz.sig* signature file to verify the *sendmail.8.12.11.tar.gz* compressed tarball:

```
# gpg --verify sendmail.8.12.11.tar.gz.sig sendmail.8.12.11.tar.gz
gpg: Signature made Sun 18 Jan 2004 01:08:52 PM EST using RSA key ID 95F61771
gpg: Good signature from "Sendmail Signing Key/2004 <sendmail@Sendmail.ORG>"
gpg: checking the trustdb
gpg: checking at depth 0 signed=2 ot(-/q/n/m/f/u)=0/0/0/0/0/1
gpg: checking at depth 1 signed=0 ot(-/q/n/m/f/u)=2/0/0/0/0/0
```

Based on this, the distribution tarball can be safely restored. The tarball creates a directory and gives it a name derived from the *sendmail* release number. The tarball

---

[*] It is necessary to download and import the *PGPKEYS* file only about once a year.

downloaded in this example would create a directory named *sendmail-8.12.11*. The files and subdirectories used to compile and configure *sendmail* are all contained within this directory.

Compiling sendmail

Compile *sendmail* using the `Build` utility provided by the *sendmail* developers. For most systems, a few commands, similar to the following, are all that is needed to compile *sendmail*:

```
# cd sendmail-8.12.11
# ./Build
```

A basic `Build` command should work unless you have unique requirements. If you do, create a custom configuration, called a *site configuration*, for the `Build` command to use. *sendmail* looks for site configurations in the *devtools/Site* directory. On a Linux system, `Build` looks for site configuration files named *site.linux.m4*, *site.config.m4*, and *site.post.m4*. If you use another filename, use the `-f` argument on the `Build` command line to identify the file. For example:

```
$ ./Build -f ourconfig.m4
```

As the file extension *.m4* file implies, the `Build` configuration is created with *m4* commands. Three commands are used to set the variables used by `Build`.

define
  The *define* command modifies the current value stored in the variable.

APPENDDEF
  The `APPENDDEF` macro appends a value to an existing list of values stored in a variable.

PREPENDDEF
  The `PREPENDDEF` macro prepends a value to an existing list of values stored in a variable.

As an example assume that the *devtools/OS/Linux* file, which defines `Build` characteristics for all Linux systems, puts the manpages in */usr/man:*[*]

```
define(`confMANROOT', `/usr/man/man')
```

Further assume that our Linux systems stores manpages in */usr/share/man*. Adding the following line to the *devtools/Site/site.config.m4* file directs `Build` to set the manpage path to */usr/share/man*:

```
define(`confMANROOT', `/usr/share/man/man')
```

Here is another example. Assume you must configure *sendmail* to read data from an LDAP server. Further, assume that you use the command sendmail -bt -d0.1 to

---

[*] Notice that m4 uses unbalanced single quotes, i.e., ` '.

check the *sendmail* compiler options and the string `LDAPMAP` does not appear in the "Compiled with:" list. You need to add LDAP support by setting LDAP values in the *site.config.m4* file and recompiling *sendmail* as shown below:

```
# cd devtools/Site
# cat >> site.config.m4
APPENDDEF(`confMAPDEF', `-DLDAPMAP')
APPENDDEF(`confLIBS', `-lldap -llber')
Ctrl-D
# cd ../../
# ./Build -c
```

Notice the `Build` command. If you make changes to the *siteconfig.m4* file and rerun `Build`, use the `-c` command-line argument to alert `Build` of the changes.

Most custom `Build` configurations are no more complicated than these examples. However, there are more than 100 variables that can be set for the `Build` configuration—far too many to cover in one chapter. See the *devtools/README* file for a complete list.

Installing the sendmail Binary

Because the *sendmail* binary is no longer installed as set-user-ID root, you must create a special user ID and group ID before installing *sendmail*. Traditionally, the *sendmail* binary was set-user-ID root so that any user could submit mail via the command line and have it written to the queue directory. However, this does not really require a set-user-ID root binary. With the proper directory permissions, a set-group-ID binary works fine, and presents less of a security risk.

Create the *smmsp* user and group for *sendmail* to use when it runs as a mail submission program. Do this using the tools appropriate to your system. Here are the */etc/passwd* and */etc/group* entries added to a sample Linux system:

```
# grep smmsp /etc/passwd
smmsp:x:25:25:Mail Submission:/var/spool/clientmqueue:/sbin/nologin
# grep smmsp /etc/group
smmsp:x:25:
```

Before installing the freshly compiled *sendmail*, back up the current *sendmail* binary, the *sendmail* utilities, and your current *sendmail* configuration files. (You never know; you might need to drop back to the old *sendmail* configuration if the new one doesn't work as anticipated.) After the system is backed up, install the new *sendmail* and utilities as follows:

```
# ./Build install
```

Running `Build install` installs *sendmail* and the utilities, and produces more than 100 lines of output. It should run without error. Notice that `Build` uses the *smmsp* user and group when it creates the */var/spool/clientmqueue* directory and when it installs the *sendmail* binary. A quick check of the ownership and permissions for the queue directory and the *sendmail* binary shows this:

```
drwxrwx---    2 smmsp    smmsp       4096 Jun  7 16:22 clientmqueue
-r-xr-sr-x    1 root     smmsp     568701 Jun  7 16:51 /usr/sbin/sendmail
```

After *sendmail* is installed, it must be configured. The topic of most of this chapter is how to configure *sendmail*.

sendmail Configuration Files

sendmail reads a configuration file (typically called */etc/mail/sendmail.cf*, or in older distributions, */etc/sendmail.cf*, or even */usr/lib/sendmail.cf*) that is simple for *sendmail* to parse, but not simple for a system administrator to read or edit. Fortunately, most *sendmail* configuration does not involve reading or editing the *sendmail.cf* file. Most *sendmail* configuration is macro driven. The macro method generates configurations to cover most installations, but you always have the option of tuning the resultant *sendmail.cf* manually.

The *m4* macro processor program processes a macro configuration file to generate the *sendmail.cf* file. For our convenience, we refer to the macro configuration file as the *sendmail.mc* file throughout this chapter. Do not name your configuration file *sendmail.mc*. Instead, give it a descriptive name. For example, you might name it after the host it was designed for—*vstout.m4*, in our case. Providing a unique name for the configuration file allows you to keep all configuration files in the same directory and is an administrative convenience.

The configuration process is basically a matter of creating a *sendmail.mc* file that includes the macros that describe your desired configuration, and then processing that *sendmail.mc* file with *m4*. The *sendmail.mc* file may include basic *m4* commands such as *define* or *divert*, but the lines in the file that have the most dramatic effect on the output file are the *sendmail* macros. The *sendmail* developers define the macros used in the *sendmail.mc* file. The *m4* macro processor expands the macros into chunks of *sendmail.cf* syntax. The macro expressions included in the *sendmail.mc* file begin with the macro name (written in capital letters), followed by parameters (enclosed in brackets) that are used in the macro expansion. The parameters may be passed literally into the *sendmail.cf* output or may be used to govern the way the macro processing occurs.

Unlike a *sendmail.cf* file, which may be more than 1,000 lines long, a basic *sendmail.mc* file is often less than 10 lines long, excluding comments.

Comments

Lines in the *sendmail.mc* file that begin with the # character are not parsed by *m4*, and, by default, are output directly into the *sendmail.cf* file. This is useful if you want to comment on what your configuration is doing in both the *sendmail.mc* and the *sendmail.cf* files.

To put comments in the *sendmail.mc* that are *not* placed into the *sendmail.cf*, use either *m4 divert* or *dnl* commands. divert(-1) causes all output to cease. divert(0) restores output to the default. Any lines between these will be discarded. Blocks of comments that should appear only in the *sendmail.mc* file are usually brackets by divert(-1) and divert(0) commands. To achieve the same result for a single line, use the dnl command at the beginning of a line that should appear as a comment only in the *sendmail.mc* file. The dnl command means "delete all characters up to and including the next newline." Sometimes *dnl* is added to the end of a macro command line, so that anything else added to that line is treated as a comment.

Often there are more comments than configuration commands in a *sendmail.mc* file! The following sections explain the structure of the *sendmail.mc* file and the commands used in the file.

Typically Used sendmail.mc Commands

A few commands are used to build most *sendmail.mc* files. Some of these typically used commands and the general sequence of these commands in the *sendmail.mc* are as follows:

```
VERSIONID
OSTYPE
DOMAIN
FEATURE
define
MAILER
LOCAL_*
```

The commands in this list that are written in uppercase are *sendmail* macros. By convention, the *sendmail* developers use uppercase letters for the names of the macros they create. There are more macros than those shown above. See the file *cf/README* for a complete list of the *sendmail* macros. In the list above, everything except the *define* command is a *sendmail* macro. The define command, which is shown in lowercase, is a basic *m4* command. All basic *m4* commands are written in lowercase letters. There are other basic *m4* commands used in *sendmail.mc* files; in fact you can use any legal *m4* command in a *sendmail.mc* file. However, the commands listed above are the basic set used to show the general order in which commands occur in a *sendmail.mc* file. We examine each of these commands in the following sections.

VERSIONID

The VERSIONID macro defines version control information. This macro is optional, but is found in most of the *sendmail m4* files. The command has no required format for the arguments field. Use any version control information you desire. Generally this is something compatible with the revision control system you use. If you don't use a revision control system, put a descriptive comment in this field. The VERSIONID macro from a *sendmail.mc* file on a system that did not use version control might look something like the following:

```
VERSIONID(`sendmail.mc, 6/11/2004 18:31 by Win Henson')
```

Notice that the argument is enclosed in single quotes and that the opening quote is ` and the closing quotes is '. When the argument passed to the *sendmail* macro contains spaces, special characters or values that may be misinterpreted as *m4* commands, the argument is enclosed in quotes, and it must be enclosed using these specific single quotes. This is true for all macros, not just VERSIONID.

OSTYPE

The OSTYPE macro is a required part of the macro configuration file. The OSTYPE macro command loads an *m4* source file that defines operating system-specific information, such as file and directory paths, mailer pathnames, and system-specific mailer arguments. The only argument passed to the OSTYPE command is the name of the *m4* source file that contains the operating system-specific information. OSTYPE files are stored in the *cf/ostype* directory. The command OSTYPE(`linux') processes the *cf/ostype/linux.m4* file.

The *sendmail* distribution provides more than 40 predefined operating system macro files in the *cf/ostype* directory, and you can create your own for a specific Linux distribution if you like. Some Linux distributions, notably the Debian distribution, include their own definition file that is completely Linux-FHS compliant. When your distribution does this, use its definition instead of the *generic-linux.m4* file. The OSTYPE macro should be one of the first commands to appear in the *sendmail.mc* file, as many other definitions depend on it.

DOMAIN

The DOMAIN macro processes the specified file from the *cf/domain* directory. A DOMAIN file is useful when configuring a large number of machines on the same network in a standard way, and typically configures items such as the name of mail relay hosts or hubs that all hosts on your network use.

To make effective use of the DOMAIN macro, you must create your own macro file containing the standard definitions you require for your site, and write it into the *domain* subdirectory. If you saved your domain macro file as *cf/domain/vbrew.m4*, you'd invoke it in your *sendmail.mc* using:

```
DOMAIN(`vbrew')
```

The *sendmail* distribution comes with a number of sample domain macro files that you can use to model your own. One is the *domain/generic.m4* file shown later in Example 12-3.

FEATURE

Use the FEATURE macro to include predefined *sendmail* features in your configuration. There are a large number of features—the *cf/feature* directory contains about 50 feature files. In this chapter we'll talk about only a few of the more commonly used features. You can find full details of all of the features in the *cf/README* file included in the source package.

To use a feature, include a line in the *sendmail.mc* that looks like:

```
FEATURE(name)
```

where *name* is the feature name. Some features take an optional parameter in a format like:

```
FEATURE(name, param)
```

where *param* is the parameter to supply.

define

Use the *m4* define command to set values for internal *sendmail.cf* macros, options, or classes. The first argument passed to the define is the *m4* name of the variable being set and the second field is the value to which the variable is set. Here is an example of how define is used to set a *sendmail.cf* macro:

```
define(`confDOMAIN_NAME', `vstout.vbrew.com')
```

The define command shown above places the following in the *sendmail.cf* file.

```
Djvstout.vbrew.com
```

This sets the *sendmail.cf* macro $j, which holds the full domain name of the *sendmail* host, to **vstout.vbrew.com**. Manually setting a value for $j is generally not necessary because, by default, *sendmail* obtains the correct name for the local host from the system itself.

Most of the *m4* variables default to a reasonable value and thus do not have to be explicitly set in the *m4* source file. The undefine command sets a variable back to its default. For example:

```
undefine(`confDOMAIN_NAME')
```

Resets confDOMAIN_NAME to the default value even if the configuration had previously set it to a specific hostname.

The list of *m4* variables that can be set by define is quite long. The *cf/README* file lists all of the variables. The listing includes the *m4* variable name, the name of the corresponding *sendmail.cf* option, macro, or class, a description of the variable, and the default value that is used if you do not explicitly define a value for the variable.

Note that the define command is not limited to setting values for *sendmail.cf* macros, options, and classes. define is also used to modify values used in the *m4* configurations and internal *sendmail* values.

MAILER

If you want *sendmail* to transport mail in any way other than by local delivery, use the MAILER macro to tell it which transports to use. *sendmail* supports a variety of mail transport protocols; some are essential, some are rarely used, and a few are experimental. The mailer arguments that can be used with the MAILER macro are shown in Table 12-2.

Table 12-2. Arguments for the MAILER macro

Argument	Purpose
local	Adds the *local* and *prog* mailers
smtp	Adds all SMTP mailers: *smtp, esmtp, smtp8, dsmtp,* and *relay*
uucp	Adds all UUCP mailers: uucp-old (*uucp*) and uucp-new (*suucp*)
usenet	Adds Usenet news support to sendmail
fax	Adds FAX support using HylaFAX software
pop	Adds Post Office Protocol (POP) support to sendmail
procmail	Adds an interface for *procmail*
mail11	Adds the DECnet *mail11* mailer
phquery	Adds the *phquery* program for CSO phone book
qpage	Adds the QuickPage mailer used to send email to a pager
cyrus	Adds the *cyrus* and *cyrusbb* mailers

Most hosts need only the SMTP transport to send and receive mail among other hosts, and the local mailer to move mail among users on the system. To achieve this, include both MAILER(`local') and MAILER(`smtp') in the macro configuration file. (The local mail transport is included by default, but is usually specified in the macro configuration file for clarity.)

The MAILER(`local') macro adds the local mailer, which delivers local mail between users of the system, and the prog mailer, which sends mail files to programs running on the system. The MAILER(`smtp') macro includes all of the mailers needed to send SMTP mail over a network. The mailers included in the *sendmail.cf* file by the MAILER(`smtp') macro are:

smtp
    This mailer handles only traditional 7-bit ASCII SMTP mail.

esmtp

> This mailer supports Extended SMTP (ESMTP), which understands the ESMTP protocol extensions and the complex message bodies and enhanced data types of MIME mail. This is the default mailer used for SMTP mail.

smtp8

> This mailer sends 8-bit data to the remote server, even if the remote server does not support ESMTP.

dsmtp

> This mailer supports the ESMTP ETRN command that allows the destination system to retrieve mail queued on the server.

relay

> This mailer is used to relay SMTP mail through another mail server.

Every system that connects to or communicates with the Internet needs the MAILER(`smtp') set of mailers, and most systems on isolated networks use these mailers because they use TCP/IP on their enterprise network. Despite the fact that the vast majority of *sendmail* systems require these mailers, installing them is not the default. To support SMTP mail, you must add the MAILER(smtp) macro to your configuration.

LOCAL_*

The LOCAL_CONFIG, LOCAL_NET_CONFIG, LOCAL_RULESET, and LOCAL_RULE_*n* macros allow you to put *sendmail.cf* configuration commands directly in the *m4* source file. These commands are copied, exactly as written, into the correct part of the *sendmail.cf* file. The list below describes where the macros place the *sendmail.cf* configuration commands that you provide.

LOCAL_CONFIG

> Marks the start of a block of *sendmail.cf* commands to be added to the local information section of the *sendmail.cf* file.

LOCAL_NET_CONFIG

> Marks the start of a section of rewrite rules that are to be added to the end of ruleset 0, which is also called ruleset *parse*.

LOCAL_RULE_*n*

> Marks the start of a section of rewrite rules to be added to ruleset 0, 1, 2, or 3. The *n* identifies the ruleset to which the rewrite rules are to be added.

LOCAL_RULESET

> Marks the start of a custom ruleset to be added to the configuration.

These macro mean that everything that can be done in the *sendmail.cf* file can be done in the *m4* macro configuration file because not only do you have access to all of the *m4* macros, you have access to all of the *sendmail.cf* commands. Of course, before you can use the *sendmail.cf* commands you need some idea of how they work. The next section briefly covers the *sendmail.cf* configuration commands.

sendmail.cf Configuration Language

There is rarely any need to use *sendmail.cf* commands in your configuration because the *sendmail* macros created by the *sendmail* developer handle most possible configurations. Yet it is useful to know something about the *sendmail.cf* command for those rare occasions when you come across a configuration that requires something that the *sendmail* developers just didn't think of. Table 12-3 lists the *sendmail.cf* configuration commands.

Table 12-3. sendmail.cf configuration commands

Command	Syntax	Meaning
Version Level	[V*level/vendor*]	Specify version level.
Define Macro	D*xvalue*	Set macro *x* to *value*.
Define Class	C*cword1*[*word2*]...	Set class *c* to *word1 word2* ....
Define Class	F*cfile*	Load class *c* from *file*.
Key File	K*name type* [*argument*]	Define database *name*.
Set Option	O*option=value*	Set *option* to *value*.
Trusted Users	T*user1*[*user2* ...]	Trusted users are *user1 user2* ....
Set Precedence	P*name=number*	Set *name* to precedence *number*.
Define Mailer	M*name*, [*field=value*]	Define mailer *name*.
Define Header	H[*?mflag ?*]*name* :*format*	Set header format.
Set Ruleset	S*n*	Start ruleset number *n*.
Define Rule	R*lhs rhs comment*	Rewrite *lhs* patterns to *rhs* format.

All of the commands in this table, except the last two, can be used with the LOCAL_CONFIG macro. The LOCAL_CONFIG macro is the one that heads a section of *sendmail.cf* commands used to define values for the configuration. These can be *sendmail.cf* database declarations, macros, or class values. Essentially anything except rewrite rulesets. Despite this, several of the *sendmail.cf* commands shown in Table 12-3 are simply not needed in the *sendmail.mc* file, even when you create a special configuration.

There is no real reason to add *sendmail.cf* 0 commands to the *sendmail.mc* configuration because all *sendmail.cf* options can be set using the define command and *m4* variables. Likewise, all necessary M commands are added to the *sendmail.cf* file by the *m4* MAILER macros, and therefore it is very unlikely you would use LOCAL_CONFIG to add M commands to your configuration. The T and P commands have limited roles. The T command adds usernames to the list of users who are allowed to send mail under someone else's username. Because of security considerations, you should be very careful about extending this list, and even if you do, you can use the confTRUSTED_USERS define in the *m4* file, or the FEATURE(use_ct_file) macro and define the usernames in the */etc/mail/trusted-users* file. The P command defines mail precedence, and frankly the default *sendmail.cf* configuration already has more mail precedence defined you will ever need.

The *sendmail.cf* commands that most commonly follow the LOCAL_CONFIG macro are D, C, F, and K. All of these can be used to define custom values that are later use, in a custom ruleset. The D command sets the value for a *sendmail.cf* macro. The C command adds values to a *sendmail.cf* class from the command line. The F command adds values to a *sendmail.cf* class from a file. The K command defines a database from which *sendmail* can obtain values. All of the standard *sendmail.cf* macros, classes, and databases can be used through standard *m4* macros. D, C, F, or K commands are added to the *sendmail.mc* configuration only on those rare occasions when you create your own private macros, classes, or databases.

The H command defines a mail header. All of the standard mail headers are already defined in the default configuration, and it is unlikely you will ever need to define a new header type. Calling special header processing is the most common reason to add a header definition to the configuration. (See the *cf/cf/knecht.mc* file for an example of a header definition that calls special processing, and see Recipe 6.9 in the *sendmail Cookbook* [O'Reilly] by Craig Hunt for a good description of how special header processing is invoked.) Of course, if you do call special header processing, you must also write the ruleset that performs the processing. The S and R commands used to write custom rulesets are our next topic.

sendmail.cf R and S Commands

Arguably the most powerful feature of *sendmail* is the rewrite rule. Rewrite rules determine how *sendmail* processes a mail message. *sendmail* passes the addresses from the *headers* of a mail message through collections of rewrite rules called *rulesets*. In the *sendmail.cf* file, each ruleset is named using an S command, coded as S*n*, where *n* specifies the name or number that is to be assigned to the current ruleset.

The rules themselves are defined by R commands grouped together as rulesets. Each rule has a left side and a right side, separated by at least one tab character.[*] When *sendmail* is processing a mail address, it scans through the rewrite rules looking for a match on the left side. If the address matches the left side of a rewrite rule, the address is replaced by the right side and processed again. In this manner, the rewrite rules transform a mail address from one form to another. Think of them as being

---

[*] Only tabs can separate the left and right side.

similar to an editor command that replaces all text matching a specified pattern with another.

A *sendmail* ruleset therefore looks like this:

```
Sn
Rlhs    rhs
Rlhs2   rhs2
```

The Left Side

The left side of a rewrite rule specifies the pattern an address must match to be transformed. The pattern may contain literals, *sendmail.cf* macros and classes, and the metasymbols described in the following list:

$@   Match exactly zero tokens

$*   Match zero or more tokens

$+   Match one or more tokens

$-   Match exactly one token

$=x Match any value in class *x*

$~x Match any value not in class *x*

A token is either a string of characters delimited by an operator or a delimiting operator. The operators are defined by the *sendmail.cf* OperatorChars option, as shown below:

```
O OperatorChars=.:%@!^/[ ]+
```

Assume the following address:

```
alana@ipa.vbrew.com
```

This email address contains seven tokens: alana, @, ipa, ., vbrew, ., and com. Three of these tokens, two dots (.), and an @, are operators. The other four tokens are strings. This address would match the symbol $+ because it contains more than one token, but it would not match the symbol $- because it does not contain exactly one token.

When a rule matches an address, the text matched by each of the patterns in the expression is assigned to special variables, called *indefinite tokens*, which can then be used in the right side. The only exception to this is the $@, which matches no tokens and therefore will never generate text to be used on the right side.

The Right Side

When the left side of a rewrite rule matches an address, the original text is deleted and replaced by the right side of the rule. Literal values in the right side are copied to the new address verbatim. Righthand side *sendmail.cf* macros are expanded and copied to the new address. Just as the left side has a number of metasymbols used for pattern matching, the right side has a special syntax for transforming an address, as described in the following list:

$n

> This metasymbol is replaced with the *n*'th indefinite token from the left side.

$[*name*$]

> This string is replaced by the canonical form of the hostname supplied.

$(*map key* $:*default* $)

> This special syntax returns the result of looking up *key* in the database named *map*. If the lookup is unsuccessful, the value defined for *default* is returned. If a default is not supplied and lookup fails, the *key* value is returned.

$>*n*

> This metasymbol calls ruleset *n* to process the rest of the line.

A rewrite rule that matches is normally tried repeatedly until it fails to match, then parsing moves on to the next rule. This behavior can be changed by preceding the right side with one of two special loop control metasymbols:

$@   This metasymbol terminates the ruleset.

$:   This metasymbol terminates this individual rule.

There is also a special right side syntax used to create the mail delivery triple of mailer, host and user. This syntax is most commonly seen in ruleset 0, which parses the mail delivery address. These symbols are:

$#*mailer*

> This metasymbol causes ruleset evaluation to halt and specifies the mailer that should be used to transport this message in the next step of its delivery. The special mailer *error* can be invoked in this manner to return an error message.

$@*host*

> This metasymbol specifies the host to which this message will be delivered. If the destination host is the local host, this syntax may be omitted from the mail delivery triple. The *host* may be a colon-separated list of destination hosts that will be tried in sequence to deliver the message.

$:*user*

> This metasymbol specifies the recipient user for the mail message.

A Simple Rule Pattern Example

To better see how the macro substitution patterns operate, consider the following left side:

    $* < $+ >

This rule matches "Zero or more tokens, followed by the < character, followed by one or more tokens, followed by the > character."

If this rule were applied to brewer@vbrew.com or Head Brewer < >, the rule would not match. The first string would not match because it does not include a < character, and the second would fail because $+ matches *one or more* tokens and there are no tokens between the <> characters. In any case in which a rule does not match, the right side of the rule is not used.

If the rule were applied to Head Brewer < brewer@vbrew.com >, the rule would match, and on the right side $1 would be substituted with Head Brewer and $2 would be substituted with brewer@vbrew.com.

If the rule were applied to < brewer@vbrew.com > the rule would match because $* matches *zero* or more tokens, and on the right side $1 would be substituted with the empty string.

A Complete Rewrite Rule Example

The following example uses the LOCAL_NET_CONFIG macro to declare a local rule and to insert the rule near the end of ruleset 0. Ruleset 0 resolves a delivery address to a mail delivery triple specifying the mailer, user, and host. Example 12-1 shows a sample rewrite rule.

Example 12-1. Sample rewrite rule

```
LOCAL_NET_CONFIG
R$*<@$*.$m.>$*      $#esmtp $@$2.$m. $:$1<@$2.$m.>$3
```

The LOCAL_NET_CONFIG macro is used to direct *m4* to place the rewrite rule in ruleset 0. The rule itself is the line beginning with R. Let's look at the rule's left side and the right side in turn.

The left side looks like: $*<@$*.$m.>$*.

< and > are focus characters, inserted by ruleset 3 early on in the address processing, which enclose the host part of the mail address. All addresses get rewritten with these focus characters. The @ is literally the @ used in an Internet email address to separate the user part from the host part. The dots (.) are literally the dots used in domain names. $m is a *sendmail.cf* macro used to hold the local domain name. The three remaining items are all $* metasymbols.

This rule matches any mail address that looks like: *DestUser<@somehost.ourdomain.> Some Text*. That is, it matches mail for any user at any host within our domain.

Text matched by metasymbols on the left side of a rewrite rule is assigned to indefinite tokens for use on the right side. In this example, the first $* matches all text from the start of the address until the <@ characters. All of this text is assigned to $1 for use on the right side. Similarly, anything matching the second $* in this rewrite rule is assigned to $2, and anything matching the last $* is assigned to $3.

When this rule matches an address of any user at any host within our domain, it assigns the username to $1, the hostname to $2, and any trailing text to $3. The right side is then used to process these values.

The right side of our example rewrite rule looks like this: $#esmtp $@$2.$m. $: $1<@$2.$m.>$3.

When the right side of our ruleset is processed, each of the metasymbols are interpreted and relevant substitutions are made.

The $# metasymbol causes this rule to resolve to a specific mailer—*esmtp*, in our case.

The $@ metasymbol specifies the target host. In our example, the target host is specified as $2.$m., which is the fully qualified domain name of the host in our domain. The FQDN is constructed of the hostname component assigned to $2 from our left side with our domain name (.$m.) appended.

The $: metasymbol specifies the recipient user's address. This is the full email address of the recipient, constructed in this case by $1 < @ $2.$m. > $3—user, bracket, at, host, dot, domain, dot, bracket, trailing text.

Since this rule resolves to a mailer, the message is forwarded to the mailer for delivery. In our example, the message would be forwarded to the destination host using the SMTP protocol.

Creating a sendmail Configuration

Using the *sendmail.mc* and *sendmail.cf* information covered so far in this chapter you should be able to read or create a basic *sendmail* configuration. Let's get started by looking at a sample *sendmail.mc* file.

The *sendmail* distribution comes with a large number of sample macro configuration files located in the *cf/cf* directory. Many are generic configuration files for different operating systems, including the *generic-linux.mc* file for Linux. Example 12-2 shows the contents of this file.

Example 12-2. The generic-linux.mc file

```
divert(-1)
#
# Copyright (c) 1998, 1999 Sendmail, Inc. and its suppliers.
#       All rights reserved.
# Copyright (c) 1983 Eric P. Allman.  All rights reserved.
# Copyright (c) 1988, 1993
#       The Regents of the University of California.  All rights reserved.
#
```

Example 12-2. The generic-linux.mc file (continued)

```
# By using this file, you agree to the terms and conditions set
# forth in the LICENSE file which can be found at the top level of
# the sendmail distribution.
#
#


#
#  This is a generic configuration file for Linux.
#  It has support for local and SMTP mail only.  If you want to
#  customize it, copy it to a name appropriate for your environment
#  and do the modifications there.
#

divert(0)dnl
VERSIONID(`$Id: ch12,v 1.6 2005/01/19 03:22:50 free2 Exp adam $')
OSTYPE(`linux')dnl
DOMAIN(`generic')dnl
MAILER(`local')dnl
MAILER(`smtp')dnl
```

A few things are obvious about this configuration file without knowing anything about the file syntax. First, the name *sendmail.mc* is obviously not sacrosanct. *generic-linux.mc* works just as well and is clearly a more descriptive name. Second, the configuration file is very short. The bulk of the lines in Example 12-1 are comments; only the last five lines are really *sendmail* configuration commands. Third, the *sendmail* configuration commands are short with a relatively simple syntax.

The five active lines in the *generic-linux.mc* file are composed of four different macros. The VERSIONID macro from the *generic-linux.mc* file is:

```
    VERSIONID(`$Id: ch12,v 1.6 2005/01/19 03:22:50 free2 Exp adam $')
```

From this we know that the *generic-linux.mc* file was last updated in September 1999 by Greg Shapiro, one of the Linux developers.

The OSTYPE(`linux') command in the *generic-linux.mc* file loads the *cf/ostype/linux. m4* file, which we will look at shortly. The DOMAIN(`generic') macro processes the *cf/ domain/generic.m4* file, which is also discussed shortly.

Finally, the MAILER(`local') and MAILER(`smtp') macros are used to add the local, prog, smtp, esmtp, smtp8, dsmtp, and relay mailers to the *sendmail.cf* configuration.

These five macro lines create the entire generic Linux *sendmail* configuration. There are, however, additional details to be found in the *linux.m4* and *generic.m4* file.

The linux.m4 OSTYPE File

The *cf/ostype/linux.m4* file is shown in Example 12-3.

Example 12-3. The linux.m4 OSTYPE file

```
divert(-1)
#
# Copyright (c) 1998, 1999 Sendmail, Inc. and its suppliers.
#       All rights reserved.
# Copyright (c) 1983 Eric P. Allman.  All rights reserved.
# Copyright (c) 1988, 1993
#       The Regents of the University of California.  All rights reserved.
#
# By using this file, you agree to the terms and conditions set
# forth in the LICENSE file which can be found at the top level of
# the sendmail distribution.
#
#

divert(0)
VERSIONID(`$Id: ch12,v 1.6 2005/01/19 03:22:50 free2 Exp adam $')
define(`confEBINDIR', `/usr/sbin')
ifdef(`PROCMAIL_MAILER_PATH',,
        define(`PROCMAIL_MAILER_PATH', `/usr/bin/procmail'))
FEATURE(local_procmail)
```

The file begins with a block of comments and a VERSIONID macro. It then defines the path to the directory that holds executable binaries. The path is stored in the *m4* variable confEBINDIR. The *linux.m4* file sets that path value to */usr/sbin*. Next, if the path to procmail has not yet been defined, it is set to */usr/bin/procmail*. The last line in the file is a FEATURE macro that loads the local_procmail feature, which cause *sendmail* to use *procmail* as the local mailer. *m4* uses the path defined for PROCMAIL_MAILER_PATH when constructing the local_procmail feature. This is an excellent example of how a value is first defined and then used in building a configuration. The *linux.m4* file is also a good example of the type of configuration commands normally found in an OSTYPE file.

The generic.m4 DOMAIN File

The *cf/domain/generic.m4* file is a sample DOMAIN file provided by the *sendmail* developers. It is used by the *generic-linux.mc* file shown in Example 12-1. The *generic.m4* file is shown in Example 12-4.

Example 12-4. The generic.m4 DOMAIN file

```
divert(-1)
#
# Copyright (c) 1998, 1999 Sendmail, Inc. and its suppliers.
#       All rights reserved.
# Copyright (c) 1983 Eric P. Allman.  All rights reserved.
# Copyright (c) 1988, 1993
#       The Regents of the University of California.  All rights reserved.
#
# By using this file, you agree to the terms and conditions set
```

Example 12-4. The generic.m4 DOMAIN file (continued)

```
# forth in the LICENSE file which can be found at the top level of
# the sendmail distribution.
#
#


#
#  The following is a generic domain file.  You should be able to
#  use it anywhere.  If you want to customize it, copy it to a file
#  named with your domain and make the edits; then, copy the appropriate
#  .mc files and change `DOMAIN(generic)' to reference your updated domain
#  files.
#
divert(0)
VERSIONID(`$Id: ch12,v 1.6 2005/01/19 03:22:50 free2 Exp adam $')
define(`confFORWARD_PATH', `$z/.forward.$w+$h:$z/.forward+$h:$z/.forward.$w:$z/.
forward')dnl
define(`confMAX_HEADERS_LENGTH', `32768')dnl
FEATURE(`redirect')dnl
FEATURE(`use_cw_file')dnl
EXPOSED_USER(`root')
```

Again the file begins with a large block of comments and a VERSIONID macro. This is followed by a define that sets the search path *sendmail* will use when looking for a user's *.forward* file. This command sets the ForwardPath option in the *sendmail.cf* file. $z, $w, and $h are internal *sendmail.cf* macros.[*]

The second define sets the maximum length for all headers in a single piece of mail to 32,768 bytes. It does this by setting the MaxHeadersLength option in the *sendmail.cf* file.

The next two lines add features to the *sendmail* configuration. The FEATURE(`redirect') macro adds support for the .REDIRECT pseudo-domain. A pseudo-domain is a domain-style extension internally added to an email address by *sendmail* to define special handling for the address. The .REDIRECT pseudo-domain works together with the *aliases* database to handle mail for people who no longer read mail at your site but who still get mail sent to an old address.[†] After enabling this feature, add an alias for each obsolete mailing address in the form:

old-address new-address.REDIRECT

This returns the following error to the sender telling them to try a new address for the recipient:

```
551 User not local; please try <new-address>
```

---

[*] See the *cf/README* file for more information about these *sendmail.cf* macros and the *Sendmail Installation and Operations Guide*, found in file *doc/op.ps*, for a full list of all *sendmail.cf* macros.

[†] The *aliases* database is covered later in this chapter.

The FEATURE(`use_cw_file') command reads */etc/mail/local-host-names* and adds the hostnames listed there to *sendmail.cf* class $=w. Class $=w contains the names of hosts for which the local computer will accept local mail. Normally, when a system running *sendmail* receives mail from the network that is addressed to another hostname, it assumes that the mail belongs to that host and forwards the mail to that host if the local host is configured as a relay, or discards the mail if the local host is not configured as a relay. If the system should accept, as local mail, mail that is addressed to another host, the name of the other host is added to class $=w. Any hostname listed in the *local-host-names* file is added to class $=w when the use_cw_file feature is used.

The last line in the *generic.m4* file is the EXPOSED_USER macro. The EXPOSED_USER macro adds usernames to class $=E. The users listed in class $=E are not masqueraded, even when masquerading is enabled. (Masquerading hides the real hostname in outbound mail and replaces it with the hostname you wish to advertise to the outside world.) Some usernames, such as *root*, occur on many systems and are therefore not unique across a domain. For those usernames, converting the host portion of the address makes it difficult to sort out where the message really came from and makes replies impossible. The EXPOSED_USER command in the *generic.m4* file prevents that from happening by ensuring that *root* is not masqueraded.

Given the commands contained in the *generic-linux.mc* file, the *linux.m4* file and the *generic.m4* file, the generic Linux configuration does the following:

- Sets */usr/sbin* as the path to executable binaries
- Sets the procmail path to */usr/bin/procmail*
- Uses procmail as the local mailer
- Defines the search path for *.forward* files
- Adds support for the .REDIRECT pseudo-domain to the configuration
- Loads class $=w from the */etc/local-host-names* file
- Adds root to class $=E
- Adds the local, prog, smtp, esmtp, smtp8, dsmtp, and relay mailers to the configuration

You can configure *sendmail* by modifying the configuration provided in your Linux distribution or create a custom configuration by modifying the *generic-linux.mc* file provided with the *sendmail* distribution. In the next section we build a *sendmail* configuration based on the *generic-linux.mc* file.

Creating a Sample Linux sendmail Configuration

We begin building our custom configuration by changing to the configuration directory and copying the *generic-linux.mc* configuration file to a working file. Because we are creating the configuration for **vstout.vbrew.com**, we call the working file *vstout.mc*.

```
$ cd sendmail-8.12.11/cf/cf
$ cp generic-linux.mc vstout.mc
```

We are configuring *vstout* to be a mail server for our group. We want it to:

- Accept inbound mail for various clients that plan to store mail on the server. No modifications to the *m4* configuration are needed to support this because the *domain/generic.m4* file used in the Linux configuration already includes the FEATURE(`use_cw_file') command.

- Relay mail for clients in the **vbrew.com** domain. Implementing this requires no changes to the *m4* configuration. By default, *sendmail* configurations support relaying for any domain defined in the *relay-domains* file. We will see how to configure the *relay-domains* file later in the chapter when we discuss *sendmail* databases.

- Rewrite the sender address on outbound mail to a generic format used by everyone at **vbrew.com**. We will add support for the *genericstable* database to do this. The contents of the *genericstable* database is covered in the *sendmail* databases section of this chapter.

- Provide some anti-spam support. We will use the *access* database for this task.

- Be easy to configure with additional security measures. The *access* database added for its anti-spam capabilities has many other easily configured features. We will see more about the *access* database in *sendmail* databases section later in this chapter.

To configure *sendmail* to do the tasks listed above, we edit the *vstout.mc* file and add the following features:

```
FEATURE(`genericstable')
GENERICS_DOMAIN(`vbrew.com')
FEATURE(`generics_entire_domain')
FEATURE(`access_db')
```

This first line adds support for the *genericstable*. The second line defines **vbrew.com** as the domain to which the *genericstable* will be applied. The third line tells *sendmail* to apply the *genericstable* to every host in the **vbrew.com** domain. The final line adds support for the *access* database.

After removing unneeded comments, updating the VERSIONID and adding the new lines, the *vstout.mc* configuration file is as shown below in Example 12-5:

Example 12-5. Sample custom configuration

```
VERSIONID(`Sample vstout configuration by Craig Hunt')
OSTYPE(`linux')dnl
DOMAIN(`generic')dnl
```

Example 12-5. Sample custom configuration (continued)

```
dnl Add support for the genericstable
FEATURE(`genericstable')
dnl Apply the genericstable to the vbrew.com domain
GENERICS_DOMAIN(`vbrew.com')
dnl Apply the genericstable to every host in the domain
FEATURE(`generics_entire_domain')
dnl Add support for the versatile access database
FEATURE(`access_db')
MAILER(`local')dnl
MAILER(`smtp')dnl
```

We now need to build a *sendmail.cf* file from our master configuration file, install the new *sendmail.cf* file, and ensure that *sendmail* reads it.

Building the sendmail.cf File

The *sendmail.cf* file is normally built in the same *cf/cf* directory where the master configuration file is created. If you're not currently in that directory, change to the *cf/cf* directory before attempting the build.

Run Build to create the *sendmail.cf* file from the *m4* master configuration file. The Build script is easy to use. Provide the name of the output file you want to create as an argument on the Build command line. The script replaces the *.cf* extension of the output file with the extension *.mc* and uses the macro configuration file with that name to create the output file. Thus, putting *vstout.cf* on the Build command line means that *vstout.mc* is used to create *vstout.cf*. Here is an example:

```
$ ./Build vstout.cf
Using M4=/usr/bin/m4
rm -f vstout.cf
/usr/bin/m4 ../m4/cf.m4 vstout.mc > vstout.cf || ( rm -f vstout.cf && exit 1 )
chmod 444 vstout.cf
```

Despite the simplicity of the Build command, many administrators never use it to build a *sendmail* configuration because the *m4* command line used to build a *sendmail* configuration is also very simple. The *m4* command line that would build the *vstout.cf* file from the *vstout.mc* file is:

```
$ m4 ../m4/cf.m4 vstout.mc > vstout.cf
```

For the average *sendmail* administrator, the Build script doesn't offer any critical advantages. For most of us, deciding to use the Build script or the *m4* command is primarily a matter of personal preference. It is even possible to invoke the *Makefile* directly with a basic make command. Use whatever method you prefer.

After building the new *.cf* file, test it thoroughly as described later in this chapter before copying that file to the location where *sendmail* expects to find the *sendmail.cf* configuration file, which is usually */etc/mail/sendmail.cf*. In most cases this is simply done with a cp command

```
# cp vstout.cf /etc/mail/sendmail.cf
```

However, it can also be done with the Build command, as follows:

```
# mv vstout.cf sendmail.cf
# ./Build install-cf
Using M4=/usr/bin/m4
../../devtools/bin/install.sh -c -o root -g bin -m 0444 sendmail.cf /etc/mail/
sendmail.cf
../../devtools/bin/install.sh -c -o root -g bin -m 0444 submit.cf /etc/mail/submit.cf
```

The Build install-cf command used above installs two configuration files: the *sendmail.cf* file, and a second file named *submit.cf*. *sendmail.cf* doesn't exist unless you create it. (In this case we created it as *vstout.cf* and renamed that file *sendmail.cf*.) But a full *submit.cf* file is delivered with the *sendmail* distribution, and does not normally need to be created or modified by you. The *submit.cf* file is the special configuration used by *sendmail* when it acts as a mail submission program, while *sendmail.cf* is the configuration file used by the *sendmail* daemon. The Build install-cf command is generally used when a new *sendmail* distribution is first installed to ensure that both the *sendmail.cf* and *submit.cf* files are installed. Other than the initial installation, however, there is generally no need to copy both files at the same time because it is not usually necessary to create a new *submit.cf* file when you create a new *sendmail.cf* file.

Once the configuration is installed, restart *sendmail* to force it to read the new configuration by sending it a HUP signal. This method of restarting *sendmail* uses standard *sendmail* signal processing that is available on any Linux system:

```
# kill -HUP `head -1 /var/run/sendmail.pid`
```

Some Linux systems provide their own tools for managing daemons. For example, some systems can start *sendmail* with the service command:

```
# service sendmail start
Starting sendmail: [  OK  ]
```

Regardless of how *sendmail* is restarted, when the daemon starts it reads in the configuration file */etc/mail/sendmail.cf*, which now contains the new configuration.

sendmail Databases

The sample configuration created above uses several *sendmail* databases. (Here we use the term "database" loosely to include both real databases and flat files.) *sendmail* databases are an often overlooked component of *sendmail* configuration. Yet *sendmail* databases play an important role in *sendmail* configuration. It is in these databases, not in the *m4* files or the *sendmail.cf* file, that day-to-day configuration changes are made. The *sendmail* databases used in our sample configuration are as follows:

aliases

> The *aliases* database is included in the configuration by default. This database is an essential component in local mail delivery and in mail forwarding. Nothing needs to be added to the configuration to use the *aliases* database.

local-host-names

> The *local-host-names* file is added to a configuration by the *use_cw_file* feature. This file is used to define which mail is accepted for local delivery.

relay-domains

> The *relay-domains* file is included in the configuration by default. Therefore, no changes are needed in the *sendmail* configuration to use this file. The *relay-domains* file can authorize relaying, which, by default, is disabled.

genericstable

> The *genericstable* feature adds support for this database. The *genericstable* is used to rewrite the email addresses an organization uses internally into the format it wishes to present to the outside world.

access

> The *access_db* feature adds support for this database. The *access* database is useful in a wide variety of ways.

Each of these databases, and others not used in the sample configuration, are described in the following sections.

The aliases Database

Mail aliases are a powerful feature for routing mail on a destination host. For example, it is common practice to direct feedback or comments relating to a World Wide Web server to "webmaster." Often there isn't a user known as "webmaster" on the target machine; instead, it is an alias for another user. Another common use of mail aliases is to create mailing lists by directing a single alias to many recipients or to use an alias to direct incoming messages to the list server program. Aliases can:

- Provide a shorthand or well-known name for mail to be addressed to in order to go to one or more persons. For example, all systems require aliases for the well-known names *Postmaster* and *MAILER-DAEMON* in order to be RFC compliant.

- Invoke a program with the mail message as the input to the program. Always be extremely aware of security when defining aliases that invoke programs or write to programs, since *sendmail* sometimes runs with root permissions.

- Deliver mail to a file.

Details concerning mail aliases may be found in the *aliases(5)* manpage. A sample *aliases* file is shown in Example 12-6.

Example 12-6. Sample aliases file

```
#
# The following two aliases must be present to be RFC-compliant.
# It is important to resolve them to 'a person' who reads mail routinely.
#
postmaster:    root                         # required entry
MAILER-DAEMON: postmaster                    # required entry
#
#
# demonstrate the common types of aliases
#
usenet:        janet                         # alias for a person
admin:         joe,janet                      # alias for several people
newspak-users: :include:/usr/lib/lists/newspak # read recipients from file
changefeed:    |/usr/local/lib/gup            # alias that invokes program
complaints:    /var/log/complaints            # alias writes mail to file
#
```

Whenever you update the */etc/aliases* text file, be sure to run the command:

```
# /usr/bin/newaliases
```

This command rebuilds the database that *sendmail* uses internally. The newaliases command is a symbolic link to the *sendmail* executable, which behaves exactly as if *sendmail* was invoked with the -bt command line argument.

The *sendmail* program consults the *aliases* database to determine how to handle an incoming mail message that has been accepted for local delivery. If the user portion of the delivery address in the mail message matches an entry in the *aliases* database, *sendmail* redirects the message as described by the entry. But this happens only if *sendmail* accepts the mail message for local delivery. The *local-host-names* file helps *sendmail* decide which messages should be accepted for local delivery.

The local-host-names File

Inbound mail is either delivered directly to the addressee or relayed to another mail host for delivery. *sendmail* accepts only mail for local delivery that is addressed to the local host. All other mail is relayed. The system checks class $=w to decide whether or not it should accept inbound mail for local delivery. Class $=w is an array that contains all of the names that *sendmail* considers valid for local mail delivery.

The *use_cw_file* feature directs *sendmail* to load the */etc/mail/local-host-names* file into class $=w. It does this by placing the following F command in the *sendmail.cf* file:

```
Fw/etc/mail/local-host-names
```

Once the *use_cw_file* feature is added to the configuration, *sendmail* expects to find the *local-host-names* file and displays a non-fatal error message when it doesn't. If you're not ready to add hostnames to the file, simply create an empty file.

To configure the *sendmail* server to accept inbound mail for other hosts, simply add the hostnames of those hosts to the *local-host-names* file. The *local-host-names* file is just a list of hostnames—one hostname to a line. Here is a sample *local-host-names* file for the **vbrew.com** domain:

```
vbrew.com
vporter.vbrew.com
vale.vbrew.com
vlager.vbrew.com
vpils.vbrew.com
vipa.vbrew.com
```

The values stored in the *local-host-names* file are added to the other values in class $=w. The other values stored in $=w are all of the hostnames, hostname aliases, and IP addresses assigned to this host that *sendmail* was able to determine by probing the various network interfaces. It is possible to limit the interface probing done by *sendmail* by adding the following define to the *sendmail* configuration:

```
define(`confDONT_PROBE_INTERFACES', `true')
```

The confDONT_PROBE_INTERFACES define is generally only used when probing the interfaces gives *sendmail* erroneous information, or when a large number of virtual interfaces are used.

It is also possible to add hostnames to class $=w inside the *sendmail* configuration file using the LOCAL_DOMAIN macro:

```
LOCAL_DOMAIN(`vbrew.com')
LOCAL_DOMAIN(`vipa.vbrew.com')
```

However, every time a LOCAL_DOMAIN macro is added to the configuration the *sendmail.cf* file must be rebuilt, tested, and moved to the */etc/mail* directory. When the *local-host-names* file is used, there is no need to rebuild *sendmail.cf* just because the *local-host-names* file has been edited.

The bestmx_is_local feature

The *bestmx_is_local* feature is another way to accept mail for local delivery that is addressed to another hostname. It works well if the only reason why hostnames are being added to the *local-host-names* file is because the local host is the preferred mail exchanger for those hosts. Mail addressed to any system that lists the local host as its preferred mail exchanger is accepted as local mail when the *bestmx_is_local* feature is used. To use this approach, put the following line in the configuration:

```
FEATURE(`bestmx_is_local', `vbrew.com')
```

The great advantage of the *bestmx_is_local* feature is that it is easy—the hostnames of MX clients do not need to be added to the *local-host-names* file. However, a potential problem with the *bestmx_is_local* solution is that it increases the processing overhead for each piece of mail. This is not a problem for a small system, but it could be a problem if the system deals with a high volume of mail. Another limitation is that *bestmx_is_local* depends completely on MX records, but it is possible to have other reasons to accept mail as local mail. The *local-host-names* file can store any hostnames that you wish; it is not limited to hosts that define your system as their mail exchanger.

Mail that is not addressed to the local host is relayed. The *relay-domains* file is one way to configure relaying.

The relay-domains File

By default, *sendmail* does not permit relaying—even relaying from other hosts within the local domain. Attempts to relay through a system using the default configuration returns the "Relaying denied" error to the sender. *sendmail* will, however, relay mail for any domain listed in class $=R, and anything listed in the *relay-domains* file is added to class $=R. For example, the following commands extend the *relay-domains* file to enable relaying for the **vbrew.com** domain:

```
# cat >> /etc/mail/relay-domains
vbrew.com
Ctrl-D
```

Restart *sendmail* to ensure that it reads the *relay-domains* file:

```
# kill -HUP `head -1 /var/run/sendmail.pid`
```

Now, hosts within the local domain are allowed to relay through **vstout.vbrew. com**—all without any changes to the *m4* configuration or any need to rebuild the *sendmail.cf* file. Mail from or to hosts in the **vbrew.com** domain is relayed. Mail that is neither from nor to a host in the **vbrew.com** domain is still blocked from relaying mail.

There are other ways to enable relaying. However, none is as easy as adding the local domain to the *relay-domains* file, and some are potential security risks. A good alternative is to add the local domain name to class $=R by using the RELAY_DOMAIN macro. The following lines added to the macro configuration would have the same effect as the *relay-domains* file defined above:

```
dnl RELAY_DOMAIN adds a domain name to class R
RELAY_DOMAIN(`vbrew.com')
```

However, the RELAY_DOMAIN command requires modifying the *m4* configuration, and rebuilding and reinstalling the *sendmail.cf* file. Using the *relay-domains* file does not, which makes the *relay-domains* file simpler to use.

Another good alternative is the *relay_entire_domain* feature. The following command added to a macro configuration would enable relaying for hosts in the local domain:

```
dnl A feature that relays mail for the local domain
FEATURE(`relay_entire_domain')
```

The *relay_entire_domain* feature relays mail from any host in a domain listed in class $=m. By default, class $=m contains the domain name of the server system, which is *vbrew.com* on a server named *vstout.vbrew.com*. This alternative solution works, but is slightly more complex than using the *relay-domains* file. Additionally, the *relay-domains* file is very flexible. It is not limited to the local domain. Any domain can be listed in the *relay-domains* file and mail from or to any host in that domain will be relayed.

There are some techniques for enabling relaying that should be avoided for security reasons. Two such alternatives are:

promiscuous_relay

This feature turns on relaying for all hosts. Of course, this includes the local domain so this feature would work. However, it would create an open relay for spammers. Avoid the *promiscuous_relay* feature even if your host is protected by a firewall.

relay_local_from

This feature enables relaying for mail if the email address in the envelope sender address of the mail contains the name of a host in the local domain. Because the envelope sender address can be faked, spammers can possibly trick your server into relaying spam.

Once the *relay-domains* file is configured to relay mail to and from the local domain, clients on the local network can start sending mail through the server to the outside world. The *genericstable*, discussed next, allows you to rewrite the sender address on the mail as it passes through the server.

The genericstable Database

To provide support for the *genericstable*, we added the *genericstable* feature, the GENERICS_DOMAIN macro, and the *generics_entire_domain* feature to our sample *sendmail* configuration. The following commands were added:

```
FEATURE(`genericstable')
GENERICS_DOMAIN(`vbrew.com')
FEATURE(`generics_entire_domain')
```

The *genericstable* feature adds the code *sendmail* needs to make use of the *genericstable*. The GENERICS_DOMAIN macro adds the value specified on the macro command line to *sendmail* class $=G. Normally, the values listed in class $=G are interpreted as hostnames, and only exact matches enable *genericstable* processing. The generics_entire_domain feature causes *sendmail* to interpret the values in class $=G as domain names, and any host within one of those domains is processed through the *genericstable*. Thus the hostname **vipa.vbrew.com**, because it contains the domain name **vbrew.com**, will be processed through the *genericstable* with this configuration.

Each entry in the *genericstable* contains two fields: the key and the value returned for that key. The key field can be either a full email address or a username. The value returned is normally a full email address containing both a username and a hostname. To create the *genericstable*, first create a text file that contains the database entries and then run that text file through the *makemap* command to build the *genericstable* database. For the **vstout.vbrew.com** server, we created the following *genericstable*:

```
# cd /etc/mail
# cat > genericstable
kathy                      kathy.mccafferty@vbrew.com
win                        winslow.smiley@vbrew.com
sara                       sara.henson@vbrew.com
dave                       david.craig@vbrew.com
becky                      rebecca.fro@vbrew.com
jay                        jay.james@vbrew.com
alana@vpils.vbrew.com      alana.darling@vbrew.com
alana@vale.vbrew.com       alana.henson@vbrew.com
alana                      alana.sweet@vbrew.com
Ctrl-D
# makemap hash genericstable < genericstable
```

Given this *genericstable*, the header sender address *win@vipa.vbrew.com* is rewritten to *winslow.smiley@vbrew.com*, which is the value returned by the *genericstable* for the key win. In this example, every *win* account in the entire *vbrew.com* domain belongs to Winslow Smiley. No matter what host in that domain he sends mail from, when the mail passes through this system it is rewritten into *winslow.smiley@vbrew. com*. For replies to the rewritten address to work correctly, the rewritten hostname must resolve to a host that will accept the mail and that host must have an alias for *winslow.smiley* that delivers the mail to the real *win* account.

The *genericstable* mapping can be anything you wish. In this example, we map login names to the user's real name and the local domain name formatted as *firstname. lastname@domain*.* Of course, if mail arrives at the server addressed to *firstname. lastname@domain*, aliases are needed to deliver the mail to the users' real address. Aliases based on the *genericstable* entries shown above could be appended to the *aliases* database in the following manner:

---

* The *firstname.lastname@domain* format is not universally endorsed. See the sendmail FAQ for some reasons why you might not want to use this address format.

```
# cd /etc/mail
# cat > aliases
kathy.mccafferty: kathy
win.strong:       craig
sara.henson:      sara
david.craig:      dave
rebecca.fro:      becky
alana.smiley:     alana
alana.darling:    alana@vpils.vbrew.com
alana.henson:     alana@vale.vbrew.com
jay.james:        jay
Ctrl-D
# newaliases
```

The aliases that map to a username store the mail on the server, where it is read by the user or retrieved by the client using POP or IMAP. The aliases that map to full addresses forward the mail to the host defined in the full address.

Most of the entries in the sample *genericstable* (*kathy*, *sara*, *dave*, *becky*, and *jay*) are any-to-one mappings that work just like the *win* entry described above. A more interesting case is the mapping of the username *alana*. Three people in the **vbrew.com** domain have this username: Alana Henson, Alana Darling, and Alana Sweet. The complete addresses used in the *genericstable* keys for Alana Darling and Alana Henson make it possible for *sendmail* to do one-to-one mappings for those addresses. The key used for Alana Sweet's entry, however, is just a username. That key matches any input address that contains the username *alana*, except for the input addresses *alana@vpils.vbrew.com* and *alana@vale.vbrew.com*. When a system handles mail that originates from several hosts, it is possible to have duplicate login names. The fact that the key in the *genericstable* can contain a full email address allows you to map these overlapping usernames.

The last database used in the sample Linux *sendmail* configuration is the *access* database. This database is so versatile that it should probably be included in the configuration of every mail server.

The access Database

The *access* database offers great flexibility and control for configuring from which hosts or users mail is accepted and for which hosts and users mail is relayed. The *access* database is a powerful configuration tool for mail relay servers that provides some protection against spam and that provides much finer control over the relay process than is provided by the *relay_domains* file. Unlike the *relay_domains* file, the *access* database is not a default part of the *sendmail* configuration. To use the *access* database, we added the *access_db* feature to our sample Linux *sendmail* configuration:

```
FEATURE(`access_db')dnl
```

The general idea of the *access* database is simple. When an SMTP connection is made, *sendmail* compares information from the envelope header to the information in the *access* database to see how it should handle the message.

The *access* database is a collection of rules that describe what action should be taken for messages from or to specific users or hosts. The database has a simple format. Each line in the table contains an access rule. The left side of each rule is a pattern matched against the envelope header information of the mail message. The right side is the action to take if the envelope information matches the pattern.

The left pattern can match:

- An individual defined by either a full email address (*user@host.domain*) or a username written as *username@*.
- A host identified by its hostname or its IP address.
- A domain identified by a domain name.
- A network identified by the network portion of an IP address.

By default, the pattern is matched against the envelope sender address, and thus the action is taken only if the mail comes from the specified address. Adding the *blacklist_recipient* feature to the *sendmail* configuration applies the pattern match to both source and destination envelope addresses. However, an optional tag field that can be prepended to the left side to provide finer control over when the pattern match is applied. Beginning the pattern with an optional tag tells *sendmail* to limit pattern matching to certain conditions. The three basic tags are:

To:
> The action is taken only when mail is being sent to the specified address.

From:
> The action is taken only when mail is received from the specified address.

Connect:
> The action is taken only when the specified address is the address of the system at the remote end of the SMTP connection.

There are five basic actions that may be defined on the right side of an access rule. These are:

OK
> Accept the mail message.

RELAY
> Accept the mail messages for relaying.

REJECT
> Reject the mail with a generic message.

DISCARD
> Discard the message using the $#discard mailer.

ERROR:*dsn*:*code text*

> Return an error message using the specified DSN code, the specified SMTP error code, and the specified text as the message.

An example */etc/mail/access* might look like this:

```
friends@cybermail.com    REJECT
aol.com                  REJECT
207.46.131.30            REJECT
postmaster@aol.com       OK
linux.org.au             RELAY
example.com              ERROR:5.7.1:550 Relaying denied to spammers
```

This example would reject any email received from *friends@cybermail.com*, any host in the domain **aol.com** and the host **207.46.131.30**. The next rule would accept email from *postmaster@aol.com*, despite the fact that the domain itself has a reject rule. The fifth rule allows relaying of mail from any host in the **linux.org.au** domain. The last rule rejects mail from **example.com** with a custom error message. The error message includes delivery status notification code 5.7.1, which is a valid code as defined by RFC 1893, and SMTP error code 550, which is a valid code from RFC 821.

The *access* database can do much more than shown here. Note that we explicitly said "basic" tags and "basic" actions because there are several more values that can be used in advanced configurations. If you plan to tackle an advanced configuration, see the "More Information" section later in the chapter.

The *access* database is the last database we used in our sample configuration. There are several other databases that are not used in our sample Linux *sendmail* configuration. These are described in the following section.

Other Databases

Some of the available *sendmail* databases were not used in our sample configuration either because their use is discouraged or because they focus on outdated technologies. These databases are:

define(`confUSERDB_SPEC', `*path*')

> The confUSERDB_SPEC option tells *sendmail* to apply the *user* database to local addresses after the *aliases* database is applied and before the *.forward* file is applied. The path argument tells *sendmail* where the database is found. The *user* database is not widely used because the *sendmail* developers discourage its use in their responses to questions 3.3 and 3.4 of the FAQ.

FEATURE(`use_ct_file', `*path*')

> The *use_ct_file* feature tells *sendmail* to add trusted usernames from the specified file to the class $=t. Because users listed in $=t are allowed to send mail using someone else's username, they present a security risk. There are fewer files to secure against tampering if trusted users are defined in the macro configura-

tion file using confTRUSTED_USERS, and because so few users should be trusted, defining them in the macro configuration file is no burden.

FEATURE(`domaintable', `specification')

The *domaintable* feature tells *sendmail* to use the domain table to map one domain name to another. An optional database specification can be provided to define the database type and pathname, which, by default, are *hash* type and */etc/mail/domaintable*. The *domaintable* eases the transition from an old domain name to a new domain name by translating the old name to the new name on all mail. Because you are rarely in this situation, this database is rarely used.

FEATURE(`uucpdomain', `specification')

The *uucpdomain* feature tells *sendmail* to use the *uucpdomain* database to map UUCP site names to Internet domain names. The optional database specification overrides the default database type of *hash* and the default database path of */etc/mail/uucpdomain*. The *uucpdomain* database converts email addresses from the .UUCP pseudo-domain into old-fashioned UUCP bang addresses. The key to the database is the hostname from the .UUCP pseudo-domain. The value returned for the key is the bang address. It is very unlikely that you will use this database because even sites that still use UUCP don't often use bang addresses because current UUCP mailers handle email addresses that look just like Internet addresses.

FEATURE('bitdomain', 'specification')

The *bitdomain* feature tells *sendmail* to use the *bitdomain* database to map BIT-NET hostnames to Internet domain names. BITNET is an outdated IBM mainframe network that you won't use, and therefore you won't use this database.

There are two other databases, *mailertable* and *virtusertable*, that, although not included in the sample configuration, are quite useful.

The mailertable

The *mailertable* feature adds support to the *sendmail* configuration for the *mailertable*. The syntax of the *mailertable* feature is:

```
FEATURE(`mailertable', `specification')
```

The optional database specification is used to override the default database type of *hash* and the default database path is */etc/mail/mailertable*.

The *mailertable* maps domain names to the internal mailer that should handle mail bound for that domain. Some mailers are used only if they are referenced in the *mailertable*. For example, the MAILER(`smtp') command adds the *esmtp, relay, smtp, smtp8,* and *dsmtp* mailers to the configuration. By default, *sendmail* uses only two of these mailers. The *esmtp* mailer is used to send standard SMTP mail, and the *relay* mailer is used when mail is relayed through an external server. The other three mailers are unused unless they are reference in a *mailertable* entry or in a custom rewrite rule. (Using the *mailertable* is much easier than writing your own rewrite rules!)

Let's use the *smtp8* mailer as an example. The *smtp8* mailer is designed to send 8-bit MIME data to outdated mail servers that support MIME but cannot understand Extended SMTP. If the domain **example.edu** used such a mail server, you could put the following entry in the *mailertable* to handle the mail:

```
.example.edu        smtp8:oldserver.example.edu
```

A *mailertable* entry contains two fields. The first field is a key containing the host portion of the delivery address. It can either be a fully qualified hostname—**emma. example.edu**—or just a domain name. To specify a domain name, start the name with a dot, as in the example above. If a domain name is used, it matches every host in the domain.

The second field is the return value. It normally contains the name of the mailer that should handle the mail and the name of the server to which the mail should be sent. Optionally, a username can be specified with the server address in the form *user@server*. Also, the selected mailer can be the internal error mailer. If the error mailer is used, the value following the mailer name is an error message instead of a server name. Here is an example of each of these alternative entries:

```
.example.edu        smtp8:oldserver.example.edu
vlite.vbrew.com     esmtp:postmaster@vstout.vbrew.com
vmead.vbrew.com     error:nohost This host is unavailable
```

Normally, mail passing through the *mailertable* is sent to the user to which it is addressed. For example, mail to *jane@emma.example.edu* is sent through the *smtp8* mailer to the server **oldserver.example.edu** addressed to the user *jane@emma. example.edu*. Adding a username to the second field, however, changes this normal behavior and routes the mail to an individual instead of a mail server. For example, mail sent to any user at **vlite.vbrew.com** is sent instead to *postmaster@vstout.vbrew. com*. There, presumably, the mail is handled manually. Finally, mail handled by the *mailertable* does not have to be delivered at all. Instead, an error message can be returned to the sender. Any mail sent to **vmead.vbrew.com** returns the error message "This host is unavailable" to the sender.

The virtusertable

The *sendmail virtusertable* feature adds support for the virtual user table, where virtual email hosting is configured. Virtual email hosting allows the mail server to accept and deliver mail on behalf of a number of different domains as though it were a number of separate mail hosts. The virtual user table maps incoming mail destined for some *user@host* to some *otheruser@otherhost*. You can think of this as an advanced mail alias feature—one that operates using not just the destination user, but also the destination domain.

To configure the *virtusertable* feature, add the feature to your *m4* macro configuration as shown:

```
FEATURE(`virtusertable')
```

By default, the *virtusertable* source file is */etc/mail/virtusertable*. You can override this by supplying an argument to the macro definition; consult a detailed *sendmail* reference to learn about what options are available.

The format of the virtual user table is very simple. The left side of each line contains a pattern representing the original destination mail address; the right side has a pattern representing the mail address that the virtual hosted address will be mapped to. The following example shows three possible types of entries:

```
samiam@bovine.net    colin
sunny@bovine.net     darkhorse@mystery.net
@dairy.org           mail@jhm.org
@artist.org          $1@red.firefly.com
```

In this example, we are virtual hosting three domains: **bovine.net**, **dairy.org**, and **artist.org**.

The first entry redirects mail sent to a user in the **bovine.net** virtual domain to a local user on the machine. The second entry redirects mail to a user in the same virtual domain to a user in another domain. The third example redirects all mail addressed to any user in the **dairly.org** virtual domain to a single remote mail address. Finally, the last entry redirects any mail to a user in the **artist.org** virtual domain to the same user in another domain; for example, *julie@artists.org* would be redirected to *julie@red.firefly.com*.

Testing Your Configuration

Email is an essential service. It is also a service that can be exploited by intruders when it is misconfigured. It is very important that you thoroughly test your configuration. Fortunately, *sendmail* provides a relatively easy way of doing this.

sendmail supports an "address test" mode that allows a full range of tests. In the following examples we specify a destination mail address and a test to apply to that address. *sendmail* then processes that destination address displaying the output of each ruleset as it proceeds. To place *sendmail* into address test mode, invoke it with the -bt argument.

The default configuration file used for the address test mode is the */etc/mail/sendmail.cf* file. To specify an alternate configuration file, use the -C argument. This is important because you will test a new configuration before moving it to */etc/mail/sendmail.cf*. To test the sample Linux *sendmail* configuration created earlier in this chapter, use the following *sendmail* command:

```
# /usr/sbin/sendmail -bt -Cvstout.cf
ADDRESS TEST MODE (ruleset 3 NOT automatically invoked)
Enter <ruleset> <address>
>
```

The > prompt shown above indicates that *sendmail* is ready to accept a test mode command. While in address test mode, *sendmail* accepts a variety of commands that examine the configuration, check settings, and observe how email addresses are process by *sendmail*. Table 12-4 lists the commands that are available in test mode.

Table 12-4. Sendmail test mode commands

Command	Usage
ruleset [,ruleset...] address	Process the address through the comma-separated list of rulesets.
=Sruleset	Display the contents of the ruleset.
=M	Display all of the mailer definitions.
$v	Display the value of macro v.
$=c	Display the values in class c.
.Dvvalue	Set the macro v to value.
.Ccvalue	Add value to class c.
-dvalue	Set the debug level to value.
/tryflags flags	Set the flags used for address processing by /try.
/try mailer address	Process the address for the mailer.
/parse address	Return the mailer/host/user delivery triple for the address.
/canon hostname	Canonify hostname.
/mx hostname	Lookup the MX records for hostname.
/map mapname key	Look up key in the database identified by mapname.
/quit	Exit address test mode.

Several commands (=S, =M, $v, and $=c) display current *sendmail* configuration values defined in the *sendmail.cf* file, and the /map command displays values set in the *sendmail* database files. The -d command can be used to change the amount of information displayed. A great many debug levels can be set by -d, but only a few are useful to the *sendmail* administrator. See a detailed *sendmail* reference for valid debug values.

Two commands, .D and .C, are used to set macro and class values in real time. Use these commands to try alternate configuration settings before rebuilding the entire configuration.

Two commands display the interaction between *sendmail* and DNS. /canon displays the canonical name returned by DNS for a given hostname. /mx shows the list of mail exchangers returned by DNS for a given host.

Most of the remaining commands process an email address through *sendmail*'s rewrite rules. /parse displays the processing of a delivery address and shows which mailer is used to deliver mail sent to the address. /try displays the processing of addresses for a specific mailer. (The /tryflags command specifies whether the sender or the recipient address should be processed by the /try command.) Use the *ruleset address* command to display the processing of an address through any arbitrary list of rulesets that you wish to test.

First we'll test that *sendmail* is able to deliver mail to local users on the system. In these tests we expect all addresses to be rewritten to the *local* mailer on this machine:

```
# /usr/sbin/sendmail -bt -Cvstout.cf
ADDRESS TEST MODE (ruleset 3 NOT automatically invoked)
Enter <ruleset> <address>
> /parse issac
Cracked address = $g
Parsing envelope recipient address
canonify          input: issac
Canonify2         input: issac
Canonify2         returns: issac
canonify          returns: issac
parse             input: issac
Parse0            input: issac
Parse0            returns: issac
ParseLocal        input: issac
ParseLocal        returns: issac
Parse1            input: issac
Parse1            returns: $# local $: issac
parse             returns: $# local $: issac
2                 input: issac
2                 returns: issac
EnvToL            input: issac
EnvToL            returns: issac
final             input: issac
final             returns: issac
mailer local, user issac
```

This output shows us how *sendmail* processes mail addressed to *isaac* on this system. Each line shows us what information has been supplied to a ruleset or the result obtained from processing by a ruleset. We told *sendmail* that we wished to parse the address for delivery. The last line shows us that the system does indeed direct mail to *isaac* to the *local* mailer.

Next we'll test mail addressed to our SMTP address: *isaac@vstout.vbrew.com*. We should be able to produce the same end result as our last example:

```
> /parse isaac@vstout.vbrew.com
Cracked address = $g
Parsing envelope recipient address
canonify          input: isaac @ vstout . vbrew . com
Canonify2         input: isaac < @ vstout . vbrew . com >
Canonify2         returns: isaac < @ vstout . vbrew . com . >
canonify          returns: isaac < @ vstout . vbrew . com . >
```

```
parse              input: isaac < @ vstout . vbrew . com . >
Parse0             input: isaac < @ vstout . vbrew . com . >
Parse0             returns: isaac < @ vstout . vbrew . com . >
ParseLocal         input: isaac < @ vstout . vbrew . com . >
ParseLocal         returns: isaac < @ vstout . vbrew . com . >
Parse1             input: isaac < @ vstout . vbrew . com . >
Parse1             returns: $# local $: isaac
parse              returns: $# local $: isaac
2                  input: isaac
2                  returns: isaac
EnvToL             input: isaac
EnvToL             returns: isaac
final              input: isaac
final              returns: isaac
mailer local, user isaac
```

Next we will test that mail addressed to other hosts in the *vbrew.com* domain is delivered directly to that host using SMTP mail:

```
> /parse issac@vale.vbrew.com
Cracked address = $g
Parsing envelope recipient address
canonify           input: issac @ vale . vbrew . com
Canonify2          input: issac < @ vale . vbrew . com >
Canonify2          returns: issac < @ vale . vbrew . com . >
canonify           returns: issac < @ vale . vbrew . com . >
parse              input: issac < @ vale . vbrew . com . >
Parse0             input: issac < @ vale . vbrew . com . >
Parse0             returns: issac < @ vale . vbrew . com . >
ParseLocal         input: issac < @ vale . vbrew . com . >
ParseLocal         returns: issac < @ vale . vbrew . com . >
Parse1             input: issac < @ vale . vbrew . com . >
MailerToTriple     input: < > issac < @ vale . vbrew . com . >
MailerToTriple     returns: issac < @ vale . vbrew . com . >
Parse1             returns: $# esmtp $@ vale . vbrew . com . $: issac < @ vale . vbrew
. com . >
parse              returns: $# esmtp $@ vale . vbrew . com . $: issac < @ vale . vbrew
. com . >
2                  input: issac < @ vale . vbrew . com . >
2                  returns: issac < @ vale . vbrew . com . >
EnvToSMTP          input: issac < @ vale . vbrew . com . >
PseudoToReal       input: issac < @ vale . vbrew . com . >
PseudoToReal       returns: issac < @ vale . vbrew . com . >
MasqSMTP           input: issac < @ vale . vbrew . com . >
MasqSMTP           returns: issac < @ vale . vbrew . com . >
EnvToSMTP          returns: issac < @ vale . vbrew . com . >
final              input: issac < @ vale . vbrew . com . >
final              returns: issac @ vale . vbrew . com
mailer esmtp, host vale.vbrew.com., user issac@vale.vbrew.com
```

We can see that this test has directed the message to the default SMTP mailer (*esmtp*) to be sent to the host *vale.vbrew.com* and the user *issac* on that host.

Our final test checks the *genericstable* we created for the *vstout.cf* configuration. We check the mapping of the username *alana* for all three people in the *vbrew.com* domain that have this username. The following test shows how the *genericstable* maps each variation of this name:

```
# sendmail -bt
ADDRESS TEST MODE (ruleset 3 NOT automatically invoked)
Enter <ruleset> <address>
> /tryflags HS
> /try esmtp alana@vpils.vbrew.com
Trying header sender address alana@vpils.vbrew.com for mailer esmtp
canonify          input: alana @ vpils . vbrew . com
Canonify2         input: alana < @ vpils . vbrew . com >
Canonify2         returns: alana < @ vpils . vbrew . com . >
canonify          returns: alana < @ vpils . vbrew . com . >
1                 input: alana < @ vpils . vbrew . com . >
1                 returns: alana < @ vpils . vbrew . com . >
HdrFromSMTP       input: alana < @ vpils . vbrew . com . >
PseudoToReal      input: alana < @ vpils . vbrew . com . >
PseudoToReal      returns: alana < @ vpils . vbrew . com . >
MasqSMTP          input: alana < @ vpils . vbrew . com . >
MasqSMTP          returns: alana < @ vpils . vbrew . com . >
MasqHdr           input: alana < @ vpils . vbrew . com . >
canonify          input: alana . darling @ vbrew . com
Canonify2         input: alana . darling < @ vbrew . com >
Canonify2         returns: alana . darling < @ vbrew . com . >
canonify          returns: alana . darling < @ vbrew . com . >
MasqHdr           returns: alana . darling < @ vbrew . com . >
HdrFromSMTP       returns: alana . darling < @ vbrew . com . >
final             input: alana . darling < @ vbrew . com . >
final             returns: alana . darling @ vbrew . com
Rcode = 0, addr = alana.darling@vbrew.com
> /try esmtp alana@vale.vbrew.com
Trying header sender address alana@vale.vbrew.com for mailer esmtp
canonify          input: alana @ vale . vbrew . com
Canonify2         input: alana < @ vale . vbrew . com >
Canonify2         returns: alana < @ vale . vbrew . com . >
canonify          returns: alana < @ vale . vbrew . com . >
1                 input: alana < @ vale . vbrew . com . >
1                 returns: alana < @ vale . vbrew . com . >
HdrFromSMTP       input: alana < @ vale . vbrew . com . >
PseudoToReal      input: alana < @ vale . vbrew . com . >
PseudoToReal      returns: alana < @ vale . vbrew . com . >
MasqSMTP          input: alana < @ vale . vbrew . com . >
MasqSMTP          returns: alana < @ vale . vbrew . com . >
MasqHdr           input: alana < @ vale . vbrew . com . >
canonify          input: alana . henson @ vbrew . com
Canonify2         input: alana . henson < @ vbrew . com >
Canonify2         returns: alana . henson < @ vbrew . com . >
canonify          returns: alana . henson < @ vbrew . com . >
MasqHdr           returns: alana . henson < @ vbrew . com . >
HdrFromSMTP       returns: alana . henson < @ vbrew . com . >
final             input: alana . henson < @ vbrew . com . >
```

```
final              returns: alana . henson @ vbrew . com
Rcode = 0, addr = alana.henson@vbrew.com
> /try esmtp alana@foobar.vbrew.com
Trying header sender address alana@foobar.vbrew.com for mailer esmtp
canonify           input: alana @ foobar . vbrew . com
Canonify2          input: alana < @ foobar . vbrew . com >
Canonify2          returns: alana < @ foobar . vbrew . com . >
canonify           returns: alana < @ foobar . vbrew . com . >
1                  input: alana < @ foobar . vbrew . com . >
1                  returns: alana < @ foobar . vbrew . com . >
HdrFromSMTP        input: alana < @ foobar . vbrew . com . >
PseudoToReal       input: alana < @ foobar . vbrew . com . >
PseudoToReal       returns: alana < @ foobar . vbrew . com . >
MasqSMTP           input: alana < @ foobar . vbrew . com . >
MasqSMTP           returns: alana < @ foobar . vbrew . com . >
MasqHdr            input: alana < @ foobar . vbrew . com . >
canonify           input: alana . smiley @ vbrew . com
Canonify2          input: alana . smiley < @ vbrew . com >
Canonify2          returns: alana . smiley < @ vbrew . com . >
canonify           returns: alana . smiley < @ vbrew . com . >
MasqHdr            returns: alana . smiley < @ vbrew . com . >
HdrFromSMTP        returns: alana . smiley < @ vbrew . com . >
final              input: alana . smiley < @ vbrew . com . >
final              returns: alana . smiley @ vbrew . com
Rcode = 0, addr = alana.smiley@vbrew.com
> /quit
```

This test uses the /tryflags command that allows us to specify whether we want to process the header sender address (HS), the header recipient address (HR), the envelope sender address (ES), or the envelope recipient address (ER). In this case, we want to see how the header sender address is rewritten. The /try command allows us to specify which mailer the address should be rewritten for and the address to be rewritten.

This test was also successful. The *genericstable* tests work for Alana Darling, Alana Henson, and Alana Smiley.

Running sendmail

The *sendmail* daemon can be run in either of two ways. One way is to have to have it run from the *inetd* daemon; the alternative, and more commonly used method, is to run *sendmail* as a standalone daemon. It is also common for mailer programs to invoke *sendmail* as a user command to accept locally generated mail for delivery.

When running *sendmail* in standalone mode, place the *sendmail* command in a startup file so that it runs at boot time. The syntax used is commonly:

```
/usr/sbin/sendmail -bd -q10m
```

The -bd argument tells *sendmail* to run as a daemon. It will fork and run in the background. The -q10m argument tells *sendmail* to check its queue every ten minutes. You may choose to use a different time interval to check the queue.

To run *sendmail* from the *inetd* network daemon, you'd use an entry such as this:

```
smtp  stream  tcp nowait  nobody  /usr/sbin/sendmail -bs
```

The -bs argument here tells *sendmail* to use the SMTP protocol on *stdin/stdout*, which is required for use with *inetd*.

When *sendmail* is invoked this way, it processes any mail waiting in the queue to be transmitted. When running *sendmail* from *inetd*, you must also create a cron job that runs the *runq* command periodically to service the mail spool periodically. A suitable cron table entry would be similar to:

```
# Run the mail spool every fifteen minutes
0,15,30,45    *    *    *    *    /usr/bin/runq
```

In most installations *sendmail* processes the queue every 15 minutes as shown in our *crontab* example. This example uses the *runq* command. The *runq* command is usually a symlink to the *sendmail* binary and is a more convenient form of:

```
# sendmail -q
```

Tips and Tricks

There are a number of things you can do to make managing a *sendmail* site efficient. A number of management tools are provided in the *sendmail* package; let's look at the most important of these.

Managing the Mail Spool

Mail is queued in the */var/spool/mqueue* directory before being transmitted. This directory is called the mail spool. The *sendmail* program provides the *mailq* command as a means of displaying a formatted list of all spooled mail messages and their status. The */usr/bin/mailq* command is a symbolic link to the *sendmail* executable and behaves identically to:

```
# sendmail -bp
```

The output of the *mailq* command displays the message ID, its size, the time it was placed in the queue, who sent it, and a message indicating its current status. The following example shows a mail message stuck in the queue with a problem:

```
$ mailq
                Mail Queue (1 request)
--Q-ID-- --Size-- -----Q-Time----- ------------Sender/Recipient------------
RAA00275      124 Wed Dec  9 17:47 root
                        (host map: lookup (tao.linux.org.au): deferred)
                                 terry@tao.linux.org.au
```

This message is still in the mail queue because the destination host IP address could not be resolved.

To force *sendmail* to immediately process the queue, issue the */usr/bin/runq* command. *sendmail* will process the mail queue in the background. The *runq* command produces no output, but a subsequent *mailq* command will tell you if the queue is clear.

Forcing a Remote Host to Process Its Mail Queue

If you use a temporary dial-up Internet connection with a fixed IP address and rely on an MX host to collect your mail while you are disconnected, you will find it useful to force the MX host to process its mail queue soon after you establish your connection.

A small *perl* program is included with the *sendmail* distribution that makes this simple for mail hosts that support it. The *etrn* script has much the same effect on a remote host as the *runq* command has on the local server. If we invoke the command as shown in this example:

```
# etrn vstout.vbrew.com
```

we force the host **vstout.vbrew.com** to process any mail queued for our local machine.

Typically you'd add this command to your PPP startup script so that it is executed soon after your network connection is established.

Mail Statistics

sendmail collects data on the volume of mail traffic and some information on the hosts to which it has delivered mail. There are two commands available to display this information, *mailstats* and *hoststat*.

mailstats

The *mailstats* command displays statistics on the volume of mail processed by *sendmail*. The time at which data collection commenced is printed first, followed by a table with one row for each configured mailer and one showing a summary total of all mail. Each line presents eight items of information, which are described in Table 12-5.

Table 12-5. The fields displayed by mailstat

Field	Meaning
M	The mailer (transport protocol) number
msgsfr	The number of messages received from the mailer

Table 12-5. The fields displayed by mailstat (continued)

Field	Meaning
bytes_from	The Kbytes of mail from the mailer
msgsto	The number of messages sent to the mailer
bytes_to	The Kbytes of mail sent to the mailer
msgsreg	The number of messages rejected
msgsdis	The number of messages discarded
Mailer	The name of the mailer

A sample of the output of the *mailstats* command is shown in Example 12-7.

Example 12-7. Sample output of the mailstats command

```
# /usr/sbin/mailstats
Statistics from Sun Dec 20 22:47:02 1998
 M    msgsfr  bytes_from   msgsto    bytes_to  msgsrej msgsdis  Mailer
 0        0          0K       19        515K        0       0  prog
 3       33        545K        0          0K        0       0  local
 5       88        972K      139       1018K        0       0  esmtp
=============================================================================
 T      121       1517K      158       1533K        0       0
```

This data is collected if the StatusFile option is enabled in the *sendmail.cf* file and the status file exists. The StatusFile option is defined in the generic Linux configuration and therefore defined in the *vstout.cf* file we built from the generic configuration, as shown below:

```
$ grep StatusFile vstout.cf
O StatusFile=/etc/mail/statistics
```

To restart the statistics collection, make the statistics file zero length and restart *sendmail*.

hoststat

The *hoststat* command displays information about the status of hosts to which *sendmail* has attempted to deliver mail. The *hoststat* command is equivalent to invoking *sendmail* as:

```
sendmail -bh
```

The output presents each host on a line of its own, and for each the time since delivery was attempted to it, and the status message received at that time.

Persistent host status is maintained only if a path for the status directory is defined by the HostStatusDirectory option, which in turn is defined in the *m4* macro configuration file by confHOST_STATUS_DIRECTORY. By default, no path is defined for the host status directory and no persistent host status is maintained.

Example 12-8 shows the sort of output you can expect from the *hoststat* command. Note that most of the results indicate successful delivery. The result for **earthlink.net**, on the other hand, indicates that delivery was unsuccessful. The status message can sometimes help determine the cause of the failure. In this case, the connection timed out, probably because the host was down or unreachable at the time delivery was attempted.

Example 12-8. Sample Output of the hoststat Command

```
# hoststat
-------------- Hostname ---------- How long ago ---------Results---------
mail.telstra.com.au                  04:05:41 250 Message accepted for
scooter.eye-net.com.au            81+08:32:42 250 OK id=0zTGai-0008S9-0
yarrina.connect.com.a             53+10:46:03 250 LAA09163 Message acce
happy.optus.com.au                55+03:34:40 250 Mail accepted
mail.zip.com.au                      04:05:33 250 RAA23904 Message acce
kwanon.research.canon.com.au      44+04:39:10 250 ok 911542267 qp 21186
linux.org.au                      83+10:04:11 250 IAA31139 Message acce
albert.aapra.org.au                  00:00:12 250 VAA21968 Message acce
field.medicine.adelaide.edu.au    53+10:46:03 250 ok 910742814 qp 721
copper.fuller.net                 65+12:38:00 250 OAA14470 Message acce
amsat.org                          5+06:49:21 250 UAA07526 Message acce
mail.acm.org                      53+10:46:17 250 TAA25012 Message acce
extmail.bigpond.com               11+04:06:20 250 ok
earthlink.net                     45+05:41:09 Deferred: Connection time
```

The *purgestat* command flushes the collected host data and is equivalent to invoking *sendmail* as:

```
# sendmail -bH
```

The statistics will continue to grow until you purge them. You might want to periodically run the *purgestat* command to make it easier to search and find recent entries, especially if you have a busy site. You could put the command into a *crontab* file so it runs automatically, or just do it yourself occasionally.

More Information

sendmail is a complex topic—much too complex to be truly covered by a single chapter. This chapter should get you started and will help you configure a simple server. However, if you have a complex configuration or you want to explore advanced features, you will need more information. Here are some sources to start you on your quest for knowledge.

- The *sendmail* distribution is delivered with some excellent *README* files. The *README* file in the top-level directory created when the distribution is installed is the place to start. It contains a list of other informational files, such as *sendmail/README* and *cf/README*, that provides essential information. (The *cf/README* file, which covers the *sendmail* configuration language, is also available on the Web at *http://www.sendmail.org/m4/readme.html*.)

- The *sendmail Installation and Operations Guide* is an excellent source of information. It is also delivered with the *sendmail* source code distribution, and can be found in *doc/op/op.me* or *doc/op/op.ps*, depending on your preferred format.

- The *sendmail* web site provides several excellent papers and online documents. The *Compiling Sendmail* documentation, available at *http://www.sendmail.org/compiling.html*, is an excellent example.

- The *sendmail* site provides a list of available *sendmail* books at *http://www.sendmail.org/books.html*.

- Formal *sendmail* training is available. Some training classes are listed at *http://www.sendmail.org/classes.html*.

Using these resources, you should be able to find out more about *sendmail* than you will ever need to know. Go exploring!

## CHAPTER 13

Configuring IPv6 Networks

IPv4 space is becoming scarcer by the day. By 2005, some estimates place the number of worldwide Internet users at over one billion. Given the fact that many of those users will have a cellular phone, a home computer, and possibly a computer at work, the available IP address space becomes critically tight. China has recently requested IP addresses for each of their students, for a total of nearly 300 million addresses. Requests such as these, which cannot be filled, demonstrate this shortage. When IANA initially began allotting address space, the Internet was a small and little-known research network. There was very little demand for addresses and class A address space was freely allocated. However, as the size and importance of the Internet started to grow, the number of available addresses diminished, making obtaining a new IP difficult and much more expensive. NAT and CIDR are two separate responses to this scarcity. NAT is an individual solution allowing one site to funnel its users through a single IP address. CIDR allows for a more efficient division of network address block. Both solutions, however, have limitations.

With new electronic devices such as PDAs and cellular phones, which all need IP addresses of their own, the NAT address blocks suddenly do not seem quite as large.

Researchers, realizing the potential IP shortage, have redesigned the IPv4 protocol so that it supports 128-bits worth of address space. The selected 128-bit address space provides 340 trillion possible addresses, an exponential increase that we hope will provide adequate addressing into the near (and far) future. This is, in fact, enough addresses to provide every person on Earth with one billion addresses.

Not only does IPv6 solve some of the address space logistics, it also addresses some configuration and security issues. In this section, we'll take a look at the current solutions available with Linux and IPv6.

The IPv4 Problem and Patchwork Solutions

At the beginning, IANA gave requestors an entire class A network space thereby granting requestors 16.7 million addresses—many more than necessary. Realizing their error, they began to assign class B networks—again, providing far too many addresses for the average requestor. As the Internet grew, it quickly became clear that allocating class A and class B networks to every requestor did not make sense. Even their later action of assigning class C banks of addresses still squandered address space, as most companies didn't require 254 IP addresses. Since IANA could not revoke currently allocated address space, it became necessary to deal with the remaining space in a way that made sense. One of these ways was through the use of *Classless Inter-Domain Routing* (CIDR).

CIDR

CIDR allows network blocks to be allocated outside of the well-defined class A/B/C ranges. In an effort to get more mileage from existing class C network blocks, CIDR allows administrators to divide their address space into smaller units, which can then be allocated as individual networks. This made it easier to give IPs to more people because space could be allocated by need, rather than by predefined size-of-space. For example, a provider with a class C subnet could choose to divide this network into 32 individual networks, and would use the network addresses and subnet masks to delineate the boundaries. A sample CIDR notation looks like this:

    10.10.0.64/29

In this example, the /29 denotes the subnet mask, which means that the first 29 bits of the address are the subnet. It could also be noted as **255.255.255.248**, which gives this network a total of six usable addresses.

While CIDR does deal with the problem in a quick and easy way, it doesn't actually create more IP addresses, and it does have some additional disadvantages. First, its efficiency is compromised since each allocated network requires a broadcast IP and a network address IP. So if a provider breaks a class C block into 32 separate networks, a total of 64 individual IPs are wasted on network and broadcast IPs. Second, complicated CIDR networks are more prone to configuration errors. A router with an improper subnet mask can cause an outage for small networks it serves.

NAT

Network Address Translation (NAT) provides some relief for the IP address space dilemma, and without it, we'd currently be well out of usable IP space. NAT provides a many-to-one translation, meaning that many machines can share the same IP address. This also provides some privacy and security for the machines behind the NAT device, since individually identifying them is more difficult. There are also some disadvantages to NAT—primarily that some older protocols aren't designed to handle redirection.

IPv6 as a Solution

In order to combat the shrinking IP space problem, the concept of IPv6 was born. Future-minded designers chose to have 128 bits of address space, providing for a total of 340,282,366,920,938,463,463,374,607,431,768,211,456 (3.4 × 1,038) addresses or, in more visual terms, 655,570,793,348,866,943,898,599 (6.5 × 1,023) addresses for every square meter of the earth's surface. This provides a sizable extension over the current 32-bits of address space under IPv4.

IPv6 Addressing

The first noticeable difference between IPv4 and IPv6 is how the addresses are written. A typical IPv6 address looks like:

    fe80:0010:0000:0000:0000:0000:0000:0001

There are eight sets of four hex values in every IP address. These addresses can be long and cumbersome, which is why a shortening method was developed. A single string of zeroes can be replaced with the double colon. For example, the previous example could be written in shortened form as.

    fe80:0010::1

However, this can be done only one time in an address in order to avoid ambiguity about what has been removed. Let us consider the following example IP which has separate strings of zeroes:

    2001:0000:0000:a080:0000:0000:0000:0001

Since only one string of zeroes can be replaced, the IP can not be shortened to:

    2001::a080::1

Generally, the longest string is shortened. In this example, with the longest set replaced, the shortened IP is:

    2001:0000:0000:a080::1

Within IPv6, there are several different types of addresses that define the various functions available within the specification:

Link-local address

> This address is automatically configured when the IPv6 stack is initialized using the MAC address from your network card. This kind of address is generally considered a client-only type of address, and would not be capable of running a server or listening for inbound connections. Link-local addresses always begin

with *FE8x, FE9x, FEAx,* or *FEBx,* where the x can be replaced with any hex digit.

Site-local addresses

While a part of the original specification, and still described in various texts, site-local addresses have been deprecated and are no longer considered to be part of IPv6.

Global unicast address

This address type is Internet routable and is expected to be the outward facing IP on all machines. This kind of address is currently identified by its starting digits of either *2xxx* or *3xxx,* though this may be expanded in the future as necessary.

IPv6 Advantages

While the most obvious benefit of IPv6 is the dramatically increased address space, there are several other key advantages that come with it. For example, there are numerous performance gains with IPv6. Packets can be processed more efficiently because option fields in the packet headers are processed only when actual options are present; additional performance gains come from having removed packet fragmentation. A second advantage is a boost in security through the inclusion of embedded IPSec. As it will be part of the protocol, implementation of encryption and non-repudiation will be more natural. Quality of Service (QoS) is another advantage that is developing with IPv6. Enabling this functionality would allow network administrators to prioritize groups of network traffic. This can be critical on networks that handle services like Voice over IP because even small network disruptions can make the service less reliable. Finally, advances in address auto-configuration make on-the-fly networking much easier. Additional benefits will emerge as adoption and research continue. Hopefully, some of these will come with advances in Mobile IP technologies that promise to make it possible for any device to keep the same IP address regardless of its current network connection.

IPv6 Configuration

IPv6 support has come a long way recently and is now supported in nearly all Linux distributions. It has been a part of the 2.4 kernel for the last few releases and is included in kernel 2.6.

Kernel and system configuration

Enabling IPv6 support in Linux has become much easier now that it is distributed with the kernel sources. Patching is no longer necessary, but you will need to install a set of tools, which will be described later in this section.

If IPv6 support isn't already built into your kernel, it may already be compiled as a module. A quick test to see whether or not the module is present can be accomplished with the following command:

```
vlager# modprobe ipv6
vlager#
```

If there is no response the module was most likely successfully loaded. There are several ways to verify that support is enabled. The fastest is by checking the /proc directory:

```
vlager# ls -l /proc/net/if_inet6
-r-r-r--  1 root    root       0  Jul 1 12:12  /proc/net/if_inet6
```

If you have a compatible version of *ifconfig*, it can also be used *to* verify:

```
vlager# ifconfig eth0 |grep inet6

    inet6 addr:  fe80::200:ef99:f3df:32ae/10 Scope:Link
```

If these tests are unsuccessful, you will likely need to recompile your kernel to enable support. The kernel configuration option for IPv6 in the *.config* file is:

```
CONFIG_IPV6=m
```

By using a "make menuconfig," the option to enable IPv6 under the 2.4 kernel is found under "Network Options" section. Under the 2.6 kernel configuration, it is found under "Network Support/Network Options". It can either be compiled into the kernel or built as a module. If you do build as a module, remember that you must *modprobe* before attempting to configure the interface.

Interface configuration

In order to configure the interface for IPv6 usage, you will need to have IPv6 versions of the common network utilities. With most Linux distributions now supporting IPv6 out of the box, it's likely that you'll already have these tools installed. If you're upgrading from an older distribution or using Linux From Scratch, you will probably need to install a package called *net-tools*, which can be found at various places on the Internet. You can find the most recent version by searching for "net-tools" on Google or FreshMeat.

To verify that you have compatible versions, a quick check can be done with either *ifconfig* or *netstat*. The quick check would look like this:

```
vlager# /sbin/netstat grep inet6
```

Before proceeding, you'll also want to make sure you have the various network connectivity checking tools for IPv6, such as *ping6*, *traceroute6*, and *tracepath6*. They are found in the *iputils* package and, again, are generally installed by default on most current distributions. You can search your path to see whether or not these tools are available and install them if necessary. Should you need to find them, the author has placed them at *ftp://ftp.inr.ac.ru/ip-routing*.

If everything has gone smoothly, your interface will have been auto-configured using your MAC address. You can check this by using *ifconfig*:

```
vlager# ifconfig eth0
eth0       Link encap:Ethernet  HWaddr 00:07:E9:DF:32:AE
           inet addr:10.10.10.19  Bcast:10.10.10.255  Mask:255.255.255.0
           inet6 addr: fe80::207:e9ff:fedf:32ae/10 Scope:Link
           UP BROADCAST RUNNING MULTICAST  MTU:1500  Metric:1
           RX packets:2272821 errors:0 dropped:0 overruns:0 frame:73
           TX packets:478473 errors:0 dropped:0 overruns:0 carrier:0
           collisions:4033 txqueuelen:100
           RX bytes:516238958 (492.3 Mb)  TX bytes:54220361 (51.7 Mb)
           Interrupt:20 Base address:0x2000
vlager#
```

The third line in the output displays the link-local address of vlager. It is easy to identify it as such because any address starting with fe80 will always be a link-local type IP address. If you are concerned about privacy issues in using your MAC as your main IP address, or if you are configuring a server and wish to have an easier IP address, you can configure your own IP address according to the following example:

```
vlager# ifconfig eth0 inet6 add 2001:02A0::1/64
vlager#
```

At this point, however, you may not have a global address type to assign, as we've done above. So, your IP may be a link- or site-local address. These will work perfectly for any non-Internet routable traffic that you want to pass, but if you wish to connect to the rest of the world, you will need to have either a connection directly to the IPv6 backbone or an IPv6 tunnel through a *tunnel broker*, which we'll discuss in the next section.

Establishing an IPv6 Connection via a Tunnel Broker

To join the wonderful world of IPv6 you will need a path through which to connect. A tunnel is currently the only way to access the IPv6 backbone for most users, as few sites have direct IPv6 connectivity. Attempting to route IPv6 traffic directly over IPv4 networks won't get you very far, as the next-hop router will most likely not know what to do with your seemingly odd traffic. For most users, the easiest path to establish a tunnel is through a tunnel broker. There are a number of different brokers on the Internet who will provide you with your very own IPv6 address space. One of the fastest and most popular tunnel brokers is Hurricane Electric (Figure 13-1), which has an automated IPv6 tunnel request form. They require only that you have a "ping-able" IPv4 address that is constantly connected to the Internet. This is the IPv4 address that they will expect to be the source of your tunnel.

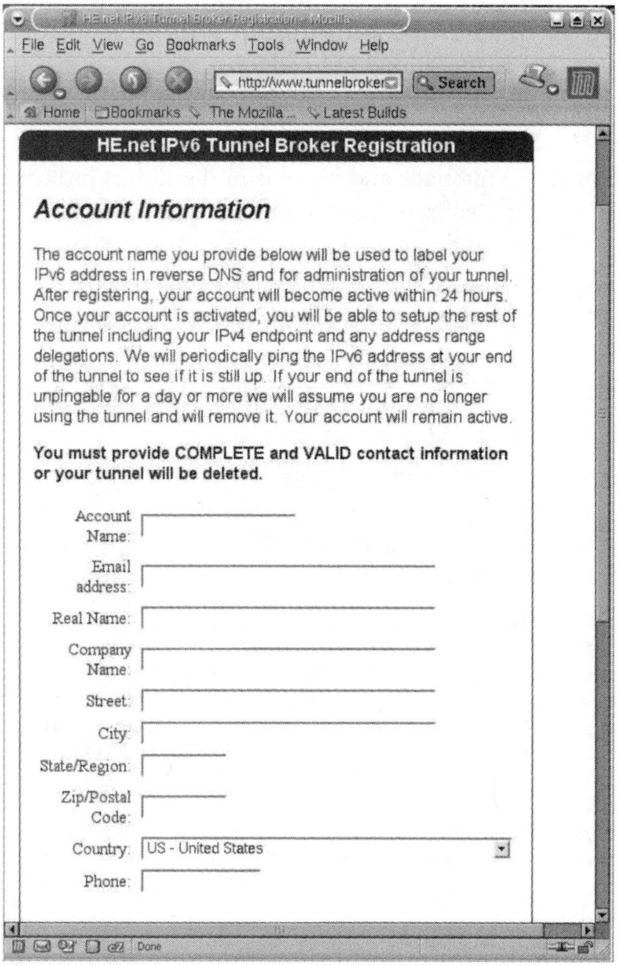

Figure 13-1. Obtaining a tunnel from he.net

Building your tunnel

Once you have received your IPv6 address space, you're ready to build your tunnel. In order to accomplish this, you will need to use the additional Link encapsulation interfaces that exist after installing the IPv6 module.

To build your tunnel, you will need to configure both the sit0 and sit1 interfaces. The sit interfaces are considered virtual adapters, because they do not directly represent hardware in your system. However, from a software perspective, these will be treated in almost the same way any other interface is treated. We will direct and route traffic through them. The sit virtual interfaces allow you to map your IPv4 address to an IPv6 address, and then create an IPv6 interface on your machine. This process is started by enabling the sit0 interface and assigning it your IPv4 address. For this example, **10.10.0.8** is the tunnel broker's IPv4 endpoint, and `2001:FEFE:0F00::4B` is **vlager**'s IPv6 tunnel endpoint IP address.

```
vlager# ifconfig sit0 up
vlager# ifconfig sit0 inet6 tunnel ::10.10.0.8
```

This step enables the sit0 interface and binds it to the tunnel broker's IPv4 address. The next step is to assign your IPv6 address to the sit1 interface. That is accomplished with the following commands:

```
vlager# ifconfig sit1 up
vlager# ifconfig sit1 inet6 add 2001:FEFE:0F00::4B/127
```

The tunnel should now be operational. However, in order to test, you will need to route IPv6 traffic to the sit1 interface. This is most easily handled by using *route*.

```
vlager$ route -A inet6 add ::/0 dev sit1
```

This command tells the OS to send all IPv6 traffic to the sit1 device. With the route in place, you should now be able to verify your IPv6. The connectivity can now be tested by using *ping6*. In this example, we will ping the IPv6 address of the remote side of our newly created tunnel.

```
vlager# ping6 2001:470:1f00:ffff::3a
PING 2001:470:1f00:ffff::3a(2001:470:1f00:ffff::3a) 56 data bytes
64 bytes from 2001:470:1f00:ffff::3a: icmp_seq=1 ttl=64 time=26.2 ms
64 bytes from 2001:470:1f00:ffff::3a: icmp_seq=2 ttl=64 time=102 ms
64 bytes from 2001:470:1f00:ffff::3a: icmp_seq=3 ttl=64 time=143 ms
64 bytes from 2001:470:1f00:ffff::3a: icmp_seq=4 ttl=64 time=130 ms
Ctrl-c
--- 2001:470:1f00:ffff::3a ping statistics ---
4 packets transmitted, 4 received, 0% packet loss, time 3013ms
rtt min/avg/max/mdev = 26.295/100.590/143.019/45.339 ms
vlager#
```

 At this point, you now have a system configured to a pubic IPv6 network. You can see the whole IPv6 world, and they can see you. It is important to note that at this point you should verify exactly which services are listening, and that they are patched and not exploitable. While IPv6 netfilter support is under development, it may not be stable enough to rely on.

IPv6-Aware Applications

There are currently quite a few IPv6-aware applications that are also commonly in use on the IPv4 networks. Among the more popular are the Apache web server and OpenSSH. In this section, we'll detail common configuration for enabling IPv6 within these applications.

Apache web server

Although Apache v1.3 is commonly used due to its stability, it does not support IPv6 without source code modification. Should you absolutely need v1.3 and IPv6 support, IPv6 patches do exist, but they are unsupported and likely untested. There has been a great deal of discussion about whether to include official IPv6 support in the stable v1.3, and the general consensus has been to leave v1.3 alone and use v2.0 for the continued support and development of Apache's IPv6 support. The Apache web server Versions 2.0 and higher support IPv6 without modification. Therefore, we will focus on this version in this section.

Configuring Apache v2.0.x for IPv6 support

The configuration of Apache with IPv6 is fairly straightforward. The build process requires no special options and can be installed from either source or RPM. One option that can be set at compile time that may be of interest to IPv6 users is *-enable-v4-mapped* tag. This is most often the default in pre built packages. It enables you to have a line with a general Listen directive such as:

```
Listen 80
```

This will bind the web server process to all available IP addresses. Administrators of IPv6 systems may find this behavior insecure and inefficient, as unnecessary sockets will be opened for the large number of default IPv6 addresses. It is for this reason that you can use *-disable-v4-mapped* when compiling and force explicit configuration of listening interfaces. With this option disabled, you can still have interfaces listen on all ports, but you must specify to do so.

When the server is compiled and installed as you wish, a single change to the configuration file is required to enable a listener. This step is very similar to the IPv4 configuration of Apache. To enable a web listener on **vlager**'s IPv6 IP, the following change to the *apache.conf* file is required:

```
Listen [fec0:ffff::2]:80
```

Once Apache is started, it opens up a listener on port 80 on the specified IP. This can be verified through the use of *netstat*:

```
vlager# netstat -aunt
Active Internet connections (servers and established)
Proto Recv-Q Send-Q  Local Address       Foreign Address     State
tcp        0      0  10.10.0.4:22        0.0.0.0:*           LISTEN
tcp        0      0  fec0:ffff::2:80     :::*               LISTEN

vlager#
```

The second entry in the table is the IPv6 apache listener, and it is noted in exactly the same format as the IPv4 addresses.

If you would like to have your Apache server listen on all available IPv6 addresses, a slightly different configuration option can be used:

```
Listen [::]:80
```

This is very similar to the 0.0.0.0 address used to accomplish the same thing in IPv4. To enable listeners on ports other than 80, either replace the existing port number or add additional Listen lines. For a more detailed discussion of Apache, please refer to Chapter 14.

OpenSSH

The OpenSSH project has been compatible with IPv6 since its early days, and support within the program is now considered mature. It is also quite easy to configure. No additional options need to be passed during compile time, so installing from binary package will cause no problems.

This section assumes that you have OpenSSH operational under IPv4 and know where your configuration files are installed. In our case, the configuration files are installed in */etc/ssh*. To add an IPv6 listener, we need to add a line to the *sshd_config* file:

```
ListenAddress fec0:ffff::2
Port 1022
```

When OpenSSH is restarted with the -6 command-line option, it will now be listening on our IPv6 address at port 1022.

Accessing IPv6 hosts with the OpenSSH client is also quite easy. It is only necessary to specify the -6 command-line option as follows:

```
othermachine$ ssh -6 fec0:ffff::2 -p 1022
bob@fec0:ffff::2's password:
bob@vlager $
```

That's really all there is to configuring OpenSSH for IPv6 usage. At this point you should have a server with an OpenSSH IPv6 listener and be able to use *ssh* to connect to other machines on the IPv6 network. If not, please see the "Troubleshooting" section, next.

Troubleshooting

As IPv6 networking is often uncharted territory, it is not uncommon for things to go wrong. One of the most common mistakes made when dealing with IPv6 initially involves the address notation. The change from the period to the colon for subset separation can cause errors, as most administrators' hands are used to reaching for the period. A second notation problem when writing out addresses comes with shortening them. As discussed earlier in the section, when omitting series of zeroes, a double colon is used. Should you forget the double colon, the machine will generate an error informing you that you have entered an incomplete IP address. Here are some examples of incorrect IPv6 notation:

```
fe80.ffff.0207.3bfe.0ddd.bbfe.02
3ffe:0001:fefe:5
2001:fdff::0901::1
```

If the problem is more severe, and you're not seeing the IPv6 stack at all, you should review your kernel configuration. If you've compiled support for IPv6 directly into the kernel, check your system log and see if you're receiving any errors when it attempts to load. A successful IPv6 installation will yield the following message at boot time:

```
NET4: Linux TCP/IP 1.0 for NET4.0
IP Protocols: ICMP, UDP, TCP
IP: routing cache hash table of 4096 buckets, 32Kbytes
TCP: Hash tables configured (established 32768 bind 65536)
NET4 Unix domain sockets 1.0/SMP for Linux NET4.0.
IPv6 v0.8 for NET4.0
IPv6 over IPv4 tunneling driver
```

This section shows the network stack initialization, and the last two lines are specific to IPv6. If you don't see these two lines, or see an error, you need to check your kernel configuration file and perhaps consider building IPv6 as a module.

If you've built IPv6 support as a module, make sure you have it configured to load automatically. There are as many ways to do this as there are Linux distributions, so consult your distribution's documentation for specific details.

When properly loaded, the module should appear when you enter the *lsmod* command.

```
vlager# lsmod |grep ipv6
Module              Size Used by    Not tainted
ipv6              162132 -1
```

When loading the module, you should also see the following lines in your system log:

```
Jul  7 16:13:43 deathstar kernel: IPv6 v0.8 for NET4.0
Jul  7 16:13:43 deathstar kernel: IPv6 over IPv4 tunneling driver
```

If you are confident that your IPv6 stack has installed properly, and you are able to send traffic on your local LAN but cannot send traffic through your IPv6 tunnel, check your IPv4 connectivity. The first step in this process would be double-checking the IPv4 tunnel addresses specified in the sit0 configuration. If the configuration is accurate, test the remote IPv4 endpoint. The inability to send IPv4 traffic to the tunnel endpoint IP will also prevent you from sending any IPv6 traffic.

Other connectivity issues could be the result of a misconfigured firewall. If you have decided to use Netfilter for IPv6, make certain that your firewall rules are accurate by attempting to send traffic both with and without your rules enabled. It is possible that there may be problems within Netfilter for IPv6 that prevent certain configurations from working properly.

## CHAPTER 14

Configuring the Apache Web Server

One of the most widely used software packages under Linux currently is the Apache web server. Starting in 1995 as small group of developers, the Apache Software foundation incorporated in 1999 to develop and support the Apache HTTP server. With a base of more than 25 million operational Internet web servers, Apache's HTTP server is known for its flexibility and performance benefits. In this section, we will explore the basics of building and configuring an Apache HTTP server and examine some options that will assist in the security and performance of its operation. In this chapter, we'll be looking at Apache v1.3, which is currently the most widely deployed and supported version.

Apache HTTPD Server—An Introduction

Apache is in itself just a simple web server. It was designed with the goal of serving web pages. Some commercial web servers have tried to pack many different features into a web server product, but such combination products tend to be open to substantial numbers of security vulnerabilities. The simplicity and modular design of the Apache HTTPD server brings a more secure product, and its track record especially when compared to other web servers shows it to be a stable and robust product.

This is not to say that Apache servers are incapable of providing dynamic content to users. There are many Apache modules that can be integrated to provide an almost infinite number of new features. Add-on products, such as PHP and *mod_perl*, can be used to create powerful web applications and generate dynamic web content. This chapter, however, will concentrate on the configuration of Apache itself. Here, we will discuss how to build and configure an Apache HTTPD web server and look at the different options that can be used to build a stable and secure web server.

Configuring and Building Apache

If your Linux distribution does not currently have Apache, the easiest way to get it is from one of the many Apache mirror sites. A list can be found at the main Apache

Software Foundation site, *http://www.apache.org*. At present, there are two branches of the Apache HTTPD version tree, 1.3 and 2.0. The new version tree, v2.0 offers new features and is being actively developed, but is more likely to be susceptible to bugs and vulnerabilities. In this chapter, we will be using the most recent version of the 1.3 branch because of its proven reliability and stability. Many of the configuration options, however, are similar in both versions.

Getting and Compiling the Software

You have the option of obtaining Apache in either source format or package format. If you are installing from package, you will not have the same amount of initial configuration flexibility as you would building from source. Packages generally come with the most common options pre-built into the binaries. If you are looking for specific features or options or if you want to build a very minimal version of the server, you should consider building from source.

Building Apache from source is similar to building other Linux source packages and follows the "configure-make-make install" path. Apache has many options that need to be set at source configuration time. Among these is the ability to select the modules which you would like to build or have disabled. Modules are a great way to add or remove functionality to your web server and cover a wide range of functions—from performance to authentication and security. Table 14-1 shows a sample list taken from the Apache documentation of a number of the available modules.

Table 14-1. Apache modules

Type	Enabled or disabled by default	Function
Environment creation		
mod_env	Enabled	Set environment variables for CGI/SSI scripts
mod_setenvif	Enabled	Set environment variables based on HTTP headers
mod_unique_id	Disabled	Generate unique identifiers for request
Content-type decisions		
mod_mime	Enabled	Content type/encoding determination (configured)
mod_mime_magic	Disabled	Content type/encoding determination (automatic)
mod_negotiation	Enabled	Content selection based on the HTTP Accept* headers
URL mapping		
mod_alias	Enabled	Simple URL translation and redirection
mod_rewrite	Disabled	Advanced URL translation and redirection
mod_userdir	Enabled	Selection of resource directories by username
mod_spelling	Disabled	Correction of misspelled URLs
Directory handling		
mod_dir	Enabled	Directory and directory default file handling
mod_autoindex	Enabled	Automated directory index file generation

Table 14-1. *Apache modules (continued)*

Type	Enabled or disabled by default	Function
Access control		
mod_access	Enabled	Access control (user, host, and network)
mod_auth	Enabled	HTTP basic authentication (user and password)
mod_auth_dbm	Disabled	HTTP basic authentication via UNIX NDBM files
mod_auth_db	Disabled	HTTP basic authentication via Berkeley DB files
mod_auth_anon	Disabled	HTTP basic authentication for anonymous-style users
mod_digest	Disabled	Digest authentication
HTTP response		
mod_headers	Disabled	Arbitrary HTTP response headers (configured)
mod_cern_meta	Disabled	Arbitrary HTTP response headers (CERN-style files)
mod_expires	Disabled	Expires HTTP responses
mod_asis	Enabled	Raw HTTP responses
Scripting		
mod_include	Enabled	Server Side Includes (SSI) support
mod_cgi	Enabled	Common Gateway Interface (CGI) support
mod_actions	Enabled	Map CGI scripts to act as internal "handlers"
Internal content handlers		
mod_status	Enabled	Content handler for server runtime status
mod_info	Disabled	Content handler for configuration summary
Request logging		
mod_log_config	Enabled	Customizable logging of requests
mod_log_agent	Disabled	Specialized HTTP User-Agent logging (deprecated)
mod_log_referer	Disabled	Specialized HTTP Referrer logging (deprecated
mod_usertrack	Disabled	Logging of user click-trails via HTTP cookies
Miscellaneous		
mod_imap	Enabled	Server-side image map support
mod_proxy	Disabled	Caching proxy module (HTTP, HTTPS, FTP)
mod_so	Disabled	Dynamic Shard Object (DSO) bootstrapping
Experimental		
mod_mmap_static	Disabled	Caching of frequently served pages via *mmap()*
Developmental		
mod_example	Disabled	Apache API demonstration (developers only)

When you have decided which options to use, you can add them to the configure script as follows. To enable a module, use:

```
vlager# ./configure -enable-module=module_name
```

To disable a default module, you can use the following command:

```
vlager# ./configure -disable-module=module_name
```

If you choose to enable or disable any of the default modules, make sure you understand exactly what that modules does. Enabling or disabling certain modules can adversely affect performance or security. More information about the specific modules can be found on the Apache web site.

The next step after configuration is to compile the entire package. Like many other Linux programs, this is accomplished by the *make* command. After you have compiled, *make install* will install Apache in the directory you specified via the -prefix= option at configuration time.

Configuration File Options

When the Apache software has been installed in the directory you have selected, you are ready to begin configuration of the server. Earlier versions of the Apache server used multiple configuration files. However, now only the *httpd.conf* file is required. It is still quite handy to have multiple configuration files (for example, to make version upgrades easier). The include option will allow you to read additional configuration files from the main *httpd.conf* file.

Apache comes with a default configuration file that has the most common options set. If you are in a hurry to have your server running, this default configuration should cover the requirements to launch Apache. While functional, this configuration is not acceptable to many administrators. To begin fine-tuning the configuration, the first option most administrators choose is selecting the IP address and port information of the server.

Binding Addresses and Ports

Listen and BindAddress are the first two options that you may want to change.

```
# Listen: Allows you to bind Apache to specific IP addresses and/or
# ports, instead of the default. See also the <VirtualHost>
# directive.
#
#Listen 3000
Listen 172.16.0.4:80
```

This configuration change enables the Apache server to listen only on the specified interface and port. You can also use the BindAddress option to specify the IP address to which the server will bind. With this option, you are only specifying the IP address, not the port as above.

```
# BindAddress: You can support virtual hosts with this option. This directive
# is used to tell the server which IP address to listen to. It can either
# contain "*", an IP address, or a fully qualified Internet domain name.
```

```
# See also the <VirtualHost> and Listen directives.
#
BindAddress 172.16.0.4
```

Logging and Path Configuration Options

When building Apache, you may have specified the installation directory. If so, the installation has automatically set the paths for your server root documents and all of your logfiles. If you need to change this, the following options will be useful:

ServerRoot

> The location of the server's main configuration and logfiles

DocumentRoot

> The location of your HTML documents, or other web content

By default, Apache will log to a path under its main server root path. If you have a different place on your system where you collect logs and would like to change the logfile paths, the following options will require changes:

CustomLog

> The location of your access logfile

ErrorLog

> The location of your error logfile

There are also some other useful options that can be set when configuring the logging settings on Apache:

HostnameLookups

> Tells Apache whether it should look up names for logged IP addresses. It is a good idea to leave this setting turned off, since logging can be slowed if the server is attempting to resolve all names.

LogLevel

> This option tells Apache how much information it should save to the logfiles. By default it is set at warn, but possible values are debug, info, notice, warn, error, crit, alert, and emerg. Each increasing level logs less information.

LogFormat

> With this option, administrators can choose which format the logs are written in. Items such as date, time, and IP address can be rearranged to any format desired. The default settings are usually not changed.

Server Identification Strings

By default, Apache is very friendly and will provide requesting users with a great deal of information about itself, including version information, virtual hostname, administrator name, and so on. Security conscious administrators may wish to disable this information, as it allows attackers a much quicker way of enumerating your server.

While it is not a foolproof method of protecting your site, it can slow down would-be attackers who use automated scanning tools. The following two configuration options can help you limit the amount of information your server discloses:

ServerSignature

With this option turned on, the server adds a line to server-generated pages that includes all of its version information.

ServerTokens

Setting this option to Prod will prevent Apache from ever disclosing its version number.

Performance Configuration

Sites will always have different performance requirements. For many sites, the default settings provided with Apache will deliver all the required performance. However, busier sites will need to make some changes to the configuration to increase performance capabilities. The following options can be used in performance tuning a server. More information on Apache performance tuning can be found at the Apache Software Foundation's web site.

Timeout

The number of seconds before Apache will timeout receive and send requests.

KeepAlive

Enable this option if you want persistent connections enabled. It can be set to either on or off.

MaxKeepAliveRequests

Set this option to the number of keep-alive requests that you want the server to allow in persistent connections. Having a higher value here may increase performance.

KeepAliveTimeout

This is the number of seconds that Apache will wait for a new request from the current connected session.

Min/MaxSpareServers

These options are used to create a pool of spare servers that Apache can use when it is busy. Larger sites may wish to increase these numbers from their defaults. However, for each spare server, more memory is required on the server.

StartServers

This option tells Apache how many servers to start when first launched.

MaxClients

This is the option an administrator can use to limit the number of client sessions to a server. The Apache documentation warns about setting this option too low because it can adversely affect availability.

Starting and Stopping Apache with apachectl

If you are feeling confident that your server is configured, and you're ready to run it, you will need to use *apachectl*, a tool provided with Apache that allows for the safe startup and shutdown of the server. The available options of *apachectl* are as follows:

start
    Starts the standard HTTP server

startssl
    Starts the SSL servers in addition to the regular server

stop
    Shuts down the Apache server

restart
    Sends a HUP signal to the running server

fullstatus
    Prints out a full status of the web server, but requires *mod_status*

status
    Displays a shorter version of the above status screen. Requires *mod_status*

graceful
    Sends a SIGUSR1 to the Apache server

configtest
    Inspects the configuration file for errors

While it's not mandatory to start Apache with *apachectl*, it is the recommended and easiest way to do so. *apachectl* makes shutting down the server processes quicker and more efficient, as well.

VirtualHost Configuration Options

One of the more powerful features of Apache is the ability to run multiple web servers on one machine. This functionality is accomplished using the VirtualHost functionality found within the *httpd.conf* file. There are two types of virtual hosts that can be configured—named virtual hosts and IP virtual hosts. With named virtual hosts, you can host multiple TLDs on a single IP, while with IP virtual hosting, you can host only one virtual host per IP address. In this section, we will give examples of each, and list some common configuration options.

IP-Based Virtual Hosts

For those who have only one site to host or have multiple IPs for all sites they wish to run, IP-based virtual hosting is the best configuration choice. Consider the following example where the Virtual Brewery decides to host a web site for its Virtual

Vineyard. The following is the minimum amount of configuration that would need to be added to the *httpd.conf* file in order to create the new web site.

```
Listen www.virtualvineyard.com:80
.
.
.
<VirtualHost www.virtualvineyard.com>
ServerAdmin webmaster@vbrew.com
DocumentRoot /home/www/virtualvineyard.com
ServerName www.virtualvineyard.com
ErrorLog /var/www/logs/vvineyard.error_log
TransferLog /var/www/logs/vvineyard.access_log
</VirtualHost>
```

You would also want to make sure that *www.virtualvinyard.com* was added to your */etc/hosts* file. This is done because Apache will need to look up an IP address for this domain when it starts. You can rely entirely on your DNS, but should your DNS server be unavailable for some reason when the web server restarts, your web server will fail. Alternately, you can hardcode the IP address of your server at the beginning of the configuration in the <VirtualHost> tag. Doing so may seem more efficient, however, should you wish to change your web server IP address, it will require changing your Apache configuration file.

In addition to the configuration options listed in the example, any of the options discussed earlier in the chapter can be added to the VirtualHost groups. This provides you with maximum flexibility for each of your separate web servers.

Name-Based Virtual Hosting

The configuration of name-based virtual hosting is very similar to the previous example, with the exception that multiple domains can be hosted on a single IP address. There are two caveats to this functionality. The first—perhaps the biggest drawback—is that SSL can be used only with a single IP address. This is not a problem with Apache, but rather with SSL and the way certificates work. The second potential drawback is that some older web browsers, such as those without the HTTP 1.1 specification, will not work. This is because name-based virtual hosting relies on the client to inform the server in the HTTP request header of the site they wish to visit. Nearly any browser released within the past few years, however, will have HTTP 1.1 implemented, so this isn't a problem for most administrators.

Proceeding to an example configuration, we will use the same example given earlier in the chapter, except this time the Virtual Brewery has only one public IP address. You will first need to inform Apache that you are using named virtual hosting, and then provide the detail on your sites as is shown in this example.

```
NameVirtualHost 172.16.0.199
<VirtualHost 172.16.0.199>
ServerName www.vbrew.com
DocumentRoot /home/www/vbrew.com
```

```
</VirtualHost>
<VirtualHost 172.16.0.199>
ServerName www.virtualvineyard.com
DocumentRoot /home/www/vvineyard.com
</VirtualHost>
```

For the sake of clarity, the additional options were omitted, but any of the previously discussed options can be added as necessary.

Apache and OpenSSL

After having configured and tested your Apache web server configuration, the next thing you may wish to do is configure an SSL page. From protecting web-based email clients, to providing secure e-commerce transactions, there are many reasons why one would use SSL. Within the Apache realm there are two options for providing SSL, Apache-SSL and *mod_ssl*. In this section, we'll focus on the older and more commonly used *mod_ssl*.

As with any SSL-based application, certificates are required. These provide the basis on which the trust relationship between client and server is established. This being said, if you are hosting a site for a business, you will likely want to get a certificate signed by a third party, such as Verisign or Thawte. Since these certificates are somewhat costly, if you aren't hosting a business, you also have the option of generating your own certificate. The disadvantage of this method is that when clients access your site, an error will be generated telling them that your certificate is not trusted since it hasn't been signed by a third party. This means that they will be required to click through the error message and decide whether or not they want to trust your certificate. In this chapter we will provide configuration examples for administrators generating their own certificates. Alternately, the *cacert.org* organization offers free certificates for individuals.

Generating an SSL Certificate

In order to enable an SSL session, you will first need to create a certificate. To do this, you will need to make sure you have OpenSSL installed. It can be found at *http://www.openssl.org*, in both source and binary package format. This package comes installed with many Linux distributions, so you may not have to install it. Once you have installed or verified the installation of OpenSSL, you can proceed to create the required SSL certificate.

The first step in this process is to create a certificate signing request. You will need to enter a temporary PEM pass phrase and some information about your site:

```
vlager# openssl req -config openssl.cnf -new -out vbrew.csr
Using configuration from openssl.cnf
Generating a 1024 bit RSA private key
...............................++++++
```

```
....++++++
writing new private key to 'privkey.pem'
Enter PEM pass phrase:
Verifying password - Enter PEM pass phrase:
-----
You are about to be asked to enter information that will be incorporated
into your certificate request.
What you are about to enter is what is called a Distinguished Name or a DN.
There are quite a few fields but you can leave some blank
For some fields there will be a default value,
If you enter '.', the field will be left blank.
-----
Country Name (2 letter code) [AU]:US
State or Province Name (full name) [Some-State]:California
Locality Name (eg, city) [ ]:Berkeley
Organization Name (eg, company) [Internet Widgits Pty Ltd]:www.vbrew.com
Organizational Unit Name (eg, section) [ ]:
Common Name (eg, YOUR name) [ ]:www.vbrew.com
Email Address [ ]:webmaster@vbrew.com
Please enter the following 'extra' attributes
to be sent with your certificate request
A challenge password [ ]:
An optional company name [ ]:
```

The next step is to remove the private key PEM pass phrase from your certificate. This will allow the server to restart without having to input the password. For paranoid administrators, this step can be bypassed, but should your server fail at any point, you will have to manually restart it.

```
vlager # openssl rsa -in privkey.pem -out vbrew.key
read RSA key
Enter PEM pass phrase:
writing RSA key
```

Having separated the pass phrase, you will now need to self-sign your certificate file. This is accomplished using the x509 option with OpenSSL:

```
apache ssl # openssl x509 -in vbrew.csr -out vbrew.cert -req -signkey vbrew.key -days
365
Signature ok
subject=/C=US/ST=California/L=Berkeley/O=www.vbrew.com/CN=www.vbrew.com/
Email=webmaster@vbrew.com
Getting Private key
```

Once this has been completed, your certificate is ready for use. You should copy the certificate files to your Apache directory so the web server can access them.

Compiling mod_ssl for Apache

If you compiled Apache from source as in the earlier example in the chapter, you will need to patch the Apache source and recompile in order to use *mod_ssl*. If you installed Apache from a binary package for your Linux distributions, then there's a good chance that it is already compiled in. To see whether you need to recompile, check which modules are built into Apache by using the following command:

```
vlager # /var/www/bin/httpd -l
Compiled-in modules:
  http_core.c
  mod_env.c
  mod_log_config.c
  mod_mime.c
  mod_negotiation.c
  mod_status.c
  mod_include.c
  mod_autoindex.c
  mod_dir.c
  mod_cgi.c
  mod_asis.c
  mod_imap.c
  mod_actions.c
  mod_userdir.c
  mod_alias.c
  mod_access.c
  mod_auth.c
  mod_setenvif.c
```

In this case, *mod_ssl* is not present, so we will have to download and compile it into our Apache server. Fortunately, this isn't as difficult as it might sound. The source for *mod_ssl* can be found at *http://www.modssl.org*. You will need to unpack it along with the source to OpenSSL. For ease, we have put all three source trees under the same directory. When you have everything unpacked, you are ready to continue. First, you will need to configure the build of *mod_ssl*:

```
vlager # ./configure --with-apache=../apache_1.3.28 --with-openssl=../openssl-0.9.6i
Configuring mod_ssl/2.8.15 for Apache/1.3.28
 + Apache location: ../apache_1.3.28 (Version 1.3.28)
 + Auxiliary patch tool: ./etc/patch/patch (local)
 + Applying packages to Apache source tree:
   o Extended API (EAPI)
   o Distribution Documents
   o SSL Module Source
   o SSL Support
   o SSL Configuration Additions
   o SSL Module Documentation
   o Addons
Done: source extension and patches successfully applied.
```

Now, assuming that you built your OpenSSL from source and it is in line with your Apache source directory, you can configure and build Apache as follows:

```
vlager # cd ../apache_1.3.28
vlager # SSL_BASE=../openssl-0.9.6i ./configure -prefix=/var/www --enable-module=ssl
Configuring for Apache, Version 1.3.28
 + using installation path layout: Apache (config.layout)
Creating Makefile
Creating Configuration.apaci in src
```

```
Creating Makefile in src
 + configured for Linux platform
 + setting C pre-processor to gcc -E
 + using "tr [a-z] [A-Z]" to uppercase
 + checking for system header files
 + adding selected modules
    o ssl_module uses ConfigStart/End
      + SSL interface: mod_ssl/2.8.15
      + SSL interface build type: OBJ
      + SSL interface compatibility: enabled
      + SSL interface experimental code: disabled
      + SSL interface conservative code: disabled
      + SSL interface vendor extensions: disabled
      + SSL interface plugin: Built-in SDBM
      + SSL library path: /root/openssl-0.9.6i
      + SSL library version: OpenSSL 0.9.6i Feb 19 2003
      + SSL library type: source tree only (stand-alone)
 + enabling Extended API (EAPI)
 + using system Expat
 + checking sizeof various data types
 + doing sanity check on compiler and options
Creating Makefile in src/support
Creating Makefile in src/regex
Creating Makefile in src/os/unix
Creating Makefile in src/ap
Creating Makefile in src/main
Creating Makefile in src/modules/standard
Creating Makefile in src/modules/ssl
```

When the source configuration has completed, you can now rebuild Apache with *make install*. You can also repeat the *httpd -l* command used above to verify that *mod_ssl* has been compiled into Apache.

Configuration File Changes

Only a few minor changes are required. The easiest way to enable SSL within Apache is by using the Virtual Host directives discussed earlier. However, first, outside of the Virtual Host section, at the end of your configuration file, you will need to add the following SSL directives:

```
SSLRandomSeed startup builtin
SSLSessionCache None
```

Now you need to build your VirtualHost configuration to enable the SSL engine. Again, in the *httpd.conf* file, add the following lines:

```
<VirtualHost www.vbrew.com:443>
SSLEngine On
SSLCipherSuite ALL:!ADH:!EXPORT56:RC4+RSA:+HIGH:+MEDIUM:!SSLv2:+EXP:+eNULL
SSLCertificateFile conf/ssl/vbrew.cert
SSLCertificateKeyFile conf/ssl/vbrew.key
</VirtualHost>
```

This section enabled the SSLEngine and configured the cipher suites. You can select which you would like to allow or disallow. The "!" is used for entries that are explicitly disallowed, and the "+" is for those that are allowed. If you have stored your certificates in any other directory, you will need to make the necessary changes to the SSLCertificateFile and KeyFile entries. For more information about the options available with *mod_ssl*, consult the documentation found on the *mod_ssl* web site.

Troubleshooting

As complex as Apache configurations can be, it's not unlikely that there will be problems. This section will address some common errors and resolutions to those problems.

Testing the Configuration File with apachectl

Fortunately for administrators, Apache comes with a configuration checker, which will test changes made to the configuration before bringing down an operational server. If it finds any errors, it will provide you with some diagnostic information. Consider the following example:

```
vlager # ../bin/apachectl configtest
Syntax error on line 985 of /var/www/conf/httpd.conf:
Invalid command 'SSLEgine', perhaps mis-spelled or defined by a module not included
in the server configuration
```

The configuration testing tool has found an error on line 985, and it appears that the SSLEngine directive was spelled incorrectly. This configuration checker will catch any syntactical errors, which certainly helps. Administrators should always run this before stopping and restarting their servers.

The configtest option won't solve all of your problems, however. Transposed digits in an IP, a misspelled domain name, or commented out requirements will all pass the test, but cause problems for the operational server.

Page Not Found Errors

This is a very general error, and a variety of circumstances can cause it. This is Apache's way of telling you that it can't find or read the page. If you are getting an error of this nature, first check all of your paths. Remember with Apache, you are operating within a virtual directory environment. If you have links to files outside of this structure, it is likely that the server will not be able to server them. Additionally, you should verify the permissions of the files and make sure that the user who owns the web server process can read them. Files owned by *root*, or any other user, set to mode 700 (read/write/execute user) may cause the server to fail, since it will be unable to read them.

Pathnames, along with domain names, are often misspelled. While configtest may catch some of them, it is unlikely that it will catch all of them. One typo can cause a whole site to fail. Double-check everything if you are having a problem.

SSL problems

If your SSL server isn't working, there are a number of things that could have gone wrong. If your server isn't delivering the pages, you should check the *error_log* file. It will often provide you with a wealth of troubleshooting options. For example, our example web server was not serving up SSL pages, but unencrypted pages were being served without issue. Checking the *error_log*, we see:

```
[Wed Aug  6 14:11:33 2003] [error] [client 10.10.0.158] Invalid method in request
\x80L\x01\x03
```

This type of error is quite common. The invalid request is the client trying to negotiate an SSL session, but for some reason the web server is serving only unencrypted pages on the SSL port. We can even verify this by pointing the browser at port 443 and initiating a normal HTTP session. The reason why this is occurring is that the server does not think it has been told to enable the SSLEngine, or doesn't think it has.

To fix this problem, you need to verify that you have the line in your *httpd.conf* file:

```
SSLEngine On
```

You should also check the Virtual Host entry that you created for the SSL server. If there is an error with the IP address or DNS name on which it was told to create the server, the server will create this kind of error. Consider the following excerpt of our configuration file:

```
<VirtualHost www.vbrew.cmo:443>
SSLEngine On
SSLCipherSuite ALL:!ADH:!EXPORT56:RC4+RSA:+HIGH:+MEDIUM:+LOW:!SSLv2:+EXP:+eNULL
SSLCertificateFile conf/ssl/vbrew.cert
SSLCertificateKeyFile conf/ssl/vbrew.key
</VirtualHost>
```

A typo in the VirtualHost directive has caused the server to try to start for a name in the **.cmo** rather than the **.com** top-level domain. Of course, Apache doesn't realize this is an error, and is doing exactly what you've asked it to do.

Other SSL-related problems are likely to center on key locations and permissions. Make sure that your keys are in a location known to the server and that they can be read by the necessary entities. Also, note that if you are using a self-signed key— some clients may be configured not to accept the certificate, causing them to fail. If this is the case, either reconfigure your client workstations or purchase a third-party signed certificate.

## CHAPTER 15

IMAP

Internet Message Access Protocol (IMAP) was developed from a need for mobile email access. Many workers read mail from a variety of locations (the office, home, hotel rooms, and so on) and want such flexible features as the ability to download headers first and then selectively download mail messages. The main mail delivery protocols before IMAP, for the Internet, was POP, which offers more rudimentary mail delivery-only functionality

With IMAP, traveling users can access their email from anywhere and download it or leave it on the server as desired. POP, on the other hand, does not work well when users access email from many different machines; users end up with their email distributed across many different email clients. IMAP provides users with the ability to remotely manage multiple email boxes, and store or search as well as archive old messages.

IMAP—An Introduction

IMAP, fully documented in RFC 3501, was designed to provide a robust, mobile mail delivery and access mechanism. For more detail on the protocol and how it functions on the network layer, or for additional information on the numerous specification options, please consult the RFC documentation.

IMAP and POP

POP and IMAP tend to be grouped together or compared, which is a bit unfair since they are dissimilar in many ways. POP was created as a simple mail delivery vehicle, which it does very well. Users connect to the server and obtain their messages, which are then, ideally, deleted from the server. IMAP takes an entirely different approach. It acts as the keeper of the messages and provides a framework in which the users can efficiently manipulate the stored messages. While administrators and users can configure POP to store the messages on the server, it can quickly become inefficient since a POP client will download all old messages each time the mail is queried. This can get messy quickly, if the user is receiving any quantity of email. For users who do not need any kind of portability, or receive little email, POP is probably an acceptable choice, but those seeking greater functionality will want to use IMAP.

Which IMAP to Choose?

Once you've decided that IMAP is for you, there are two primary options. The two main flavors are Cyrus IMAP and the University of Washington IMAP server. Both follow the RFC specification for IMAP and have their advantages and disadvantages. They also use different mailbox formats and therefore cannot be mixed. One key difference between the two is found in Cyrus IMAP. It does not use */etc/passwd* for its mail account database, so the administrator does not have to specially add mail users to the system password file. This is more secure option for system administrators, because creating accounts on systems can be construed as a security risk. However, the ease of configuration and installation of UW IMAP often makes it more appealing. In this chapter, we'll primarily focus on the two most common IMAP servers: UW IMAP, because of its popularity and ease of installation, and Cyrus IMAP, because of its additional security features.

Getting an IMAP client

The UW IMAP, as its name suggests, can be found at the University of Washington. Their web site, *http://www.washington.edu/imap/*, contains various documentation and implementation suggestions, as well as the link to their software repository FTP site. There are a number of different versions available in various forms. For simplicity, the UW IMAP team offers a link a direct link to the most current version: *ftp:// ftp.cac.washington.edu/mail/imap.tar.Z*.

Installing UW-IMAP

Once the server software has been downloaded and decompressed, it can be installed. However, because of UW-IMAP's large portability database, it does not support GNU automake, meaning that there isn't a *configure* script. Instead, a *Makefile* that relies on user-specified parameters is used. There are many supported operating systems, including a number of Linux distributions. Here's a list of a few of the supported Linuxes distributions:

```
# ldb    Debian Linux
# lnx    Linux with traditional passwords and crypt( ) in the C library
#          (see lnp, sl4, sl5, and slx)
# lnp    Linux with Pluggable Authentication Modules (PAM)
# lrh    RedHat Linux 7.2
# lsu    SuSE Linux
# sl4    Linux using -lshadow to get the crypt( ) function
# sl5    Linux with shadow passwords, no extra libraries
# slx    Linux using -lcrypt to get the crypt( ) function
```

The lrh version will probably work on newer Red Hat versions as well. If your distribution isn't listed, try one of the matching generic options. lnp is a good guess for most modern versions of Linux.

If you don't have OpenSSL installed, you will need to edit a part of the Makefile. Find the section where SSL is being configured, and look for the following line:

```
SSLTYPE=nopwd
```

The nopwd option needs to be set to none in order to tell IMAP that you aren't using OpenSSL.

If you have OpenSSL installed but the installer is still failing, the cause is most likely that it is looking for OpenSSL in the wrong place. By default, the *Makefile* searches a predefined path based on your build selection at the beginning of the process. For example, if you have used the lnp option to build IMAP, it is looking for SSL in the */usr/ssl* directory. But if you're using Gentoo Linux, your SSL directory is */usr* and you will need to search for the SSLPATH option in the Makefile and correct the path. The same process will need to be followed for the SSLCERTS option, which should be in the same area of the *Makefile*.

Having successfully compiled the IMAP server, you should install it in your *inetd. conf* file (or use *xinetd*, if appropriate). To use *inetd.conf*, you need to add the following line:

```
imap    stream tcp    nowait root    /path/to/imapd    imapd
```

Note that you will need to change the actual path to reflect the location where you installed your *imapd* binary.

Most modern Linux systems have a fairly complete */etc/services* file, but you should verify that IMAP is present by searching for or, if necessary, adding, the following line:

```
imap            143/tcp
imaps           993/tcp
```

When these steps have been completed, the installation can be tested with the *netstat*. If you installation is successful, you will see a listener on TCP port 143.

```
vlager# netstat -aunt
 Active Internet connections (servers and established)
Proto Recv-Q Send-Q Local Address        Foreign Address        State
tcp       0      0 0.0.0.0:143          0.0.0.0:*              LISTEN
tcp       0      0 0.0.0.0:22           0.0.0.0:*              LISTEN
```

As with any service, it may also be necessary to make adjustments to the firewall to allow the new connections.

IMAP configuration

One of the great joys of UW IMAP is that once it is installed, it is almost always fully functional. The default options, including the use of standard */etc/passwd* authentication and the Unix mailbox format, are considered acceptable by most administrators. If you need more flexibility or features, UW IMAP offers extended configuration options such as anonymous logins, IMAP alert messages, alternate mailbox formats, and the possibility of shared mailboxes, which we'll take a look at in the next section.

Advanced UW IMAP configuration options

There are a number of additional options that can be added to a UW IMAP server, based on your requirements. One feature that may be useful is the potential to allow anonymous logins. This can be used as a way to provide information to users without creating specific accounts for them. This has been used at universities as a method of distributing information, or providing read-only access to discussion lists. To enable this functionality, the only step required is to place a file in your */etc* directory called *anonymous.newsgroups*. Once this has been completed, anonymous users will have access to commonly shared mailboxes.

Another potentially useful feature is the ability to create an alert message for IMAP users. When enabled, this feature will generate an alert message for any user logging in to check their mail. As the message is displayed every time a user checks their mail, it should be used only in emergency situations. It would not be a good place to put a banner or disclaimer. To create the alert message, you need to create a file called *imapd.alert*. The contents consist of your message.

Using alternate mailbox formats

The default mailbox format configured by UW IMAP was selected because it provides the greatest flexibility and compatibility. While these are two definite advantages, they come at a cost of performance. The mbx format supported by UW IMAP provides better capabilities for shared mailboxes, since it supports simultaneous reading and writing.

Configuring IMAP to use OpenSSL

IMAP provides many useful conveniences required by users when dealing with their email, but lacks one very important feature—encryption. For this reason, IMAP-SSL was developed. When it is installed, an IMAP user with compatible client software can enjoy all the functions of IMAP without worrying about eavesdropping. In order to install IMAP with SSL support, you will first need to make sure that your IMAP server is properly installed and functioning. You will also need a functional OpenSSL installation. Most Linux distributions are shipped with OpenSSL, but if for some reason your distribution does not have it, please consult the Apache chapter in this book for more information on building OpenSSL.

To begin the configuration process, create digital certificates for your IMAP server to use. This can be done with the OpenSSL command-line utility. A sample certificate can be created as follows:

```
vlager# cd /path/to/ssl/certs
vlager# openssl req -new -x509 -nodes -out imapd.pem -keyout imapd.pem -days 365
Using configuration from /etc/ssl/openssl.cnf
Generating a 1024 bit RSA private key
..............++++++
.......................................................++++++
writing new private key to 'imapd.pem'
-----
You are about to be asked to enter information that will be incorporated
into your certificate request.
What you are about to enter is what is called a Distinguished Name or a DN.
There are quite a few fields but you can leave some blank
For some fields there will be a default value,
If you enter '.', the field will be left blank.
-----
Country Name (2 letter code) [AU]:
.
.
Common Name (eg, YOUR name) []: mail.virtualbrewery.com
Email Address []:
vlager # ls -l
total 4
-rw-r--r--    1 root     root             1925 Nov 17 19:08 imapd.pem
vlager #
```

When creating this certificate, make sure that you've entered the domain name of your mail server in the common name field. If this is not set, or is set improperly, you will at best get error messages when clients try to connect, and at worst have a broken server.

There is a good chance that your IMAP server will need to be recompiled and configured to use OpenSSL. Fortunately, this is a fairly easy process. If you are using Red Hat, SuSE, or any of the other mentioned distributions, substitute them in the command line; otherwise, the following command-line options will work for most other Linux distributions:

```
vlager#  make lnp PASSWDTYPE=pam SSLTYPE=nopwd
```

If you receive errors regarding OpenSSL, you may need to adjust the path settings. You can do this by making changes to the SSLDIR, SSLLIB, and SSLINCLUDE path options found in the *Makefile*. For most users, this will not be necessary.

After compiling the new IMAP server, copy it from the build directory to the location on your system where your other daemon files are located. Since IMAP-SSL uses a different port from the standard IMAP, you will need to make a change to your *inetd.conf* file.

```
imaps stream tcp nowait root /path/to/imapd imapd
```

If you're using *xinetd*, you will need to create a file in your */etc/xinetd.d* directory, which looks like this:

```
service imaps
{
        socket_type             = stream
        wait                    = no
        user                    = root
        server                  = /path/to/imapd
        log_on_success          += DURATION USERID
        log_on_failure          += USERID
        disable                 = no
}
```

It is also important, at this point, to make certain that you have an *imaps* entry in your */etc/services* file.

```
vlager # cat /etc/services |grep imaps
imaps           993/tcp                         # IMAP over SSL
imaps           993/udp                         # IMAP over SSL
vlager #
```

You can now test your server from any number of clients. Make certain that you've specified in the client configuration that you will be using SSL. In a number of clients, upon connection, you will receive a message asking you if you wish to trust the certificate. This message will appear only if you've generated your own certificate, as we did in the above example. Some administrators, especially if the server is being used for production use, will likely want to purchase a certificate to avoid this.

Cyrus IMAP

Another option IMAP administrators have is the product from CMU called Cyrus. It is similar to UW IMAP as far as general functionality goes—from the user standpoint, there will be little difference. The majority of the differences come on the administrative side. This is also where its benefits can be seen.

Getting Cyrus IMAP

The Cyrus software can be obtained in a number of places, but the most reliable choice, with the latest source releases, will be the central CMU Cyrus distribution site, *http://asg.web.cmu.edu/cyrus/download/*. Here, both current and previous releases can be downloaded. The availability of previous releases could be an advantage for sites with polices against using the most recent versions of software.

To begin the installation of the Cyrus server, download and decompress the latest version. You will need to download both the IMAP and SASL packages.

SASL is the authentication mechanism used by Cyrus IMAP, and will need to be configured and installed first. It is easily built using the standard "configure-make" order.

```
vlager# cd cyrus-sasl-2.1.15
vlager# ./configure
loading cache ./config.cache
checking host system type... i686-pc-linux-gnu
.
creating saslauthd.h
Configuration Complete. Type 'make' to build.
vlager# make
make  all-recursive
make[1]: Entering directory `/tmp/cyrus-sasl-2.1.15'
```

Assuming the compile is completed without failure and you've successfully executed the make install, you can now proceed to configuring and installing the Cyrus IMAP server itself.

After decompressing the Cyrus IMAP source, prepare the configuration using the following command:

```
vlager# ./configure --with-auth=unix
```

This will prepare Cyrus IMAP to use the Unix *passwd/shadow* files for user authentication. It is also possible to enable Kerberos for authentication at this point.

Next, you will need to create all of the dependency files, and then build and install the package:

```
vlager# make depend
...
vlager# make all CFLAGS=-O
...
vlager# make install
...
```

With that successfully completed, your Cyrus IMAP server is now ready to be configured.

Configuring Cyrus IMAP

You will need to create a user for the Cyrus server to use. It should be something that you can easily relate to your Cyrus server, and it also needs to be a part of the mail group.

Once the user is created, you can begin configuring your Cyrus server. The */etc/imapd.conf* file is the primary configuration file for the server. Verify that it looks something like the example below. You may need to add some of these lines.

```
configdirectory:           /var/imap
partition-default:         /var/spool/imap
sievedir:                  /var/imap/sieve
# Don't use an everyday user as admin.
admins:                    cyrus root
hashimapspool:             yes
allowanonymouslogin:       no
allowplaintext:            no
```

Troubleshooting Cyrus IMAP

Building Cyrus IMAP can be somewhat tricky, as it tends to be pickier about files and locations. If the configure process is failing, take special note of what exactly is causing the failure. For example, when building Cyrus-SASL, if the build fails with an error complaining about undefined references in the berkeley_db section, it is likely that you do not have BerkeleyDB installed, or you installed it in a place where the configure script isn't looking. The path to the installed BerkeleyDB can be set at the command line when the configure script is run. This method of tracing the root of the error, and remedying it can solve many problems.

Another common problem when building Cyrus IMAP involves the location of a file called *com_err.h*. It is expected by Cyrus IMAP to be in the */usr/include* directory. However, it often tends to be found in the */usr/include/et* directory. Therefore, it will be necessary to copy this file to the */usr/include* directory for the installation to proceed.

CHAPTER 16
Samba

The presence of Microsoft Windows machines in the network environment is often unavoidable for the Linux network administrator, and often interoperability is critical. Fortunately, a group of developers has been hard at work for the last 10 years, and has created one of the most advanced Windows-to-UNIX interoperability packages—Samba. It has, in fact, become so successful and practical that system administrators can completely replace Windows servers with Samba servers, keeping all functionality, while adding additional stability.

Samba—An Introduction

Samba, still actively developed in order to maintain feature compatibility with the ever-changing Microsoft software, provides a framework to allow Linux machines to access Windows network resources, such as shared drives and printers. Samba not only lets Linux machines access these services, but also allows Linux to offer these same services to Windows machines. With Samba, it's possible to completely replace a Windows-based file server, a Windows print server, and even, with advanced options, replace the Primary Domain Controller (PDC). Recent versions of Samba even allow Active Directory compatibility. The open-source flexibility of Samba means that development will be able to continue, and new features will be introduced when the Windows architecture changes. More information on Samba can be found in *Using Samba*, Second Edition (O'Reilly), by Jay Ts, Robert Eckstein, and David Collier-Brown.

SMB, CIFS, and Samba

The underlying technology used in Samba is based on *Server Message Blocks* (SMB), which was originally developed in the early 80s by Dr. Barry Feigenbaum while he was working at IBM. Initially, IBM was actively involved with the development, but Microsoft soon took charge and heavily continued the development work. In later years, Microsoft renamed the SMB protocol to *Common Internet File System* (CIFS), by which it is now known. One sees the terms used interchangeably.

There is little accurate and official documentation about how CIFS functions. Unlike most other network protocols, there is no official RFC documentation, though Microsoft did submit specifications to the IETF in the 1990s that expired due to numerous inaccuracies and inconsistencies. Newer documentation attempts by Microsoft have not been as helpful to the Samba development group, due to the licensing restrictions place upon it as well as a general lack of new information.

Obtaining Samba

There are a number of options available for obtaining Samba. Many distributions now come with Samba as a part of their default installation. If this is the case with your distribution, you will not necessarily need to build from source. Red Hat, Mandrake, and SuSE users may install the package from RPM, available via a number of Samba mirrors. Gentoo users need only use *emerge samba* to install the package, and Debian users do the same with *apt-get*. Other users, or those who prefer to do so, can install the Samba package from source. Often this provides the greatest amount of flexibility because of the options available at compile time.

Building from source

In order to build from source, you will need to obtain the latest source tarball, found at any of the Samba mirrors listed on the main *http://www.samba.org* site. Once the tarball has downloaded, extract it to a directory and build the binaries using the provided configuration file.

```
vlager#  tar xzvf samba-current.tgz
vlager#  cd samba-3.0.0
vlager#  cd source
vlager#  ./configure
...
...
vlager#  make
...
vlager#  make install
```

Once the software has compiled and installed, you will need to choose how you wish to have it run at startup. It can be run as an *inetd* service or as a daemon. Either way is acceptable, but running Samba from *inetd* may require the update of your */etc/services* file. You will need to make sure that the following lines, which define the Samba protocol, are inserted:

```
netbios-ns      137/tcp                        # NETBIOS Name Service
netbios-ns      137/udp
netbios-dgm     138/tcp                        # NETBIOS Datagram Service
netbios-dgm     138/udp
netbios-ssn     139/tcp                        # NETBIOS session service
```

```
netbios-ssn     139/udp
microsoft-ds    445/tcp         Microsoft-DS
microsoft-ds    445/udp         Microsoft-DS
```

After this has been added or confirmed, you are should add Samba to your *inetd.conf* file, or to your *xinetd* configuration. You should also check to verify that your firewall is configured to allow the necessary ports.

Alternately, if you're planning to have Samba run as a daemon process, you will need to add it to your *rc* startup scripts. This is different for each of the various Linux distributions, so if you're unsure of how to do this, check your distribution's documentation.

Getting Started with Samba

Once you've compiled or installed Samba, you now have the potentially lengthy task of configuration ahead of you. The enormous flexibility offered by Samba means that there are a number of configuration options. Fortunately, for file server functionality, the configuration is fairly straightforward. In this section, we'll cover some of the basic options and discuss how to create shared file directories. For additional information, refer to *Using Samba* (O'Reilly).

Basic configuration options

The easiest way to get started configuring Samba is to start with the minimal configuration and add to it. So, to start, we'll just create a workgroup, name our server, and add a simple file share.

```
{global}

workgroup = Brewery
netbios name = vlager

[share]

path = /home/files
comment = Some HomeBrew recipes
```

You can test your Samba configurations with *testparm*. It will parse your configuration files and point out any typos or incorrect options you've entered. At this point, it's not too likely that you'll have any mistakes, but it's still good to get to know how to use the tool.

If everything works, you can start or restart your Samba server and attempt to view your new file share. The *smbclient* program, which is a part of the Samba package, can be used to view file shares. In this example, we're going to look at the file shares we've just created on **vlager** (**10.10.0.5**)

```
client# smbclient -L 10.10.0.5
Password:
```

```
        Sharename        Type      Comment
        ---------        ----      -------
        share            Disk      Some HomeBrew recipes
client#
```

After the successful completion of this step, we're now ready to tackle some more sophisticated configuration options, which will make Samba much more useful.

Configuring Samba user accounts

The above configuration is great if you're only interested in having an open file share, but you may have been wondering about access control. In the above example configuration, anyone can connect to the file share. This is generally not a desirable configuration on a network. It is for that reason that Samba does, in fact, have user authorization functionality.

Staring with the previous configuration file, authentication can be added by adding the following lines:

```
security = user
encrypt passwords = yes
smb passwd file = /etc/samba/private/smbpasswd
username map = /etc/samba/smbusers
```

The first line enables user security. This means that you will need to manage the users file on the Samba server. The second line establishes that the Samba password file will be encrypted. The third and fourth lines provide the path locations for the password and user files. It isn't necessary to have a separate users file, but it is possible with Linux.

When this has been configured, you will now be required to create users on your system. The Samba suite provides *smbpasswd* to manage user accounts. This isn't required, because Samba can reference the users in your */etc/passwd* file. However, if there are users from Microsoft environments accessing files on your new Samba server, you will need to have this file.

Creating users is pretty straightforward and is done with the *smbpasswd* utility.

```
vlager# smbpasswd -a larry
New SMB password:
Retype new SMB password:
vlager#
```

Once the user has been created, it can be tested with either a Windows machine or a Linux machine using *smbmount*. After entering **\\<server.ip>** into the Explorer address bar, the Windows user will be presented with a dialog box, as shown in Figure 16-1.

For Linux, and other Unixes, *smbmount* is invoked as follows:

```
vlager#  mount -t smbfs -o username=larry //server.ip /mnt/samba
```

Figure 16-1. Windows network login request

If everything has been successful, you will now be able to access the shared directory at */mnt/samba*.

Additional Samba Options

So far, we've discussed the bare minimum configuration of a Samba server. This is great for those who just want to quickly get something on the network. In order to get a little bit more out of Samba, we'll now take a look at some additional options.

Access control

The Samba server offers some additional security, which can prove very useful in large networks. IP-based access control is available with what are likely very familiar commands:

```
hosts allow = 10.10.
hosts.deny = any
```

This will allow connections only from the **10.10** network. The Samba IP access control follows the same logic used by *tcpwrappers*. You can either explicitly allow or deny IP addresses or ranges. This option is really convenient because it can be used at the global or the share level, meaning that you can have a list of IP addresses that are either allowed or banned from all of your server's file shares, or you can break it down so that only certain IP addresses have access to certain shared directories. This type of granular access is not even offered by Windows itself!

The Samba server is also flexible as to which interface it will bind to. By default, it will bind to all available interfaces, including loopback. To remove any unwanted access, such as binding Samba to the external interface of a dual-homed machine, the bind interface can be specified.

```
bind interfaces only = True
interfaces = eth1 10.10.0.4
```

This will make sure that Samba listens only on the specified interface on the provided IP address. If you are concerned about security, it is best to restrict access at the application level, rather than rely on a firewall to protect you.

Another type of access control offered by Samba is the ability to mark a shared directory as browsable. If it is browsable, it will be immediately visible and users will be able to peruse its contents. The command to manipulate this feature is:

```
browsable = yes|no
```

If you would like to be able to give people access to certain files, perhaps by sending them a URI pointing to a specific file, while not wanting them to be able to see all the files in the directory, this option should be set to no. A URI of this kind should look familiar; for example, \\vlager.vbrew.com\recipe\secret.txt would work for Windows users, while for Unix users, one might use smb://vlager.vbrew.com/recipe/secret.txt. In either case, the user would be allowed access to just the secret.txt file only. For most purposes it is set to yes, as the Samba server tends to be more functional when users can browse the filesystem.

Along the same lines, shared directories can be marked as to whether or not they're publicly available. If a folder is not public, even with a specific URI a user cannot access a file. It is important to note, though, that anyone with a Samba account will be able to view folders that are labeled public.

```
public = yes|no
```

Having granted viewing rights to a user, the Samba administrator can also choose whether or not shared directories are writable. This is done with the writable command:

```
writable = yes|no
```

When this option is set to no, nothing can be written to the directory.

Should you wish to have a fairly open Samba server for something like an open, browsable documentation server, you might wish to enable the Samba guest account. This is easily done with the guest directive:

```
guest ok = yes|no
```

Finally, one of the most useful features of Samba is that it allows access to shared directories to be controlled with user access lists. The easiest way to accomplish this is by using the valid users option.

```
valid users = sharon paul charlie pat
```

You can also simplify this by using an already defined group from your */etc/group* file:

```
valid users = @brewers
```

The at sign (@) tells Samba that the *brewers* value is the group name. Having controlled access to the point where you're comfortable, you're probably interested in making sure that your configuration is working. One of the best ways to see what's happening with Samba is through its excellent logging capabilities.

Logging with Samba

Using the log functions with Samba is quite simple. There are a number of additional modifiers that can be added to expand on the logging capabilities. The most basic logging can be accomplished with the following command:

```
log file = /var/log/samba.log
```

This will provide basic logging of all Samba transactions to the file specified. However, in some instances, these logfiles can be a bit unwieldy if many machines are accessing the Samba server. To make the logging easier to sift through, Samba offers the ability to log by each host that connects. Enabling this functionality requires only the following addition:

```
log file = /var/log/samba.log.%m
```

As with most logging functions on Linux, the administrator has the ability to configure how much logging occurs. In Samba, these log levels follow a 0 to 10 scale, starting from light to intensive logging. For most uses, the Samba documentation suggests using log level 2, which provides a good amount of information for debugging, without overdoing it. Levels 3 and higher are designed for Samba programmers and aren't for normal usage. To specify the log level in your Samba configuration file, add this line:

```
log level = 2
```

If you have a fairly busy server, it is likely that your logfiles will grow very quickly. For this reason, Samba offers a maximum size logfile directive.

```
max log size = 75
```

This example sets the maximum logfile size to 75 KB. When the logfile reaches this size, it is automatically renamed by adding *.old* to the file, and a new logfile is created. When the new logfile reaches 75 KB, the previous *.old* file is overwritten. If you have logfile retention requirements in your environment, make sure that you have a script that automatically archives your Samba logs.

Logging with syslog

In addition to its own logging capabilities, Samba, when compiled with the `--with-syslog` option, will also use the system logger. In situations when administrators have automated log-watching tools, like *swatch*, this can be more useful. To have Samba use syslog, just add the following line to your Samba configuration file:

```
syslog = 2
```

This will send all of Samba's Level 2 logging detail to the syslogfile. If you're happy with this, and would like to use the syslog exclusively, specify the following in your *smb.conf*:

```
syslog only = yes
```

Printing with Samba

Samba is fully functional as a Windows print server, enabling users to connect and print, and even download relevant print drivers. According to the Samba team, this was one of the biggest interoperability issues they faced because of complexities with the Windows print job queuing system. There are a number of ways to configure Samba for printing, but the two most common are the traditional BSD printing, and more recent CUPS.

BSD Printing

The older, traditional method of printing is the BSD print system which is based around the RFC 1179 framework. It uses commands such as *lpr* that most Unix administrators are familiar with. Samba works well with this environment, and it is easily configured. The basic configuration to enable BSD printing looks like this:

```
[global]
printing = bsd
load printers = yes

[printers]
path = /var/spool/samba
printable = yes
public = yes
writable = no
```

At this point, if you're thinking that this seems really simplistic, it is! This is thanks to the fact that Samba makes a great number of assumptions with its default configuration. To see what the configuration *really* looks like, you can use the *testparm* program:

```
ticktock samba # testparm -s -v |egrep "(lp|print|port|driver|spool|\[)"
Processing section "[printers]"
[global]
        smb ports = 445 139
        nt pipe support = Yes
        nt status support = Yes
        lpq cache time = 10
        load printers = Yes
        printcap name = /etc/printcap
```

```
disable spoolss = No
enumports command =
addprinter command =
deleteprinter command =
show add printer wizard = Yes
os2 driver map =
wins support = No
printer admin =
nt acl support = Yes
min print space = 0
max reported print jobs = 0
max print jobs = 1000
printable = No
printing = bsd
print command = lpr -r -P'%p' %s
lpq command = lpq -P'%p'
lprm command = lprm -P'%p' %j
lppause command =
lpresume command =
printer name =
use client driver = No
[printers]
path = /var/spool/samba
printable = Yes
```

This is the point at which you can readjust some of the default options that might not be right for your system. One item to consider is whether the *lp* commands are in your default path. You can also add anything to the *lp* command lines that you see fit.

A sample */etc/printcap* file is also included here. As all systems are different, this configuration file may not work properly for you, but it is provided to give you an idea of the configuration format. For more detailed information, check the *printcap* manpages.

```
# /etc/printcap: printer capability database.

/lp|Generic dot-matrix printer entry
        :lp=/dev/lp1
        :sd=/var/spool/lpd/lp
        :af=/var/log/lp-acct
        :lf=/var/log/lp-errs
        :pl#66
        :pw#80
        :pc#150
        :mx#0
        :sh
```

Printing with CUPS

The *Common Unix Printing System* (CUPS) is quickly replacing BSD-style printing in most Linux distributions. There are numerous reasons why CUPS is displacing the status quo, which we will leave for another discussion. However, no discussion of printing in the Samba environment would be complete without now including a section on CUPS printing.

To introduce printing with CUPS, let's have a look at a simple CUPS configured *smb. conf* file:

```
[global]
load printers = yes
printing = cups
printcap name = cups

[printers]
comment = Brewery Printers
path = /var/spool/samba
browsable = no
public = yes
guest ok = yes
writable = no
printable = yes
printer admin = root, @wheel
```

This is all that is required for basic configuration to make Samba work with CUPS, provided that CUPS itself is functional on your system.

The global section establishes that the */etc/printcap* file is enumerated with the load printers option, which automatically parses the printcap and enables the printers configured within. This feature can be both really helpful and a bit frightening for some system administrators. While it makes configuration much easier, it does somewhat reduce the administrators ability to control what is visible to users. If this option turned off, you must individually create each printer share in the Samba configuration files.

The printing option, which we had previously set to bsd, has been changed to cups. We've also named the printcap *cups* for clarity.

The next section, printers, is also very similar to the previous example; however, we've now configured a printer administration group. This is a basic option that will allow the group specified to have administrative access to the CUPS aspects of the printing.

While not necessary, there are a number of additional options that can be added to a cups-based printer configuration to customize it based on need. For more detail and advanced configuration with CUPS and Samba, check the Samba web site at *http:// www.samba.org* and the CUPS web site at *http://www.cups.org*.

Using SWAT

Samba Web Administration Tool (SWAT) is used to simplify administration and configuration of Samba. For those who like to use a GUI, this is one of the best options because it is written by the Samba team and contains all possible configuration options. Other GUI frontend programs will work, but may not be as current.

Enabling SWAT

SWAT is basically a web server as well as an administration tool. In order to get it working, you will need to add it to your *inetd.conf* or *xinetd* configurations. With *xinetd*, your configuration for swat should look something like this:

```
service swat
{
        port            = 901
        socket_type     = stream
        wait            = no
        user            = root
        server          = /usr/sbin/swat
        log_on_failure += USERID
        disable         = no
}
```

You will also need to add the SWAT port to your */etc/services* file, if it's not already there.

```
swat            901/tcp                         # Samba configuration tool
```

After you restart your *xinetd* process, you are ready to use the service, which you would do by pointing your web browser at your Samba server's IP address on port 901.

SWAT and SSL

You may have noticed that SWAT doesn't use SSL, which is probably OK if you are using it from only *localhost*. If you are interested in using it over the network, however, encryption is a good idea. Though SWAT doesn't support encryption, it can be added using the popular SSL tunneling tool called *stunnel*.

The easiest method to configure this was developed by Markus Krieger. In order to use this method, you will need to have both OpenSSL and *stunnel* installed. Documentation and source code for *stunnel* can be found at *http://www.stunnel.org*. Once both are installed and operational, you will need to generate a private key, which can be done like this:

```
vlager# /usr/bin/openssl req -new -x509 -days 730 -nodes -config /path/to/stunnel/
stunnel.cnf -out /etc/stunnel/stunnel.pem -keyout /etc/stunnel/stunnel.pem
```

Once you have created your keys, you need to make sure that you remove the original SWAT from your *inetd.conf* file and send a SIGHUP signal to the daemon, if necessary. You will no longer be calling the standard SWAT daemon through *inetd*, so be sure that it has been removed.

stunnel can now be started. You can launch it from the command line or create a small script to launch it automatically. To start *stunnel*, as *root*, type:

```
vlager# stunnel -p /etc/stunnel/stunnel.pem -d 901 -l /path/to/samba/bin/swat swat
```

Troubleshooting Samba

If you've built your Samba server and everything has worked perfectly the first time, consider yourself a part of the lucky minority. For everyone else, we'll now discuss a few tips on how to track down and fix some common problems.

Configuration file woes

When troubleshooting Samba, one important issue to keep in mind is that the default options always take priority. This means that if a default configuration option is set, simply commenting it out does not change its value. For example, you can try to disable the load printers option by simply commenting it out.

```
[printers]
path = /var/spool/samba
#load printers = yes
```

However, using *testparm*, you will see that the option is still set to yes.

```
ticktock samba # testparm -s -v |grep "load printers"
        load printers = Yes
```

With Samba, you must always explicitly define the options you wish to have; commenting out will not necessarily guarantee success. If something isn't working as expected, check this first.

As basic as it sounds, you should also check to see whether the *smbd* and *nmbd* processes exist. It is not uncommon for something to cause them to fail silently, and you will not realize they are not running.

Account problems

One of the more common login problems with Samba occurs with the root, but can happen with any user on the system. For each Samba user, it is important to remember that a separate Samba password must be created because Samba does not use the Linux */etc/shadow* hash. For example, if you try to access a Samba file share as *root*, the system *root* password will fail, unless you've already created a Samba password for the *root* account using the same *root* password (which is definitely not advised). To correct this issue, a separate account must be created as follows:

```
vlager# smbpasswd -a root
New SMB password:
Retype new SMB password:
Added user root.
```

## CHAPTER 17

OpenLDAP

OpenLDAP is a freely available, open source LDAP solution designed to compile on a number of different platforms. Under Linux, it is currently the most widely used and best supported free LDAP product available. It offers the performance and expected functionality of many commercial solutions, but offers additional flexibility because the source is available and customizable. In this section, we will discuss possible uses for an OpenLDAP server as well as describe installation and configuration.

Understanding LDAP

Before proceeding, a brief explanation of LDAP is required. *Lightweight Directory Access Protocol* (LDAP) is a directory service that can be used to store almost anything. In this way, it is very similar to a database. However, it is designed to store only small amounts of data, and is optimized for quick searching of records. A perfect example of an application for which LDAP is suited is a PKI environment. This type of environment stores only minimal amount of information and is designed to be accessed quickly.

The easiest way to explain the structure of LDAP is to imagine it as a tree. Each LDAP directory starts with a root entry. From this entry others branch out, and from each of these branches are more branches, each with the ability to store a bit of information. A sample LDAP tree is shown in Figure 17-1.

Another critical difference between LDAP and regular databases is that LDAP is designed for interoperability. LDAP uses predefined schemas, or sets of data that map out specific trees. The X.500 structure is outlined by RFC 2253 and contains the following entries:

```
String  X.500 AttributeType
------------------------------
CN        commonName
```

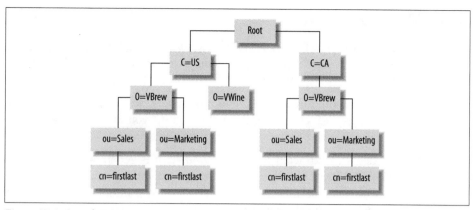

Figure 17-1. Sample LDAP tree.

```
L          localityName
ST         stateOrProvinceName
O          organizationName
OU         organizationalUnitName
C          countryName
STREET     streetAddress
DC         domainComponent
UID        userid
```

Another useful schema is inetOrgPerson. It is designed to represent people within an organizational structure and contains values such as telephone numbers, addresses, user IDs, and even employee photos.

Data Naming Conventions

LDAP entries are stored in the directory as *Relative Distinguished Names* (RDN), and individual entries are referred to by their *Distinguished Names* (DN). For example, the user Bob Jones might have an RDN of:

    cn=BobJones

And his DN might look like this:

    c=us,st=California,o=VirtualBrewery,ou=Engineering,cn=BobJones

While this section barely scratches the surface of the entirety of LDAP, it serves as the necessary background to install and operate OpenLDAP. For a more detailed look at LDAP, consult RFC 2251, "The Lightweight Directory Access Protocol (v3)."

Obtaining OpenLDAP

The current home of OpenLDAP is *http://www.openldap.org*. All current stable and beta versions can be acquired from this site along with an "Issue Tracking" engine, should you encounter any bugs that you wish to report.

While the temptation of downloading and using beta versions is always there, because of the promise of increased functionality, unless you are installing the software on a test server, it is best to use only known stable versions.

Having downloaded and extracted the source archive, it is generally a good idea to briefly review any README files that may be contained within the archive. The five minutes spent reading these files can save five times the initial time investment should there be any problems during install.

Dependencies

Like many software packages, OpenLDAP is not without its dependencies. With OpenLDAP, you will need to have the latest version of OpenSSL installed and configured. If you do not yet have this package, it can be found at *http://www.openssl. org*, along with installation instructions.

SASL from Cyrus is also required for OpenLDAP. As defined by its name, *Simple Authentication and Security Layer* (SASL) provides an easy-to-use security framework. Many Linux distributions have this package installed by default; however, should you need to install this yourself, it can be found at *http://asg.web.cmu.edu/ sasl/sasl-library.html* or by using a package search engine such as RPMfind.

OpenLDAP supports Kerberos as an option rather than a requirement. If you are currently using Kerberos in your environment, you will want to make sure that you have it installed on your OpenLDAP server machine. If you're not currently using Kerberos, it may not be of great value to enable it especially for OpenLDAP. There is a great deal of Kerberos information available on which you can base your decision as to whether or not to enable it.

Another optional component is for the OpenLDAP backend database (BDB). In order to use BDB, you will need something like the BerkeleyDB from Sleepycat Software. This is a very commonly used package that is often installed by default on many Linux distributions. If your system does not have this installed, you can find it at *http://www.sleepycat.com*. Alternately, other BDBs exist; for example, MySQL may be appropriate in your environment. It is important to note that this is a matter of personal preference, and for most users the default OpenLDAP database is acceptable.

Compiling OpenLDAP

Building OpenLDAP is fairly straightforward once you have selected the options you wish to have built into the software. A list of available options can be retrieved with the *configure* program. One option that you may wish to enable is *-with-tls*. This will enable SSL support in OpenLDAP, which we will discuss later in this chapter.

```
vlager# ./configure -with-tls
Copyright 1998-2003 The OpenLDAP Foundation,  All Rights Reserved.
        Restrictions apply, see COPYRIGHT and LICENSE files.
Configuring OpenLDAP 2.1.22-Release ...
checking host system type... i686-pc-linux-gnu
checking target system type... i686-pc-linux-gnu
checking build system type... i686-pc-linux-gnu
checking for a BSD compatible install... /bin/install -c
checking whether build environment is sane... yes
checking for mawk... no
checking for gawk... gawk
checking whether make sets ${MAKE}... yes
checking for working aclocal... found
checking for working autoconf... found
checking for working automake... found
checking for working autoheader... found
checking for working makeinfo... found
checking for gnutar... no
checking for gtar... no
.
.
.
vlager#
```

After configuring the *makefile*, the next step is to attempt to compile the package. With most software, the next step is to run *make*. However, it is recommended when building OpenLDAP to run a *make depend* first. The configure script will even remind you of this, should you forget.

When the dependencies have been built, you can now safely issue the *make* command and wait for the software to build. Upon completion, you may wish to verify that the build process has completed properly. Using *make test* will run a series of checks and inform you of any problems with the build.

Assuming all has gone successfully, you can now become root and install the software automatically by using the make install option. By default, OpenLDAP will place its configuration files in */usr/local/etc/openldap*. Users of some distributions will choose to have these files placed in */etc/openldap* for consistency. The option to do this should be set in the *./configure* command line.

Configuring the OpenLDAP Server

If you were watching the installation of the software, you may have noticed that it created two programs, *slapd* and *slurpd*. These are the two daemons used with an OpenLDAP installation.

The first step in understanding how to configure the OpenLDAP server is to look at its configuration files. On our sample host, **vlager**, we have placed the configuration scripts in the */usr/local/etc/openldap* directory. Looking at the *slapd.conf* file, we see a few places that must be customized. It will be necessary to update any of the following values to make them consistent with your site:

```
include         /usr/local/etc/openldap/schema/core.schema
include         /usr/local/etc/openldap/schema/cosine.schema
include         /usr/local/etc/openldap/schema/inetorgperson.schema

database        ldbm
suffix          "o=vbrew"
suffix          "dc=ldap,dc=vbrew,dc=com"
rootdn          "cn=JaneAdmin,o=vbrew"
rootpw          secret
directory       /usr/local/var/openldap-vbrew
defaultaccess   read
schemacheck        on
lastmod         on
```

You should also change the `rootpw` from `secret` to something that makes sense to you. This is the password you will need to use to make changes to your LDAP directory.

With these changes made, you are now ready to run the OpenLDAP server, which we will discuss in the next section.

Running OpenLDAP

The standalone OpenLDAP server is called *slapd* and, if you have not changed any of the default paths, it will have installed in */usr/local/libexec/*. This program simply listens on the LDAP port (TCP 389) for incoming connections, and then processes the requests accordingly. Since this process runs on a reserved port, you will need to start it with root privileges. The quickest way to do this is as follows:

```
vlager# su root -c /usr/local/libexec/slapd
```

To verify that the service has started, you can use *netstat* to see that it is listening on port 389:

```
vlager# netstat -aunt | grep 389
tcp        0      0 0.0.0.0:389          0.0.0.0:*          LISTEN
```

At this point, you should also verify that the service itself is working by issuing a query to it using the *ldapsearch* command:

```
vlager# ldapsearch -x -b '' -s base '(objectclass=*)' namingContexts
version: 2

#
# filter: (objectclass=*)
# requesting: namingContexts
#

#
dn:
namingContexts: dc=vbrew,dc=com

# search result
search: 2
result: 0 Success

# numResponses: 2
# numEntries: 1
vlager#
```

This query is designed to do a wildcard search on your database; it should therefore retrieve everything stored within. If your configuration was completed properly, you will see your own domain name in the dc field.

Adding entries to your directory

Now that the LDAP server is operational, it makes sense to add some entries. OpenLDAP comes with a utility called *ldapadd*, which inserts records into your LDAP database. The program only accepts additions from LDAP Data Interchange files (LDIF), so in order to add a record, you will need to create this file. More information about the LDIF file format can be found in RFC 2849. Fortunately, creating LDIF files is a very easy step—a sample file looks like:

```
# Organization for Virtual Brewery Corporation
dn: dc=vbrew,dc=com
objectClass: dcObject
objectClass: organization
dc: example
o: VirtualBrew Corporation
description: The Virtual Brewery Corporation

# Organizational Role for Directory Manager
dn: cn=Manager,dc=vbrew,dc=com
objectClass: organizationalRole
cn: Manager
description: Directory Manager

dn: dc=ldap,dc=vbrew,dc=com
objectClass: top
```

```
objectClass: dcObject
objectClass: orginization
dc: vbrew
o: vbrew
description: Virtual Brewing Company LDAP Domain

dn: o=vbrew
objectClass: top
objectClass: organization
o: vbrew
description: Virtual Brewery

dn: cn=JaneAdmin,o=vbrew
objectClass: organizationalRole
cn: JaneAdmin
description: Linux System Admin Guru

dn: ou=Marketing,o=vbrew
ou: Marketing
objectClass: top
objectClass: organizationalUnit
description: The Marketing Department

dn: ou=Engineering,o=vbrew
ou: Engineering
objectClass: top
objectClass: organizationalUnit
description: Engineering team

dn: ou=Brewers,o=vbrew
ou: Brewers
objectClass: top
objectClass: orginazationalUnit
description: Brewing team

dn: cn=Joe Slick,ou=Marketing,o=vbrew
cn: Joe Slick
objectClass: top
objectClass: person
objectClass: organizationalPerson
objectClass: inetOrgPerson
mail: jslick@vbrew.com
firstname: Joe
lasname: Slick
ou: Marketing
uid: 1001
postalAddress: 10 Westwood Lane
l: Chicago
st: IL
zipcode: 12394
phoneNumber: 312-555-1212

dn: cn=Mary Smith,ou=Engineering,o=vbrew
cn: Mary Smith
```

```
objectClass: top
objectClass: person
objectClass: organizationalPerson
objectClass: inetOrgPerson
mail: msmith@vbrew.com
firstname: Mary
lasname: Smith
ou: Engineering
uid: 1002
postalAddress: 123 4th Street
l: San Francisco
st: CA
zipcode: 12312
phoneNumber: 415-555-1212

dn: cn=Bill Peris,ou=Brewing,o=vbrew
cn: Bill Peris
objectClass: top
objectClass: person
objectClass: organizationalPerson
objectClass: inetOrgPerson
mail: per@vbrew.com
firstname: Bill
lasname: Peris
ou: Brewing
uid: 1003
postalAddress: 8181 Binary Blvd
l: New York
st: NY
zipcode: 12344
phoneNumber: 212-555-1212
```

Once the LDIF file is ready, it is added to the LDAP directory using the following command:

```
vlager# ldapadd -x -D "cn=Manager,dc=vbrew,dc=com" -W -f goo.ldif
Enter LDAP Password:
adding new entry "dc=vbrew,dc=com"

adding new entry "cn=Manager,dc=vbrew,dc=com"

vlager#
```

You can search for your new directory entries using the *ldapsearch* command described earlier.

Using OpenLDAP

There are a number of uses for an LDAP server—too many to mention. However, authentication is among the more useful to Linux network administrators. For an administrator of many different machines, the task of managing the password and authentication details for a large number of users can quickly become daunting. An

OpenLDAP directory can be used to centrally manage the user accounts for a group of systems, making it possible for an administrator to enable or disable user accounts quickly and efficiently—a process that, on multiple systems, can be a chore.

The first step in configuring this is to install the LDAP NSS and PAM libraries. Under Linux, NSS and PAM handle authentication and tell the system where to look to verify users. It is necessary to install two packages, *pam_ldap* and *nss_ldap*, which can be found at *http://www.padl.com/OSS* in the software subsection. Most distributions have packages for these, and they are often combined and named *libnss-ldap*. If you are installing from source, the building of this software is straightforward and can be accomplished with the standard *configure, make install* method. Along with installing this on your LDAP server, you will also need to install these libraries on your client machines.

When these libraries have been installed, you can now start configuring your *slapd* OpenLDAP process. You will need to make a few changes to your *slapd.conf* file, similar to those which were covered earlier. The schema section as configured earlier is sufficient; however, you will need to add some new definitions in the database section.

```
#######################################################################
# ldbm database definitions
#######################################################################

database        ldbm
suffix          "o=vbrew,dc=com"
rootdn          "uid=root,ou=Engineering,o=vbrew,dc=com"
rootpw          secret
directory       /usr/local/etc/openldap/data
# Indices to maintain
index   objectClass,uid,uidNumber,gidNumber    eq
index   cn,mail,surname,givenname              eq,subinitial
```

This section will create the directory definitions for the structure in which you will be storing your user data.

Adding access control lists (ACLs)

As this type of directory should not be writable by any anonymous users, it is a good idea to include some type of access list as well. Fortunately, OpenLDAP makes this type of control quite easy.

```
# Access control listing - basic
#

access to dn=".*,ou=Engineering,o=vbrew,dc=com"
   attr=userPassword
 by self write
 by dn="uid=root,ou=Engineering,o=vbrew,dc=com" write
 by * auth
```

```
access to dn=".*,o=vbrew,dc=com"
  by self write
  by dn="uid=root,ou=Engineering,o=vbrew,dc=com" write
  by * read

access to dn=".*,o=vbrew,dc=com"
  by * read

defaultaccess read
```

This list does some basic locking down of the directory and makes it more difficult for anyone to write to the directory. Once this configuration has been completed, you can now safely start (or restart) the OpenLDAP daemon.

Migrating to LDAP authentication

You now have your empty directory created awaiting input and queries. For administrators who have hundreds or thousands of user accounts across many machines, the next step, migrating the authentication data into the directory, may sound like a nightmare. Fortunately, there are tools created to assist with this potentially difficult step. The OpenLDAP migration tools from *http://www.padl.com/OSS* make the task of populating the LDAP database from existing */etc/passwd* files simple. Each distribution or package will likely place the files in the */usr/share* directory, but check the documentation in your package for specifics.

In order for these scripts to work properly, you will need to make a few minor changes to one of them. The first one to update is *migrage_common.ph*. Search for the following lines:

```
#Default DNS domain
$DEFAULT_MAIL_DOMAIN = "padl.com";

#Default base
$DEFAULT_BASE = "dc=padl,dc=com";
```

And replace them with the values that are correct for your environment. For our example, this would be:

```
$DEFAULT_MAIL_DOMAIN = "vbrew.com";
$DEFAULT_BASE = "o=vbrew,dc=com";
```

Now, verify that your OpenLDAP server is listening and that you've saved the changes to the migration configuration file. When all of this has been completed, you are now ready to execute *migrate_all_online.sh*, which will begin the process of moving your */etc/passwd* entries into your LDAP directory.

```
vlager# ./migrate_all_online.sh
Enter the Name of the X.500 naming context you wish to import into: [o=vbrew, dc=com]
Enter the name of your LDAP server [ldap]: vlager
Enter the manager DN: [cn=manager,o=vbrew,dc=com] cn=root,o=vbrew,dc=com
Enter the credentials to bind with: password
Importing into o=vbrew,dc=com...
```

```
Creating naming context entries...
Migrating aliases...
Migrating groups...
    .
    .
vlager#
```

At this point, you will now see that all of your */etc/passwd* entries have been automatically entered into your LDAP directory. You may wish to use the *ldapsearch* query tool now to see some of your entries. With your directory service functional and now populated with user entries, you now need to configure your clients to query the LDAP server, which we will discuss in the next section.

Client LDAP configurations

Linux distributions come configured by default to look at the */etc/passwd* file for authentication. This default option is easily configurable once the *nss-ldap* and PAM libraries are installed, as described earlier. The first of the configuration files that need to be changed is the */etc/nsswitch.conf* file. You simply need to tell the system to query LDAP.

```
passwd:    files ldap
group:     files ldap
shadow:    files ldap
```

You might be wondering why we've left the `files` entry in the configuration. It is strongly recommended that it be left in so accounts such as *root* can still have access should something happen to the LDAP server. If you delete this line, and the LDAP server fails, you will be locked out of all of your systems! This is, of course, where multiple servers come in handy. Replication between LDAP servers is possible and a fairly straightforward exercise. For information on building backup OpenLDAP servers, check the *OpenLDAP HOWTOs* found on the Linux Documentation Project web site.

Some Linux distributions (Debian, for example) have the client configuration in */etc/openldap.conf*. Be careful not to mistake this for the server configuration files found in */etc/openldap*.

The next file you need to modify is the *openldap.conf* file. Like the other configuration files, the location of this will vary between the distributions. This file is very simple and has only a few configurable options. You need to update it to reflect the URI of your LDAP server and your base LDAP information.

```
URI  ldap://vlager.vbrew.com
BASE o=vbrew,dc=com
```

You should now attempt an LDAP query on one of your client machines.

```
client$ ldapsearch -x 'uid=bob'
version: 2
```

```
#
# filter: uid=bob
# requesting: ALL
#

# bob,Engineering,vbrew,com
dn: uid=bob,ou=Engineering,o=vbrew,c=com
uid: bob
cn: bob
sn: bob
mail: bob@vbrew.com
objectClass: person
objectClass: organizationalPerson
objectClass: inetOrgPerson
objectClass: account
objectClass: posixAccount
objectClass: top
objectClass: shadowAccount
shadowMax: 99999
shadowWarning: 7
loginShell: /bin/bash
uidNumber: 1003
gidNumber: 1003
homeDirectory: /home/bob
gecos: bob

# search result
search: 2
result: 0 Success

# numResponses: 2
# numEntries: 1

client$
```

If your query resembled the above entry, you know that your queries are working. Your OpenLDAP server is now fully populated, can be queried from client machines, and is ready for real use.

Adding SSL to OpenLDAP

As LDAP was designed to be a secure and efficient method of serving up small amounts of data, by default it runs in clear text. While this may be acceptable for certain uses, at some point you may wish to add encryption to the data stream. This will help preserve the confidentiality of your directory inquiries and make it more difficult for attackers to gather information on your network. If you are using LDAP for any kind of authentication, encryption is highly recommended.

If you configured your OpenLDAP at compile time using the -with-tls option, your server is ready to use SSL. If not, you will need to rebuild OpenLDAP before continuing.

Adding SSL to OpenLDAP requires only a few simple changes to the OpenLDAP configuration file. You will need to tell OpenLDAP which SSL cipher to use and tell it the locations of your SSL certificate and key files, which you will create later.

```
TLSCipherSuite HIGH:MEDIUM:+SSLv3
TLSCertificateFile /etc/ssl/certs/slapd.pem
TLSCertificateKeyFile /etc/ssl/certs/slapd.pem
```

In this case, we've specified that our OpenSSL certificates will be stored in the */etc/ssl* directory. This will vary between the distributions; however, you can choose to store your SSL in certificates any place you like. We've also specified the type of cipher to use. Note that there are a number of different choices available; you can choose whichever you prefer. Since the server now expects to find certificate files when it is restarted, we will need to create them. Information on how to do this is covered in previous sections of this book or is available in the OpenSSL documentation.

It is important to realize that this creates a self-signed certificate, as opposed to one that is purchased from one of the certificate providers. If an LDAP client were to check the validity of your certificate, it would likely generate an error, just as a web browser would when it detects a non-third-party signed certificate. However, most LDAP clients do not check certificate validity, so this isn't likely to create many issues. If you would like to have a third party certificate, there are numerous vendors who provide them.

Before you restart your server, you should also make sure that your certificates are readable only by your LDAP server. They should not be accessible or writable by any other user on the system. You should also clean up any temporary files, such as those created in the previous step before continuing. When these steps have been taken, you can safely restart your LDAP server.

Testing SSL availability

There are a couple of quick tests that can be done to see whether or not the SSL support has been enabled. The easiest way to test whether or not the server is listening is to use *netstat*, as we did in the earlier example.

```
vlager# netstat -aunt | grep 636
tcp      0      0 0.0.0.0:636            0.0.0.0:*           LISTEN
```

Seeing that the server is listening on the LDAP SSL port is a good start. This means that the server understood the request to run SSL and is listening on the correct port. Next, you can choose to see whether or not the process is actually working. An easy way to do this is to request to see its digital certificates. The OpenSSL package comes with a client that can be used to do this.

```
vlager# openssl s_client -connect vlager:636 -showcerts
```

The output of this command will display the full technical information about the digital certificate that you created at the beginning of this section. If you aren't seeing any output from this command, verify that you've started the service and that something is listening on port 636. If you are still receiving no response, check the troubleshooting section found later in this chapter.

LDAP GUI Browsers

For those administrators who prefer a GUI to a command line, there are a number of LDAP browsers available for Linux. One of the more functional offerings is from Argonne National Laboratory and is a Java applet available at *http://www-unix.mcs. anl.gov/~gawor/ldap/applet/applet.html*. As seen in Figure 17-2, the GUI allows you to easily browse your directories and modify entries. This software also has the advantage of running from any platform, easily and without any installation hassles, provided that Java is available.

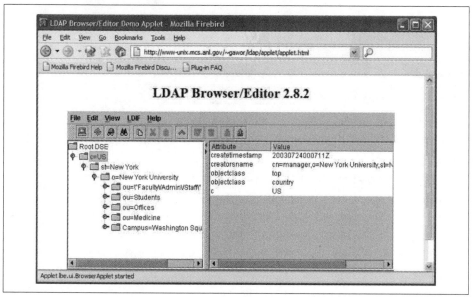

Figure 17-2. Java LDAP browser

Another popular and very powerful LDAP frontend for Linux is GQ, illustrated in Figure 17-3. It uses a GTK+-style interface and gives administrators full control over their directories, allowing them to add, modify, and remove entries, build templates, execute advanced searches and more. GQ can be found at *http://www.biot.com/gq*, and requires a Linux GTK+-compatible interface.

Troubleshooting OpenLDAP

Installing and configuring OpenLDAP can be a tricky process, and there are a number of things that can go wrong. As with many Linux server processes, the best place

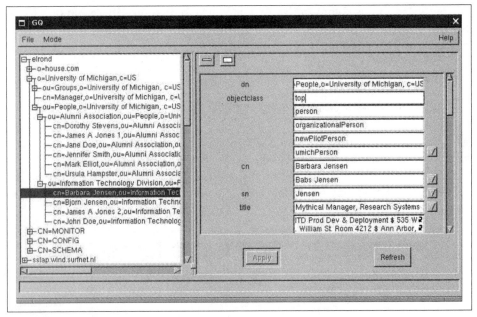

Figure 17-3. GQ in browsing mode

to start debugging is the system log. There, you should see a line somewhat similar to this one, which should give you an indication as to whether your server has started properly.

```
Jun 15 11:33:39 vlager slapd[1323]: slapd starting
```

If you make a typo in the *slapd.conf* file, the process is often smart enough to just ignore the line and proceed. However, if you happen to make a critical error, as we have in the following example, *slapd* will fail to start.

```
Jul 25 11:45:25 vlager slapd[10872]: /etc/openldap/slapd.conf: line 46: unknown
directive "odatabase" outside backend info and database definitions (ignored)
Jul 25 11:45:25 vlager slapd[10872]: /etc/openldap/slapd.conf: line 47: suffix line
must appear inside a database definition (ignored)
Jul 25 11:45:25 vlager slapd[10872]: /etc/openldap/slapd.conf: line 49: rootdn line
must appear inside a database definition (ignored)
Jul 25 11:45:25 vlager slapd[10872]: /etc/openldap/slapd.conf: line 54: rootpw line
must appear inside a database definition (ignored)
Jul 25 11:45:25 vlager slapd[10872]: /etc/openldap/slapd.conf: line 57: unknown
directive "directory" outside backend info and database definitions (ignored)
Jul 25 11:45:25 vlager slapd[10872]: /etc/openldap/slapd.conf: line 59: unknown
directive "index" outside backend info and database definitions (ignored)
Jul 25 11:45:25 vlager slapd[10873]: backend_startup: 0 databases to startup.
Jul 25 11:45:25 vlager slapd[10873]: slapd stopped.
Jul 25 11:45:25 vlager slapd[10873]: connections_destroy: nothing to destroy.
```

In this example, we mistyped the word "database," which is a critical option in the configuration. As you can see, the server failed to start, but still provided us with enough information to figure out what went wrong.

If you have verified that everything is running on the server, but clients are unable to connect, you should verify that the LDAP ports 389 and 636 are not being blocked by a firewall. If your server is running *iptables* with a default policy denying any incoming connections, you will need to explicitly allow these two ports.

Other common issues are caused by missing or incomplete SSL certificates. An indication from the system log that something is wrong with the SSL functioning is:

```
Jul 25 12:02:15 vlager slapd[11135]: main: TLS init def ctx failed: 0
Jul 25 12:02:15 vlager slapd[11135]: slapd stopped.
Jul 25 12:02:15 vlager slapd[11135]: connections_destroy: nothing to destroy.
```

The error in this case is very terse; however, the fact that TSL is mentioned indicates a problem with SSL. If you are receiving this error, you should check your certificate paths and permissions. Often, the certificate files cannot be read by the LDAP server because they are set to be readable only by the root account.

CHAPTER 18
Wireless Networking

Wireless networking is a promising and increasingly popular technology, offering a wide range of benefits compared to traditional wired technology. These advantages range from increased convenience to users and decreased deployment cost to ease of network installation. A new wireless deployment can save substantial amounts of money since there is no need for additional cables, jacks, or network switches. Adding new users to a network can be as easy as plugging in a wireless card and powering up a machine. Wireless networking has also been used to deliver network access to areas where there is little or no traditional network infrastructure.

Perhaps the biggest impact of wireless networking can be seen within its widespread acceptance among consumers. The most obvious example of this popularity can be seen with new laptop systems, where nearly every unit is shipped with integrated 802.11b or g. The practical benefits have consequently insured good sales, allowing manufacturers to lower the equipment costs. At the time of this writing, the price of client wireless cards is comparable to that of traditional Ethernet adapter cards.

These benefits, however, do not come without some disadvantages, the most severe of these being the security issues.

History

Wireless LANs are based on spread spectrum technology, initially developed for military communications by the U.S. Army during World War II. Military technicians considered spread spectrum desirable because it was more resistant to jamming. Other advances at this time allowed an increase in the radio data rate. After 1945, commercial enterprises began to expand on this technology, realizing its potential benefits to consumers.

Spread spectrum technology evolved into the beginnings of the modern wireless LAN in 1971 with a University of Hawaii project called AlohNet. This project allowed seven computers around the various islands to communicate bidirectionally with a central hub on Oahu.

The university research on AlohNet paved the way for the first generation of modern wireless networking gear, which operated at the 901–928 MHz frequency range. Primarily used by the military, this phase of wireless development saw only limited consumer use, due to crowding within this frequency and the relatively low speed.

From this point, the 2.4 GHz frequency was defined for unlicensed use, so wireless technology began to emerge in this range and the 802.11 specification was established. This specification evolved into the widely accepted 802.11b standard, and continues to evolve into faster, more secure implementations of the technology.

The Standards

The standards based around wireless networking for PCs are established by the Institute of Electrical and Electronics Engineers (IEEE). LAN/MAN technology has been broadly assigned number 802, which is then broken down into working groups. Some of the most active wireless working groups include 802.15, designed for wireless personal area networks (Bluetooth), 802.16 which defines support for broadband wireless systems, and finally, 802.11, assigned to wireless LAN technology. Within the 802.11 definition, there are more specific definitions that are assigned letters. Here is a list of the most important 802.11 wireless LAN definitions:

802.11a
> This definition provides wireless access on the 5 GHz band. It offers speeds of up to 54 MBps, but has not caught on, perhaps due to relatively higher priced equipment and short range.

802.11b
> This is still the standard to which most people refer when talking about wireless networking. It establishes 11 MBps speeds on the 2.4 GHz band, and can have a range extending more than 500 meters.

802.11g
> This standard has been established to provide higher data rates within the 2.4 GHz band and provides added security with the introduction of WiFi Protected Access, or WPA. 802.11g devices are now being deployed in place of 802.11b devices and have nearly reached mainstream acceptance.

802.11i
> While still in the development phase, this standard seeks to resolve many of the security issues that have plagued 802.11b and provide a more robust system of authentication and encryption. At the time of this writing, the specification has not been finalized.

802.11n

802.11n is being touted as the high-speed answer to current wireless network speed shortcomings. With an operational speed of 100 Mbps, it will roughly double existing wireless transfer speeds, while maintaining backward compatibility with b and g. At the time of this writing, the specification is not complete; however, several vendors have released "pre-n" products, based on the early drafts of the specification.

802.11b Security Concerns

When the IEEE created the 802.11b standard, they realized that the open nature of wireless networking required some kind of data integrity and protection mechanism and thus created Wired Equivalent Privacy (WEP). Promised by the standard to provide encryption at the 128-bit level, users were supposed to be able to enjoy the same levels of privacy found on a traditional wired network.

Hopes for this kind of security, however, were quickly dashed. In a paper called "Weaknesses in the Key Scheduling Algorithm of RC4" by Scott Fluhrer, Itsik Mantin, and Adi Shamir, the weaknesses in the key generation and implementation of WEP were described in great detail. Although this development was a theoretical attack when the paper was written, a student at Rice University, Adam Stubblefield, brought it into reality and created the first WEP attack. Although he has never made his tools public, there are now many similar tools for Linux that will allow attackers to break WEP, making it an untrustworthy security tool.

Still, it should be acknowledged that staging a WEP attack requires a considerable amount of time. The success of the attack relies upon the amount of encrypted data the attacker has captured. Tools such as AirSnort require approximately 5 to 10 million encrypted packets. A busy wireless LAN, which is constantly seeing the maximum amount of traffic, can still take as long as 10 hours to crack. Since most networks do not run at capacity for this long, it can be expected that the attack would take considerably longer, stretching out to a few days for smaller networks.

However, for true protection from malicious behavior and eavesdropping, a VPN technology should be used, and wireless networks should never be directly connected to internal, trusted networks.

Hardware

Different manufacturers use a slightly different architecture to provide 802.11b functionality. There are two major chipset manufacturers, Hermes and Prism, and within each, hardware manufacturers have made modifications to increase security or speed. For example, the USRobotics equipment, based on the Prism chipset, now offers 802.11b at 22 MBps, but it will not operate at these speeds without the DLink 802.11b 22 MBps hardware. However, they are interoperable at the 11 MBps speed.

801.11g versus 802.11b on Linux

Due to new chipsets and manufacturer differences, 802.11g support on Linux has been somewhat difficult. At the time of writing, support for 802.11g devices under Linux was still emerging and was not yet as stable and robust as the 802.11b support. For this reason, this chapter focuses on 802.11b drivers and support. Mainstream Linux support for g devices, however, is not far off. With the work of groups such as Prism54.org, which is developing g drivers, and Intel's announcement that it will release drivers for its Centrino chipset, full support is less than a year away.

Chipsets

As mentioned, there are two main 802.11b chipsets, Hermes and Prism. While initially Hermes cards were predominant due to the popularity of Lucent WaveLAN (Orinoco) cards, a majority of card makes today use Prism's prism2 chipset. Some well-known Prism cards are those from D-Link, Linksys, and USR. You'll get roughly the same performance with either card, and they are interoperable when operating within the 802.11b standard, meaning that you can connect a Lucent wireless card to a D-Link access point, and vice versa. A brief listing of major card manufacturers and their chipsets follows. If your card is not listed, check your operation manual or the vendor web site.

- Hermes chipset cards:

  Lucent Orinoco Silver and Gold Cards
  Gateway Solo
  Buffalo Technologies

- Prism 2 Chipset cards:

  Addtron
  Belkin
  Linksys
  D-Link
  ZoomMax

Client Configuration

802.11b networks can be configured to operate in several different modes. The two main types you're likely to encounter are infrastructure mode (sometimes referred to as managed mode) and ad-hoc. Infrastructure mode is the most common and uses a hub-and-spoke architecture in which multiple clients connect to a central access point, as shown in Figure 18-1. The ad-hoc wireless network mode is a peer-to-peer network, in which clients connect to each other directly, as shown in Figure 18-2. Infrastructure mode deployments are an effective means to replace wires on a traditional network, making them ideal for office environments where wireless clients need access to servers that are connected to the wired network. Ad-hoc networks are beneficial to those who simply wish to transfer files between PCs, or do not require access to any servers outside of the wireless network.

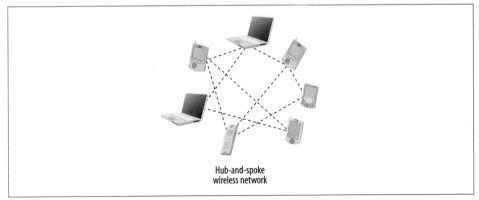

Figure 18-1. Hub-and-spoke wireless network

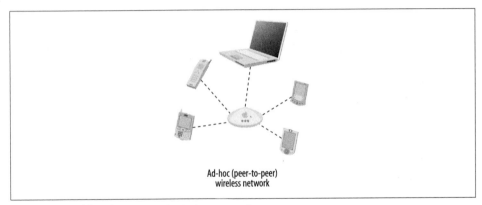

Figure 18-2. Ad-hoc (peer-to-peer) wireless network

802.11b networks operate on a predetermined set of frequencies known as a channel. The specification allows for 14 separate channels, though in North America users are limited to the first 11 and in Europe, the first 13. Only Japanese users have access to the full range of channels. In North America, the eleven channel span from 2400 to 2483 MHz, with each channel set to 22 MHz wide. Clearly there is some overlap between the channels, so it is important to conduct a site survey before selecting a channel to save future headaches by avoiding possible interference from other wireless networks.

As it is the most commonly used mode, this section will focus primarily on the infrastructure mode, which works on a hub-and-spoke model. The access point is the hub, and the clients are the spokes. An access point can either be a packaged unit bought from a store, or be built from a Linux machine running HostAP, which we'll discuss later.

An 802.11b network utilizes an access point that transmits a signal known as a *beacon*. This is basically just a message from the access point informing any nearby clients that it is available for connections. The beacon contains a limited amount of information that is necessary for the client to connect. The most important content of the beacon is the ESSID, or the name of the access point. The client, on seeing an access point, sends a request to associate. If the access point allows this, it grants an associate frame to the client, and they attach. Other types of authentication can also occur at this point. Some access points allow only clients with a prespecified MAC address, and some require further authentication. Developers are working on the standard 802.1x in an effort to establish a good authentication framework. Unfortunately, however, this is unlikely to prove effective, as there are already known vulnerabilities for it.

Drivers

A Linux wireless driver can either be built into your kernel when you compile, or created as a *loadable kernel module* (LKM). It is recommended that you create a kernel module, since drivers may require frequent updates. Building a new module is much easier and less time consuming than rebuilding the entire kernel. Either way, you need to enable the wireless extensions in the kernel configuration. Most distributions now come with this enabled; however, if you are upgrading from scratch, the configuration looks like this:

```
# Loadable module support
#
CONFIG_MODULES=y
# CONFIG_MODVERSIONS is not set
CONFIG_KMOD=y
```

You may also notice that MODVERSIONS has been disabled. Having this option disabled makes it easier to compile modules separate from the kernel module tree. While not a requirement, this can save time when trying to patch and recompile kernel modules. Whichever chip architecture your card is using, if you're using a PC card, or even some PCI cards, pcmcia-cs, the Linux PCMCIA card manager, will be able to detect your card and will have the appropriate driver installed for you. There are a number of drivers available, but only two are currently and actively maintained.

The Orinico_cs drivers, written by David Gibson, are generally recognized as the best for the Hermes cards. They are actively developed and patched, and work with most wireless applications. The Orinoco_cs drivers have been included in the Linux kernel since Version 2.4.3 and have been a part of the pcmcia-cs since version 3.1.30. The driver included with your distribution may not be as current, so you may wish to upgrade.

Confusingly enough, some prism2 cards are now supported in the Orninoco_cs drivers. That number is increasing with each new release, so despite the name of the driver, it is beginning to be a solid option for prism2 users, and may emerge as a standard in the future.

However, should your card not be supported by the Orinoco_cs driver, Prism cards are also supported by the linux-wlan-ng driver from Absolute Value Systems. This is the best known and maintained client driver for this chipset at the moment. It is also included with most Linux distributions and supports PCI, USB, and PCMCIA versions of Prism 2.x and 3.0 cards.

Once you have installed the driver of your choice and everything is working, you'll need to install the Linux Wireless Extension Tools, a collection of invaluable configuration tools written by Jean Tourrilhes, found at his site: http://*www.hpl.hp.com/personal/Jean_Tourrilhes/Linux/Tools.html*.

Using the Linux Wireless Exension Tools

Linux Wireless Extension Tools are very useful for configuring every aspect of your wireless networking devices. If you need to change any of the default wireless options or want to easily configure ad-hoc networks, you will need to familiarize yourself with these tools. They are also required for building a Linux access point, which will be discussed later in the chapter.

The toolkit contains the following programs:

iwconfig
> This is the primary configuration tool for wireless networking. It will allow you to change all aspects of your configuration, such as the ESSID, channel, frequency, and WEP keying.

iwlist
> This program lists the available channels, frequencies, bit rates, and other information for a given wireless interface.

iwspy
> This program collects per node link quality information, and is useful when debugging connections.

iwpriv
> With this program, you can modify and manipulate parameters specific to your driver. For example, if you are using a modified version of the Orinoco_cs driver, *iwpriv* will allow you to place the driver into promiscuous mode.

Linux Access Point Configuration

A very useful tool in the Linux wireless arsenal is HostAP, a wireless driver written by Jouni Malinen. It allows prism2 card users to turn their wireless cards and Linux servers into access points. Since there are many inexpensive access points on the market, you might be asking yourself why you'd ever want to turn a server into an access point. The answer is simply a matter of functionality. With most inexpensive dedicated access points, there is little functionality other than simply serving up the wireless network. There is little option for access control and firewalling. This is where Linux provides immeasurable advantages. With a Linux-based access point, you will be able to take advantage of Netfilter, RADIUS, MAC authentication, and just about any other type of Linux-based software you may find useful.

Installing the HostAP driver

In order to install HostAP, your system must have the following:

- Linux Kernel v2.4.20 or higher (kernel patches for 2.4.19 are included)
- Wireless extensions toolkit
- Latest HostAP driver, found at *http://hostap.epitest.fi/releases*

Obtaining and building the HostAP driver

While RPM and .deb packages may be available, it's likely that you will have to build HostAP from scratch in order to have the most recent version of the driver. Untar the source to a working directory. HostAP will also look for the Linux kernel source code in */usr/src/linux*. Some distributions, such as Red Hat, place kernel source in */usr/src/linux-2.4*. In that case, you should make a symbolic link called *linux* that points at your kernel source directory. Preparing the source for installation is fairly straightforward and looks like this:

```
[root@localhost root]# tar xzvf hostap-0.0.1.tar.gz
hostap-0.0.1/
hostap-0.0.1/COPYING
hostap-0.0.1/ChangeLog
hostap-0.0.1/FAQ
 .
 .
 .
hostap-0.0.1/Makefile
hostap-0.0.1/README
hostap-0.0.1/utils/util.h
hostap-0.0.1/utils/wireless_copy.h
```

Unlike many packages, HostAP has no configuration script to run before building the source. You do, however, need to choose which modules you would like to build. HostAP can currently support PCMCIA, PLX, or PCI devices. USB devices are not compatible, though support may be added in the future. For this example, we'll be building the PC Card version.

```
[root@localhost root]# make pccard
gcc -I/usr/src/linux/include  -O2 -D__KERNEL__ -DMODULE -Wall -g -c  -I/usr/src/
linux/arch/i386/mach-generic -I/usr/src/linux/include/asm/mach-default -fomit-frame-
pointer -o driver/modules/hostap_cs.o driver/modules/hostap_cs.c
gcc -I/usr/src/linux/include  -O2 -D__KERNEL__ -DMODULE -Wall -g -c  -I/usr/src/
linux/arch/i386/mach-generic -I/usr/src/linux/include/asm/mach-default -fomit-frame-
pointer -o driver/modules/hostap.o driver/modules/hostap.c
```

```
     .
     .
     .
Run 'make install_pccard' as root to install hostap_cs.o

[root@localhost root]# make pccard_install
Installing hostap_crypt*.o to /lib/modules/2.4.20-8/net
mkdir -p /lib/modules/2.4.20-8/net
     .
     .
     .
Installing /etc/pcmcia/hostap_cs.conf
[root@localhost hostap-0.0.1]#
```

After compiling, take note of the *hostap_cs.conf* file that's now installed in */etc/ pcmcia*. It is the module configuration file and tells the module to load when seeing a matching card. The list comes with configurations for a number of popular cards, but if yours isn't listed, you will need to add it. This is an easy process, and entries are generally only three lines long:

```
card "Compaq WL100 11Mb/s WLAN Card"
   manfid 0x0138, 0x0002
   bind "hostap_cs"
```

To determine the exact make of your card, this command can be used:

```
[root@localhost etc]# cardctl ident
Socket 0:
  no product info available
Socket 1:
  product info: "Lucent Technologies", "WaveLAN/IEEE", "Version 01.01", ""
  manfid: 0x0156, 0x0002
  function: 6 (network)
[root@localhost etc]#
```

After these steps, you can either use *modprobe* to install your device, or reboot, and it will automatically load. You can check your syslog for the following message, or something similarly reassuring, to confirm that it has been loaded properly:

```
hostap_crypt: registered algorithm 'NULL'
hostap_cs: hostap_cs.c 0.0.1 2002-10-12
  (SSH Communications Security Corp, Jouni Malinen)
hostap_cs: (c) Jouni Malinen
PCI: Found IRQ 12 for device 00:0b.0
hostap_cs: Registered netdevice wlan0
prism2_hw_init( )
prism2_hw_config: initialized in 17775 iterations
wlan0: NIC: id=0x8013 v1.0.0
wlan0: PRI: id=0x15 v1.0.7
wlan0: STA: id=0x1f v1.3.5
wlan0: defaulting to host-based encryption as a workaround for
  firmware bug in Host AP mode WEP
wlan0: LinkStatus=2 (Disconnected)
wlan0: Intersil Prism2.5 PCI: mem=0xe7000000, irq=12
wlan0: prism2_open
wlan0: LinkStatus=2 (Disconnected)
```

Configuring HostAP

As discussed earlier, the *iwconfig* program is necessary to configure HostAP. First, you have to tell HostAP that you wish to use it in infrastructure mode. This is done with the following command:

```
vlager# iwconfig wlan0 mode Master
```

Next, the ESSID must be set. This will be the name of the access point, seen by all of the clients. In this example, we'll call ours "pub":

```
vlager#  iwconfig wlan0 essid pub
```

Then you should set the IP address as follows:

```
vlager# iwconfig wlan0 10.10.0.1
```

Selecting a channel is an important step, and as mentioned earlier, a site survey should be conducted to find the least congested channel available:

```
vlager# iwconfig channel 1
```

Now, once this has been completed, you can check to make sure that it's all been entered properly. The following command will produce:

```
vlager# iwconfig wlan0
wlan0      IEEE 802.11-DS  ESSID:"pub"  Nickname:" "
           Mode:Managed  Frequency:2.457GHz  Access Point:00:04:5A:0F:19:3D
           Bit Rate=11Mb/s   Tx-Power=15 dBm   Sensitivity:1/3
           Retry limit:4   RTS thr:off   Fragment thr:off
           Encryption key:off
           Power Management:off
           Link Quality:21/92  Signal level:-74 dBm  Noise level:-95 dBm
           Rx invalid nwid:0  Rx invalid crypt:0  Rx invalid frag:2960
           Tx excessive retries:1  Invalid misc:0   Missed beacon:0
```

The configuration of HostAP is complete. You should now be able to configure clients to connect to your Linux server through the wireless network.

Additional options

As you get more comfortable with HostAP, you may wish to configure some additional options, such as MAC filtering and WEP configurations. It is a good idea to implement one or both of these security measures, since the default configuration results in an open access point that can be sniffed or used by anyone within range. Using WEP will make sniffing more difficult but not impossible, and will also make unauthorized use a more complex process. MAC address filtering provides another good way to keep out unwanted guests. Again, it is important to note that because of flaws in the 802.11b protocol, neither of these steps will guarantee a safe and secure computing environment. In order to secure a wireless installation properly, traditional security methods, like VPNs, should be used. A VPN provides both confidentiality and authentication, since after all, a client on a wireless LAN should be classified in the same way as a client from the Internet—untrusted.

Enabling WEP is simple and accomplished through the *iwconfig* command. You can choose whether you wish to use a 40-bit or 104-bit key. A 40-bit WEP key is configured by using 10 hexadecimal digits:

```
# iwconfig wlan0 key 1234567890
```

A 104-bit WEP key is configured with 26 hexadecimal digits, grouped in four, separated by a dash:

```
# iwconfig wlan0 key 1000-2000-3000-4000-5000-6000-70
```

Using the following command will confirm your key:

```
# iwconfig wlan0
```

It is also important to note that a WEP key can also be configured with an ASCII string. There are a number of reasons why this method isn't particularly good, but perhaps the most important is that ASCII keys don't always work when entered on the client side. However, should you decide you'd like to try, ASCII key configuration is accomplished by specifying *s:* followed by the key in the *iwconfig* command, as follows:

For 40-bit keys, 5 characters, which equate to a 10-digit hexadecimal, are requred:

```
# iwconfig wlan0 key s:smile
```

For 104-bit keys, 13 characters, which equate to the 26 hexadecimal digits in the earlier example, are required:

```
# iwconfig wlan0 key s:passwordtest3
```

If you wish to disable WEP, it can be done with:

```
# iwconfig wlan0 key off
```

HostAP also provides another useful feature that allows clients to be filtered by MAC address. While this method is not a foolproof security mechanism, it will provide you with a certain amount of protection from unauthorized users.

There are two basic ways to filter MAC addresses: you can either allow the clients in your list, or you can deny the clients in your list. Both options are enabled with the *iwpriv* command. The following command will enable MAC filtering, allowing the clients in the MAC list:

```
# iwpriv wlan0 maccmd 1
```

The MAC filtering command `maccmd` offers the following options:

maccmd 0
> Disables MAC filtering

maccmd 1
> Enables MAC filtering and allows specified MAC addresses

maccmd 2
> Enables MAC filtering and denies specified MAC addresses

maccmd 3
     Flushes the MAC filter table

To begin adding MAC addresses to your list, *iwpriv* is again used as follows:

```
# iwpriv wlan0 addmac 00:44:00:44:00:44
```

This command adds the client with the MAC address **00:44:00:44:00:44**. Now this user will be allowed to participate in our wireless network. However, should we decide that we don't want to allow this MAC at some point in future; it can be removed with the following command:

```
# iwpriv wlan0 delmac 00:44:00:44:00:44
```

Now this MAC has been removed, and will no longer be able to associate. If you have a large list of client MAC addresses and wish to remove them all, you can flush the MAC access control list by invoking:

```
# iwpriv wlan0 maccmd 3
```

This clears the access control list, and you will need to either disable filtering or re-enter the valid MAC addresses you wish to authorize.

Troubleshooting

Because of their wireless nature, 802.11b networks can be much more prone to problems than traditional wired networks. There are a number of issues you may face when planning a wireless deployment.

The first is that of the signal strength. You want to make sure that your signal is strong enough to reach all of your clients, and yet not so strong that you're broadcasting to the world. The signal strength can be controlled with an antenna, through access point placement and some software controls. Experiment with different configurations and placements to see what works the best in your environment.

Interference may also be an issue. Many other devices now share the same 2.4 GHz frequency used by 802.11b. Cordless phones, baby monitor, and microwave ovens may all cause certain amounts of interference with your network. Neighboring access points operating on the same channel, or close to the channel you have selected, can also interfere with your network. While it's not likely that this particular issue will cause an outage, there will certainly be performance degradation. It is recommended, again, that experimentation be conducted prior to any major deployment.

Besides the physical issues, there are a number of software issues that are fairly common. Most issues are caused by driver or card incompatibility. The best way to avoid these kinds of problems is to know precisely which hardware you're using. Being able to identify your chipset will make finding the correct driver much easier.

Card identification is accomplished with the *cardctl* command, or by looking at the system log:

```
[root@localhost etc]# cardctl ident
Socket 0:
  no product info available
Socket 1:
  product info: "Lucent Technologies", "WaveLAN/IEEE", "Version 01.01", ""
  manfid: 0x0156, 0x0002
  function: 6 (network)
[root@localhost etc]#
```

In this example, we're using the easily identifiable WaveLAN card. Of course, this only works after successful configuration and module loading.

Bridging Your Networks

Once the HostAP software and drivers have been properly configured, a useful next step is to grant the client's access to your wired LAN. This is done via bridging, which requires software located at *http://bridge.sourceforge.net*. Some distributions have ready-to-install packages containing all necessary tools and kernel modifications. Red Hat RPMs contain both. Debian users can just enter *apt-get install bridge-utils*. Check your distribution for specifics.

The bridging software is controlled with a program called *brctl*. It is the main configuration tool for the software and has quite a few options. We'll be using only a few of the available choices, but for a more comprehensive listing, check the brctl manpages, which install with the software.

The first step in bridging is to create our virtual bridging interface by typing:

```
vlager#  brctl addbr br0
```

This command creates an interface on the machine that is used to bridge the two connections. You'll see it when running *ifconfig*:

```
vlager# ifconfig br0
br0       Link encap:Ethernet  HWaddr 00:00:00:00:00:00
          BROADCAST MULTICAST  MTU:1500  Metric:1
          RX packets:0 errors:0 dropped:0 overruns:0 frame:0
          TX packets:0 errors:0 dropped:0 overruns:0 carrier:0
          collisions:0 txqueuelen:0
          RX bytes:0 (0.0 b)  TX bytes:0 (0.0 b)
```

Additionally, you can tell by looking at the system log whether the bridge has been enabled:

```
Jan 22 13:17:54 vlager kernel: NET4: Ethernet Bridge 008 for NET4.0
```

The next step is to add the two interfaces that you wish to bridge. In this example, we'll be bridging wlan0, our wireless interface, and eth0, our wired Ethernet interface. First, however, it is important to clear the IP addresses from your interfaces. Since we're bridging the networks at layer two, IP addresses are not required.

```
Vlager#  ifconfig eth1 0.0.0.0 down
Vlager#  ifconfig wlan0 0.0.0.0 down
```

Once the IP addresses have been removed, the interfaces can be added to the bridge.

```
vlager# brctl addif br0 wlan0
vlager# brctl addif br0 eth1
```

The addif option adds interfaces that you'd like to have bridged. If you have another wired or wireless interface to add to the bridge, do so now in the same way.

The final step in the bridging process is to bring up the interfaces. You can also decide at this point whether you wish to assign an IP to your bridging interface. Having an IP makes it possible to remotely manage your server; however, some would argue that not having an IP makes the device more secure. For most purposes, however, it is helpful to have a management IP. To enable the bridge, you will need to enable the bridge interface, as well as both hardware interfaces.

```
vlager#  ifconfig br0 10.10.0.1 up
vlager#  ifconfig wlan0 up
vlager#  ifconfig eth0 up
```

With the successful completion of these commands, you will now be able to access your bridge using the IP **10.10.0.1**. Of course, this address must be one that is accessible from either side of the bridge.

Now you may wish to configure all of this to load at startup. This is done in a different way on just about every Linux distribution. Check the documentation specific to your distribution regarding the modification and addition to startup scripts.

Example Network: The Virtual Brewery

Throughout this book we've used the following example that is a little less complex than Groucho Marx University and may be closer to the tasks you will actually encounter.

The Virtual Brewery is a small company that brews, as the name suggests, virtual beer. To manage their business more efficiently, the virtual brewers want to network their computers, which all happen to be PCs running the brightest and shiniest production Linux kernel. Figure A-1 shows the network configuration.

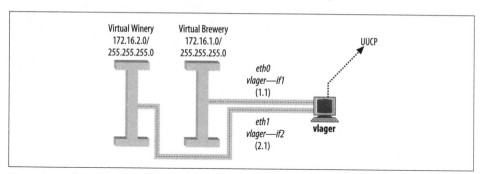

Figure A-1. The Virtual Brewery and Virtual Winery subnets

On the same floor, just across the hall, there's the Virtual Winery, which works closely with the brewery. The vintners run an Ethernet of their own. Quite naturally, the two companies want to link their networks once they are operational. As a first step, they want to set up a gateway host that forwards datagrams between the two subnets. Later, they also want to have a UUCP link to the outside world, through which they exchange mail and news. In the long run, they also want to set up PPP connections to connect to offsite locations and to the Internet.

The Virtual Brewery and the Virtual Winery each have a class C subnet of the Brewery's class B network, and gateway to each other via the host *vlager*, which also supports the UUCP connection. Figure A-2 shows the configuration.

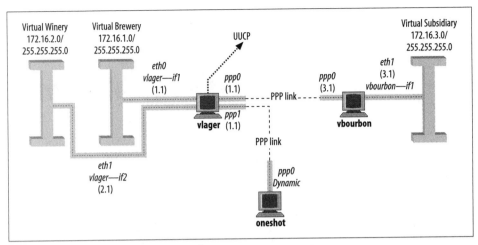

Figure A-2. The Virtual Brewery Network

Connecting the Virtual Subsidiary Network

The Virtual Brewery grows and opens a branch in another city. The subsidiary runs an Ethernet of its own using the IP network number **172.16.3.0**, which is subnet 3 of the Brewery's class B network. The host **vlager** acts as the gateway for the Brewery network and will support the PPP link; its peer at the new branch is called **vbourbon** and has an IP address of **172.16.3.1**. This network is illustrated in Figure A-2.

Index

We'd like to hear your suggestions for improving our indexes. Send email to *index@oreilly.com*.

broadcast option (ifconfig), 59
broadcasting
    defined, 19
    eavesdropping and, 122
    Ethernet and, 56, 60
browsable command (Samba), 271
-bs argument (sendmail), 228
BSD print system, 273
BSD remote services, 120, 121
BSD routed daemon, 25
buffers, UART chips and, 34
bug databases, 120
Bugtraq database, 120
Build utility, 190–191, 209
Burgiss, Hal, 116
BUSY message, 102
bytes_from field (mailstats), 230
bytes_to field (mailstats), 230

C

-c argument (Build), 191
.C command (sendmail), 223
C command (sendmail), 198, 199
-c option (iptables), 135
cable modems, 30
cacert.org organization, 252
cache option (named.conf), 79
caching-only servers, 75, 78, 83, 98
Callahan, Michael, 97
callout (cua) devices, 31
/canon command (sendmail), 223
canonical hostname
    A record and, 81
    aliases and, 82
    defined, 75
    SOA record and, 80
card identification, 305
cardctl command, 305
carriage return, 102
case sensitivity, 113, 193
Cc: field (mail header), 181
CCITT, 179
cellular phones, 233
certificates
    OpenLDAP and, 290
    OpenSSL and, 262
    SSL and, 252, 253
    troubleshooting, 293
chains
    iptables and, 126, 130, 134
    packets and, 131

policies for, 131
rules and, 149
Challenge Handshake Authentication
        Protocol (see CHAP)
channels
    defined, 298
    HostAP and, 303
    iwconfig tool and, 300
    troubleshooting and, 305
CHAP (Challenge Handshake Authentication
        Protocol)
    authorization and, 96
    chap-secrets file, 109, 111
    mgetty program and, 113
    PAP and, 108, 109
    PPP and, 108, 113
    pppd and, 97, 99
chap-secrets file, 109, 111
chargen internal service, 161
chat program, 97, 100–102
checksums, 15, 96, 129
chipsets, 296, 297
choke points, 122
CIDR (Classless Inter-Domain Routing)
    address scarcity and, 233
    block notation, 19
    IP addresses and, 18
    notation used, 138
    overview, 234
CIFS (Common Internet File System), 266,
        267
cipher, SSL, 290
Class A networks
    address ranges, 18
    IANA and, 45, 233, 234
    nslookup and, 89
    overview, 17
Class B networks
    address ranges, 18
    IANA and, 45, 234
    overview, 17
    subnetting and, 48
Class C networks
    address ranges, 18
    CIDR and, 234
    IANA and, 45
    overview, 17
    subnetting and, 48
Class D networks, 17
Class E networks, 17
Class F networks, 17

cyrus argument (MAILER macro), 196
Cyrus IMAP, 259, 263–265

D

-d built-in match (iptables), 137
.D command (sendmail), 223
D command (sendmail), 198, 199
-d command (sendmail), 223
-d option (arp), 64
-D subcommand option (iptables), 136
daemon facility (syslog), 101, 112
daemon wrapper, 163
daemons, 160, 162, 171
daemontools program, 92, 93
DARPA (Defense Advanced Research
        Projects Agency), 2
Data Carrier Detect (DCD), 38, 101
data communications equipment, 5
data terminal equipment, 5
Data Terminal Ready (DTR), 40
databases
    LDAP and, 278
    sendmail, 210–222
datagrams
    broadcasting, 19
    congested networks and, 55
    firewall packet logging and, 133n
    hops for, 26
    hosts and, 20, 21
    netstat command and, 61
    packets as, 2, 7
    routing, 24–26
    subnets and, 21
    traceroute and, 63
    UDP and, 9
    Van Jacobson header compression, 97
data-only keyword (mgetty), 40
Date: field (mail header), 182
daytime internal service, 161
DCC (Direct Communications
        Channels), 157
DCD (Data Carrier Detect), 38, 101
DDI (Device Driver Interface), 12
Debian, 120, 288, 306
debug keyword (mgetty), 40
debugging, PPP and, 112
DECnet, 196
default route, 18, 24, 25
default-lease-time option (DHCP), 47
defaultroute option (pppd), 99, 104
Defense Advanced Research Projects Agency
        (DARPA), 2

define command (sendmail)
    databases and, 219
    lowercase and, 193
    overview, 190, 195
    sendmail.cf and, 198
    sendmail.mc and, 192
    setting maximum headers, 206
del argument (route), 50
--delete subcommand option (iptables), 136
--delete-chain subcommand option
        (iptables), 136
delimiters, 200
demand dialing, 114, 115
demand option (pppd), 114
denial of service attacks, 121, 150
dependencies, OpenLDAP and, 280
--destination built-in match (iptables), 137
Destination NAT (DNAT), 121, 156, 159
--destination-port match option
        (iptables), 140
-detach option (pppd), 101, 113
/dev directory, 30
device argument (ip-up), 105
Device Driver Interface (DDI), 12
device drivers, Net-4 and, 11
dgram sockets, 161
DHCP (Dynamic Host Configuration
        Protocol), 44–48
dhcpcd program, 46
dhcpd.conf file, 47
diald command, 114
dial-up configuration
    authorization and, 96
    dumb terminals and, 38
    IP addresses and, 103
    nameservers and, 69
    persistent dialing and, 115
    proxy ARP and, 64
dig tool (BIND), 84, 87, 88
Direct Communications Channels
        (DCC), 157
direct keyword (mgetty), 40
directory services, 278
disable configuration option (xinetd), 167
-disable-v4-mapped tag (IPv6), 241
DISCARD action (access rule), 218
discussion lists, 261
Distinguished Names (DN), 279
divert command (m4), 192, 193
djbdns resolver, 66, 92–93
DMZ (demilitarized zone) networks, 122
DN (Distinguished Names), 279

H

H command (sendmail), 198, 199
H flag (netstat), 61
-h option (iptables), 135
handshakes, 33, 36, 105
hardware, 802.11b standard and, 296
hardware Ethernet option (DHCP), 47
hardware field (HINFO RR), 83
hardware handshaking (see handshakes)
hash sign (see pound sign)
HDLC (High-Level Data Link Control), 96, 97, 112
help command (nslookup), 91
--help option (iptables), 135
Hermes chipsets, 296, 297, 299
Hesiod addresses, 75, 79
hexadecimal characters, 106, 304
High-Level Data Link Control (HDLC), 96, 97, 112
HINFO record, 83
holdoff option (pppd), 114, 115
hook points, 127, 129, 131
hops, 26, 26n
host field (MX RR), 82
host keys, 172, 175
host numbers, 17
-host option (route), 50
HOST suboption (xinetd), 166
host tool, 91
HostAP tool, 298, 300–303, 306
hostap_cs.conf file, 302
hostcvt tool (BIND), 91
hostlist, 164
hostname
    A record and, 81
    access database and, 218
    canonical, 75, 80, 81, 82
    chap-secrets file, 110
    dot and, 164n
    FEATURE macro and, 207
    FQDNs and, 203
    genericstable database and, 216
    hostlist and, 164
    IP addresses and, 67, 81, 103
    IP masquerade and, 207
    localhost, 51, 52
    mapping, 79, 82
    networks file and, 50n
    scp program and, 177
    setting, 44
    uniqueness of, 73
    xinetd and, 165

hostname command, 44
hostname option (nslookup), 89
hostname resolution
    defined, 8
    local nameservers and, 71
    nsswitch.conf and, 67
    overview, 27
    pppd and, 98
    TCP/IP networking and, 48–50
HostnameLookups option (Apache), 248
hosts
    access database and, 218
    adding, 93
    broadcasting and, 19
    communications and, 5
    defined, 1
    DHCP lease and, 47
    eavesdropping and, 122
    filtering and, 122
    firewalls and, 122
    as gateways, 7, 22
    IP addresses and, 8, 20, 45
    IP masquerade and, 156
    MAC addresses, 48
    mail and, 183, 184
    names for, 70, 75
    ports on, 9
    relay-domains file and, 214
    remote login to, 176
    security and, 163
    serial communications and, 29
    sizes of, 17
    spoofing and, 121
    thin Ethernet and, 4
    trusted, 163
    updating files for, 27
    zones and, 74
hosts database, 67
hosts: dns files, 71
hosts file
    backup host table in, 71
    configuring gateways and, 55
    hostcvt tool and, 91
    ifconfig and, 51
    nameservers and, 69
    writing, 48–50
hosts.allow file, 163
hosts.deny file, 163
hoststat command, 230, 231
HostStatusDirectory option, 230
HOSTS.TXT database, 27
HTTP, 123, 124, 148

httpd -l command, 255
httpd.conf file, 247, 250–252, 255
hub-and-spoke model, 298
hubs, active, 4
Hunt, Craig, 16, 199
hwaddr argument (arp), 64
HylaFAX software, 196
hyphen (-), 102, 110

I

-i built-in match (iptables), 138
-I subcommand option (iptables), 136
IANA (Internet Assigned Numbers
    Authority), 45, 233, 234
IBM, 5, 220, 266
ICMP (Internet Control Message Protocol)
    IP accounting and, 150, 151
    IP filtering and, 124
    iptables matches, 139
    netstat options and, 61
    TCP/IP and, 26–28
    traceroute and, 63
--icmp-type match option (iptables), 139
identity file, 174, 175
identity.pub file, 174, 178
idle option (pppd), 115
IEEE (Institute of Electrical and Electronics
    Engineers), 295, 296
IETF (Internet Engineering Task Force), 10,
    267
if argument (route), 50
iface argument (ip-up), 105
ifconfig command
    bridging interface and, 306
    compatibility considerations, 52
    Ethernet interfaces, 53
    interface configuration and, 50
    IPv6 and, 237
    multicast support, 46
    network devices and, 30
    overview, 57–60
    PPPoE clients and, 118
IMAP (Internet Message Access Protocol)
    aliases and, 217
    choosing, 259–263
    Cyrus, 263–265
    email and, 180
    POP and, 258, 259
    purpose, 258
imapd.alert file, 261
imapd.conf file, 264
in-addr.arpa domain, 82

include option (Apache), 247
indefinite tokens, 200
inetd daemon, 160–163, 227, 267
inetd.conf file
    disabling r* commands, 171
    finger daemon, 163
    IMAP and, 260, 262
    overview, 161–162
    Samba in, 268
    SWAT and, 276
inetOrgPerson schema, 279
info top-level domain, 72
infrastructure mode, 297, 298, 303
--in-interface built-in match (iptables), 138
init command, 40
inittab file, 40
INPUT hook point (iptables)
    chains and, 127
    filter table and, 131, 134
    functionality, 129
    MAC match option, 139
    mangle table and, 131
input redirection (<), 37
--insert subcommand option (iptables), 136
install-cf command (Build), 210
installing
    Apache considerations, 248
    LDAP libraries, 286
    sendmail, 186–192
    ssh tools, 171–178
    UW IMAP, 259–261
instances option (xinetd), 165
Institute of Electrical and Electronics
    Engineers (IEEE), 295, 296
interfaces
    bind, 270
    bridging and, 306, 307
    configuring aliases for, 57
    defined, 16
    displaying netstat statistics, 62
    Ethernet, 16, 52–54
    GTK+-style, 291
    incompatible changes and, 169
    IP and, 50n
    IPv6 and, 237, 238
    packets and, 18
    packet-switching and, 26
    PPP, 57
    procmail argument (MAILER) and, 196
    promiscuous mode, 59
    Samba and, 270
    (see also loopback interface; network
        interfaces)

LANs (Local Area Networks)
    IP masquerading and, 155
    nameservers and, 71
    prevalence of, 154
    routing tables and, 25
    wireless networking and, 295
LCP (Link Control Protocol)
    overview, 105–107
    PPP and, 96
    pppd and, 98, 108
lcp-echo-failure option (pppd), 107
lcp-echo-interval option (pppd), 107
LDAP Data Interchange files
        (LDIF), 283–285
LDAP (Lightweight Directory Access
        Protocol)
    GUI and, 291
    overview, 278–279
    sendmail and, 190
    (see also OpenLDAP)
ldapadd utility, 283
ldapsearch command, 283, 285, 288
LDIF (LDAP Data Interchange
        files), 283–285
less than (<) sign (sendmail), 202
libc library, 27, 67
Libes, Don, 100
Lightweight Directory Access Protocol (see
        LDAP)
line discipline, 30
--line-numbers option (iptables), 135
Link Control Protocol (see LCP)
link-local address, 235, 238
Linux
    documentation available, xii
    getting the code, 12
    mailing lists, xiii
    obtaining, xiv
    platforms supported, ix
    Usenet newsgroups, xiii
    user groups, xiv
Linux Documentation Project, xii
Linux File System Standard Group
        (FSSTND), xv, 32
Linux Journal, xiii
Linux Magazine, xiii
Linux Standard Base, xv
Linux Systems Labs, xii
Linux Wireless Extension Tools, 300
linux.m4 file, 204
linux-wlan-ng driver, 300
--list subcommand option (iptables), 136

Listen option (Apache), 247
listening
    IPv6 cautions, 240, 241
    OpenLDAP and, 287
    OpenSSH and, 242
    ports and, 10
    Samba and, 271
    slapd program and, 282
    testing, 290
Liu, Cricket, 67
LKM (loadable kernel module), 299
lnp option (IMAP), 260
load printers option (printcap), 275
loadable kernel module (LKM), 299
loadavg file, 43
Local Area Networks (see LANs)
local argument (MAILER macro), 196
LOCAL keyword, 164
local mailer (MAILER macro), 196, 204
local_addr option
    ip-up, 105
    pppd, 103
LOCAL_CONFIG macro (sendmail), 197,
        198
LOCAL_DOMAIN macro (sendmail), 213
localhost hostname, 51, 52
local-host-names file, 207, 211, 212–214
LOCAL_NET_CONFIG macro
        (sendmail), 197, 202
LOCAL_RULE_n macro (sendmail), 197
LOCAL_RULESET macro (sendmail), 197
lock files, 31, 32
lock keyword (pppd), 99
log file command (Samba), 272
log level command (Samba), 272
LogFormat option (Apache), 248
logins
    anonymous, 261
    PAP and, 108
    pppd and, 100
    remote, 170–178
    serial devices and, 38–41
LogLevel option (Apache), 248
log_on_failure option (xinetd), 166
log_on_success option (xinetd), 166
log_type option (xinetd), 165
Longyear, Al, 97
loopback address, 18
loopback interface
    defined, 18
    example, 24
    gated and, 26

N

N flag (stty), 38
-N option
  iptables, 136
  ssh-keygen, 172
-n option (iptables), 135
name option
  dig, 88
  pppd, 111
name resolution, DNS and, 28, 74–75
name top-level domain, 72
named program, 66
named.conf file, 77–79, 83
nameserver option
  dig, 87
  resolv.conf, 69
nameservers
  DNS and, 74, 75, 98
  handling lookups, 158, 159
  hosts file and, 69
  LANs and, 71
  nslookup and, 89
  resolv.conf and, 69–71
  root, 90
  serial number and, 80
  verifying setup of, 87, 88
namespace, 73, 77
naming conventions, LDAP and, 279
NAT (Network Address Translation)
  address scarcity and, 233
  defined, 123
  IP addresses and, 45
  IP firewalling and, 125
  IP masquerade and, 154
  iptables and, 121, 127, 134
  netfilter and, 159
  overview, 234, 235
  spoofing and, 121
nat table (iptables), 131, 134
NCP (Network Control Protocol), 96
net directory, 43
-net option (route), 50, 53
net top-level domain, 72
Net-2, 11
Net-3, 11
Net-4, 11, 12
netfilter kernel module
  access control and, 301
  backwards compatibility with, 134
  firewalls and, 243
  IP masquerade and, 157
  kernel and, 119
  loading, 134
  NAT and, 159
  overview, 125–127
  packet processing and, 123
netmask option (ifconfig), 58
netmasks, 21, 25, 164, 234
NetRom protocol, 6, 11
netstat command
  Apache web server and, 241
  checking interface configuration, 54
  checking ports and, 120
  IMAP and, 260
  IPv6 and, 237
  overview, 60–63
  testing SSL availability, 290
net-tools package, 57, 237
Network Address Translation (see NAT)
Network Control Protocol (NCP), 96
Network File System (NFS), 169
Network Information Center (NIC), 17, 27, 73
network interface card (NIC), 4
network interfaces
  configuring, 50n
  gated and, 26
  scripts and, 42
  TCP/IP, 16
network layer
  denial of service and, 122
  ebtables command and, 126
  IP filtering and, 124
  protocols, 6, 45
network numbers, 17, 21, 45
networking
  access database and, 218
  broadcast, 56
  choke points, 122
  congested, 55
  DHCP lease and, 45
  email and, 179
  gateways and, 22–24
  global village and, ix
  history, 1
  IP masquerade and, 156
  IPv6 and, 236
  Linux, 12–13
  perimeter, 122
  system maintenance, 13–15
  TCP/IP networks, 2–11
  unauthorized access, 120
  (see also wireless networks)
networks database, 67

TCP (Transmission Control Protocol)
(*continued*)
    tcpd and, 163
    ucspi-tcp program, 92
    Van Jacobson header compression, 97
tcpd access control facility, 163, 164
tcpdump tool, 59, 114
--tcp-flags match option (iptables), 140
TCP/IP networking
    ARP tables, 63, 65
    creating subnets, 48
    DHCP and, 45–48
    Ethernet interfaces, 52–54
    gateways and, 54, 55
    hostname resolution, 48–50
    ICMP and, 26–28
    ifconfig command and, 57–60
    installing tools, 43
    interfaces and, 16, 50n
    IP addresses, 17–26, 44, 45
    IP Alias, 57
    Linux and, x
    loopback interface, 51–52
    netstat command, 60–63
    overview, 2–11
    PPP interface, 57
    setting hostnames, 44
    SMTP and, 183
    socket library for, 11
    traceroute tool and, 63
    Unix and, 2
--tcp-option match option (iptables), 140
tcpwrappers, 270
teletype devices (see tty devices)
telnet, 105, 124
10-base2, 4
10-base5, 4
10-baseT, 4
Terminal Node Controller, 6
terminal programs, 29
testparm program, 268, 273, 277
tftp daemon, 162
tftp service, 164
TFTP (Trivial File Transfer Protocol), 14,
    162
Thawte, 252
thick Ethernet, 3, 4
thin Ethernet, 3, 4
time to live (see ttl)
Timeout option
    Apache, 249

chat, 102
tkrat MUA, 182
TLDs (top-level domains), 72, 73, 250
To: field (mail header), 181
To: tag field, 218
toggle-dtr keyword (mgetty), 40
Token Ring, 5, 11
tokens, 200, 202
top-level domains (TLDs), 72, 73
Torvalds, Linus, x
Tourrilhes, Jean, 300
Toxen, Bob, 121
tracepath6 tool, 237
traceroute tool, 63
traceroute6 tool, 237
TRAFFIC suboption (xinetd), 166
Transmission Control Protocol (see TCP)
tree structure, 278
tripwire tool, 15
Trivial File Transfer Protocol (TFTP), 14,
    162
troubleshooting
    802.11b standard, 305–306
    Apache web servers, 256–257
    Cyrus IMAP, 265
    IPv6 and, 242–243
    OpenLDAP, 291–293
    Samba, 277
trusted hosts, 163
/try command (sendmail), 223, 227
tryagain option (nsswitch.conf), 69
/tryflags command (sendmail), 223, 227
Ts, Jay, 266
ttl field (resource record), 79
ttl (time to live)
    defined, 75
    resource records and, 79, 81
    SOA record and, 76
tty devices
    defined, 30
    opening, 31
    PPP servers and, 112
    stty command, 37
tunnels, 238–240, 276
twisted pair Ethernet, 3, 4
type field
    inetd, 161
    resource record, 80
type option (dig), 88

U

U flag (netstat), 61
UART chips, 34
uart parameter (setserial), 35
ucspi-tcp program, 92
UDP (User Datagram Protocol)
    inetd.conf and, 161
    IP accounting and, 148, 151
    IP filtering and, 124
    iptables matches, 139
    overview, 9
    ports and, 150
    RPC and, 169, 170
    tcpd and, 163
    traceroute and, 63
unavail option (nsswitch.conf), 69
undefine command (m4), 195
Unix
    Berkeley Socket Library, 10
    counting and, 31
    daemontools program, 92
    init command, 40
    kermit and, 29
    lpr command and, 273
    m4 program, 186
    networks and, ix
    sendmail and, 179
    socket library for, 11
    TCP/IP and, 2
    tty devices and, 30
UNKNOWN keyword, 164
up option (ifconfig), 58
uppercase, 193
URIs, 271, 288
Urlichs, Matthias, 12
USB, 301
use_ct_file feature, 219
use_cw_file feature, 211, 212
usehostname option (pppd), 111
usenet argument (MAILER macro), 196
Usenet newsgroups, xiii, 196
user accounts, 269, 277, 285
user configuration option (xinetd), 167
user database, 219
User Datagram Protocol (see UDP)
user field (inetd), 161
user ID, 191
useradd utility, 112n
username
    adding to classes, 207
    eavesdropping and, 122
    FEATURE macro and, 199

    genericstable database and, 216
    login procedure and, 108
    PPP servers and, 113
    PPPoE client and, 118
    remote login and, 171
uucico program, 99
uucp argument (MAILER macro), 196
UUCP environment, 180, 184, 196, 220
uucpdomain database, 220
uucpdomain feature, 220
UW IMAP, 259–261

V

V command (sendmail), 198
-v option
    chat, 101
    iptables, 135
-V subcommand option (iptables), 136
valid users option (Samba), 271
vampire taps, 4
Van Jacobson header compression, 97, 106
van Kempen, Fred, 11
variables, 191, 195
/var/lock directory, 32
--verbose option (iptables), 135
Verisign, 252
--version subcommand option (iptables), 137
VERSIONID macro
    generic-linux.mc, 204
    generic.m4, 206, 208
    linux.m4, 205
    sendmail, 193
versions
    OpenLDAP and, 280
    RPC and, 169
Virtual Brewery, 309
virtual hosting, 57
virtual terminals, 30, 38, 100
VirtualHost functionality
    (httpd.conf), 250–252, 255, 257
virtusertable database, 220, 221, 222
virtusertable feature, 221
VJ header compression (see Van Jacobson
    header compression)
Voice over IP, 236
VPNs, 296, 303
vulnerabilities
    BIND and, 92
    RTM Internet worm, 163
    security considerations and, 15

W

wait configuration option (xinetd), 167
wait field (inetd), 161
WANs, server addresses and, 116
WaveLAN cards, 297, 306
web browsers, 251, 291
web servers, 156, 276
    (see also Apache web servers)
WEP (Wired Equivalent Privacy)
    attacks on, 296
    HostAP and, 303, 304
    iwconfig tool and, 300
whitespace, 67
WiFi Protected Access (WPA), 295
wildcards, 110, 174, 283
Windows (Microsoft), 266, 273
WinModem, 34n
Wired Equivalent Privacy (see WEP)
wireless networks
    802.11b security concerns, 296–305
    acceptance of, 294
    bridging, 306–307
    history, 294, 295
    Linux and, 4
    standards, 295–296
    troubleshooting, 305–306
--with-inet6 option (xinetd), 165
--with-syslog option (Samba), 272
-with-tls option (OpenLDAP), 281, 289
working groups, 295
World Wide Web, 124, 148, 211
    (see also Internet)
WPA (WiFi Protected Access), 295
writable command (Samba), 271

X

X- field (mail header), 182
-x option (iptables), 135
-X subcommand option (iptables), 137
X terminals, 162
X.11, 29, 30
X.25 protocol, 5, 11, 96
X.400 standard, 179, 183, 184
x509 option (OpenSSL), 253
XDR (External Data Representation)
        format, 169
xinetd super server, 164–167
xinetd.conf file, 165, 263, 268, 276
XON/XOFF handshaking, 33, 105

Y

YaST Online Update (YOU) utility, 120
YOU (YaST Online Update) utility, 120
yum utility (Red Hat), 120

Z

-Z subcommand option (iptables), 137
--zero subcommand option (iptables), 137
zeroes, double-colon and, 235, 242
zone option (named.conf), 78
zones
    domains and, 73
    nameservers and, 74
    NS records and, 82
    RFC 1912, 78
    serial numbers and, 80
    SOA records and, 80

About the Authors

Tony Bautts is an independent security consultant who has worked with Fortune 500 companies in the U.S. and Japan. He has spoken at security-related events for The Information Systems Audit and Control Association (ISACA) and has spoken and chaired events for the MIS Training Institute. Tony is the coauthor of *Hack Proofing Your Wireless Network*, *Nokia Network Solutions Handbook*, and the *Security Certification Handbook* and has, additionally, served as technical reviewer for *Implementing IPv6 on Cisco IOS*. His specialties include wireless networking, secure infrastructure design, and post-intrusion forensics.

Terry Dawson has 20 years of professional experience in telecommunications and currently leads a team engaged in operational support system research in the Telstra Research Laboratories.

Gregor N. Purdy is an engineering manager in the large account services group at Amazon.com. Before joining Amazon.com in 2003, Gregor worked for 10 years as a consultant in high-end data warehousing, system integration, and prior art research in software and Internet patents. He has also contributed to a number of open source projects, including Perl core and extension modules, the Perl shell, and the Parrot virtual machine for Perl 6.

Colophon

Our look is the result of reader comments, our own experimentation, and feedback from distribution channels. Distinctive covers complement our distinctive approach to technical topics, breathing personality and life into potentially dry subjects.

The image on the cover of *Linux Network Administrator's Guide*, Third Edition, is adapted from a 19th-century engraving from *Marvels of the New West: A Vivid Portrayal of the Stupendous Marvels in the Vast Wonderland West of the Missouri River*, by William Thayer (The Henry Bill Publishing Co., Norwich, CT, 1888). The cowboy has long been an American symbol of strength and rugged individualism, but the first cowboys, known as *vaqueros*, were actually from Mexico. In the 1800s, *vaqueros* drove their cattle north into America to graze. This practice gave ranchers in Texas ideas of moving herds away from cold weather, toward water sources, and eventually north to railheads so that their cattle could be shipped to eastern markets.

Cattle trails started from the southernmost tip of Texas and extended through Colorado, Arkansas, and Wyoming. Cowboys were hired by ranchers to brand and drive the cattle through dangerous countryside and deliver them safely to railheads. Cattle were often scared by bad weather and started stampedes powerful enough to make the ground vibrate. It was the cowboys' responsibility to calm the herds and round up any cows and steers that had wandered off. One well-known technique for calming nervous cattle was singing to them.

American cowboys were a diverse crowd. African-Americans, Indians, Mexicans, and former Confederate cavalrymen were about as common as the Hollywood, John Wayne stereotype. Cowboys were usually medium-sized, wiry fellows, and on average about twenty-four years old. They owned their saddles, but not the horses they rode day and night. Cowboys were worked so hard and paid so little that most of them made only one trail drive before finding another occupation.

Although cowboys had a large impact on American culture, they were only an important part of the West for a short time. As more and more ranchers began using barbed wire to fence cattle for branding, fewer cowboys were needed. Before long, railroads covered the former Wild West, and cattle herding turned into an event seen primarily at the rodeo.

Adam Witwer was the production editor and copyeditor for *Linux Network Administrator's Guide,* Third Edition. Ann Schirmer proofread the text. Matt Hutchinson and Claire Cloutier provided quality control. Lucie Haskins wrote the index.

Edie Freedman designed the cover of this book. Emma Colby produced the layout with Adobe InDesign CS using Adobe's ITC Garamond font.

David Futato designed the interior layout. The chapter opening images are from *Marvels of the New West: A Vivid Portrayal of the Stupendous Marvels in the Vast Wonderland West of the Missouri River.* This book was converted to FrameMaker 5.5.6 by Julie Hawks with a format conversion tool created by Erik Ray, Jason McIntosh, Neil Walls, and Mike Sierra that uses Perl and XML technologies. The text font is Linotype Birka; the heading font is Adobe Myriad Condensed; and the code font is LucasFont's TheSans Mono Condensed. The illustrations that appear in the book were produced by Robert Romano and Jessamyn Read using Macromedia FreeHand MX and Adobe Photoshop CS. The tip and warning icons were drawn by Christopher Bing. This colophon was written by Lydia Onofrei.

Buy *Linux Network Administrator's Guide, 3rd Edition* and access the digital edition

FREE on Safari for 45 days.

Go to **www.oreilly.com/go/safarienabled**
and type in coupon code **7KG5-ANJF-RAOK-UXE8-9AFF**

Better than e-books

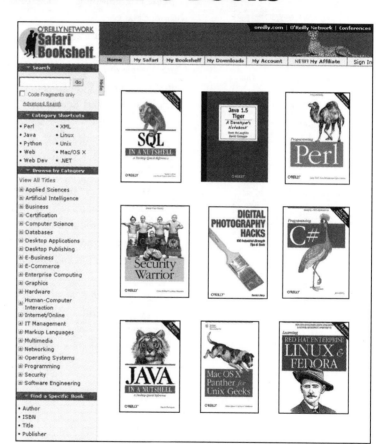

Search

over 2000 top
tech books

Download

whole chapters

Cut and Paste

code examples

Find

answers fast

Read books from cover
to cover. Or, simply click
to the page you need.

**Search Safari! The premier electronic reference
library for programmers and IT professionals**

 Addison
Wesley

 Sun
microsystems

 ALPHA

 Java
for-the-enterprise

Microsoft
Press

 Peachpit
Press

 O'REILLY

 QUE

AdobePress

 SAMS

New
Riders

Cisco Press

 macromedia
PRESS

 PRENTICE
HALL
PTR

Part# 40421

Related Titles Available from O'Reilly

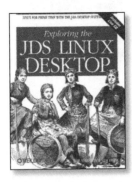

Linux

Building Embedded Linux Systems

Building Secure Servers with Linux

The Complete FreeBSD, *4th Edition*

Even Grues Get Full

Exploring the JDS Linux Desktop

Extreme Programming Pocket Guide

Knoppix Hacks

Learning Red Hat Enterprise Linux and Fedora, *4th Edition*

Linux Cookbook

Linux Device Drivers, *3rd Edition*

Linux in a Nutshell, *4th Edition*

Linux iptables Pocket Reference

Linux Pocket Guide

Linux Security Cookbook

Linux Server Hacks

Linux Unwired

Linux Web Server CD Bookshelf, *Version 2.0*

LPI Linux Certification in a Nutshell, *2nd Edition*

Managing RAID on Linux

OpenOffice.org Writer

Programming with Qt, *2nd Edition*

Root of all Evil

Running Linux, *4th Edition*

Samba Pocket Reference, *2nd Edition*

Test Driving Linux

Understanding the Linux Kernel, *2nd Edition*

Understanding Open Source & Free Software Licensing

User Friendly

Using Samba, *3rd Edition*

O'REILLY®

Our books are available at most retail and online bookstores.
To order direct: 1-800-998-9938 • *order@oreilly.com* • *www.oreilly.com*
Online editions of most O'Reilly titles are available by subscription at *safari.oreilly.com*

Keep in touch with O'Reilly

1. Download examples from our books

To find example files for a book, go to:

www.oreilly.com/catalog

select the book, and follow the "Examples" link.

2. Register your O'Reilly books

Register your book at *register.oreilly.com*

Why register your books?
Once you've registered your O'Reilly books you can:

- Win O'Reilly books, T-shirts or discount coupons in our monthly drawing.
- Get special offers available only to registered O'Reilly customers.
- Get catalogs announcing new books (US and UK only).
- Get email notification of new editions of the O'Reilly books you own.

3. Join our email lists

Sign up to get topic-specific email announcements of new books and conferences, special offers, and O'Reilly Network technology newsletters at:

elists.oreilly.com

It's easy to customize your free elists subscription so you'll get exactly the O'Reilly news you want.

4. Get the latest news, tips, and tools

www.oreilly.com

- "Top 100 Sites on the Web"—PC Magazine
- CIO Magazine's Web Business 50 Awards

Our web site contains a library of comprehensive product information (including book excerpts and tables of contents), downloadable software, background articles, interviews with technology leaders, links to relevant sites, book cover art, and more.

5. Work for O'Reilly

Check out our web site for current employment opportunities:

jobs.oreilly.com

6. Contact us

O'Reilly & Associates
1005 Gravenstein Hwy North
Sebastopol, CA 95472 USA

TEL: 707-827-7000 or 800-998-9938
        (6am to 5pm PST)

FAX: 707-829-0104

order@oreilly.com
For answers to problems regarding your order or our products. To place a book order online, visit:

www.oreilly.com/order_new

catalog@oreilly.com
To request a copy of our latest catalog.

booktech@oreilly.com
For book content technical questions or corrections.

corporate@oreilly.com
For educational, library, government, and corporate sales.

proposals@oreilly.com
To submit new book proposals to our editors and product managers.

international@oreilly.com
For information about our international distributors or translation queries. For a list of our distributors outside of North America check out:

international.oreilly.com/distributors.html

adoption@oreilly.com
For information about academic use of O'Reilly books, visit:

academic.oreilly.com

O'REILLY®

Our books are available at most retail and online bookstores.
To order direct: 1-800-998-9938 • *order@oreilly.com* • *www.oreilly.com*
Online editions of most O'Reilly titles are available by subscription at *safari.oreilly.com*

WITHDRAWN